Globalization and
the European Political Economy

Steven Weber, Editor

COLUMBIA UNIVERSITY PRESS   NEW YORK

COLUMBIA UNIVERSITY PRESS
Publishers Since 1893
New York, Chichester, West Sussex
Copyright © 2001 Columbia University Press
All rights reserved

Library of Congress Cataloging-in-Publication Data

Globalization and the European political economy / Steven Weber, editor.
    p. cm.
Includes bibliographical references and index.
ISBN 0-231-12148-2 (cloth : alk. paper)—ISBN 0-231-12149-0 (pbk. : alk. paper)
1. Europe—Economic conditions. 2. Globalization. 3. Europe—Foreign
economic relations. I. Weber, Steven.

HC240 .G535 2001
337.4—dc21

                                                                00-064425

∞

Casebound editions of Columbia University Press books
are printed on permanent and durable acid-free paper.
Printed in the United States of America

c 10 9 8 7 6 5 4 3 2 1
p 10 9 8 7 6 5 4 3 2 1

Contents

Preface

The Center for German and European Studies at Berkeley graciously supports a number of research "convenor groups" on topics related to European integration, political economy, and society and culture. In 1998, Gerald Feldman and Beverly Crawford (Director and Associate Director of the Center, respectively) asked if I would be interested in putting together a group of scholars to collaborate on a study of how globalization was affecting governance structures in European political economy. This book is the product of that group. We met three times physically (and innumerable times in cyberspace) over the course of two years, to develop and refine an analytic framework and our individual contributions. It was a fruitful and fun collaboration that leaves us all with pleasant memories, new ideas, and (hopefully) better research agendas. It has certainly left me with some new friends.

Several outsiders participated in one or another of our meetings, to offer valuable feedback and criticism. In addition to the people mentioned in the individual papers, we thank Beverly Crawford, Nicolas Jabko, Kirsten Rodine, Neil Fligstein, Jonah Levy, and Barbara Connolly. Two anonymous reviewers for Columbia University Press gave helpful comments on the volume as a whole. The staff of the Center for German and European Studies, particularly Gia White, handled all the logistical arrangements for our meetings with efficiency and good cheer. And the cooks at Restaurant Tra Vigne made the whole thing seem worthwhile, even in our deepest darkest moments of analytical confusion.

Putting together a coherent edited volume is not a task for the faint of heart. I hope that I have met the challenge in a way that adds value to each of the individual contributions.

Steven Weber
Berkeley, California
September 2000

Contributors

Christopher K. Ansell is associate professor of political science at University of California, Berkeley. He teaches organization theory and public Administration, and is currently developing a project on changing forms of governance in subnational regions of Western Europe.

John Campbell is professor in and Chair of the Department of Sociology at Dartmouth College, and adjunct professor of political science at the University of Copenhagen. His research has focused on comparative nuclear energy policy, governance of the U.S. economy, institutional change in post-communist Europe, shifts in U.S. tax policy regimes, and the role of ideas in policy making.

Vanna Gonzales is a graduate student in the department of political science at UC Berkeley. She is currently planning a dissertation project on the decentralization of the Italian welfare state.

Paulette Kurzer is associate professor of political science at University of Arizona. She is the author of *Business and Banking* (Ithaca: Cornell University Press 1993) and a forthcoming book tentatively titled *Markets versus Morality Norms: Cultural Change in Europe*.

Conor O'Dwyer is a graduate student in the department of political science at UC Berkeley. His dissertation project examines political strategies of decentralization in Eastern Europe.

Elliot Posner is a doctoral candidate in Political Science at the University of California, Berkeley. He is working on a dissertation about the institutional foundations of Europe's new economic sector for entrepreneurial companies.

Vivien A. Schmidt, professor of international relations at Boston University, has written extensively on European political economy and public policy, including *From State to Market?* (Cambridge, 1996), *Democratizing France* (Cambridge, 1990), and many articles. She is working on a book on the impact of European integration on economies, institutions, and discourse in France, Britain, and Germany.

Steven Weber is associate professor of political science at University of California, Berkeley. He is the author of *Cooperation and Discord in US-Soviet Arms Control* (Princeton: Princeton University Press, 1991) and a number of articles in the area of international institutions, European Union, and the political and economic consequences of technological change.

J. Nicholas Ziegler teaches comparative politics and management at the University of California, Berkeley. He is author of *Governing Ideas: Strategies for Innovation in France and Germany* (Ithaca: Cornell University Press, 1997), and is currently working on the politics of institutional redesign for capital markets and white-collar training in Europe.

Globalization and the European Political Economy

Introduction

Steven Weber

This book examines consequences of "globalization" for governance structures in the modern European political economy. The authors bring together, through empirical research in a number of different issue-areas, two sets of ideas that generally have been apart from one another. The first is a discussion about "globalization." The second is a broad set of notions about new or unconventional governance structures that are developing or propagating (or are being seen more clearly) in domestic politics, political economy, and international relations. How do these sets of ideas relate to each other, in Europe specifically? What are the implications for Europe's relationship with more macro, global structures and institutions? Is there an autonomous set of causal forces operating at the regional level? If so, is Europe "special" in any sense?

Changing governance structures in political economy are the major "dependent variable" of this book. Paulette Kurzer examines the consequences of European integration for socially sensitive policy areas (alcohol in Sweden, drugs in the Netherlands, abortion in Ireland) and for attempts by these states to maintain distinctive policies. John Campbell compares efforts by the Czech Republic, Poland, and Hungary during the 1990s to bring fiscal policies under control in national budgeting. Nick Ziegler examines ongoing changes in corporate governance in Germany. Chris Ansell, Vanna Gonzales, and Connor O'Dwyer look at the changing relationship between subnational regions, national governments, and the EU in Tuscany and North Rhine-Westphalia. Vivien Schmidt compares French, German, and British efforts to construct a political discourse that supports and legitimizes social and institutional changes connected to globalization. Elliot Posner and I look at efforts to create a pan-European stock market for small high-technology firms in Europe.

There is plenty of anecdotal evidence that many countries are currently tinkering with, or in some cases revising more deeply, a range of institutions and organizations that are important parts of the governance structures in their political economies. These changes are more profound than simply shifting policies. Why is this happening? The most generic causal argument is simply that governance structures as institutions respond to some set of pressures that arise from external and/or domestic sources. "Globalization" arguments (even though often ambiguously specified) share a common trait in that they emphasize external forces as the primary causal driver.

The ongoing debate about globalization tends to focus on the external as the "global," and to pose it as a set of causes against a distinct set of causes at the "national" (or domestic) level. The "regional" level, by which I mean a supranational aggregation that is bigger than a nation state but less extensive than global in scope, plays a weak role in this discussion. That is a peculiar omission, particularly now as regional organizations are proliferating throughout the world. It is particularly peculiar for Europe, which has the most elaborate and extensive network of regional institutions. Of course, there is a large literature on the impact of Europe's regional architecture on domestic and local governance structures in various issue areas. There is also literature on the impact of "globalization" in particular European states.[1]

This book begins the process of tying these literatures together. It explores the question of what driving forces are located at what levels, what the relationships between them are, and whether there is an important autonomous set of causal drivers at the European level that makes Europe different. Three questions make up the motivating agenda:

- what are the causal forces in globalization?
- what are the mechanisms of change in governance structures?
- what is the relationship between European-level causes, global-level causes, and national institutions?

Progress toward understanding these issues will be a contribution toward greater understanding of how "tied in to" or "insulated from" Europe as a region is to the global economy and security systems. This, in turn, should refine conceptualizations of what globalization actually means and what "it" is causing. Explicating mechanisms of change will help to reveal more precisely how these causal forces operate within, against, and in conjunction with national institutions. Ultimately the question becomes simply this: what kinds of politics does globalization engender in Europe?

This introductory chapter has four sections. First, I offer a preliminary definition of globalization and use this to motivate the focus on Europe. Second, I discuss in greater detail the more complex meaning(s) of globalization and review some of the recent relevant literature. I organize the discussion around key concepts and analytical advances. This section concludes with suggestions about where the debate about globalization might go next, and situates this book within that agenda. Section Three explains the research strategy of this book. It defines the explanatory framework for the succeeding case studies and justifies the broad spectrum of case selection. Section Four is a short "plan of the book." The Concluding chapter to the book considers possible implications in three areas—the value of differentiating between mechanisms of change; the conceptualization of what governance structures are and what they do; and a revised set of understandings about what globalization means in practice.

1. Why Europe?

Consider, to start, a fundamental and stark definition of globalization. I believe that globalization is most simply a story about the causes and consequences of an increase in *mobility*.[2] For most of human history, neither goods nor capital nor most people nor many ideas moved very far from their place of origin. Over the last several hundred years, mobility of many (not all) things has increased. As I will discuss in the next section, this has happened unevenly across time and with some setbacks. The next section will also explore in more detail contending arguments about how political-economic and social structures and practices react to, or change in the face of, increased mobility. These arguments share at least one element: the idea that there has been an enhancement of markets as a way of organizing economic activity. Mobility, among other consequences, makes possible the expansion of markets beyond physical and other kinds of borders that previously contained them. I portray the globalization debate as largely about the ramifications of that possibility.

Europe appears in many ways a possible microcosm of the globalization process. Another way to put this, is to say that Europe as a region may be a prototype of reactions to globalization. At a minimum, Europe appears set to pose some of the issues that follow from globalization in a particularly clear manner. "Completion" of Europe's internal market and the move to monetary union place Europe in a position where product, capital, and (to a lesser degree) labor markets are much more deeply integrated than is true worldwide. The parallel process of political integration, although incomplete in many respects, nonetheless has led to the creation of central political institutions with some capacity to regulate, standardize, and create non-market incentives for private actors.

How Europe responds to globalization may foreshadow some of the pressures, dilemmas, and possibilities that other regions face over the next decades.[3] The twentieth-century European "welfare state" was in part a Polanyi-esque response to the prospect that markets, organized mainly on a national basis, would be expanding into more and more aspects of human existence. The question today naturally becomes: are there similar responses to an emerging era of global capitalism, where at least some markets are increasingly organized without regard to national boundaries? It is not the purpose of this book to answer that question.

But Europe is an obvious place to look for signals of (at least) one possible version of a *political, macro-level* response. The European Union is an elaborate set of institutions. This reflects and builds on the premise that Europe—although not a single polity by most measures—does have more deeply shared conceptions of civil society than other "regions" in the world economy do. Europe also has two relevant histories: one of trying to remove barriers and free the market, and (a sometimes competing) one of attempts to create a supranationally based welfare capitalist system. To the extent that globalization is sometimes perceived as "Americanization" (or the insinuation of American-style capitalism into distinct national systems) the EU has also the history of trying to assert an independent vision, often against the bogeyman of US "hegemony." In today's ideological environment, it is reasonable to ask, is anyone willing to do anything politically more significant *at the supranational level*, than constructing markets? Europe may not yet have answers, but it is certainly posing that question more actively and sharply than are other regions of the world economy.

For these reasons Europe could simply be "out ahead" of the global and thus in some significant ways an early window into aspects of a future world political economy. Alternatively, Europe could be very different and its evolution may represent a process of distinguishing and insulating itself off from the global. It is also possible that Europe may come to be subsumed by the global. This could happen, for example, if European integration proceeds but the driving forces from (even a much less deeply integrated) world are so much stronger than regional forces, that they overwhelm whatever is distinctly European. In each case the relationship between what is regional/European and what is global would be different. We are not yet in a position to say definitively in this book what that relationship will be. Indeed, the case studies illustrate some aspects of each in particular settings. I draw out implications of this later in the chapter. First it is necessary to look more closely and deeply at the meaning(s) of globalization and at some of the recent research projects and conceptual advances the notion has motivated.

2. Globalization

Different authors use the term "globalization" in a variety of ways, and often not as a precisely defined concept. Analysts argue a great deal about what "it" means, *and* about what the consequences of "it" are expected to be. At times they argue about both, without delineating clearly the logical and causal distinctions. This leads easily to confusion. Sometimes, analysts with different definitions tend to focus on empirical cases that most affect their own interests or with which they feel most comfortable. The tendency then is to designate these as "effects" and reason backward toward "causes," which in turn get labeled as globalization. Other times, the debate slides into a "glass half full, glass half empty" discussion where analysts disagree over whether globalization as a cause of institutional change is more or less powerful than they expect. This is more interesting for what it says about expectations (and how those expectations are derived) than for what it says about the data.

I suggested earlier the kernel of a simple globalization story that skips over all these complexities. It consists of a very sparse cause—mobility. Consider the following caricature: mobility leads to the diffusion of value-added processes and consumption around the globe. This in turn causes an increase in the level of ambient competition in the world economy, which tends to drive prices to a common level. As prices converge, institutions reshape themselves and become more similar as well in order to compete at an equal level.

Of course, this kind of caricature is at best a gross oversimplification that covers up the interesting disagreements among analysts who take the basic idea of mobility more seriously. But it can be used to put some context and perspective around those disagreements. The point is, there is logical "slip-page" at each stage of the story. Mobility does not necessarily lead to the geographic diffusion of production and consumption. Geographic diffusion might not enhance competition. Only under certain restrictive conditions does competition drive prices to a common level. And even if prices converge and institutions need to perform to a set level of competitiveness in order to survive, it is not at all necessary that they become more similar or converge in order to do so. "Functionally equivalent institutional constellations" exist which might be truly equivalent.[4] Or they might look that way, in a competitive environment that is not discriminating enough in a fine grained way to show different performance features.[5]

The contingencies surrounding these causal links make up the bulk of the contemporary research agenda around globalization. Much (but not all) of the debate is about the logical derivation of expectations for institutional change. Some disagreement is about the nature and magnitude of the causal forces per se.

Take the latter issue first. Skeptics make the important point that the process of globalization did not begin in 1989 or for that matter in 1889. If the primary causal force at play is mobility, this of course has been increasing for several hundred years (although not in a linear fashion). Today's integration of national economies is not unprecedented. During the "belle époque" of the late 1800s, declining transportation costs and reductions in trade barriers among advanced industrial countries drove large movements of capital, goods, and people across national borders. By some calculations capital moved just as freely at the end of the nineteenth century as it does at the beginning of the twenty-first. Trade in goods for many countries has only recently surpassed levels (measured in percent of GNP) achieved a hundred years ago. And in certain places, people moved across national borders *more* freely then than they do now. About 60 million people left Europe for the U.S. in the last half of the 1800s.[6]

Most of these trends reversed themselves during the world war years of the first half of the twentieth century. They re-emerged after World War II and in certain aspects accelerated in the 1990s. One major difference between the belle époque and the current era is simply this acceleration and the speed with which things move from place to place. Mobility used to be relatively slow. Now it is fast and in many cases effectively instantaneous. The marginal cost of sending a piece of information around the world in real time is approaching zero. Another difference is size. The late 1800s certainly saw deep integration of sorts, but only among a fraction of the world's nations and population. The "world" in which the "world economy" operates is now much larger. Another important difference may be the very perception of globalization. If people, companies, and state leaders believe in a causal force, their behavior is sure to reflect the consequences. After all, relative prices do not make decisions or change institutions. Only people do that, and they do it in response to their perceptions of relative prices and most certainly other things as well.

These are just a few of the complexities that make globalization a much messier proposition than "the ultimate triumph of markets homogenizing politics and erasing boundaries." It is the complexities that also make globalization a much more interesting proposition.

Globalization arguments blur the boundaries between international relations and comparative politics. The perspective would be valuable even if it did nothing more than encourage the ongoing development of constructive dialogue between these disciplines. We have tried consciously to capitalize on this opportunity within this book. The basic globalization idea is a consummately systemic argument and clearly resonates with neo-realist styles of explanation, which remain popular in IR. Many IR scholars emphasize the importance of global or "systemic" pressures that act on states (or other international actors) to constrain strongly or drive their behavior and institutional structures. Comparativists emphasize the study of national institutional change. The basic globalization idea locates a major driving force of that kind change at a level above the nation-state and forces a deeper dialogue between the two perspectives. In both cases there is something to be learned by taking globalization seriously. IR-type theorists are forced to delineate more clearly the links between supposed systemic pressures and structures, and the consequences of those for national politics. Comparativist-type theorists are forced to look more intently at systemic sources of pressure that may be driving change in particular national sets of institutions. Of course, these are some of the directions in which both subfields are currently heading, and substantial contributions to modern understandings of political economy have resulted from the challenges that emerge.

3. Political Economy and Globalization

The most recent round of globalization arguments centers on the question of convergence and divergence among different forms of capitalism at the end of the twentieth century. But the fundamental notion of course is not new. In the nineteenth century, Durkheim, Marx, and Spencer, had implicit notions of convergence embedded in their respective arguments about the emergence of modern societies.[7] The 1950s and 1960s modernization theorists saw the end of ideology and the rise of "technostructures" in a set of growth and technological imperatives that would gradually put all nations on a single path toward industrial society and modernity. These views fell out of favor in the wake of the 1970s oil crisis. States responded very differently to this "global" shock, and—contra Rostow—it appeared as if much of the developing world was going backwards through the "stages" of economic growth, or had stepped off the train entirely.[8]

The end of the Cold War, along with Europe's practical commitment to monetary union within the Maastricht Treaty, brought the convergence notion back into prominent focus. The explosive growth of foreign exchange markets in the wake of cascading decisions to scrap capital controls provided a presumptive driving force motivating a new round of convergence debates. Of course, it soon became obvious that history was not in fact over as Frances Fukuyama had thought, and that national systems of production and innovation (lumped together under the umbrella term "capitalist") in fact remained quite different even within the supposed "West."[9]

Some scholars questioned whether this diversity would remain in the future. They argued that increasing integration of goods and capital markets as well as the diffusion of ideas and cultural norms were driving a convergence among these distinct national systems, which were becoming more like each other over time.[10] Other scholars responded that the convergence glass was actually more empty than full. National systems had changed (and presumably, would change) considerably less than the convergence school anticipated. Or systems were changing but in directions that would make them more, not less diverse. A rich variety of institutions, practices, and cultural ways of being would remain the rule and might even increase despite the relative globalization of certain kinds of markets.[11] National politics and institutions were so deeply ingrained in political-economic life in Western countries that they would either refract or block price signals and other kinds of pressures from the international environment. Even if systemic pressures were quite strong, there remained "functionally equivalent" institutional configurations that could compete successfully with each other, from very different starting points. And going back to the critique of the independent variable, it was also possible that the pressures themselves were not so potent as some scholars had said.[12]

This book is not going to settle the debate among these viewpoints. In fact, I believe there is quite a lot of common ground present in the discussion, which then goes off along two different visions of a future world political economy that we cannot yet see evidence of. No one really argues that convergence means a future Germany would be institutionally indistinguishable from the United States. The convergence vision (and it is not a precise argument) is one of a surprising degree to which national systems will tend to become more similar.[13] The most strongly competing vision (also not a precise argument in this context) is one of historical institutionalism. Here the driving forces of mobility tend to push national systems further down their own path of development as the world economy spawns a more deeply developed division of labor. Competition acts upon different preexisting structures in different ways. In other words, "common" international pressures are perceived differently by actors who live in different institutional settings because those pressures are, in practical terms, functionally different.[14]

Countries might then look more different from each other in twenty years than they do today.[15] But even if the implications of these visions are different enough from each other not to blur the distinctions, much of the evidence is still to come. And since the driving force of mobility is much weaker in some aspects of the world economy than it is in others, the causal force behind the independent variable in either argument may not be so strong as to provide a good test. Of course, there are also many other forces operating in this complex story, and some of these could turn out to be much more important as causes of institutional change than mobility.[16] These are salutary reminders of an important point: big abstract arguments can be wrong in more than one way.

Yet big abstract arguments also have advantages—they tend to generate provocative ideas with possibly major implications. Globalization arguments have produced at least one very interesting proposition of this sort, about states' ability to control macroeconomic variables within national borders and thus to make effective choices about macro policies. The modal argument is that this ability has declined as a result of globalization, most importantly but not only as a result of the progressive freeing of capital from constraints on mobility.

At least three interesting questions have emerged from this discussion. One question is how much has state capacity and efficacy really declined. Garrett (along with others) argues against the hypothesis that it has dissolved in global capital flows. There is still plenty of difference in how much governments spend and for what purpose.[17] A second question is whether the changes in capital mobility are voluntary and reversible, or an overdetermined and irreversible development outside the control of political decisions. Helleiner argued that capital was made mobile through a series of state decisions more than through technological or other structural changes, and that state choices can always be reversed if the decision calculus should change.[18] A third question is how does it affect the prospects for policy coordination and cooperation among states. Webb argues that coordination and cooperation are not prevalent, but that this may not be much of a change since cooperation was less common than generally thought during the earlier, Cold War era which serves as an analytic baseline.[19]

Clearly the debate over globalization has moved beyond the stage of bashing a naïve convergence scenario. This has produced a general sense of consensus around a few important points. Mobility does change relative prices in economies that were previously insulated from world markets, as Keohane and Milner emphasize.[20] This will change the interests and capabilities of many political and economic actors, but even if prices everywhere were the same (and it is unlikely that they can or will be) those effects do not manifest themselves in a straightforward fashion. Political coalitions, bargaining, extant institutions, and—most fundamentally in my view—uncertainty about the nature of relative prices, where they are coming from and where they are going to, impact upon the ways in which actors see themselves and calculate their interests.[21] There is a fairly definitive empirical observation in place: not everyone is acting the same in response to globalization—not governments, not transnational corporations, and certainly not people.[22]

Political and economic actors are differently situated in terms of their abilities to benefit from globalization. One analytic lever that might help in gaining a more distinct understanding of the interests at play is the "mobile vs. non-mobile cleavage." The basic economic argument is quite simple: owners of mobile assets are likely to be advantaged by globalization while owners of nonmobile assets tend to lose out. This argument can be developed along different units of analysis. Following Rogowski, the emphasis would be on factors of production; following Frieden, the emphasis would be on economic sectors; following Milner, the emphasis would be on firms. Each approach generates a set of hypotheses about the preferences of the relevant actors depending on their inherent mobility, and particularly how those preferences and power resources should be changed by globalization.

On first glance it might seem possible (even obvious) to "test" the predictions of these arguments against each other. That is actually a very complicated proposition, and the reason is simple. Consider the underlying claim: globalization acts upon relative prices which in turn affect the preferences of actors. But countries do not respond solely on the basis of actors' changing preferences in a way that can be modeled clearly. And lots of other things besides globalization could change actors' preferences as well.[23] It is obvious that simple economic pluralism is not a very helpful model of political outcomes, but it is not so obvious what should replace it in this kind of theoretical experiment. If many things could change actors' preferences, and then actors' preferences do not translate very clearly into policy or institutional change, it quickly becomes very difficult to test the predictions about which actors' preferences are making a difference in a way that would distinguish among contending theoretical claims. There are simply too many degrees of freedom in any political equation that could be written on the basis of these theories.[24]

Clearly the next step would be to articulate more refined models of how political and societal institutions modulate the impact of these kinds of changing preferences. Garrett and Lange did this in one relatively simple way, and it was a positive move toward contextualizing the globalization argument by focusing more closely on processes of political change.[25] They added to the story labor union strength as a proxy measure of (one aspect of) societal institutions, and focused attention on the variance in formal political institutions among regime type, number of veto points for policy action, and the relative insulation of bureaucratic agencies. In a related argument, Torben Iversen develops a more complicated, multiple equilibria model that identifies a set of institutional configurations consistent with superior economic performance in the context of a "rational expectations" response to globalization-induced pressures.[26] No one claims that these are fully developed models of the process of political change in globalization, or that this is the only way to approach the problem. It is a useful step, because it starts to elucidate from the micro level upwards, some of the mechanisms through which the driving forces of globalization cause observable political and policy change.

Approaching the problem in this way, from a micro level aiming upwards, is good for generating more specific hypotheses about discrete aspects of process. It is also possible to approach the problem from a macro level, aiming downwards, by conceptualizing mechanisms in a more abstract and generalized way. Berger and Dore did this, building off a critique of naïve convergence arguments as lacking a good general sense of the mechanism(s) by which convergence might happen. If globalization means the further extension of market competition, it is important to remember that markets do not automatically lead to convergence in the absence of other conditions. Put simply, factor price equalization and even the equalization of costs of production does not demand convergence of patterns of organizations and institutions—even in a world of perfect information. An alternative possible scenario would have systems that are equally successful at solving problems, but develop different institutional means for doing so that are "functional equivalents" price-wise. This would be a form of divergence rather than convergence. Or, systems might specialize in solving different problems. This would be segregation into market niches.[27] It is also the case that other things, not simply market competition, could produce convergence. For example, actors might copy institutions from elsewhere for the sake of legitimacy rather than efficient performance. Even if convergence (or some relative degree of convergence) is the expected outcome of globalization's driving forces, the mechanisms by which this happens will be complex and politically precarious.

Berger and Dore offered three general views about the nature of possible mechanisms, from a wide angled or macro perspective. These three mechanisms are not exhaustive of the possibilities; nor are they exclusive of each other (any individual case may demonstrate elements of more than one).[28] The analytic step forward here nonetheless is considerable.[29] Their three general mechanisms differ from each other in interesting ways, and point to distinct visions of the kinds of politics globalization might be leading or contributing to.

The first mechanism is essentially an argument about convergence as the triumph of market forces. Over time, as markets spread geographically and sectorally, competition forces the costs of production to equalize. Associated with this idea (although not strictly required by it in economic theory) is the notion that patterns of organizing production, and common institutional configurations for doing that, would also emerge. The functional equivalence of different institutional configurations that I discussed earlier is, in this argument, only an interim stable state. As markets expand, competition becomes sufficiently intense and fine-grained to differentiate among what were functional equivalents in performance. A set of "optimal" institutions emerges. Governments and other political actors don't disappear from this story, but they take a backseat role as passive or complicit actors in a process that is being pushed forward principally by market forces.[30] When market rationality is the fundamental driving force, it is hard to envision (through neoclassical lenses at least) a condition of long-term stability in a world with highly diverse ways of organizing economic life.

The second mechanism relies on diffusion among institutional forms of something like "best practice." Markets are important in this story because they do create competitive conditions, but since there are few markets in the real world that come anywhere near to the ideal of a perfect market, competition is often much less intense and constraining of possibilities than stark economic theories portray. In the real world, and in the foreseeable future, goods are not standardized; information is highly imperfect and impacted in organizations and tacit knowledge; factors of production are not homogeneous. Thus market pressures, real as they may be, are almost always indeterminate, uncertain, and confusing to the participants. Organizations trying to survive and succeed in this kind of an environment will look outside themselves to other organizations for clues and signals about what works. They will copy or mimic practices primarily from other organizations that seem to be doing well.

Aggregate this kind of process over many organizations (including but not limited to governments and firms) and the result is the diffusion of "best practice," which is really just a socially sanctioned legitimate way of doing things that observers generally think is the "sensible" or "proper" way to do it. Ultimately there is no presumption of "optimal" or efficient outcomes in this story. "Best practice" could simply be what the biggest and most visible players in the game are doing, so long as they do it well enough to survive. Satisficing is the operative image here. It is easy to imagine this mechanism producing a low-efficiency equilibrium "trap" where best practice is in fact only an apparently successful option among a very bad set of socially-available alternatives, with other more efficient possibilities unable to gain a foothold. As a broad image of political economy this looks very different to the outcome of the market-competition mechanism that I discussed above.

The third mechanism sees convergence emerging from the development of internationally negotiated (or coerced) sets of rules that firms and governments participating in the global economy will come to follow. This notion points out that mobility (and thus globalization) raises the stakes of *both* cooperation and competition between states and firms in different countries. And it may be just as hard, if not harder, to cooperate effectively at a high level as it is to compete effectively, between firms or states that have very different social structures and organizations.

Powerful actors may try to influence the shape of other actors in their organizational field, either to create a so-called level playing field for competition, or to facilitate effective cooperation (or some combination). In the European Union, for example, integration stalled out in the 1970s in part because of a lack of convergence among national systems of production and regulation. To move further along, it became necessary to negotiate, through some mixture of harmonization and mutual recognition, a set of rules and institutional structures for a common base. Kahler and Ostry, writing in the Berger and Dore book, develop similar ideas about "systems friction" that emerges when very differently organized economies interact at higher levels. Kahler interprets the Structural Impediments Initiative (1989–90) talks between the U.S. and Japan as an effort to generate, through political processes, enough convergence to maintain the possibilities of trade and cooperation between these two very different economies.[31]

This is a distinct mechanism of convergence, since it depends heavily on domestic and international political processes, ideas, bargaining, and ultimately the power of the actors to shape others in their organizational field of action. By some reckonings, globalization of this sort really might simply be a euphemism for "Americanization" (just as it might have been thought of as a euphemism for the spread of Japanese models in the 1980s). If the resulting configuration of institutions reinforces the power structure that underlay its construction, by continuing to favor the actors that are already most powerful rather than diffusing power around to others, then convergence around negotiated or coerced set of rules is a plausible stable state and potentially for a long time.

4. Where to from Here?

My co-authors and I write from a perspective that is closer to the macro, "top down" view of how to approach the mechanisms of globalization. This represents simply a shared analytic bet, made on pragmatic grounds. In other words, we are not making some absolute claim about the "best" or "most scientific" means of approaching the problem. It seems self-evident to us that bottom-up and top-down approaches will yield different kinds of insights. Ideally, points of agreement or complementarity in these arguments would emerge over time.

We see at least three possible directions in which to develop a set of arguments. We aim to explore more deeply the mechanisms by which globalization drives changes in the European political economy. A major part of our effort here is to attach specific *agents* to stories that sometimes lack them and as a result tend to rely heavily on nebulous driving forces ("efficiency," "the market"). We also examine *obstacles* and *intervening variables* to diffusion processes, from an inductive point of view. In the several cases in this book, we ask what are the major political, social, and economic actors that stand in the way of globalization-induced change in Europe. How do these intervening variables filter, transform, or translate global-level driving forces? Our objective finally is to use these pieces of knowledge to go back *and refine or revise our understanding of what globalization is really about.*

We started with a very stark and parsimonious notion of globalization as an independent variable. It seems certain that confronting empirical cases will complicate that. In the real world, even the cleanest markets are quite messy. The social and political structures that surround them are even more so. We try to bring some order to that subject by focusing our energy around three possible contributions to understanding. What is globalization and what does it cause? What are the mechanisms of globalization-induced change in governance and social structures in Europe? And if Europe per se does figure significantly in the explanations of change, what is special about Europe's regional order and what are the consequences for Europe's interface with other regions and the global system?

The next section details the research strategy through which we aim to make progress on these questions.

Figure 1 is an orienting framework for the book. This chart lays out several steps in a structured causal argument. There is variation possible at each step. But ignore that for the moment and consider the diagram as a simple flow chart. I discuss first the overall structure as if this were such a flow chart, and specify the path through it that we use as a practical null hypothesis. After that, I go back to consider the variations that can arise at each step along the way.

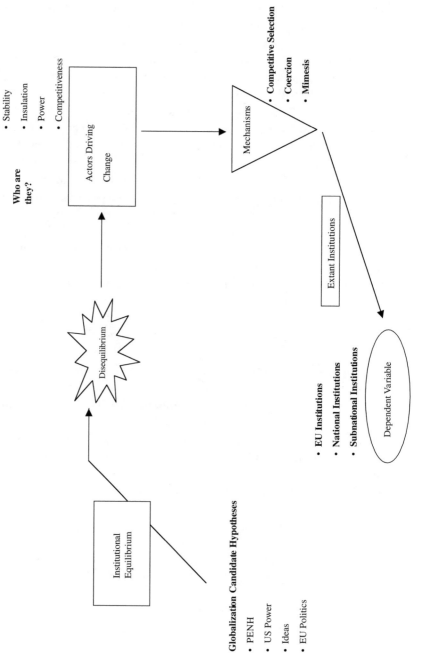

FIGURE 1

The flow chart begins with a de facto *institutional equilibrium*. This is in principle a social steady state. I mean this in a practical sense, that absent any major exogenous driving forces the institutional structure would not change dramatically but rather would evolve gradually along a consistent trajectory without any substantial discontinuities. Think of it simply as an extant set of institutions, governance structures, laws, or ways of doing things.

Globalization creates *disequilibrium*. Under the pressure of this disequilibrium, *actors mobilize and press for change*. This reflects some underlying motivation structure—what is it that actors want to achieve in the face of, or by responding to, this pressure? Step 4 contains the *mechanism(s)* by which institutional change happens. Mechanisms operate through elements of the existing structure to yield some kind of change that can be seen in step 5, the "outcome" of the process or *dependent variable* of the argument.

This is a complex causal framework. To unravel something like this in empirical cases is easier, if there is an explicit null hypothesis to bounce off from. In depicting such a null hypothesis, we do not intend to privilege the causal path it represents, or even to say implicitly that it is the most likely explanation of the outcomes we seek to explain. Simply, we propose it as a pragmatic baseline that is relatively clear and parsimonious.

We call it the Political Economy Null Hypothesis (PENH). It represents the following simple story about globalization—with sparse causes, simple motivations and mechanisms, and a clear expected outcome. Mobility (as defined earlier in this chapter) is the major driving force. There are changes in relative prices that are perceived by economic actors.[32] These actors experience an increase in the ambient level of competition in the world economy—creating disequilibrium. Actors are motivated to respond by the perceived need to maintain competitiveness. Actors who fail to do this are eliminated through the mechanism of competitive selection, according to efficiency. Existing institutions may hinder or slow down adjustment, but not stop it. The process "ends" with changes in institutions or governance structures—the observed dependent variable. In short, the PENH is a story about mobility, converging prices, increased competition, and adaptive institutions.

Each author in this volume evaluates the explanatory power of the PENH in the individual case. A simple null hypothesis like this easily generates a set of theoretical expectations about potential outcomes and these expectations should be testable. We ask, are the changes we see in institutional structure the result of the PENH causal path, as a first cut? The authors then move to refine the argument by seeking out more precise renditions of the driving forces, the agents, and the mechanisms of change.

Globalization Candidate Hypotheses

The PENH captures only one of several systemic causes that could be important driving forces for change in the first step of the model. We consider three candidate alternatives—U.S. power, ideas, and EU politics.[33] The first stresses the power and capabilities of the United States to set the terms and the rules of market competition.[34] The second stresses a set of ideas, many of which may be about the nature of global economic change but are analytically distinct from material economic forces themselves. For example, firms may believe that they are subject to new constraints from global markets even if they are not, and low-wage workers in the United States may believe that they are suffering declining real wages because of workers in Indonesia even if economists assure them that this is not the cause.

EU politics stresses constraints and incentives that emanate from EU institutions. With our special interest in parsing out the contribution of European-level causes to change in domestic institutions, we have three broad hypotheses about the possible role of Europe as a causal force.

- The EU may be an autonomous source of driving forces that would be significant even in the absence of global-level driving forces.
- The EU may be a strategic environment within which other kinds of causes are played out, and manipulated by actors. In this view Europe acts as a "filter" and a playing field where states and firms try to moderate and control how they are affected by global driving forces.
- Europe may be a causally "empty" level. In this view Europe is simply a pipeline that transmits global causes to states and firms. In this case the explanation of change will focus on the causal importance of national-level institutions.

Actors

Who are the actors that are pushing for, and against, change? They may be the economic interest groups that are the familiar stuff of modern pluralist political economy arguments. Or they may be state officials; international organizations; powerful transnational actors (including but not limited to large consulting firms, investment banking houses, institutional money managers); epistemic communities of one or another kind; or some other relevant set.

Some of these suggestions about who the relevant actors might be follow (by deduction) from standard theoretical perspectives in political economy. For example, realist arguments point to the importance of state actors while some "world system" arguments from sociology highlight the role of transnational knowledge networks such as those embedded in consulting and accountancy firms.[35] Our shared analytic bet here is that the theoretical field is still open in the sense that we do not know, a priori, what the range of possible generalizations might be.[36] Hence we look for the relevant actors regardless of whether they fall into these suggested categories.

This mix of deductive and inductive approaches is somewhat less neat than we would like. But it retains the possibility of surprise, and that is an advantage. It is particularly valuable here because if globalization is indeed a significant driving force for political-economic change, it is possible that new categories of actors and interest groups may emerge out of rapidly changing constellations of interests not parsed out neatly by existing theoretical arguments.[37] We believe also that sacrificing deductive parsimony is a tolerable cost here, since the actors who are both forcing and impeding change tend to be the most easily visible elements in an empirical investigation. Thus we are inclined to work with a greater degree of openness at this juncture in the argument than we are elsewhere, where we rely more heavily on deductive style reasoning to focus the empirical research.

Motivations and Mechanisms

Ultimately, it is actors and not structural forces that change institutions. Actors have a motivation structure upon which driving forces for change operate. Actors may be motivated by "competitiveness," in the sense that selection would act to weed out institutions that do not perform to a particular standard. This is the motivation typically stressed by economistic models. Or actors may try to insulate themselves from competitive pressures. They may be seeking stability and predictability (not efficiency) in a rapidly changing environment, where the standards of performance may not become clear. This is a motivation that sociologists pay more attention to.[38] Or actors may look for sources of power that can be used to restructure elements of the environment in ways that advantage them, as realist arguments in international politics tend to stress. It is also possible that actors may be seeking not to *compete* with each other per se, but to find ways to *cooperate* more effectively for joint objectives.[39] Each case study tries to identify the operative motivations for the relevant actors who are seeking change.

The mechanisms of change themselves are linked closely to actors' motivations (though they are not identical). We make use of the framework constructed by Berger and Dore, along with the influential work of Dimaggio and Powell, to specify three general mechanisms which differ in their implications for the kinds of politics that globalization engenders.[40]

Competitive Selection is the first and most familiar of these mechanisms. It rests on the idea that as global markets become increasingly competitive there is less room for variation in performance. Competition selects among institutions, on the basis of efficiency. There is a single equilibrium as the ideal endpoint of this process.[41] Although recalcitrant vested interests and other sources of stickiness in extant institutions push back to limit the speed and possibly the magnitude of change, isomorphism—increasing similarity of institutions across different national contexts—is the asymptote which institutions approach. Politics actually takes a backseat in this story. The competitive forces are sufficiently strong and determinative, that the inevitable pushing and pulling of political actors and institutions struggling to respond to (and in some cases divert) those forces constitute a backdrop of *relatively less* significance.

Mimesis is the second general mechanism. Global markets may be increasingly competitive, but in most markets competition is still imperfect and lumpy. There remains considerable variation in performance and ways of doing things. Most important, there is simply too much uncertainty within markets for actors really to know in advance what will and will not work in any given setting, much less be "efficient."[42] Even if the relevant actors have clearly articulated goals (and they often do not), the technologies, organizational strategies, and other means for achieving those goals are poorly understood and ambiguous. For example, many states and firms may wish to create a high technology district or "Silicon Valley" of their own, but how do they actually promote that?[43]

Mimesis, then, is about institutions responding to complexity and uncertainty by copying things that seem to work. Actors will mimic characteristics of other actors that appear to be doing well. Dimaggio and Powell called this "mimesis under uncertainty." It differs from competitive selection in that it carries no presumption of optimality. Mimesis is more like a satisficing than it is like an optimizing strategy. The choice of what to do rests heavily on the perceived adequacy of success that others are achieving.

This creates legitimacy of certain practices and principles among institutions that already exist. With legitimate ways of doing things in place, meaningful competition actually tends to fall. If competitive selection is a strongly operative mechanism, we would expect more frequently to see actors experimenting with new ideas and systems in an attempt to do better than existing standards. If the mechanism is mimesis, experimentation and risk taking should be infrequent. Doing just as well by mimicking what works should be more prominent.

The third general mechanism is *coercion*, which is fundamentally about the exercise of power, by actors trying to shape the world in which they and other actors live. Powerful actors may be powerful by virtue of their economic or market status, but also by virtue of their political and ideological positions.[44] As a general mechanism, coercion does not prejudge this point.

Precisely because power comes from several different sources and can operate in a variety of ways, it is very rare that one source of power controls outcomes in a straightforward way. Thus, coercive mechanisms focus analytic attention on the bargaining processes that take place in both domestic and international politics as power meets power. Bargaining happens precisely because there are multiple ways of doing things, promulgated in different instances by actors who are sufficiently capable to try to sustain and extend their institutions and practices. The motivation for trying to bring other actors into line can vary, as I discussed above. It might be to stabilize and slow down the rate of change in a market; to "level a playing field" for continued competition; to "un-level" the playing field in favor of the powerful actor; or to facilitate cooperation at high levels of interdependence. (In real cases, of course, these motivations can be combined—as in some instances of EU regulatory harmonization where motivations often seem to mix facilitating competition and cooperation at high levels.) In all instances, coercive mechanisms emphasize the role of one actor consciously trying to change another—in contrast to impersonal selection by markets, or copying that is initiated by the actor that is undergoing change.

Outcomes

The major observed outcome or dependent variable of each case study in this book is a set of institutional changes. But no political system is a blank slate. Our causal model specifies drivers and processes of change, which operate ultimately in the context of a set of previously existing institutions. The structure of existing institutions bends and shapes the process along the way. The authors consider the impact of international, European-level, national, and subnational institutions at whatever stage in their causal argument these influences appear. But we pay particular attention in each case to the "final" step in the analytic framework, where mechanisms work themselves through into institutional change. The justification for this is simple. Extant institutions are almost certain to have a strong influence on how relevant actors perceive the situation, and on what their motivations are.[45] But the influence of these institutions is likely to be most easily visible in empirical research at the last step in our analytic framework. In practice, to demonstrate the effect at this stage in the argument makes it easier to go back and see more clearly what role existing institutions play along the way. It also provides a useful metric for making some judgments about the extent and significance of institutional change. Ultimately, however, our claims do not rest on these judgments.[46] Our claims rest on demonstrating causes, processes, and mechanisms of institutional change.

This section has laid out a multifaceted research agenda for the case studies in this book. It was my aim to make clear the structure of the overall framework for argument, the variants that are to be investigated along the way, and the logic of how the pieces tie together. I have not tried in this introductory chapter to write down specific empirical manifestations of these arguments that ought to be visible in case studies. I have not specified expectations that follow from global-level causes, European-level causes, and national-level causes in individual cases. That task is left up to the individual authors and their particular chapters. Because the case studies in this book cover a broad spectrum in European political economy, the general arguments that I presented in this chapter will work themselves out in specific ways and look contextually different in the following chapters. It is the general logic that links them together of course, not the precise empirical expectations or outcomes in diverse settings.

Plan of the Book

The next chapters are case studies of particular areas of European political economy, all of which have undergone substantial governance transformations in the last decade. Each author begins by describing the nature of the change and explaining how it might plausibly be linked in a causal sense to the driving forces of globalization. The chapters then develop alternative hypotheses about the causal impact of European-level and national-level driving forces, tying each to a set of expectations about the process of change and its outcome. The bulk of each chapter is an analytic narrative that explains, mainly through historical process-tracing, the actual causal route to the dependent variable. In each case the explanation is "tested" against the starting hypotheses, and at the same time situated within the analytic framework which guides the book as a whole.

The diversity of the cases is striking. It raises the issue of case selection and the scientific justification for looking at a fairly wide spectrum of cases, selected from a much larger possible universe. Our cases are not a random sample in the sense that would justify generalizing our conclusions a priori. Indeed, the authors in this book are writing about cases that they know well and that they investigated because they witnessed institutional changes that they believed to be surprising or at least interesting. We do not systematically compare cases of change to cases of stasis. That would be one possible way to approach the problem, but it is not the only possible way nor is it self-evidently the most useful at this stage in our understanding.[47] These are cases that demonstrate substantial change in the dependent variable and thus should demonstrate the causal stories we are searching for in a particularly prominent way.

It should be obvious that this book is a theory-enriching and hypothesis-generating exercise, not an attempt to "test" definitively or in a highly generalizable way any particular big theory about globalization. In our view, it is too early in our understanding of the process to create and engage in such tests (unless we are willing to be satisfied with falsifying "strawman" type arguments, and we are not). We believe it is more important at this stage to develop a more refined set of arguments, hypotheses, and ideas about the kinds of politics engendered by globalization.

Our measure of success is not necessarily a definitive proof of any particular statement—although the case studies in this book certainly add weight to the conclusion (shared by others of course) that simplistic globalization/convergence arguments are not correct. Similarly, our PENH is an analytic baseline only. If this book moves toward "falisifying" it, we would not want to claim that as our main contribution. Our measure of success is more demanding than that. In fact what we do should not be read as trying to "falsify" per se any particular perspective on the politics of globalization, although we do call into question the usefulness of various mainstream perspectives to capture very significant political dynamics in the real world. To take the debate a few steps further, we seek the generation of new and provocative insights into the mechanisms of institutional change in response to globalization, and the particular place that Europe as a highly organized political region holds in that story.

Endnotes

1. Recent interesting and relevant examples include the essays in Colin Crouch and Wolfgang Streeck, eds. *Political Economy of Modern Capitalism* (London: Sage, 1997); Randall W. Kindley and David F (Good, eds, *The Challenge of Globalization and Institution Building: Lessons from Small European States* (Boulder: Westview Press, 1997); Neil Fligstein, "Markets, Politics, and Globalization," Uppsala Lectures in Business 13 (Stockholm: Almquist and Wiksell, 1997); Roland Axtmann ed (*Globalization and Europe: Theoretical and Empirical Investigations* (London: Pinter, 1998); Ash Amin and Nigel Thrift, eds (*Globalization, Institutions, and Regional Development in Europe* (Oxford: Oxford University Press, 1994)); Robert Boyer and Daniel Drache, eds. *States Against Markets: The Limits of Globalization* (London: Routledge, 1996); Wayne Sandholtz and Alec Stone Sweet, eds. *European Integration and Supranational Governance* (New York: Oxford University Press, 1998); Herbert Kitschelt, Peter Lange, Gary Marks, and John D. Stephens, *Continuity and Change in Contemporary Capitalism* (Cambridge: Cambridge University Press, 1999; see in particular the essay by Liesbet Hooghe and Gary Marks, "The Making of a Polity: The Struggle over European Integration," pp. 70–100).
2. There are, of course, a large number of other definitions in the literature. The advantage of starting with such a narrow definition, is that we avoid assuming very much about effects. It is an effort to keep the driving force simple and thus highlight the causal links that lead to outcomes.
3. See for example the contributions of Peter Hall, Gosta Esping-Andersen, Kees van Kerbergen, and Hanspeter Kriesi in Herbert Kitschelt, Peter Lange, Gary Marks, and John D. Stephens, eds. *Continuity and Change in Contemporary Capitalism* (Cambridge: Cambridge University Press, 1999).
4. See for example Charles Sabel, Gary Herrigel, Richard Deeg, and R. Kazis, "Regional Prosperities Compared: Baden-Wurttemberg and Massachusetts in the 1980s," *Economy and Society* 1989, 18.

5. See Richard C. Lewontin, "The Shape of Optimality," in John Dupre, ed. *The Latest on the Best: Essays on Evolution and Optimality*. (Cambridge: MIT Press, 1987), pp. 151–62.

6. This is now a well travelled discussion. For data and interpretations see, for example, Paul Bairoch and Richard Kozul-Wright, *Globalization Myths: Some Historical Reflections on Integration, Industrialization, and Growth in the World Economy* (Geneva: UNCTAD, 1996); Richard Baldwin and Phillipe Martin, "Two Waves of Globalization: Superficial Similarities, Fundamental Differences," NBER Working Paper 6904, January 1999; James Foreman-Peck, ed. *Historical Foundations of Globalization* (Northampton: Edward Elgar, 1998); Dani Rodrik, *Has Globalization Gone Too Far?* (Washington DC: IIE, 1997); Jeffrey G. Williamson, "Globalization, Convergence, and History," NBER Working Paper 5259, 1995; Timothy J. McKewon, "The Global Economy, Post-Fordism, and Trade Policy in Advanced Capitalist States," in Kitschelt et. al. eds, p. 11–35

7. Durkheim argued that the division of labor leads to organic solidarity that replaces the mechanical solidarity of traditional societies. Marx argued that the inevitable fall in the rate of profit would affect all capitalist systems and bring them to a common finale. Spencer argued that social darwinism would extrude alternatives to yield the "one best way."

8. The articles in John Goldthorpe ed., *Order and Conflict in Contemporary Capitalism* (Oxford: Clarendon Press, 1984) summarize many of the major arguments. Some of the more influential arguments include Walt Rostow, *The Stages of Economic Growth* (Cambridge: Cambridge University Press, 1968); John Kenneth Galbraith *Economic Development* (Boston: Houghton Mifflin, 1964); Daniel Bell, *The End of Ideology: On the Exhaustion of Political Ideas in the Fifties* (Glencoe, IL: Free Press, 1960); Raymond Aron, *Democracy and Totalitarianism*, trans. Valence Ionescu (London: Weidenfeld and Nicolson, 1968).

9. See Francis Fukuyama, *The End of History and the Last Man* (New York: Free Press, 1992); Charles Hampden-Turner and Alfons Trompenaars, *The Seven Cultures of Capitalism: Value Systems for Creating Wealth in the United States, Japan, Germany, France, Britain, Sweden, and the Netherlands* (New York: Currency/Doubleday, 1993).

10. John Meyer et. al. "World Society and the Nation State," *American Journal of Sociology*, 1997; Kenichi Ohmae, *The Borderless World: Power and Strategy in the Interlinked Economy* (New York, Harper and Row, 1991); Robert Reich, *The Work of Nations: Preparing Ourselves for 21st Century Capitalism* (New York: Knopf, 1991); Malcolm Waters, *Globalization* (New York: Routledge, 1995).

11. See for example Suzanne Berger and Ronald Dore, eds. *National Diversity and Global Capitalism* (Ithaca: Cornell University Press, 1996); Paul Hirst and

Grahame Thompson, *Globalization in Question: The International Economy and the Possibilities of Governance* (Cambridge MA: Blackwell, 1996); Louis W. Pauly and Simon Reich, "National Structures and Multinational Corporate Behavior: Enduring Differences in the Age of Globalization," *International Organization* 51 (1997): 1–30.

12. For example see Suzanne Berger, "Introduction," in Berger and Dore, eds; J. Rogers Hollingsworth, Phillippe C. Schmitter, and Wolfgang Streeck, *Governing Capitalist Economies: Performance and Control of Economic Sectors* (New York: Oxford University Press, 1994); Robert O. Keohane and Helen Milner, eds. *Internationalization and Domestic Politics* (Cambridge: Cambridge University Press, 1996).

13. A powerful statement is Susan Strange, "The Future of Global Capitalism; Or, Will Divergence Persist Forever?" in Crouch and Streeck, eds, pp. 182–91. Convergence remains more a vision than a precise argument because it does not include a definite metric for how much similarity is expected and thus how much would be surprising. By the same logic, "divergence" theorists need to be just as cautious about implying that *any* degree of difference between national systems disproves the globalization thesis.

14. Some existing and relevant differences include resource endowments, the organization of labor and capital markets, formal and informal political rules, and alliances between political factions, subnational regions, and countries. A good discussion is in Herbert Kitschelt, Peter Lange, Gary Marks, and John D. Stephens, "Convergence and Divergence in Advanced Capitalist Democracies," in Kitschelt, Lange, Marks, and Stephens, eds. The point is, a single driving force pressing against such different institutional configurations is quickly refracted into what are essentially very different driving forces of change.

15. For example, one can imagine a world economy in which the U.S. specializes in health care and finance, Japan builds cars and consumer electronics, Denmark grows high value-added agricultural products; and each country has institutions set up to optimize those activities.

16. For example, if there were to be a big war.

17. Geoffrey Garrett, "Global Markets and National Politics: Collision Course or Virtuous Circle?" *International Organization* 52 (Autumn 1998): 787–824.

18. Eric Helleiner, *States and The Reemergence of Global Finance: From Bretton Woods to the 1990s* (Ithaca: Cornell University Press, 1994).

19. Michael C. Webb, "International Economic Structures, Government Interests, and International Coordination of Macroeconomic Adjustment Policies," *International Organization* 45 (1991): 307–42.

20. Robert O. Keohane and Helen V. Milner, eds. *Internationalization and Domestic Politics* (Cambridge: Cambridge University Press, 1996).

21. Keohane and Milner recognize the importance of coalitions and institutions. Steven Weber and Elliot Posner, "Emerging Markets: Good for Us? Good for Everyone?" *Brown Journal of International Affairs* Summer 1998, emphasize the importance of uncertainty about what relative prices really are and what they mean for actors' interests.

22. See also Pauly and Reich, "National Structures and Multinational Corporate Behavior: Enduring Differences in the Age of Globalization," for evidence on the behavior of multinational firms.

23. Torben Iversen and Anne Wren, "Equality, Employment, and Budgetary Restraint: The Trilemma of the Service Economy," *World Politics* 50 (July 1998): 507–46) believe that it is the shift from manufacturing toward services, *in the context* of globalization constraints, that sets up a "trilemma" between budgetary restraint, income equality, and employment growth. They explain the different choices that countries make about how to manage the trade-offs among these three objectives, as a dependent variable of a country's particular value structure and ideology, expressed in institutions such as tax codes or labor bargaining structures.

24. See for example Helen Milner and Robert Keohane, "Internationalization and Domestic Politics: A Conclusion," in Keohane and Milner eds.

25. Geoffrey Garrett and Peter Lange, "Internationalization, Institutions, and Political Change," *International Organization* 49 (Autumn 1995): 627–55.

26. Torben Iversen, *Contested Economic Institutions: The Politics of Macroeconomics and Wage Bargaining in Advanced Democracies* (Cambridge: Cambridge University Press, 1999).

27. I explore the logic of these arguments in Steven Weber, "What is Competition?" forthcoming.

28. See in particular Suzanne Berger, "Introduction" p. 16 in Berger and Dore, eds.

29. See Jon Elster, *Explaining Technical Change* Chapter 4 for a now-standard argument about this issue. A good recent discussion in sociology is Peter Hedstrom and Richard Swedberg, eds. *Social Mechanisms: An Analytical Approach to Social Theory* (New York: Cambridge University Press, 1998).

30. Suzanne Berger, "Introduction," in Berger and Dore, eds. p. 16.

31. Miles Kahler, "Trade and Domestic Differences"; Sylvia Ostry, "Policy Approaches to System Friction: Convergence Plus," in Berger and Dore, eds.

32. In the null hypothesis, the real and perceived situations of actors correspond reasonably closely. In other words, there is relatively smooth transition between changes in relative prices in the real world, and the perception of those changes by relevant economic actors.

33. Again, this represents a shared analytic bet on causal variables; it is not a claim that this represents the universe of possible systemic causes.

34. For many companies and countries outside the U.S., "globalization" in the late 1990s is seen as a codeword for increasing competition with American firms. This echoes literature in the late 1980s where "globalization"—from the U.S. perspective—was in effect the global reach of a new kind of competition from Japan. See for example Michael Best, *The New Competition: Institutions of Industrial Restructuring* (Cambridge: Harvard University Press, 1990).

35. See for example John W. Meyer, John Boli, George M. Thomas, and Francisco O. Ramirez, "World Society and the Nation State," *American Journal of Sociology* 103 (1997): 144–81.

36. This is true for all elements of the argument of course. The next paragraph in the text explains why we can afford to leave the issue more open for the actors than for mechanisms or causal driving forces.

37. John Zysman and I develop this view in "Why the Changed Relation Between Security and Economics Will Alter the Character of the European Union," in Zysman and Andrew Schwartz, eds., *Enlarging Europe: The Industrial Foundations of a New Political Reality* (Berkeley: IAS, 1998).

38. For example, see William Lazonick, *Business Organization and the Myth of the Market Economy* (Cambridge: Cambridge University Press, 1991). See also Neil Fligstein, *The Transformation of Corporate Control* (Cambridge: Harvard University Press, 1990).

39. Weber, "What is Competition?"

40. Paul J. DiMaggio and Walter W. Powell, "The Iron Cage Revisited: Institutional Isomorphism and Collective Rationality in Organizational Fields," *American Sociological Review* 48 (1983): 147–60.

41. Of course this is an "ideal" since political and economic systems are not expected to reach an equilibrium.

42. This may not be true of *all* markets, but it is true of most.

43. See Annalee Saxenian, *Regional Advantage: Culture and Competition in Silicon Valley and Route 128* (Cambridge: Harvard University Press, 1994).

44. See James C. Scott and David A. Lake, "The Second Face of Hegemony: Britain's Repeal of the Corn Laws and the American Walker Tariff of 1846," *International Organization* 43 (1989): 1–29. The proselytizing of an ideology, for example by an epistemic community of economists or multinational management consulting firms who preach the virtues of liberalization, represents a coercive mechanism in this framework.

45. Extant institutions may also modulate in an even more fundamental way who the relevant actors are.

46. For reasons specified earlier in this chapter.

47. A relevant discussion of this point is in Gary King, Robert O. Keohane, and Sidney Verba, *Designing Social Inquiry: Scientific Inference in Qualitative Research* (Princeton: Princeton University Press, 1994).

1 Market Integration and the Mobility of People: Europeanization of Values and Beliefs

Paulette Kurzer

In this chapter I examine the consequences of regional integration on policies or rules, which govern areas of policymaking that deal with socially sensitive activities. I claim that regional integration affects areas of life most of us would consider highly resistant to international pressures and adjustments. National beliefs, norms, and convictions, for example, are unlikely to fall under the spell of Europeanization or globalization since member governments and voters are keen to protect and defend their ways of doing things. By the same token, supranational institutions respect the boundaries of cultural autonomy and have no appetite for meddling in such highly controversial issues. Yet market integration is disturbing the integrity of cultural norms and collective identities in ways not anticipated by the current literature on regional institution building and globalization.

In the beginning, there is a *de facto* institutional equilibrium. Beliefs, convictions, opinions, and customs go unquestioned and are preserved and defended by social institutions. Although beliefs and social structures are far from static, they undergo gradual change and show considerable consistency across time and space. But exogenous pressures emanating from the EU create a disequilibrium and offer (disaffected) actors an opportunity to mobilize and press for change. Agents of change operate through the existing structures to yield some kind of adjustment. The outcome of the process, or dependent variable, according to the chart, consists of policy reforms and institutional change.

The chart leaves open which agents push for change and the purpose of this chapter is to analyze how the process of change and adaptation unfolds, and why discontent and resentment translates into policy adjustments. The second aim is to point out that the actual agents of change are neither economic actors, organized interests, elite decisionmakers, nor national agencies. Rather, individuals or the public exploit a new repertoire of knowledge, based on their access to new markets, to redefine the moral environment of their society. Cultural frameworks tend to persist over time in part because people believe in them and attribute some higher purpose to the existence of rules of intervention and modes of operation. This conviction impedes change and obstructs adjustment. The Single Market, however, furnishes disaffected individuals or groups with new tools to subvert political and institutional resistance to change. Market integration gives a boost to a reform agenda with implausible odds.

To document the emergence of greater cultural homogenization and the parallel abatement of national peculiarities, I focus on policy areas—alcohol in Finland and Sweden, drugs in the Netherlands, and abortion in Ireland— which define the cultural characteristic of a country and symbolize what it means to be Dutch, Finnish or Swedish, and Irish. Nordic[1] alcohol policy, Dutch drug measures, and Irish proscription on abortion contribute to the preservation of collective identity precisely because they reveal something crucial about the normative priorities and deeply held beliefs of a society. In fact, I would go so far as to claim that the discrepancy with the rest of Europe helps cement internal cohesion and external differentiation.

A striking discovery, therefore, is that Nordic alcohol control policy is becoming more liberal, that Dutch drug policy is becoming more punitive, and that Irish anti-abortion views are softening. The domestic shift in attitudes, the emergence of a new discourse, and the formulation of new policy proposals are the outgrowth of two interdependent forces. Porous borders, free circulation of people, and integrating markets expose a country or culture to alternative ideas, convictions, opinions, and arrangements, while they open a society to increased (external) scrutiny, supply novel ways of escaping domestic restrictions or regulations, and accentuate the quaintness of a cultural legacy that once upon a time handed down restrictive drinking rules, abortion ban, and drug toleration. At the same time, while exposure to different ways of organizing life is on the increase, the public has already lost faith in the indispensability of the morality regimes. In other words, purely domestic factors have already undermined public support for the peculiar normative standards and regional integration pushes change forward.

The Political Economy Null Hypothesis (PENH), as outlined in the introduction, goes some ways toward clarifying how market integration and intergovernmental cooperation interact with domestic developments and institutions. The completion of the Single Market has dramatically lowered the physical and psychological barriers of cross-border movements. Individuals pursue new strategies by seeking goods or services restricted or suppressed in their country. For example, the Irish need only to cross a narrow body of water to obtain an abortion in Britain and the Swedes and Finns can easily purchase cheap liquor in neighboring countries. Foreigners have direct access to the Netherlands' open drug market and can bring back, without much hassle, small amounts of drugs. National institutions that regulate private behavior experience an increase in the ambient level of competition, which in turn challenges the philosophical or cultural foundation of the type of policy intervention pursued by each country. Forced to respond to new challenges, institutions introduce reforms. The process ends with changes in institutions or governance structures and with a move towards policies or rules more in synchrony with the rest of Europe.

New ideas do not automatically translate into policy reforms and the PENH needs to be supplemented by additional systemic causes. European Union membership, to some extent, frames the kind of policy responses available to decisionmakers and prejudices certain outcomes, which tend to favor the larger goal of European integration. This holds true especially for the adaptation in morality standards because the agents of change are individuals who have been empowered thanks to being increasingly mobile by European Union legislation. Movement of people and disappearing frontiers prompt a critical assessment of needed adjustments, patterned along a conventional European model. Thus, membership in a supranational organization first intensifies pressures against domestic arrangements and then influences the direction of the adjustment deliberations and policy outcomes.

The next section explains the persistence of different norms in Europe. This is followed by a discussion of the actual direct impact of European Union institutions on divergent moral sensibilities. The final two sections explain how the movement of people uncovers existing contradictions in the policy narrative and deepens resentment against social arrangements out of synchrony with the rest of Europe.

Existence of Divergent Norms

Some countries some of the time identify themselves by being different from dominant concepts or driving forces in the global system. Scholars who work within the constructivist tradition contend that the community of states or world culture shape state identity and preferences (Checkel, 1998; Finnemore, 1996; Florini, 1996; Katzenstein, 1996; Ruggie, 1998). States often lack a clear sense of where they stand on an issue, and like individuals slowly develop perceptions of interests and understanding of situations through ongoing interaction with other states or transnational organizations and institutions. They assimilate templates of international meanings and, like individuals, adhere to norms and hold common expectations about appropriate behavior (Barrett and Frank, 1999; Klotz, 1995; Loya and Boli, 1999; Tannenwald, 1999). Social structures, which contain shared knowledge, material resources, and practices construct identity and are produced and reproduced by agents/actors who in turn are embedded in the social structures (Adler, 1997; Wendt, 1992 & 1994). For constructivists, state preferences are molded over time as states participate in a larger environment. This environment or social structure constructs certain norms, which then impose shared expectation about appropriate behavior.

The examples in this chapter describe another sort of relationship between identity formation and the larger international environment. Once in awhile, a state will be strongly attached to its way of doing things and decisively rejects "mainstream" (i.e. European) approaches and conventions. It is not too farfetched to imagine a situation in which state agencies embrace a frame of cognition and repertoire of action that they themselves regard as vastly superior to what other states have adopted over time. For example, the Netherlands does not buy into the global prohibitionist regime on drugs (Korf, Riper, and Bullington, 1999; Kort and Korf, 1992; Leuw and Marshall, 1994; Vliet, 1990). The Dutch claim that the entire drug problem poses what is mainly a public health challenge and successive coalition governments have set aside proportionally more funding for social assistance and medical intervention than for incarceration and prosecution. Sweden and Finland dismiss the international approval of alcoholic beverages, a chemical substance with the potential to destroy human life. National authorities in each country passed legislation to create a state monopoly to exclude private agents from the production, distribution, and retail of alcoholic drinks. Limits on the number of retail outlets and on the opening hours of liquor stores coupled with extremely high excise taxes curbs impulse buying and aggregate alcohol consumption.

Ireland disdains the individualistic culture of post-Christian Europe and fears the sexual permissiveness of the sixties era. When other countries liberalized their abortion laws, Ireland passed a constitutional ban on abortion in 1983. Dutch drug policy, Nordic alcohol policy, and Irish constitutional ban on abortion are examples of domestic norms and standards of behavior that stand in opposition to evolving international and European practices.

Probably, all countries pursue projects close to their heart and numerous examples help uncover a basic mismatch between domestic and international norms. Nevertheless, these morality policies merit special attention because they go beyond formal prescriptions on how to tackle substance misuse or how to cope with the decline of tradition and religious authority. The morality standards describe what it means to be Irish, Dutch, Swedish, or Finnish respectively. They constitute state and collective identity. Each formulation grew out of particular historical experiences, unique to a country or a group of countries, and left a legacy that presently defines what it means to be a citizen of this country. State and national identity is thus partly formed in opposition to shared international norms and differentiates a country (or geographic cluster of countries) from its (their) neighbors.[2]

For example, bookshelves are filled with autobiographical accounts of what it means to grow up Irish and thus Catholic (McCourt, 1996; O'Faolain, 1997).The unique devotion to Catholicism by the population of the Irish Republic is both a source of internal identification and external differentiation. Adherence to the Catholic ethos governs state policy in areas of central importance to the Church (family and sexuality) and prescribes how the state and society ought to behave. This pattern of state action gives Ireland its distinctive character and sharply contrasts with that of, say, Britain.

Along similar lines, restrictive drinking rules grew out of the early and successful efforts of temperance movements to impose external forms of discipline on a society undergoing the wrenching experiences of urbanization and industrialization. The strong aversion to mind-altering substances characterizes an aspect of "Nordicness" quite distinct from the personality of other European people. The Nordic apprehension of chemical dependency is commonly attributed to "communication anxiety" (being shy) and to the reliance on liquor to overcome social inhibitions (Daun, 1996; Phillips-Martinsson, 1981).[3] Long, dark winters, according to the received wisdom, deprived the Finnish and Swedish people of regular contact with strangers and thwarted the development of strong interpersonal skills. When together, to ease sociability, the Finns and Swedes drink heavily with terrible consequences for the physical and social health of the individual and society. Binge drinking (heavy drinking at one sitting) is considered typical of the

Nordic countries and this injurious and rowdy drinking style requires constant state vigilance (Levine, 1992; Mäkelä and Viikari, 1977; Mäkelä, 1985; Bruun, 1985).

Dutch drug policy is also a testimony to an essential element of Dutchness. Dutch ascribe to the idea that moral decisions are private affairs and, accordingly, that private activities should not be prohibited, banned, curbed, or restrained by outside agencies. The public health focus of Dutch drug policy emerged from a tradition that permitted society to find its moral center. If Sweden and Finland prefer to raise certain collective moral principles and to hold out certain life projects as more desirable than others, the Netherlands allows its citizens to pursue life projects even if they prove to be very harmful and destructive. The state is not actively involved in structuring the lives of its citizens along a particular dimension and does not assert a hierarchy of values (Rothstein, 1998). Citizens can form their own opinions and evaluate what is manageable or not. For this reason, the Dutch are generally considered morally permissive.[4]

All countries construct different environments to provide clues to how to regulate questionable moral activities. Most norms do not last for more than a generation because each new cohort group confronts different experiences and selects different guideposts on how to organize life. The norms described in this study, however, survived structural changes in the workplace, the family, career paths, and international fashions. The reason for their longevity is that social institutions in charge of overseeing and implementing rules, which contain these norms, maintain and reproduce the moral environment and vouch for their robustness and flexibility (Jepperson, Wendt, and Katzenstein, 1996: 63–64). State policy, formulated and administered by agents ensconced in social institutions, immerses new generations of citizens in the dominant cognitive framework.

Take, for example, the case of Dutch drug policy. Its policy stance is unconventional in that the consumption of soft drugs is largely decriminalized and cannabis products are openly traded in so-called coffee shops. Lending support to this form of drug control intervention are social welfare agencies, which define problematic drug use/abuse as a chronic disease with very disappointing rates of rehabilitation. After years of field research and experimentation, public health officials and social welfare agents believe that a critical mass of drug addicts is beyond recovery and the next best step is to prevent them from causing damage to themselves and others. Therefore, Dutch drug specialists from the fields of social work, public health, and even law enforcement argue that mandatory detoxification treatments hardly ever work and that it makes more sense to prevent criminalization of drug-driven life styles by, among other things, encouraging addicts to seek out social services and medical assistance. Social welfare officials and police officers have also been at the forefront in maintaining a sharp distinction between hard and soft drugs and in protecting recreational drug users from the criminal milieu of hard drugs. Local city councils ignore the private trade of all kinds of drugs and encourage the establishment of official sites for drug dealing (coffee shops and street scenes) (Korf, et.al., 1999; Kort, 1995; Kort and Cramer, 1999).

Finnish and Swedish institutions also define and redefine the national drinking problem. At first, it was thought that the main policy targets should be to prevent heavy drinkers from consuming excessive amounts of alcohol. Leading theories on the prevalence of heavy drinking projected a bifurcated population in which the majority consisted of modest drinkers and a small minority of heavy drinkers created much havoc and disorder. As Finnish and Swedish consumers increasingly opted for light alcoholic beverages (wine and beer) and no longer drunk as much spirits as before, complaints about the heavy regulation of the liquor market began to increase. To counter the complaints and accusations that alcohol control policy, based on a state monopoly system and exorbitantly high excise taxes, was outdated and irrelevant, public health officials, scientists, and social welfare agencies embraced and then aggressively promoted a new understanding of why the state needs to curb alcohol consumption. No longer was the population neatly divided into two separate groups of regular and abnormal drinkers, but rather statistical modeling of the distribution characteristics of the drinking population suggested that the proportion of problem drinkers in the general population corresponded to the actual level of per capita consumption. The higher the level of per capita consumption of alcohol, the larger the number of problem drinkers in society. The explanation for this phenomenon was that drinking constituted a social activity and the environment in which it took place influenced overall levels of consumption. Individuals adjusted their drinking habits consistent with prevailing social norms. A milieu of non-drinkers inhibits a person with an inclination to drink while a high-consumption culture encourages this same individual to indulge in alcohol (Bruun, et.al., 1975; Griffith, 1994; Leifman, 1996; Österberg, 1990; Skog, 1991a and 1991b). Researchers coined the concept of the "prevention paradox" to urge officials to continue to curb the alcohol intake of moderate

drinkers since they determined whether a social environment was particularly "wet" or "dry" and since they collectively contributed to a greater number of injuries and harms. The risk of injury and illness is greatest in the
group of heavy drinkers. But this group constitutes a diminutive section of
the drinking population. The emerging paradox is that the group of light
drinkers because of its size is responsible for the majority of alcohol-related
harm suffered by society.[5] In order to prevent alcohol-related harm, policy
targets should be directed to all drinkers, which means that restrictive drinking rules are a public good since it protects society from higher incidents of
accidents, violence, criminality, abuse, absenteeism, drunk-driving, and
chronic physical illnesses.

A final example is the Irish proscription on abortion. It seems self-evident
that the taboo grew out of the role played by the Irish Catholic clergy in the
long struggle for emancipation from British colonialism and is a testimony
to the outsized influence of the ecclesiastical hierarchy over legislation dealing with the family, education, Church matters, and the status of women in
Irish society. In addition, the Church itself controlled a vast network of social
institutions through which it reached the minds and souls of most Irish men
and women (Drudy and Lynch, 1993; Inglis, 1998a; Inglis, 1998b; Keating
and Desmond, 1993). Its unquestioned rejection of sexual permissiveness
goes a long way toward explaining the absolute ban on abortion.

Cultural differences persist because social institutions and agents, which
defend and articulate the dominant vision, vary across the European Union.
Morality standards as an expression of a national culture (in the anthropo-
logical sense of the term) differ because the social characteristics of institutions vary. Different institutions produce different belief systems and codes
of conduct and differentiate Ireland from Britain, the Netherlands from Germany, and the Nordic countries from their continental neighbors. The morality standards are norms, which guide action, provide a template for understanding new situations, and legitimate a set of government measures.
Because institutions themselves operate within the context of the norms,
they reproduce them through policy action.

Encounters with the European Union

The nature of the EU is such that there are no direct, immediate pressures
exerted on member states to adopt common, European-wide rules with re-

spect to the regulation of drugs, abortion, and alcohol. Neither are there direct pressures to foster cultural and moral conformity. The Council of Ministers, representing the interests and preferences of member governments, grants ample concessions to chiefs of government who request derogation to protect cultural institutions. The Commission focuses its attention on policy areas that are more likely to enhance its competence and success, and culture is not yet one of them (Majone, 1996; Wendon, 1998). Even the European Court with its reputation for judicial activism on behalf of the viability of transnational polities shies away from demanding compliance to mainstream cultural views. So many obstacles thwart the emergence of a common cultural space that EU institutions do not even try to dilute Europe's rich mélange of cultural diversity. National politicians energetically resist efforts to construct common norms if it involves the dilution of national beliefs and convictions. They act in accordance with popular preferences since voters view policies related to culture and language outside the competence of the EU (Dalton and Eichenberg, 1998).

The puzzle, therefore, is that we would expect to find cultural structures and norms to be immune from growing European governance yet the empirical evidence points to a different conclusion. Dutch drug policy is becoming more restrictive and thus less different from its neighbors. Irish views on abortion are softening and shedding their special attachment to the Catholic ethos. Nordic alcohol policy is turning into the direction of liberalization. Purely domestic factors do not fully explain either the timing or the direction of the change. The question now is how change is effected if supranational institutions tolerate diversity and national politicians resist conformity. Political leaders in all four of the countries made special efforts to guarantee the survival of the norms. Dutch negotiators insisted that the Council ought to insert a sentence or two into a final declaration or treaty to guarantee that improved European-wide coordination on international drug trafficking would not contaminate national autonomy to pursue distinctive anti-drug programs. Irish politicians under pressure from pro-life activists added a paragraph to the Treaty for European Union to shield the 1937 Constitution from European legal challenges. Finnish and Swedish officials extracted concessions from the Commission at the time of the negotiations on accession to conserve the operations of the retail branch of the state alcohol monopoly. They also received an exemption from common commercial foreign policy (Hug, 1999; Eggert and Rolston, 1994: 166; Miles, 1996; Ossebaard and Wijngaart, 1998: 267; Reid, 1992; Rüter, 1996; Tomasson, 1998).

In turn, EU institutions recognize the cultural and political sensitivities of the member states and have not pushed hard to bring about conformity. Finland and Sweden have encountered the greatest difficulties because alcohol control policy intersects with Single Market directives and Community law prohibits state monopolies. Nevertheless, in spite of the Commission's hostility to the monopoly system, it extended derogation from common foreign commercial policy (travelers' imports) for some additional years.

Drug policy falls outside the purview of the Commission and individual member states have been the main source of external pressures to adapt to European-wide rules and norms. Here, too, the Council ultimately backed off from denying one of its members the freedom to experiment with unorthodox anti-drug policies. Against their inclination, Germany and France granted the Netherlands the right to pursue divergent drug policy. Finally, the European Court missed an opportunity in the early 1990s to censor the repressive methods condoned by Irish law to suppress all information on (lawful) abortion services available abroad in the case *The Society of the Unborn Children Ltd. (S.P.U.C.) v. Groganand others* (C-159/90). The ECJ judges had no appetite for a major confrontation with the Irish judiciary and implicitly recognized the right of a member state to frame its morality standards.

In spite of these political deals and institutional restraints, abortion, alcohol, and drugs are Europeanizing in that their distinctive characteristics are disappearing and they are becoming more like that of other countries. Again, it is important to reiterate that the institutions of the European Union (the Commission, the Council, and the Court) displayed obvious restraints when confronted with the cultural peculiarities of one of its members. Equally important, national governments struck special deals with whatever EU institution was in charge of this area to protect the morality norms from pressures emanating from European integration.

The PENH provides a fruitful first step in understanding how or why cultural norms are exposed to European pressures. Movement of people and mobility of ideas have sharpened the tension between Nordic restrictions on drinking, Irish proscription on abortion, or Dutch drug toleration and conventional definitions embraced by the rest of Europe. The growing crisis in each morality regime was ultimately related to the fact that public support on behalf of the conservation of policy tools or constitutional ban had already declined. The mobility of people and the corresponding exposure to different kinds of arrangements deepened voters' skepticism and forced government agencies to take international considerations into account. The movement of people, in summation, exerts exactly the same kind of constraining influence as the mobility of capital. Asset-holders limit fiscal, monetary, and economic policies of member-governments because they raise the costs of policy nonconformity and penalize divergent macroeconomic agendas. Rational self-centered individuals operate like asset-holders in that they seek goods and services not available at home or available at exorbitant costs and engage in a form of arbitrage to take advantage of a borderless Europe by evading domestic rules and regulations without detaching themselves completely from the domestic market or society. In the process, the retention of divergent morality standards becomes prohibitively expensive and prompts a reassessment with the view of altering certain features of the domestic rules to regulate morally questionable behavior.

Ambivalence or skepticism can be traced to the late 1980s when neither Dutch drug policy or Nordic alcohol control policy were much in the news. The establishment interpreted the lack of open discussion or criticism as a tacit consensus of state practices and thus conveniently sidestepped the decline in public support. But the lack of overt opposition was really due to the feeling that there was no real alternative to the drinking restrictions or drug toleration. The public in each country had been socialized into thinking that this is how things are done in our society and could not easily envision a reasonable alternative. This is why the completion of the Single Market and the free circulation of people uncovered tensions and inconsistencies in each morality regime. Discord and dissension lingered just below the surface. Once new choices presented themselves, many consumers, whose voice had been stifled, voted with their feet and took the exit option. They bought items abroad either not available at home or obtainable at much higher prices.

Fissures in the Cultural Narrative

In chapter 6, Vivien Schmidt looks at "policy narratives"[6] to describe the way in which different countries frame complex reality and provide guideposts to knowing, analyzing, and acting. She differentiates between policy discussion and actual discourse and considers the ways in which discourse may affect values rather than simply reflect them. I look at what Schmidt calls the communicative stage of the discourse the point at which policy elites persuade the public of the validity of the policy programs they have constructed (Hall, 1989: 383). The term communicative discourse is useful for understanding how the morality norms and corresponding policy actions (or inaction in Ireland) were explicated to outsiders and how they were able to garner support from the public. Each morality regime offered strikingly similar reasons to justify their continued existence. First, public authorities touted the public health or social benefits of the policies or measures associated with the morality regime. Second, they reminded voters of the cultural specificity of the morality standards and how the norms encapsulated an essential aspect of collective identity. The free movement of people challenges both the instrumental and philosophical roots of each morality regime.

Some Finns and Swedes hated the anti-drinking rules and prayed for the rapid dismantlement of the state company system and Irish liberals looked to the EU to liberate them from the moral monopoly of the Church. Dutch conservatives were appalled at the Netherlands' reputation as Europe's drug Mecca. Although the morality norms epitomized the cultural mentality of the country, some agents disliked the arrangements tremendously.[7] The obstacle they encountered was that their objections did not fall on receptive ears. Public authorities and professional experts ignored the protests and isolated their opponents by stressing the cultural roots of their approach and their beneficial impact on society.

A good example is Nordic alcohol control policy. Ultimately, the main justification for the set of anti-drinking measures in existence since the pre-World War II era is the notion that many Swedes and Finns are reserved and introverted, and drink (excessively) when together. This is so much part of the repertoire of national knowledge that very few Swedes or Finns directly contest the image of (mostly) hard-drinking men and it is generally believed that alcohol and the Nordic personality do not mix well. Although binge drinking declined as urban, educated professionals adopted more continental-like drinking rituals, public health officials and social welfare agencies nonetheless refused to relinquish control over the alcohol trade. They observed that some people still gravitated toward binge drinking (undoubtedly true) and that restrictions on alcohol lowered overall consumption and improved public health.

The latter point became the main weapon to diffuse any suggestions of liberalization. Nordic scientists embraced the total consumption model, which linked per capita consumption of alcohol to the prevalence of alcohol-related harm. The model and subsequent public discourse presumed a strong correlation between actual alcohol consumption and alcohol-related deaths, injuries, accidents, disease, violence, absenteeism, vandalism, and abuse (Blomqvist, 1998; Leifman, 1996; Skog, 1985).

The total consumption model is not widely used as a policy tool outside the Nordic countries because officials in other countries assign very different risks to the availability of alcohol in society. The theory only becomes a policy tool if society accepts *a priori* a trade-off between individual freedom to engage in self-abuse and restrictions on psychoactive substances to prevent patterns of abuse. If the public already expresses sizable apprehensions toward psychotropic substances, then society does not mind the (minor) hassles of drinking restrictions. The problem for alcohol liberalization advocates was that they had to refute the alleged empirical correlation between aggregate alcohol consumption and the incidence of alcohol-related disease, social pathologies, deaths, accidents, injuries, and so forth in addition to having to renounce the national apprehension about destructive drinking habits.

A similar predicament faced Irish liberals, feminists, and pro-choice advocates. Abortion is contrary to the teaching of the Catholic Church and drew out frequent statements by the Catholic hierarchy. The Church's absolute rejection of abortion reflects religious doctrine although it is also connected to the Irish-Catholic conception of being female. The 1937 Constitution identified an Irish woman as a mother and designated her to the private home and the domestic sphere (Connelly, 1993; O'Connor, 1988). Against this backdrop, abortion contradicts basic female existence, which consists of finding a goal in life by having a large family and raising children to adulthood. Of course, since the 1960s, abortion has also been associated with sexual permissiveness and moral decay, both of which constitute a threat to the well being of society.

Catholicism, unlike many branches of Protestant-Christian religion, aims to direct all spheres of behavior through its priesthood and discourages individuals from developing their own ethical guidelines (Gorski, 1999; Lüthy, 1985). The particular history of the Irish nation elevated the Church as legislator and arbiter of morality with the result that a decent person was a devout Catholic. Since the Church shaped the framework for assessing a person's moral standing, Church approval, by being a good Catholic, meant a stamp of approval by society. Important individuals sought the canon of reputability by contributing to the Church and observing Catholic rules (Hempton, 1996: 72–92; Keating and Desmond, 1993:171; Whyte, 1980:

313–14). Against this background, it was difficult to openly support a pro-choice position because it meant that by the standards of society you were slightly suspect and disreputable. Not many other issues provoked the Church as much as abortion. Therefore, in Ireland, even the most ardent opponents of the absolute injunction against abortion did not campaign for its legalization. They lobbied for de-constitutionalization on the grounds that this was such a complex personal-moral question that a blanket proscription was simply unworkable (Eggert and Rolston, 1994: 167; Hug, 1999).

In the Netherlands, opponents ran into a wall of resistance because re-pression and punitive measures clashed with the ideological inclination of state institutions. When anti-drug voices faulted the establishment for the Netherlands' reputation as a drug Mecca, officials proclaimed that decrim-inalization and tolerance of drug-taking "fits" the Dutch mold. In addition, harm reduction yielded better outcomes than the sort of repressive strategies employed by neighboring countries because it shielded end users from po-lice harassment and protected them from a criminal milieu. Drug policy experts pointed out that maintenance programs and treatment centers low-ered drug-related mortality rates and enabled addicts to live relatively normal lives (Maris, 1996:144; Cohen and Sas, 1997). Critics, when pressed, found it difficult to come up with an alternative anti-drug program. The use of repression to stamp out private consumer behavior is alien to Dutch culture and ideology. Even law enforcement had doubts about the wisdom of mo-bilizing the coercive powers of the state to prosecute the consumption habits of young adults (Kort, 1995).

In summary, critics in each country had to deconstruct the "communi-cative" narrative, which was based upon a mixture of utilitarian and cultural arguments. They did not really manage to accomplish this because they, too, were socialized in this culture and recognized the legitimacy of certain features of the narrative. To overcome these hurdles, they had to find an alternative formulation that did not contradict the conventional wisdom on the national character of the country. They found unexpected support from the completion of the Single Market, which lowered both physical and psy-chological barriers against cross-border movement of people and stimulated abortion, alcohol, and drug tourism. This kind of tourism gave opponents the necessary ammunition to launch a frontal attack on the morality regime. They began to argue that "the people" no longer believed in the morality standards and that the standards were therefore no longer representative of the national culture and identity. Moreover, the flow of people uncovered inconsistencies in the narrative that had earlier been concealed or dismissed. Opponents seized on the inconsistencies to challenge the health or social benefits of the policy norms and measures.

Change of Attitudes, Policies, and Institutions

Dutch drug policy faced a slightly different situation than Nordic alcohol policy or Irish abortion ban. The threat came from an inflow of people who sought out the Netherlands for its fine choice of many different kinds of recreational drugs. Drug tourism always existed and American heroin refugees flocked to Amsterdam in the late 1960s to qualify for methadone treatments or be close to their suppliers without having to fear the law (Cuskey, Klein, and Krasner, 1972). Three new developments took place in the early 1990s that shifted the center of attention from harm reduction or minimization to more repressive steps to deal with the negative consequences of drug toleration (Korf, Riper, and Bullington, 1999: 459–61).

The first new trend was a rising concern with drug-related nuisance. The latter refers to the presence of street addicts with unconventional and alarming lifestyles, the trafficking of drugs from private residences, and cross-border trade by drug tourists. Second, the mass media and political establishment delved into the growing (or new) phenomenon of organized crime and its connections to the drug trade. Third, the effect of Dutch drug policy on other countries forced a reassessment of some features of the current situation. All three developments were to some extent related to European integration since they grew out of the removal of borders and intergovernmental agreements to bolster European-wide police and custom cooperation.

The Schengen Agreement and the free movement of people have replaced classic concerns with military security with new fears about societal security (Bigo, 1998; Waever, et al., 1993; Waever, 1993). For the Netherlands, the phenomenon of disappearing borders has generated new waves of young tourists, visiting border towns or large metropolitan cities to buy affordable drug merchandise. These visitors differed from the first generation of heroin refugees in that the latter quickly assimilated into the local drug scene and did not constitute a specific tourist phenomenon. The noisy presence of rowdy coffee shop visitors and the weekend traffic of foreign heroin users constitute a specific tourism problem because the group of drug users/buyers remain separate from the local drug scene and only stay for as long as it takes to purchase drugs. In the process, they nurture a thriving cross-border trade in illicit goods. The inflow of drug tourists is, together with asylum seekers and immigrants, associated with crime and a decline of public safety. Drug tourism annoys local residents because of an increase in traffic congestion and noise, and is blamed for scores of other (minor) inconveniences. A further aggravation is that Dutch authorities quietly tolerate open drug scenes (drug dealing in public spaces) to prevent criminalization of drug-induced lifestyles (Bless, Korf, and Freeman, 1995). But the presence of open drug scenes in downtown areas and transportation centers is a magnet for all kinds of undesirable people. Thus many commuters, shoppers, and working people frequently run into scores of disheveled homeless people, drug addicts, prostitutes, drug dealers, and other intimidating people, which only intensifies the feeling that the situation is out of control. By the early 1990s, local citizen groups in areas with a high concentration of coffee shops or in the vicinity of open drug sites mounted a new campaign to force the police to do something about the proliferation of retail trade in hard and soft drugs in private residences, public spaces, or downtown areas (Collins, 1999). Much of their anger was directed against the flow of weekend visitors, who were accused of diminishing the quality of life of the average citizen.

While local residents organized themselves and insisted on stricter supervision over the drug trade with the intention of combating drug-related nuisance, the Justice and Home Affairs section in the Treaty of European Union came into being. The formation of a Justice and Home Affairs pillar has drawn fresh attention to the uniqueness of Dutch drug policy, now blamed for Europe's drug problem by prohibitionist member states. Sweden and France, for example, accuse the Netherlands of subverting their efforts to ban drugs from society because they perceive a clear correlation between availability, demand, and use. According to their understanding of the drug issue, supplies equal demand. If the supply of drugs can be destroyed, demand for drugs will disappear. Dutch drug policy enables users who cannot find any affordable drugs at home to obtain their quota of stimulants across the border. Foreign critics claim that Dutch drug toleration keeps the demand for drugs alive in spite of their heroic efforts to destroy the supply base at home (Boekhout van Solinge, 1999). Chiefs of government of prohibitionist member states urged the Netherlands to join the fight against drugs by closing down coffee shops, getting rid of open drug scenes, and ceasing programs like syringe exchanges and mobile methadone clinics (actually a bus which stops at sites where hard drugs are dealt).

The acrimonious diplomatic debate on Dutch drug policy is also the byproduct of Europe's growing obsession with internal security. The new democracies in the East are unfortunately considered perfect breeding grounds for organized crime and the latter constitutes a direct threat to the constitutional order of the EU member states.[8] The European Parliament and the Council have had regular debates on such nefarious activities as plutonium smuggling, environmental crimes, financial fraud, or drug trafficking—all of which has elevated the combat of organized crime as one of the most pressing objectives for the European Union. *Eurobarometer* opinion polls show that the overwhelming majority of European citizens regard "crime" (in all its manifestations) as one of the greatest threats to society. The Netherlands is obviously not immune to this discussion and around 90 percent of the Dutch population is strongly in favor of European-wide coordination to fight drug trafficking in spite of domestic legislation at odds with the tenor of European discussions (European Commission, 1994: 30; European Commission, 1997: 32).

Possibly, because of the European focus on crime and its threat to the security of the state, Dutch parliament requested an in-depth analysis on the scale and scope of organized crime in the Netherlands. The expert reports, written by academics from criminal law and sociology, link the global and domestic developments in the drug trade to the growing presence of powerful, violent, and wealthy criminal syndicates in the Dutch economy. Apparently, many old-time gangsters, formerly engaged in fencing, pimping, or robbing banks, have switched to dealing drugs since no other illegal activity yields greater profits (Fijnaut, et al., 1998: 60–61).[9] Although the main contributing factor is the global drug trade, a vast illegal market at home has also created tempting incentives for the criminally inclined entrepreneur. Progress at the European level to foster improved police and customs cooperation has therefore had a twofold impact on the Dutch debate on drugs. First, the torturous efforts to enhance European police coordination is accompanied by a critical assessment of Dutch drug decriminalization by countries which hold very different views on the origins of the drug crisis and its impact on society. Second, the ongoing discussion on crime in a borderless Europe has legitimized a national debate on the relationship between Dutch drug policy and the growth of criminal organizations.

Organized crime and drug decriminalization also go hand in hand, for many analysts, because coffee shops (and open drug sites) rely on a steady supply of drugs. From the beginning, Dutch law, while permitting the existence of retail trade in drugs, has prohibited the production, distribution, and importation/exportation of drugs. Since the non-retail portion of the cannabis trade is illegal and thus subject to criminal prosecution, it draws criminal organizations or individuals, which are able to guarantee coffee shops their drug wares. As more and more city councils ignored the existence of coffee shops, more establishments were opened so that in 1991 there were between 2,400 and 4,700 cannabis outlets or 1 per 2,600 and 1 per 5,200 of the population over 15 years of age (Derks, Hoekstra, and Kaplan, 1998: 82).[10] The growing number of coffee shops required a more steady and sophisticated network of cannabis suppliers many of whom not only supplied the local market but also shipped large volumes of soft drugs to the rest of Europe.

Originally, there existed a contradiction between permissible front door trade in drugs and prosecutable back door distribution. For a while, this contradiction could be ignored because the number of actual coffee shops was small and many of them obtained their wares from amateurs who cultivated a couple of marijuana plants in their closets or on their window sills. Since those innocent days, the soft drug trade has become a serious business and is no longer run by "idealists" unconcerned about profits. The differential legal treatment of retail and wholesale trade resulted in a crime tax that helped enrich criminals (Ministers van VWS and Justitie, and Staatssecretaris van Binnenlandse Zaken, 1996).[11]

Opponents of drug toleration pounced on the fact that harm reduction came with externalities, which perpetrated a different sort of harm on society. Whereas addicts lived until a ripe old age, thanks to medical and social intervention, the concentration of drug dealing sites in particular neighborhoods or sites produced considerable nuisance and safety concerns for local residents. Harm reduction saved lives; at the same time, it undermined public safety and order because it invited a host of other problems such as drug tourism and organized crime.

Under pressure from domestic and foreign forces, the Dutch parliament has taken measures to reduce the negative externalities of drug tolerance. The local police are charged with arresting the flow of drug tourists, among other things, by checking cars with foreign license plates in neighborhoods with coffee shops and known sites of heroin dealing. The harsher actions of the police are supposed to expunge the image of carefree, everything is possible environment (Ottevanger, 1997). Dutch customs officials renewed their efforts to facilitate close and ongoing cooperation with their French counterparts to prove their new determination to intercept the transit in drugs. In the meantime, Parliament reduced the amount of cannabis a person can buy from 30 grams (sufficient for up to a 100 joints and equal to an ounce) to 5 grams. The new limit eliminates, in theory, the trade in cannabis because 5 grams is barely sufficient for 8 joints. New legislation also limits the amount of inventory a coffee shop can hold to 500 grams. In addition, local authorities have explicit responsibility for the coffee shop policy in their area and can impose additional limits such as banning them from their jurisdiction. To cope with the proliferation of hard-drug dealing sites, Parliament amended the Municipalities Act in 1995 to permit local government to evacuate and close down private residences to combat nuisance in residential neighborhoods.[12] The government also raised the penalties for various drug-related offenses (Korf, Riper, and Bullington, 1999: 466–67). Finally, in March 1999, the government amended the Opium Act to declare the professional cultivation of marijuana illegal. The small-scale growing of a couple of plants is, however, not prosecuted.

The greater emphasis on crime is ultimately related to the fact that Dutch household never fully reconciled themselves to drug decriminalization. Two-thirds of the voters agreed in surveys conducted between 1970 and 1991 that smoking marijuana and hashish should be severely punished (Rochon, 1999: 284). Since 1981, the general public's support for mandatory treatment, resolutely rejected by the professional experts as futile, fluctuated at around 75 percent. Even in Amsterdam, more tolerant than the rest of the Netherlands, 60 percent of households favored mandatory detoxification (Buning and van Brussel, 1995). In 1996, a national household survey showed that two-thirds of the population believed that a desirable drug policy included the prosecution of drug dealers and mandatory treatment of drug addicts. Forty percent of the population favored a ban on the sale of soft drugs while 29 percent favored the continuation of present practice and 23 percent preferred legalization of cannabis (Korf, Riper, and Bullington, 1999: 456–58).

All of these figures give a rough picture of a population divided about the merits of decriminalization although the response of the central administration was to dismiss these concerns by emphasizing the positive impact of decriminalization on social order and individual drug users. The steady growth of coffee shop establishments, the inflow of drug tourists, general disquiet about public safety, and diplomatic pressure prompted closer attention to the negative ramifications of drug decriminalization (Minister van

VWS, Justice, and Interior, 1996). Whereas the misgivings of the electorate were quietly ignored for years, international considerations reflecting new progress in market integration and intergovernmental coordination finally spurred a revision and some (modest) policy adjustments. The public debate, both in the media and parliament, mirrors these new concerns and highlights the need to step up inspection of coffee shops, to curtail the number of establishments which sell cannabis, to clean up open drug sites, and to act decisively against drug-related offenses.

The tension in Ireland and resulting softening of abortion attitudes also came about as domestic shifts in values coincided with new developments in the EU. The greatest source of friction, not fully anticipated by traditionalist anti-abortion forces, is that there are instances when a mother's life is at risk unless the pregnancy is ended. The question then becomes whether the life of the mother ought to be sacrificed for the sake of the unborn. The constitutional ban on abortion could not resolve this dilemma because it simply denied that there ever was any reason for an abortion. In February 1992, however, an incident occurred that underscored the cruelties and impracticalities of an absolute ban on abortion.

Referred to as the X-case, it involved the rape of a 14-year-old girl. When she was already in England to end her unwanted pregnancy, the Irish High Court passed a ruling that the girl (and her parents) were committing a crime and called them back to Ireland (Hogan, 1992: 112; Hug, 1999: 167). The logical extension of the Court ruling was that the authorities had to do pregnancy testing on all women of child-bearing age to ensure that none of them were about to commit a crime. Afraid of a major scandal and bad publicity, the government pressed the parents to seek an appeal from the Irish Supreme Court. The judges heard the case a few weeks later in late February and decided that abortion was in fact legal in Ireland if the life of the mother was at risk. The girl had threatened and tried to commit suicide, which was the basis of the new interpretation of the constitutional ban. Of course, the constitutional ban on abortion was meant to rule out for once and for all the possibility of having an abortion on Irish soil and Catholic lay forces were first shocked and then angry about the ruling. But the embattled liberal minority was also upset because the judgment effectively stipulated that only women who could prove to run the risk of losing their lives were allowed to obtain an abortion in Britain. Women who could not prove their lives were at risk were committing a crime if they traveled abroad to end their pregnancy. Neither the Catholic lay movement nor the small liberal community was satisfied with this new legal interpretation. The situation became even more muddled after it was discovered that the traditionalists had pressured the government to insert a special protocol in the Treaty on European Union to pre-empt any future Community challenges on Article 40.3.3 from the EC (Hug, 1999: 172).[13] The Irish chief of government had added a protocol to the Treaty for European Union (just a few months earlier!) to void forever the eventuality that Community law could overturn the abortion ban. After the unexpected ruling of the Irish Supreme Court in late February 1992, Protocol 17 contradicted Irish as well as European rules and practices. The protocol affirmed the absolute proscription of abortion in Ireland, no longer compatible with the new interpretation given by the Irish Supreme Court, and also upended the existing right of EU citizens to travel freely within the EU. The Court's decision left open the question whether pregnant women whose lives were not at risk were free to seek an abortion abroad.

When the Irish government attempted to redraft the protocol to account for new domestic reasoning, Brussels torpedoed that suggestion. Ireland was therefore forced to add a "solemn declaration" to the protocol reinterpreting its meaning according to the 1992 judgment. But the politicians were also forced to call for a referendum to find out if the people of Ireland were prepared to permit abortion if the life of the mother was at risk and whether pregnant women were free to seek information and travel abroad to obtain an abortion. The result of the fall 1992 abortion referendum was that the electorate turned down the substantive question on abortion but approved by a two-thirds majority the freedom to seek information and to travel abroad. After the referendum, the politicians agreed that the legislature should pass legislation to clarify the practical implications of a constitutional ban on abortion and sort out how to deal with exceptional situations (Eggert and Rolston, 1994: 168; Girvin, 1994: 209).

Abortion is a highly sensitive topic. Irish legislators repeatedly procrastinated and refused to untie the knotty problems created by a blanket proscription on abortion. Yet the number of Irish women who availed themselves of what was euphemistically called the "English option" rose steadily. After Britain first legalized abortion in 1967, approximately 64 Irish women traveled to England the following year. Since that date, the number of pregnant Irish women who cross the channel has increased every single year. In the late 1980s, around 4000 women went to England. In 1997, the number rose to 5,325—an increase of nearly nine percent on the previous year (Inglis, 1998b: 169). The 1998 figures from the UK Office for National Statistics show the number of Irish women having abortions in England to be 5,892, which represents a remarkable increase of more than 10 percent since 1997.[14] This figure only counts women who give their address in Ireland. Many Irish women have friends and relatives in England and thus do not show up as Irish citizens in a British registry. This means that the number of women who terminate an abortion in England can easily be double. In 1994, Ireland's official abortion rate was 6 percent per 1,000 women aged between 14 and 44 in contrast to Britain's 14.8 percent. Informally, its abortion rate might be closer to 12 percent per 1,000 women aged between 14 and 44 (Hardiman and Whelan, 1998: 78; Hug, 1999: 161; Kenny, 1997: 243).

Abortion tourism raises the troubling question of how the constitutional amendment protects the life of the unborn if pregnant Irish women travel to England for an abortion. What is the use of a constitutional ban if it is widely circumvented? Moreover, what does the outflow of pregnant women say about Irish sexual morality? The claim that the Irish are different because they are more attached to the principles of the Catholic faith sounds hollow when so many women ignore one of the Church's greatest taboos. Such questions were not fully articulated but hovered in the background so long as abortion itself was not debated.

The constitutional ban is still in effect. Nevertheless, after a long delay, the coalition government of Fianna Fail and the Progressive Democrats finally published a 172-page Green Paper in September 1999 to launch a discussion on precisely these issues and to seek a consensus on how to proceed next. The government paper states outright that it is very difficult to arrive at an acceptable wording to provide for a constitutional prohibition on abortion, considering the personal complications. It continues by noting that abortion, which is considered a lawful service in the rest of the EU, is available only 60 miles away and that no Constitutional amendment and virtual blanket legislative prohibition can reduce the level of pregnancy terminations among Irish women. The Green Paper lays out seven options ranging from strengthening the ban to permitting abortion on demand.

The publication of this report is an important milestone because it is the first formal admission of the difficulties of issuing legal rulings to dictate a particular sexual morality. For the first time since the 1983 referendum there is an open and frank debate on a highly sensitive and taboo topic. The launching of the debate itself, however, desensitizes Irish voters and prepares the way toward a tacit acceptance of abortion as a solution to difficult personal predicaments.

The Green Paper appears at a point when attitudes concerning abortion have already softened. In 1973, 74 percent of Irish thought that abortion was always evil and only 5 percent accepted abortion in case of rape or illegitimacy (Hug, 1999: 150). In 1981, 55 percent of the surveyed population repudiated abortion and 45 percent of the Irish respondents approved of abortion if the mother's health was at risk by the pregnancy (Hornsby-Smith and Whelan, 1994: 36). In 1994, 71 percent of the population agreed that abortion should be possible if the life of the mother was at risk and 41 percent felt that extreme mental anguish (suicidal tendencies) should be included as one of the reasons (Girvin, 1996a: 176). Thus, it seems clear that the electorate is increasingly willing to recognize the legitimacy of an abortion in well-defined circumstances although it is important to remember that the idea of abortion on demand would not get electoral approval (Kennedy, 1999: 16). Ireland remains different from its European neighbors in that respect although the gap between Irish attitudes and that of mainstream Europe has narrowed.[15]

For Sweden and Finland, alcohol control policy is also under threat because of the widespread habit of cross-border shopping trips to respectively Denmark or Estonia. As soon as both countries joined the EU, travelers' imports surged as many tourists brought back taxed though much cheaper liquor from neighboring countries. In addition, the phasing out of border controls was an open invitation to criminal organizations to enter the alcohol smuggling business. Accordingly, unregistered consumption of moonshine and legal personal imports is conservatively estimated to be around 30 percent (Österberg, et al., 1996; Österberg and Pekhonen, 1996). The question raised by opponents is why the state continues to operate a monopoly system when people have easy access to cheap liquor and increasingly satisfy their alcohol needs outside the state framework. Retail outlets in border regions in both Finland and Sweden, for example, have witnessed a dramatic decline in turnover.

The cheating and smuggling could have been ignored were it not that Sweden, in particular, faces ongoing minor conflicts with the EU. Both Finland and Sweden agreed to institute reforms in exchange for concessions from the Commission. In return for keeping the retail network of company stores intact, the Nordic applicants to the EC/EU (including Norway as participant in the European Economic Area) agreed to demonopolize the distribution and production of alcoholic beverages. After 1994, private agents were allowed to enter the alcohol beverage market and compete with state companies in production, foreign trade, and the supply to the catering industry. But the state retail monopoly continued to be the only legal sale point for off-premise consumption (Holder, et. al., 1998).

In addition, Nordic officials requested an exemption from the common trade policies of the EU. In the wake of the Single Market, the Commission had made great strides in removing barriers against the import of taxed liquor by private citizens. Thus, the Commission declared years ago that a EU citizen could import for personal use 10 liters of spirits, 90 liters of table wine, 20 liters of fortified wine, and 110 liters of beer. By contrast, until 1995, Sweden and Finland restricted traveler's imports to 1 liter of spirits, 1 liter of wine, and 2 liters of beer. Sweden and Finland asked for a transition phase during which they kept limits on personal travelers' imports. The compromise solution was to raise the maximum to 1 liter of spirits, 5 liters of table wine, and 15 liters of beer. Essentially, the Commission opposed the special arrangements for Finland and Sweden and each country is supposed to phase out the restrictions by December 2003.

Critics exploit the considerable reservations of the Commission and the ambiguities in Community law to challenge national authorities. A Swedish grocery storeowner, Harry Franzén, a member of the Swedish association of retail stores, insisted on selling wine in his store in January 1995 (immediately after accession). Once the Swedish authorities decided to prosecute Mr. Franzén for illegally selling wine, he claimed that he had not committed any crime because Article 30 of the Treaty of Rome prohibited restrictions on the importation of goods and Article 37 guarantees that state monopolies shall not impede trade or foster discrimination. *Allmänna Åklagaren vs. Harry Franzén* [C-189/95] arose after the Swedish district court requested a preliminary ruling on whether the alcohol retail monopoly was in compliance with the Treaty of Rome. In June 1995, the Landskrona Tingsrätt sought clarification on whether the monopoly is in line with Article 30 of the Treaty of Rome (free importation of goods from other member-states) and whether it must be abolished or can be adapted to Treaty requirements (trade barriers erected by state monopolies).

The European Court of Justice made its decision public in late October 1997 and considered the distribution system of the alcohol monopoly nondiscriminatory and not liable to put imported products at a disadvantage. In spite of the restricted number of sales outlets, the monopoly, it argued, is structured in order to offer customers a wide range of choices of domestic and foreign beverages. It does not promote domestic over foreign products and its entire structure never meant to create selection bias (Holder, et al., 1998: 31–49).

Nevertheless, the long wait for a resolution of the Franzén case stimulated a lengthy debate to reassess the purpose and effectiveness of the state monopoly system. By and large, the public evaluation inadvertently lent support to pro-liberalization voices by raising questions that could no longer be easily answered (Sutton, 1998, 138; Ugland, 1997). They turned the classic public health argument around by claiming that high taxes/prices forced consumers to resort to moonshine, which occasionally contained more than ethyl alcohol. In addition, since alcoholic beverages are prohibitively expensive, consumers drink at home and never get the routine down of how to drink in public and thus in moderation. The inflow of illegal or licit alcohol even irritates the state-owned distillery company and the manufacturer of the *Absolut* vodka brand. The managing director of *Vin och Sprit*, Kjell-Olof Feldt, has repeatedly appealed for more lax rules to arrest the popularity of smuggled spirits and moonshine. He suggested more stores, weekend openings, and the advertising of legal liquor to be able to compete with the popularity of black market spirits. Like conservatives (Feldt is a former social democratic finance minister), he believes that the state should focus mainly on public opinion building and measures to reduce alcohol abuse among the young and vulnerable (Feldt, 1998, 2; Nycander, 1996: 281; Sutton, 1998, 141).[16]

The attacks, couched in language that seem to indicate great concern for the health and well-being of society, receive extra resonance because of the continuing popularity of travelers' import. The inflow of (legal) alcohol suggests that the government no longer possesses the necessary instruments to meet its public health objectives.

Unanswerable questions concerning the purpose and utility of a state alcohol monopoly coupled with the flood of new rhetoric on the benefits of market forces and the "costs" of drinking restrictions influence opinions on drinking. National household surveys on drinking attitudes include a question on whether table wines should be sold in grocery stores. In 1988, 39 percent of Swedish respondents were in favor of selling table wines in grocery stores. In 1994, during the run-up of the membership referendum, the approval rate was 72 percent, but by 1997 it had fallen back to 55 percent. In Finland, 54 percent of the population was in favor of wine sales from grocery stores in 1988 and 64 percent in 1996 (Holder et al., 1998, 202–3). Sale of distilled liquors, however, should remain in state retail stores according to the majority of Swedish and Finnish citizens. In 1997, only 20 percent of the population in each country felt positive about the sale of liquor in grocery stores (Holder et al., 1998, 207).

Although distilled spirits are still considered dangerous to the fabric of society, a taboo has been lifted in that an increasing number of citizens, having become familiar with the European model, advocate some liberalization in the form of permitting the sale of light alcoholic beverages in grocery stores. The discussion itself convinces many consumers that there is really no harm in selling wine in supermarkets so long as everybody realizes the dangers of uncontrolled drinking. Younger cohorts are among the strongest advocates of further alcohol liberalization. They are more likely to travel abroad and be cognizant of drinking customs in non-Nordic countries and they are least likely to have any mental connection to the era of excessive drinking prior to the imposition of alcohol legislation.

To counter public criticism and compete with outside sources of alcoholic beverages, both *Alko* and *Systembolaget* stress customer service and downplay the public health message. Thus, in November 1999, the Swedish government decided to open half of *Systembolaget* retail outlets in northern and southern Sweden on Saturdays to cut down on long lines, which always seem to develop on Friday afternoon (Vipotnik, 1999, 3). Earlier in 1997, the Swedish government lowered the price of domestic beer to compete with Danish beer and curb smuggling and personal imports.[17] In Finland, pressure for liberalization is also strong although *Alko* had already decided to keep its store open on Saturdays in 1991 and beer is available outside the state retail stores. In Finland, the private sector, consisting of retail stores, catering industry, and brewery companies, is therefore divided about liberalization and deregulation. The brewery industry is not opposed to retail state outlets since beer is available in thousands of stores, gas stations, and newspaper kiosks while wine is only obtainable in 255 state monopoly shops (Holder, et al. 1998, 132 & 187).[18] Finnish beer breweries also sell Finnish beer in Estonia where many Helsinki residents go to stock up on cheap liquor. But the private sector wants to see lower prices out of fear that ultimately many Finnish consumers will shop abroad not only for cheap liquor but also to procure other goods, which are more expensive in the domestic market.

In March 2000, the Commission insisted that Sweden abolish all limits on personal imports by August of that year. The Swedish authorities pleaded with Fritz Bolkestein (Commissioner for Internal Market) for an extension, but the Commissioner was adamant that the exemption should run out by the summer. After much publicity and a special visit by Bolkestein to Stockholm, it was agreed that Sweden, jointly with Finland, adopt EU rules by January 1, 2003. In preparation, Sweden raised the limits on personal traveler's import for beer and wine in July 2000. Then, starting in 2003, Swedes and Finns can buy as much as liquor abroad as they want.

Will this mean the end of the state monopoly company? Most likely, Alko and Systembolaget will remain in operation. The Swedish and Finnish ministries of finance are loath to lose the equivalent of respectively 3 percent and 6 percent of tax revenues. Politicians, not only officials in the finance ministry, are aware that further liberalization will increase alcohol consumption and thus multiply alcohol-related problems. At the same time, tax revenues will be less than half owing to pressures to conform to Continental price structures so that less money will be available to deal with a higher prevalence of alcohol-related problems (Österberg and Kajalo, 1998).[19] Thus, lingering reservations or apprehensions concerning abusive drinking rituals and basic monetary calculation will keep the alcohol monopoly system intact.

Summary and Conclusion

Mobility of ideas and people has unexpected consequences for morality regimes, that is, systems of beliefs and rules that govern sensitive social areas of behavior. The disappearance of borders due to market integration leads to "sin shopping" with consumers buying goods or services not available at home or available at much higher prices. However, the movement of people succeeds in effecting domestic change because public attitudes have already undergone a shift toward a more European-like interpretation of each issue. Removal of borders constrains the cultural sovereignty of national authorities because people take advantage of the new opportunities created by regional integration. Presumably, the cheating or sin shopping would have been less if the population truly bought into the rationale and reasoning of the morality regime. Likewise, aggravation of drug users and accusations of drug-related nuisance would have been less strident if the Dutch population accepted the principles of harm reduction fully. A combination of domestic and external factors contributed to a weakening of singular cultural frameworks.

In spite of pressures to revisit morality standards, the result is a modest trend toward cultural homogenization. It is important to note that Irish opinion on abortion still diverges from the rest of Europe, that Finns and Swedes still mistrust hard liquor and engage in binge drinking rituals, and that the Dutch are still more or less in agreement on retaining the public health framework to cope with drug use/misuse. Europe's diversity is diminishing but plenty of differences continue to obstruct real political unity and close, emotional identification with the European Union.

This chapter has sought to isolate the mechanism responsible for a modest cultural convergence and has argued that the driving forces of change reside at the national level. Domestic institutions, rules, and procedures mediate the impact of regional or global forces. In addition, even across the four cases, the nature of external pressures differs. Dutch drug policy clashes with the intergovernmental level of the EU. Alcohol monopoly systems collide with Single Market rules on open competition, non-trade discrimination, and deregulation of public services. Abortion does not fall under any part of the EU and external pressures hover in the background and play a modest role. Although external pressures and domestic arrangements differ, the mechanism of adjustment is a combination of competitive selection and mimesis. On the one hand, markets reduce the room for variance as nonconformity is punished as less efficient and rational. The punishing agents are individuals, which is different from what we usually associate with market forces, namely economic agents, yet the effect is strikingly familiar. Recalcitrant "interests" (actual individuals) push for change by evading national rules and understandings. Cheating causes strain in the morality regimes and leads to a political process of reevaluating the desirability and utility of drug decriminalization, restrictive drinking laws, and abortion ban.

On the other hand, mimesis also shapes the outcome. When considering adjustment, the obvious model at hand is that which prevails in the rest of Europe. The alternative for each country is undoubtedly mainstream European conventions with respect to the age-old dilemma of substance abuse or the more recent phenomenon of a decline of religious authority. Mimesis explains why institutions, when they must respond to the uncertainty created by the elimination of borders, copy arrangements that seem to work for the rest of Europe. There is, however, one major caveat. Even if each of the four countries moves closer to a European interpretation of these morally questionable activities, they continue to assign different benefits or risks to each activity. This chapter ultimately demonstrates not only the stickiness of social institutions but also the endurance of norms, convictions, and beliefs. Finnish and Swedish consumers still view drinking of hard liquor with enormous suspicion, Dutch voters have serious qualms about police repression to rid society of drugs, and the Irish continue to reject the idea of abortion on demand. Mounting disagreements at home and friction abroad encourages a new debate on existing cultural legacies. But these legacies will, for the time being, endure regardless of how the grand project of supranational institution-building unfolds.

Endnotes

1. Please note that Nordic refers to Iceland, Finland, Norway, and Sweden. Denmark is a Nordic country but it does not share the same drinking traditions as the other four. The merry Danes, therefore, are not part of this story on anti-drinking policy.
2. For other examples, consult, Katzenstein (1996).
3. A classic joke about the painfully taciturn Finn is as follows. Two Finns sit at a bar. After hours of silence one raises a glass and says "cheers." His friend snaps back, "We didn't come here to talk."
4. Two very different analyses of Dutch tolerance, Downes (1988) and Israel, Berkvens-Stevelinck, and Meyjes (1997).
5. For an illuminating analysis of how the discourse on drinking veered from a preoccupation with alcoholism to alcohol harm, see Sutton (1998).
6. See also, Roe (1994). For empirical studies using the concept of policy narrative, Gottweis (1998) and Schmidt (forthcoming).
7. Both drug and alcohol policy had a fair share of skeptics and detractors at various times. For other examples of contested norms, which nonetheless became part of collective identity, Katzenstein (1996) and Olsen (1996).
8. In a 1992 report, the European Parliament made the bold allegation that the power of criminal organizations, which controlled the global flow of drugs, was growing at an alarming rate and was having serious effects on society and on the political institutions of the member states. It continued to note ominously that organized crime undermined the foundations of the legitimate economy and threatened the stability of the States of the Community (Hebenton and Thomas, 1995: 158).
9. The immediate reason for launching an inquiry into the growth of organized crime was a huge police scandal uncovered in 1993.
10. In 1995, the actual number of total outlets was around 2,000.

11. The government report published by the three departments in charge of drug policy (Public Health, Justice, and Interior) describes these trends exhaustively.

12. The Dutch law prohibited the police from closing down private residences so long as people were living in them.

13. A first draft of the proposal to add a protocol to the Treaty for European Union included a section on divorce. Some cabinet members found that too much and torpedoed the plan to protect the ban on divorce from European interference.

14. It appears that more than 20 percent of Irish women have an abortion after the first trimester. Only 11 percent of women resident in England and Wales had abortions after 13 weeks of pregnancy. Britain effectively permits abortion on demand and allows terminations to take place as late as the 24th week of pregnancy. Many other countries either limit abortion to the first 12 or 13 weeks or apply stricter criteria to abortions undertaken after that time-limit (Fitzgerald, 1999: 14; Irish Times, 1999: 4).

15. See, for example, on the topic of structural change and secularization Crotty and Schmitt (1998), Girvin (1996b), and O'Connor (1998).

16. Feldt (1998: 4) is on record to favor liberalization since the mid-1990s.

17. Sweden also agreed with the Commission to apply a uniform tax rate according to the alcohol percentage of the beverage. Until January 1997, medium-strength beer had been favored with an extra low tax to encourage consumption of light alcoholic beverages. After that date, the price of medium-strength beer went up because it was subject to the same tax as other beers. Excise taxes on wine decreased in Finland by 17 percent and the retail price dropped by 10 percent on January 1998 (Holder et al., 1998: 45 & 146; McIvor, 1998: 1).

18. Strong beer is sold in monopoly stores and is barely consumed. Finns drink 4 liters of alcohol of medium beer and only half a liter of alcohol of strong beer per person per year.

19. Estimates are that Finnish per capita consumption will reach 11.7 liters in 2004 and will surpass that of France.

References

Adler, Emanuel. 1997. "Seizing the Middle Ground. Constructivism in World Politics." *European Journal of International Relations* 3: 319–363.

Barrett, Deborah and David John Frank. 1999. "Population Control for National Development: From World Discourse to National Policies." In *Constructing World Culture: International Nongovernmental Organizations since 1875*, edited by John Boli and George M Thomas. Stanford: Stanford University Press.

Bigo, Didier. 1998. "L'Europe de la sécurité interieure: penser autrement la sécurité." In *Entre Union et Nations*, edited by Anne-Marie Le Gloannec. Paris: Presses de Sciences Po.

Bless, R., D.J. Korf, and M. Freeman. 1995. "Open Drug Scenes: A Cross-National Comparison of Concepts and Urban Strategies." *European Addiction Research* 1: 128–38.

Blomqvist, Jan. 1998. "The 'Swedish Model' of Dealing with Alcohol Problems: Historical Trends and Future Challenges." *Contemporary Drug Problems*. 25: 253–320.

Boekhout van Solinge, Tim. 1999. "Dutch Drug Policy in a European Context." *Journal of Drug Issues* 29: 511–28.

Bruun Kettil E. et.al. 1975. *Alcohol Control Policies*. Helsinki: Finnish Foundation for Alcohol Studies.

Bruun, Kettil E. 1985. "Sweden." In *Alcohol Policies*, edited by Marcus Grant. Copenhagen: World Health Organization/Regional Office for Europe.

Buning E. and G.H.A. van Brussel. 1995. "The Effects of Harm Reduction in Amsterdam." *European Addiction Research* 1: 92–98.

Checkel, Jeffrey. 1998. "The Constructivist Turn in International Relations Theory." *World Politics* 50: 324–48.

Cohen, Peter and Arjan Sas. 1997. "Cannabis Use, A Stepping Stone to Other Drugs? The Case of Amsterdam." In *Cannabis Science: From Prohibition to Human Rights*, edited by Lorzenz Bollinger. Frankfurt: Peter Lang.

Collins, Larry. 1999. "Holland's Half-baked Drug Experiment." *Foreign Affairs* 78: 3–21.

Connelly, Alpha. 1993. *Women and the Law in Ireland*. Dublin: Gill & Macmillan.

Crotty, William, and David E. Schmitt. 1998. *Ireland and the Politics of Change*. New York: Longman.

Cuskey, Walter R., Arnold Klein, and William Krasner. 1972. *Drug-trip Abroad. American Drug Refugees in Amsterdam and London*. Philadelphia: University of Pennsylvania Press.

Dalton, Russell J. and Richard C. Eichenberg. 1998. "Citizen Support for Policy Integration." In *European Integration and Supranational Governance*, edited by Wayne Sandholtz and Alec Stone Sweet. New York: Oxford University Press.

Daun, Åke. *Swedish Mentality*. University Park: Pennsylvania State University Press, 1996.

Derks, Jack T. M., Marten J. Hoekstra, and Charles D. Kaplan. 1998. "Integrating Care, Cure, and Control: Drug Treatment System in the Netherlands." In *Treatment Systems in an International Perspective: Drugs, Demons, and Delinquents*, edited by Harald Klingemann and Geoffrey Hunt. Thousand Oaks, CA: Sage.

Downes, David. 1988. *Contrasts in Tolerance: Postwar Penal Policy in the Netherlands, and England and Wales.* New York: Oxford University Press.

Drudy, Sheelagh and Kathleen Lynch. 1993. *Schools and Society in Ireland.* Dublin: Gill and Macmillan.

Eggert, Anna and Bill Rolston. 1994. "Ireland." In *Abortion in the New Europe: A Comparative Handbook,* edited by Anna Eggert and Bill Rolston. Westport, CT: Greenwood.

European Commission. 1994. *EuroBarometer* 41.

European Commission. 1997. *EuroBarometer* 47.

Feldt, Kjell-Olof. 1998. "Spritreklamen måste återinföras." *Sverige Nytt*: May 4.

Fijnaut, Cyrille, Frank Bovenkerk, Gerben Bruinsma, and Henk van de Bunt. 1998. *Organized Crime in the Netherlands.* Boston: Kluwer.

Finnemore, Martha. 1996. *National Interests in International Society.* Ithaca: Cornell University Press.

Fitzgerald, Garret. 1999. "Green Paper is a helpful guide to key issues in divisive topic of abortion." *Irish Times* (September 18): 14.

Florini, Ann. 1996. "The Evolution of International Norms." *International Studies Quarterly* 40: 363–90.

Girvin, Brian. 1994. "Moral Politics and the Irish Abortion Referendums 1992." *Parliamentary Affairs* 47: 222–37.

Girvin, Brian. 1996a. "Ireland and the European Union: The Impact of Integration and Social Change on Abortion Policy." In *Abortion Politics : Public Policy in Cross-Cultural Perspective,* edited by Marianne Githens and Dorothy Stetson. New York: Routledge.

Girvin, Brian. 1996b. "Church, State, and the Irish Constitution: The Secularization of Irish Politics." *Parliamentary Affairs* 49: 599–615.

Gorski, Philip S. 1999. "Calvinism and State-Formation in Early Modern Europe." In *State/Culture: State-Formation after the Cultural Turn,* edited by George Steinmetz. Ithaca: Cornell University Press.

Gottweis, Herbert. 1998. *Governing Molecules.* New York: Routledge.

Griffith, Edward, et al. 1994. *Alcohol Policy and the Public Good.* New York: Oxford University Press.

Hall, Peter A. 1989. "Conclusion." In *The Political Power of Economic Ideas: Keynesianism Across Nations,* edited by Peter A. Hall. Princeton: Princeton University Press.

Hardiman, Niamh, and Christopher Whelan. 1998. "Changing Values." In *Ireland and the Politics of Change,* edited by William Crotty and David E. Schmitt. New York: Longman.

Hebenton Bill and Terry Thomas. 1995. *Policing Europe: Cooperation, Conflict, and Control.* New York: St Martin's.

Hempton, David. 1996. *Religion and Political Culture in Britain and Ireland.* New York: Cambridge University Press.

Hogan, Gerard. 1992. "Protocol 17." In *Maastricht and Ireland: What the Treaty Means*, edited by Patrick Keating. Dublin: Studies in European Union.

Holder, Harold, Eckart Kühlhorn, Sturla Nordlund, Esa Österberg, Anders Romelsjö, and Trygve Ugland. 1998. *European Integrationand Nordic Alcohol Policies: Changes in Alcohol Controls and Consequences in Finland, Norway, and Sweden.* Brookfield: Ashgate.

Hornsby-Smith Michael P. and Christopher T. Whelan. 1994. "Religious and Moral Values." In *Values and Social Change in Ireland*, edited by Christopher T. Whelan. Dublin: Gill & Macmillan.

Hug, Chrystel. 1999. *The Politics of Sexual Morality in Ireland.* New York: St. Martin's Press.

Inglis, Tom. 1998a. *Moral Monopoly: The Rise and Fall of the Catholic Church in Modern Ireland.* Dublin: University College Dublin Press.

Inglis. 1998b. *Lessons in Irish Sexuality.* Dublin: University College Dublin Press.

Irish Times, 1999. "Abortion has increased by 10.4 percent." (June 8): 4.

Israel, Jonathan, Christiane Berkvens-Stevelinck, Posthumus G. H. M. Meyjes. 1997. *The Emergence of Tolerance in the Dutch Republic.* New York: E.J. Brill.

Jepperson, Ron Alex Wendt, and Peter Katzenstein, "Norms, Identity, and Culture in National Security." In *The Culture of National Security*, edited by Peter Katzenstein.

Katzenstein, Peter, ed. 1996. *The Culture of National Security: Norms and Identity in World Politics.* New York: Columbia University Press.

Keating, Paul and Derry Desmond. 1993. *Culture and Capitalism in Contemporary Ireland.* Brookfield, VT: Ashgate.

Kennedy, Geraldine. 1999. "Ahern is right on approach to abortion." *Irish Times* (September 20): 16.

Kenny, Mary. 1997. *Goodbye to Catholic Ireland.* London: Sinclair-Stevenson.

Klotz, Audie. 1995. *Norms in International Relations: The Struggle Against Apartheid.* Ithaca: Cornell University Press.

Korf, Dirk J., Heleen Riper, and Bruce Bullington. 1999. "Windmills in their Minds? Drug Policy and Drug Research in the Netherlands." *Journal of Drug Issues* 29: 451–72.

Kort, de Marcel and Ton Cramer. 1999. "Pragmaticism versus Ideology: Dutch Drug Policy Continued." *Journal of Drug Issues* 29: 473–92.

Kort, de Marcel. 1995. "A Short History of Drugs in the Netherlands." *Between Prohibition and Legalization: The Dutch Experiment in Drug Policy, edited by* Ed. Leuw and I. Haen Marshall. New York: Kugler.

Kort, de Marcel. 1995. *Tussen patiënt en delinquent: Geschiedenis van het Nederlandse drugbeleid.* Hilversum: Verloren.

Kort, Marcel de, and Dirk J. Korf. 1992. "The Development of Drug Trade and Drug Control in the Netherlands: A Historical Perspective." *Crime, Law, and Social Change* 17:

Leifman, Håkan. 1996. *Perspectives on Alcohol Prevention.* Stockholm: Almqvist and Wiksell.

Leifman, Håkan. 1996. *Perspectives on Alcohol Prevention.* Stockholm: Almqvist and Wiksell.

Leuw, Ed. and I. Haen Marshall, eds. *Between Prohibition and Legalization: the Dutch Experiment in Drug Policy.* New York: Kugler Publications, 1994.

Levine, Harry G. 1992. "Alcohol Problems in Nordic and English-speaking Cultures." In *The Nature of Alcohol and Drug Related Problems,* edited by Malcolm Lader, Griffith Edwards, D. Colin Drummond. New York: Oxford University Press.

Loya, Thomas A. and John Boli. 1999. "Standardization in the World Polity: Technical Rationality Over Power." In *Constructing World Culture,* edited by John Boli and George M. Thomas. Stanford: Stanford University Press

Lüthy, Herbert. 1985. "Variations on a Theme by Max Weber." In *International Calvinism,* edited by Menna Prestwich Oxford: Clarendon.

Majone, Giandomenico. 1996. *Regulating Europe.* New York: Routledge.

Mäkelä, Klaus, and Matti Viikari. 1977. "Notes on Alcohol and the State." *Acta Sociologica* 20: 169–76

Mäkelä. 1985. "Lessons from the Postwar Period." In *Alcohol Policies,* edited by Marcus Grant. Copenhagen: World Health Organization/Regional Office for Europe.

Maris, C.W. 1996. "Dutch Weed and Logic: The Logic of the Harm Principle." *International Journal of Drug Policy* 7: 142–49.

McCourt, Frank. 1996. *Angela's Ashes. A Memoir.* New York: Scribner.

McIvor, Greg. 1998. "Sweden cuts tobacco tax by 27 percent." *Financial Times* (April 15): 3.

Miles, Lee. 1996. *The Nordic Countries and the 1995 EU Enlargment.* New York: Routledge.

Minister van Volksgezondheid, Welzijn, en Sport, Minister van Justitie, and Staatsscretaris van Binnenlandse Zaken. 1996. *Het Nederlandse drugbeleid; continuïteit en verandering.* The Hague: Sdu.

Nycander, Svante 1996. *Svenskarna och spriten; Alkoholpolitik 1855–1995.* Malmö: Sober.

O'Connor, Pat. 1998. *Emerging Voices: Women in Contemporary Irish Society.* Dublin: Institute for Public Administration.

O'Connor, Paul. 1988. *Key Issues in Irish Family Law.* Dublin: Round Hall Press.

O'Faolain, Nuala. 1997. *Are you Somebody? The Life and Times of Nuala O'Faolain.* Dublin: New Island Books.

Olsen, Johan P. 1996. "Europeanization and Nation-State Dynamics." In *The Future of the Nation State,* edited by Sverker Gustavsson and Leif Lewin. New York: Routledge.

Ossebaard, H.C. and G.F. van de Wijngaart. 1998. "Purple Haze: The Remaking of Dutch Drug Policy." *International Journal of Drug Policy* 9: 264–70.

Österberg, Esa and Juhani Pekhonen. 1996. "Travellers' Imports of Alcohol into Finland: Changes caused by Finnish EU membership." *Nordisk Alkoholtidskrift* 13: 22–32.

Österberg, Esa and Sami Kajalo, et.al. 1998. "Alkoholkonsumtion och -priser i Finland till å 2004. Fyra scenarier." *Nordisk aklohol-& narkotikatidskrift*, 15: 212–22.

Österberg, Esa, Kari Haavisto, Raija Ahtola and Maija Kaivomurmi. 1996. "The Booze Rally on the Eastern Border, Alcohol Consumption and Problems Caused by Alcohol." Translation of "Itärajan viinaralli, alkoholin kulutus ja alkoholihaitat." *Alkoholipolitiikka* 61: 325–35.

Österberg, Esa. 1990. "The Relationship Between Alcohol Consumption Patterns and the Harmful Consequences of Drinking." In *Alcohol and Drugs*, edited by Martin Plant. Edinburgh: Edinburgh University Press. 82–92.

Ottevanger, C. M. 1997. "Drug Policy and Drug Tourism." In *Schengen, Judicial Cooperation and Policy Coordination*, edited by Maria den Boer. Maastricht: European Institute of Public Administration.

Phillips-Martinsson, Jean. 1981. *Swedes, as others see them*. Stockholm: Affärsförlaget.

Reid, Madeleine. 1992. "Abortion Law in Ireland after the Maastricht Referendum." In *Abortion Papers, Ireland*, edited by Ailbhe Smyth. Dublin: Attic Press.

Rochon, Thomas. 1999. *The Netherlands: Negotiating Sovereignty in an Interdependent World*. Boulder: Westview.

Roe, Emery. 1994. *Narrative Policy Analysis: Theory and Practice*. Durham: Duke University Press.

Rothstein, Bo. 1998. *Just Institutions Matter: The Moral and Political Logic of the Universal Welfare State*. New York: Cambridge University Press.

Ruggie, John Gerard. 1998. "What Makes the World Hang Together? Neo-Utilitarianism and Social Constructivist Challenge." *International Organization* 52: 855–85.

Rüter, C.F. 1996. "De grote verdwijntruc." In *Naar een consistent drugsbeleid*, edited by T. Blom, H. de Doelder, and D.J. Hessing. Gouda: Quint.

Schmidt, Vivien. Forthcoming. "Politics, Values, and the Power of Discourse in the Reform of the Welfare State." In *From Vulnerability to Competitiveness: Welfare and Work in the Open Economy*, edited by Fritz Scharpf and Vivien Schmidt. New York: Oxford University Press.

Skog, Ole-Jörgen. 1985. "The Collectivity of Drinking Cultures: A Theory of the Distribution of Alcohol Consumption." *British Journal of Addiction*, 81: 83–99.

Skog, Ole-Jörgen. 1991a. "Drinking and the Distribution of Alcohol Consumption." In *Society, Culture, and Drinking Patterns Reexamined*, edited by David J. Pittman and Helene Raskin White. New Brunswick: Rutgers Center for Alcohol Studies.

Skog. 1991b. "Implications of the Distribution Theory for Drinking and Alcoholism." In *Society, Culture, and Drinking Patterns Reexamined.*

Sutton, Caroline. 1998. *Swedish Alcohol Discourse: Constructions of a Social Problem.* Uppsala: Studia Sociologica Upsaliensia.

Tannenwald, Nina. 1999 "The Taboo on Nuclear Weapons." *International Organization* 53: 433–68.

Tomasson, Richard F. 1998. "Alcohol and Alcohol Control in Sweden." *Scandinavian Studies,* 70: 261–79.

Ugland, Trygve. 1997. "Europeanization of the Nordic Alcohol Monopoly Systems: Collisions between Ideologies and Political Cultures." *Nordic Studies on Alcohol and Drugs* 14: 7–15.

Vipotnik, Matej. 1999. "Wine and Swedes can mix on a Saturday night." *Financial Times* (November 29): 3.

Vliet, van Henk Jan. 1990. "A Symposium on Drug Decriminalization: The Uneasy Decriminalization: A Perspective on Dutch Drug Policy." *Hofstra Law Review* 18: 718–30.

Waever, Ole, B. Buzan, M. Kestrup, and P. Lemaître. 1993. *Identity, Migration, and the New Security Agenda in Europe.* London: Pinter.

Waever, Ole. 1993. *Securitization and Desecuritization.* Copenhagen: Center for Peace and Conflict Research.

Wendon, Bryan. 1998. "The Commission as Image-Venue Entrepreneur in EU Social Policy." *Journal of European Public Policy* 5: 339–53.

Wendt, Alexander. 1992. "Anarchy is What States Make of It: The Social Construction of Power Politics." *International Organization* 46: 391–425.

Wendt. 1994. "Collective Identity Formation and the International State." *American Political Science Review* 88: 384–96.

Whyte, John H. 1980. *Church and State in Modern Ireland, 1923–79.* Dublin: Gill and Macmillan.

2 The Variable Geometry of European Regional Economic Development

Chris Ansell, Vanna Gonzales, and Conor O'Dwyer

Globalization is our fate and we can't escape it.
—Official with the North Rhine-Westphalia Ministry of Economics

Globalization is something that we watch carefully because we view this new type of internationalization in a very positive way.
—Official in Tuscan Regional Government

In this volume, we have defined globalization in terms of the increased mobility of goods, capital, labor, and ideas. Our Political Economy Null Hypothesis (PENH) predicts that this increased mobility will be experienced by actors as an increase in the ambient level of competition in the world economy; to remain competitive, actors are compelled to adopt more efficient strategies and practices, and consequently new institutions of governance. The explanatory mechanism here is competitive selection. In Darwinian fashion, actors who do not adopt new strategies, practices, and institutions will not survive—or, to adopt a more plausible standard for the subnational governments we analyze—their performance will be greatly impaired. We then offered three alternative explanations of changing governance structures—U.S. power, ideas, and EU politics. In each case, coercion or mimesis rather than competitive selection is the expected explanatory mechanism. Finally, and most broadly, we anticipate that extant institutional structures and practices will act as major intervening variables in explaining the precise nature of any change in governance structure.

In this chapter, we examine changing forms of subnational governance of economic development in two European regions: the German Länder of North Rhine-Westphalia and the Italian region of Tuscany. Interviews with officials in these two regions suggest that at least a part of the null hypothesis (PENH) is valid: these subnational governments do experience an increase in the ambient level of competition in the world economy, though it is unclear how much of this experience should be attributed to increased mobility. We also found that subnational governments were adopting new strategies of governance or adapting existing strategies in ways that they believed would increase the economic competitiveness of their regions. We even found a degree of convergence in the types of governance strategies being adopted by the two regions. At this very crude level, then, the Political Economy Null Hypothesis cannot be easily rejected. At the same time, we found that the precise nature of governance change could only be fully understood in terms of new ideas about economic development, broad changes in the distribution of political authority, and the emerging role of the European Union. Most importantly, we found that specific adaptations in subnational governance can only be understood in terms of extant institutional structures and practices.

The broad context for understanding changes in subnational governance of economic development is a macro-institutional shift in political authority over regional economic development. After World War II, advanced industrial nations became increasingly concerned about spatial inequalities in economic development. They responded with *national* policies and programs that promoted greater economic equality across *subnational* regions. Beginning in the 1970s, however, the institutional structure of these programs underwent two major changes in European nations. The first change was a *decentralization* or *devolution* of these policies and programs. Faced with fiscal pressures and major structural transitions in declining manufacturing regions, national governments gradually reduced their overall level of financial commitment and gave greater policy autonomy to subnational governments or quasi-public development agencies. The second change was a *europeanization* of regional development policy. The deepening of European political and economic integration in the 1970s led to the creation of European-wide regional development institutions designed to ameliorate regional inequalities in economic growth, thereby safeguarding European "cohesion." In the late 1980s and early 1990s, these programs and policies were greatly expanded and have become increasingly prominent in shaping regional development strategy.[1] In the language of our alternative hypotheses, the relative "coercive" power of national governments declined relative to that of subnational and European institutions.

At both the subnational and European level, regional development strategy has gravitated towards the idea of an "endogenous development" strategy as a particular conception of economic development (Coffey and Polese 1984, 1985; Molle and Cappellin 1988; Garfoli 1992; Musyck 1995; Rhodes 1995; Wilson 1995; Behrens and Smyrl 1997). Broadly speaking, endogenous development entails adopting policies that utilize and develop indigenous resources to create self-sustaining economic development. The strategy places greater weight on cultivating local growth potential than on attracting external investment to the region. Obviously, this development philosophy sounds attractive in a context in which subnational governments have greater autonomy in fashioning their own development strategies, where external development funds are scarce, and where capital is globally mobile. It is also attractive to a European Union with limited political and administrative capacity that fears permanent underdevelopment of certain regions as a threat to deepened market integration and European "cohesion."[2] Indeed, we find some degree of convergence among both subnational governments and European authorities on the standard precepts of development philosophy—the importance of cultivating technological innovation, human capital and a focus on small and medium enterprises. This convergence must be partly attributed to the European Regional Development Fund's institutionalization of this idea as a criterion for receiving project funding (coercion).[3]

As a response to either globalization or europeanization, the idea of endogenous development is relatively vague and policy prescriptions remain ambiguous. Even when regions embrace this philosophy, they may still develop very different development strategies and very different relationships with the EU. Despite a degree of convergence on the idea of development, our reading of the development literature and our research in two European regions found that subnational governments interpret the challenges and possibilities of globalization and europeanization quite differently. To describe the spectrum of differences baldly: "endogenous development" can be understood as making the regional economy autonomous from the pressures of globalization or it can be understood as mirroring the logic of global competition at the regional level. The first perspective seeks to insulate the subnational economy from global competition while the second seeks to more fully integrate the subnational into the global economy. As we shall argue, these divergent interpretations reveal different institutional lenses through which globalization is viewed. The more insular perspective interprets regional development and globalization from a "statist" perspective while the more integrative perspective sees the subnational region not so much as a self-contained state as a node of territorial governance in a broader political and economic "network."[4]

We can describe each of these perspectives in somewhat more detail, beginning with the "statist" perspective, which understands the regional economy to be a bounded territorial unit coincident with, and ultimately defined by, a sovereign political jurisdiction. This territorial market represents the productive assets of this sovereign political association. As a political association, the region is a corporate actor that has the rights and responsibilities of a sovereign to manage these assets for the good of the collectivity as a whole. Economic assets are therefore treated as part of the regional state's investment and management portfolio and the political economy of the region is viewed in accounting terms as achieving the proper balance between revenues and expenditures. As a territorially bounded corporate actor, the state views globalization as a set of external factors that have impacts upon its political assets—impacts partly beyond its control. It is happy when it has a positive trade balance and strong exports, but views other territories as threatening its assets when the trade balance is negative and exports are weak. Thus, a positive view of globalization would see it as an opportunity to expand exports but a negative view is likely to be quite defensive—seeing globalization as something the subnational government must protect and buffer itself from. The state can be seen as a gatekeeper between the local economy and the global economy—redressing any outflow of assets through investment and management of structural change. Finally, the state will see other political associations as corporate actors having their own distinctive set of interests flowing from a different portfolio of assets. Cooperation with these other actors will be measured in terms of favorable exchange opportunities and will be structured as intergovernmental relations between corporate actors with clearly bounded commitments. Dyadic relations will be preferred over multilateral relations because dyadic exchange safeguards corporate autonomy.

The "network" perspective sees the economy as standing in a different relationship to the political unit.[5] Instead of seeing the subnational government as defining the region, this perspective understands the region as a natural economic system. The local market is seen as a social unit marked by dense fabric of interdependent exchange, by historical traditions of production, and also by the characteristic social relations associated with certain forms of production. The economy is not a bundle of assets, but a way of life. Since the economy is not defined in the first place by the territorial boundaries of a sovereign political association, the subnational state does not primarily see its role as a portfolio manager for the territory's productive assets. Instead, the state is an extension of the social economy itself and seeks to reproduce the economy as a social institution. The state will act more as a facilitator of a network of social and economic relationships than as a corporate sovereign. The market will appear as a cluster of spatially concentrated but only fuzzily bounded interpersonal and interorganizational relations. It is seen as deeply interconnected with (rather than demarcated from) the larger world economy. Thus, rather than seeing the global economy as a potential hierarchy of competing territories, the network state understands the local economy to be a social and political constellation within a continuous market network. Subnational government is seen as serving in a gateway as opposed to a gatekeeper role between the local and the global economies. Other political actors are seen as partners in an open-ended project to be negotiated as you go rather than in corporate and intergovernmental terms.[6] Consequently, multilateral relations will be viewed as expanding downstream opportunities rather than as potential threats to future sovereignty.

The differences between these two perspectives are summarized in table 2.1. We argue that they will have important implications for the evolving character of region-EU relationships. The "statist" region will approach the EU in intergovernmental terms, seeing it as a corporate actor with its own distinctive interests. The two can work together if there is a clear mutual advantage, but the respective commitments of each party must be clearly delineated. As a sovereign state, it will also be uncomfortable about the possible hierarchical relationship between the EU and the subnational government, seeing it as a potential infringement on local sovereignty. For these reasons, it will prefer to engage in cooperation with its political equals— engaging other subnational governments of equal stature in dyadic cooperation. In contrast, the network state will see the EU as an institution much like itself: a facilitator of market networks at the European-wide level. They will see it as neither a corporate actor nor in hierarchical terms. Rather, the EU facilitates social and economic relations at a different scale than does the subnational government. Therefore, cooperation is less threatening and more complementary. Most importantly, it envisions the EU as a multilateral institution that potentially offers access to this higher level of market integration. Finally, since the region sees its engagement with the EU as being open-ended, flexible, and ongoing, it does not feel the same pressure to clearly specify subnational and EU commitments.

TABLE 2.1 The Spectrum of Regional Economic Geometry

Statist ⟵――――――――――――――――――――――→	Network
Regional economy seen as demarcated from global economy	Regional economy seen as interpenetrated by global economy
Regional economy seen as a portfolio of assets	Regional economy seen as way of life
Regional economy defined by political sovereignty over a particular territory	Regional economy seen as a natural system of spatially concentrated social and economic networks
Regional state as a gatekeeper to global economy	Regional state as gateway to global economy
Other political actors seen as corporate actors with distinct interests	Other political actors seen as network partners
Cooperation with other actors based on clearly bounded and specified interests	Cooperation with other actors based on open-ended continuously negotiated relations
Dyadic relations with other actors preferred so as to preserve sovereignty	Multilateral relations seen as maximizing network access to information and resources

This description of an ideal-typical "statist" and "network" region suggest very different strategies of "endogenous" development, responses to globalization, and visions for a "Europe of Regions." In illustrating these differences in the rest of the paper, we have selected to study two powerful regions that both lie at the core of the European economy — North Rhine-Westphalia in Germany and Tuscany in Italy. Both of these regions have moved beyond neoclassical development strategies and have been held up as models for subnational economic development. They are both at the cutting edge of change in the relationship between subnational governments and European integration and have both promoted the idea of a "Europe of Regions." Yet despite these similarities, North Rhine-Westphalia (NRW) illustrates our "statist" region while Tuscany exemplifies our "network" region.

In the remainder of the essay we will examine the similarities and differences between these two regions. First, we shall describe the economic structure and the different political contexts of each region. Second, we shall examine their respective perceptions of globalization and the challenges it entails. Third, we shall compare their economic development strategies. Finally, we will conclude by showing how the two regions construe their relationships with other regions and with the EU in very different terms.

The Economic and Political Contexts

While NRW and Tuscany are both prosperous European regions, their economic fundamentals and political context differ considerably. In this section we provide a basic sketch of these differences.

Historically, NRW has been a center of German industry. It is the largest of the Länder, both in terms of territory and population. Though its sheer size has guaranteed NRW a measure of sectoral diversification in the economy—with bases in manufacturing, mining, chemicals, textiles, and agriculture—it must also be noted that, historically, the core of the NRW economy was in heavy industry, especially coal and steel.[7] Indeed, Alexander Gerschenkron's famous thesis about the nature of late industrialization was drawn from the study of regions such as NRW, in which an interventionist state provided the financial and administrative wherewithal for the development of capital-intensive, vertically and horizontally integrated manufacturing concerns. Late industrialization affected the nature of both the state and the firm, both of which became centralized and hierarchical. Gary Herrigel (1996) categorizes this style of economic and political development as autarchic. In an autarchic region, both the state and large-scale, integrated industrial firms defend their autonomy within their respective spheres. The result is a distinctive pattern of arms-length government-business relations. Unlike the neoclassical "night watchman" state, which also maintains arms-length relations with the private sector, the German State's early and extensive participation in the process of industrialization led it to feel a greater stake in economic outcomes. Once the region's firms had come of age, however, they became more sensitive toward state intervention.

For most of the period from the nineteenth century to the present, NRW fit this model of autarky. The core of the region's heavy industry was located in the Ruhr Valley. In this area, the overwhelming majority of employment was in the coal and steel sectors. As late as 1984, NRW accounted for 60 percent of Germany's steel production and 90 percent of its coal extraction,

and a full 28 percent of Germany's GDP was produced in NRW. The manufacturing sector employed 56.2 percent of the labor force in 1961, as opposed
to a national average of 48.1 percent (Anderson 1992, 159). Consequently,
the NRW's economic policies were to a very great extent synonymous with
its steel and coal policies.

For most of this period, this model was very successful. But in the late
1960s and 1970s, the NRW model came under attack, as international competition threw the Ruhr Valley into a state of more or less permanent crisis.
From the middle of the 1980s to 1994, the coal industry lost some 70,800
jobs, which represented 46 percent of the sector's work force. In the same
period, the steel industry lost 45,800 jobs, which represented a more than
45 percent loss (NRW-EU-Programme 1995: 10–11). According to the government's 1996 regional development report, coal and steel now employ less
than four percent of the work force in NRW. Even in the *Ruhrgebiet*, the
traditional home of the region's heavy industry, less than eight percent were
employed in coal and steel (Landesentwicklungsbericht 1994, 11).

Because of these problems, NRW has undergone dramatic economic
restructuring. As one regional government report described the economic
developments in the region, "The Land of coal and steel has become a Land
with coal and steel" (Landesentwicklungsbericht 1994, 19). The service sector has grown from 42 percent of gross regional product in 1970 to 62 percent
in 1996. Small and medium-sized enterprises (SMEs) have grown rapidly
in number. Today, there are some 600,000 SMEs in NRW, employing approximately 4.6 million people (Landesentwicklungsbericht 1994, 23; and
ibid. 1996, 11, respectively). Despite the precipitous decline of its coal and
steel industries, NRW remains the biggest regional economy in Germany.
It still accounts for approximately one quarter of Germany's exports and
GDP (Landesentwicklungsbericht 1994, 35). The challenge for the regional
government has been to adapt economic policy to the region's changing
economic base. Doing so has required it to alter its long-standing model of
regional policy. With the decline of the massive firms in coal and steel, the
state's traditional arms-length policies are no longer sufficient. The regional
state is trying to move toward a more endogenous growth-oriented model,
but the special problems of industrial decline have led that model to take a
different form than in regions such as Tuscany.

Located in the heart of what has come to be known as the "Third Italy,"
Tuscany exemplifies an economic structure that distinguishes the central
Northeast from the rest of the country (Bagnasco 1977). The most salient
features of this model include a diffuse pattern of industrialization and active

urban centers combined with an urbanized countryside. Beyond these characteristics, three factors are particularly salient to Tuscan economic development: its industrial districts, its small and medium sized enterprises (SMEs), and the interlocking of its social and economic infrastructures. Together, these elements create a regional economic base that exemplifies the localized model of "post-fordist" flexible specialization developed theoretically by Piore and Sabel (1984).[8]

Industrial districts serve as the predominant organizational feature of the Tuscan economy and have been widely acknowledged as a key component of its success (See for example Beccatini 1987; Sforzi 1995; Trigilia 1986). According to Regional Councilor Sergio Siliani, industrial districts such as Empoli and Prato, characterized as specialized, interconnected production processes, are among the strongest elements of the Tuscan economy. Although the service sector has become increasingly more important in the 1990s, the centerpiece of Tuscan regional development remains its industrial specialization (Sforzi 1995). This feature sets it apart from its northwestern neighbors, Lombardy and Piedmont, as well as from NRW in Germany. In contrast to these regions, Tuscany has never been dominated by heavy industry or large-scale enterprises. Instead, its industrial districts are rooted in localized industrial complexes based primarily on textiles, luxury goods (leather and ceramic), and minerals. Because the enterprises within these districts tend to be small, they rely heavily on regional networks to sustain themselves (Grassi interview 1997). Due to this infrastructure, regional development has been predicated on flexible specialization, applicable to light industry and to high quality craft products in particular.

This leads to the second important characteristic of Tuscany's economic structure, the predominance of small and medium-sized enterprises. According to Doccioli (1993), 58 percent of those employed in the region work in enterprises with less than twenty employees while companies with less than ten employees represent 89 percent of the total. Compared to most regions characterized by small-scale industry, Tuscany operates with an unusually diffuse system of SMEs. SMEs are the dominant organizational characteristic of the service sector, which in recent years has evolved alongside industry as a significant factor in the development of the region (Grassi interview 1997). Financing in Italy is made more readily available to big companies and national legislation is geared toward enhancing the capacity of the biggest enterprises, but Tuscany's critical mass of SMEs allows the region to rely predominately on pooled resources or joint ventures rather than state intervention to promote its' economic and commercial interests

(Bartolini 1995). This in turn creates a kind of regional infrastructure similar to the polycentric networks described by Locke (1995) in his analysis of Italian industrial relations.

The third, but arguably most important, structural characteristic of the Tuscan economy is its interlocking social and economic infrastructures. Both Italian and American scholars have commented extensively on the primacy of "social capital" and sociopolitical networks within Tuscany (See Bagnasco 1988; Bartolini 1995; Leonardi and Nanetti 1994; Putnam 1993; Trigilia 1986). This is supported by our interviews in the region; regional officials expressed a sense that the social means of negotiation and cooperation and the high quality of these interactions are intrinsic to Tuscany's regional identity. As Mauro Grassi, a researcher at a Tuscan economic institute told us, in Tuscany "there is considerable emphasis on retaining and building the small enterprise system. Here, it is tremendously important to maintain high levels of flexibility while also retaining a high level of collective, social life" (Grassi interview 1997). In this way regional officials strive to continually reassess and reformulate the balance between market and state intervention in the economy.

Beyond these differences in economic context, NRW and Tuscany are situated in very different political contexts—the most important of which is the constitutional position of the region in relation to the larger national state. In Germany, the federal structure of the national state promotes a statist, inward-looking regional identity on the part of the Länder. In German federalism, the Länder enjoy official representation in the federal legislative process through the Bundesrat, executive power in the implementation of much of that legislation, and near total policy autonomy in such areas as education.

Italy's regions do not enjoy the same scope of institutional jurisdiction in determining regional development policy as do the Länder. Indeed commentators working on Italian politics have tended to stress the weaknesses of regional government powers (for example, see Dente 1997; Freddi 1980, Hine 1993, Pasquino 1996), often portraying regional government largely as a byproduct of unintended consequences.[9] Although reforms of the past two decades have granted considerable legislative authority to regions in important policy domains such as social services and territorial planning (King 1987; Putnam 1993), they are considerably more restricted in their ability to craft economic policy than are the German Länder.

In general, the Italian regions lack adequate instruments of governance and most policy areas pertaining to the region remain in the legislative domain of the central government. As a result, the areas of "exclusive," as opposed to concurrent, legislative powers attributed to the regions remains limited (Hine 1993). For example, while the Länder have exclusive competence in the realms of education and vocational training, the Italian regions do not. Moreover, despite their constitutional authority to set out procedures and establish overall goals within their own policy process, Italian subnational governments have limited financial autonomy and regional discretion in dispensing funds.[10] According to Sergio Siliani (interview 1997), state principles significantly restrict the expression of regional legislation in practice. Whereas, in Germany, the Bundesrat provides a formal arena of exchange for the Länder, the Italian regions do not enjoy formal representation in the legislature. Thus, despite recent emphasis on devolution within the Italian political and administrative structures, in practice regions in Italy continue to act predominately on a voluntary basis with little national institutional support.

To recapitulate, Tuscany and NRW differ considerably in terms of political and economic structure. Whereas development in NRW traditionally followed a path of ever-greater formal institutionalization, Tuscany has cultivated highly embedded networks of development. Tuscany operates more as a monitor while NRW acts more as a regulator. In NRW, the regional state enjoyed extensive powers within a federal sphere, and, mirroring this organizational logic, its firms were horizontally and vertically integrated giants. In contrast, state-region relations in Italy are less regulated and regions are more specialized in their responsibilities. Tuscany enjoys considerable autonomy because it is less institutionally connected to a cohesive, well-defined governance structure, but its economic and political capacities to *direct or steer* regional development are also restricted vis-à-vis those of NRW. This has enabled the region to act as a support structure for SMEs and industrial districts, which have been the region's central engine of growth. Of course, things are changing in both regions. In NRW, the old model is under threat, and the state is looking for alternative models. Tuscany's version of endogenous growth, by contrast, has proven successful, and therefore the region seeks to maintain its flexibility by upgrading rather than radically altering this model.

Perceptions of Globalization

The different political and economic contexts in Tuscany and NRW contribute to different evaluations of globalization in each region. While regional officials in NRW view globalization defensively, as a threat, Tuscany sees it more optimistically, as an opportunity.

As is true for much of Germany, globalization is seen in NRW as a development that highlights the uncompetitiveness of the native economy. People associate globalization with unemployment, the considerable problems of structural adaptation, downward pressure on wages, opposition from unions, and an insufficiently flexible legal code (Fischer interview). As Professor Franz Lehner of the *Institut für Arbeit und Technik* in NRW described the perception of globalization in Germany:

> The Europeans, and in particular the Germans, have considered glob-
> alization to be a big threat, and they have discussed it in a very pes-
> simistic mood. It is seen is as a huge competitiveness problem. Our
> problem with globalization, or what we assign to globalization, is huge
> unemployment, which is rapidly growing. (Lehner interview 1997)

Such fears about globalization are especially prevalent in NRW, which in the last forty years has seen the prolonged decline of its traditional economic bases, the coal and steel industries, from positions of world preeminence to virtual oblivion.

While the problem of unemployment has led the region to interpret globalization defensively, it has not led it to withdraw from global markets. Traditionally the region has had a strong export orientation, and exports still account for around 26 percent of the region's economic production (Landesentwicklungsbericht 1994, 61). In fact, NRW's economic policies aggressively promote the region in trade. For all the criticisms of the EU that emerged in the interviews we conducted, state officials praised it for expanding export markets (Jakoby, Messalla, and Noll interviews 1997). If anything, globalization seems to have heightened NRW's export orientation. But these policies seem to rest less on conviction that there are new opportunities than on the fear of doing nothing.

At the same time that this perception of globalization spurs NRW to remain strongly export-oriented, it inclines the region toward an inward-looking understanding of subnational economic development. The subnational region is, in this view, the primary defense against the market forces that threaten employment. Because "globalization has put a question mark over the nation-state, the regions must play an ever bigger role in economic policy" (Jakoby interview 1997). Economic restructuring focuses the region inward on the transformation of its economic structure. The preoccupation with structural adjustment manifests itself in a heightened concern about the powers of the subnational government vis-à-vis the federal government and the EU. As a result globalization produces in NRW the seeming paradox of an export-oriented but inward-looking subnationalism: it is preoccupied with increasing its export market in order to defend the integrity of its regional economy in a globalized international economy.

In contrast to the defensiveness of NRW, Tuscan identity is built around a more optimistic attitude toward the opportunities presented by globalization. Tuscan officials tend to view globalization as a challenge rather than a threat. It is seen as promoting the importance of regional economies at the international level and providing pressure to adopt "modernizing" practices. As expressed by one Regional Councilor, "Globalization diminishes the weight of the central state while promoting the region. Within this framework, the role of regions like Tuscany become more critical both economically and politically" (Siliani interview 1997). Tuscan officials perceive of globalization as a process that can interject the region with a new vitality. Thus, globalization is interpreted as an opportunity set which generates more benefits than costs:

> We [the region] are very present in the process of globalization. For example, we are a leading exporter and have developed extensive international linkages, both socio-cultural and more market-oriented . . . [Globalization] is something that we watch carefully because we view this new type of internationalization in a very positive way (Pizzanelli, interview 1997).

At a general level, regional officials appear to have cultivated an outward-looking perspective predicated on a high level of openness toward the international system. Increased competition from abroad has led to a perception that globalization promotes a healthy reorientation of local means toward the exterior. This viewpoint deviates considerably from an alternative conception of globalization as causing regional deindustrialization (Giovannini and Perulli 1995; Sforzi 1995) and the transformation of the regional economy into a stage of what Amin and Thrift (1992) have identified as an "international value-added chain."[11] In line with this perspective, recent scholarship on the Tuscan economy has focused on external pressure to abandon internal production networks for an internationalization of inter-

mediary stages of production which would pose a severe strain on the much
heralded Tuscan model of regional development (Cavalieri 1995). Given
the prospect that industrial districts could be vertically reintegrated into a
more globalized production system, thereby undermining regional development, it is particularly striking that Tuscan officials remain confident in
the region's ability to adjust and readapt.

This seeming anomaly can be understood in the context of Tuscany's
position within the broader political economy of Italy. Because Tuscan officials perceive their region as capable of adapting to the changing needs of
a global economy, they are led to interpret interventionist efforts of the central government as constraining at best and detrimental at worst. This view
is further reinforced by the fact that Tuscany does not shoulder the principal
responsibility for the economic and social welfare of the region, allowing it
a considerable cushion. Because the central government is primarily responsible for financing regional spending and is committed to providing
particular services directly to the local population, the region is able to fi-
nesse its position of dependency, and promote its own legitimacy, by attrib-
uting its regional economic problems to national level dysfunctions. Moreover, Tuscany's record of relative economic successes, combined with
scandals in the central government, converge so that Italy's bureaucratic
inertia is perceived to be more costly to the region than the potential negative
impacts of globalization. Thus, Tuscany's bounded administrative capacity
and political responsibility enables the region to take a relatively benign view
of globalization.

Due to a faith in mutually reinforcing patterns of interaction and firmly
embedded social traditions, regional officials remain confident of the region's ability to meet new challenges presented by globalization. The regional economy has tended to be seen as *interpenetrated* by the global economy. This perspective allows the regional government to view globalization
as signaling the need for a shift in emphasis within the region as opposed to
a wholesale reorientation of the local economy. It has faith that sociocultural
factors, now considered part of Tuscany's regional identity, will persist in
making globalization functional for the region. Together with a regional
philosophy that values cross-fertilization, globalization provides a way to en-
large the space of operation and open new synergies by increasing resources.

Although these two perceptions of globalization differ in most respects,
it is important to emphasize two broad similarities. Regional officials in both
Tuscany and NRW believe that international economic pressures impact the

region by highlighting the subnational role vis-à-vis the national state and increasing pressure for subnational competitiveness. Prescriptions for regional development vary considerably, however. NRW sees globalization as threatening its traditional model of regional policy and necessitating significant structural changes. Tuscany, on the other hand, is more of a willing participant, viewing globalization as an opportunity for positive change that involves more minor adjustment at the margins. These different orientations relate to the political and economic context introduced in the previous section. In NRW, the assessment of problems associated with globalization stems predominantly from an economic concern about unemployment. Because of the relative autonomy and access to policy resources provided by German federalism, the regional state is seen as a gatekeeper to the national and international economy, and therefore, as somehow "responsible" for dealing with globalization. To pursue the metaphor, in Tuscany the subnational state is more of a gateway to the international economy. The locus of local economic problems is perceived to be the dysfunctioning of the national state administrative structure and the lack of regional independence in economic planning. Therefore, the problem is seen as political rather than economic and globalization is viewed as helping more than hindering local growth.

Two Interpretations of "Endogenous Growth"

Although officials in both regions embrace the desirability of "endogenous growth," in practice their different perceptions of globalization have led Tuscan and NRW policymakers to implement different strategies of regional development. In NRW, where gradual economic decline is coupled with a relatively strong regional state, policymakers have embarked on a program of radical economic restructuring (*Strukturwandel*).[12] For state officials in NRW, the task is to reorient the regional economy away from coal and steel to industries with better prospects for growth. At the same time, however, they must deal with the persistent problem of unemployment as heavy industry sheds jobs. In some ways, the execution of this task has closely mirrored the goals of the classical conception of endogenous growth. For example, industrial policy planners in NRW sought to adapt old industrial facilities, especially in coal and steel, to new markets such as environmental technologies. In Tuscany, on the other hand, the combination of a relatively benign view of globalization and a dominant national state has inclined regional policymakers to opt for an incremental vision of reform. Rather than radical restructuring, the goal has been to fine tune existing production networks.

When we interviewed regional officials in NRW, we found an overwhelming concern with the problem of unemployment. Even with the growth of services and SMEs described earlier, the rate of overall job creation is slower than the rate of job loss in heavy industry (Landesentwicklungsbericht 1994, 21), and the unemployment rate is above the German average. As a result, the current regional government names the fight against unemployment as its most important task. In fact, the fight against unemployment serves as the unifying rationale for most areas of regional economic policy. Energy policy, technology policy, promotion of the region abroad, commercial advising, all are designed to complement the goal of reducing unemployment (Landesentwicklungsbericht 1996, 24).

Beyond the immediate problem of unemployment, however, there is also the sense that the NRW model is no longer adequate. As surfaced again and again in the interviews conducted among officials in the regional state, the root cause of NRW's economic troubles is seen to be its uncompetitiveness in a global market. As a result, there is an attempt to move toward more endogenous growth-oriented policies. Where before the regional model was that of an autarkic industrial order as described by Herrigel—with vertically and horizontally integrated firms that managed their own R&D and maintained arms-length relations with the state—now the regional state wants to promote SMEs, government-mediated technology transfer, and decentralized governance. However, because of the region's legacy of statism, coupled with the problem of unemployment, this endogenous growth strategy has taken a statist cast. The same policies to restructure the economy in the long term are used to reduce unemployment in the short term. This is reflected in NRW's SME policy as well as its technology policy. A paradox emerges: NRW's attempt to bring about decentralized endogenous growth relies on radical state-led restructuring. A centralized state is necessary to decentralize the economy.

First, consider the policy promoting SMEs. This policy is justified in terms of leading the economy away from large, capital-intensive, manufacturing concerns in the steel, coal, and energy sectors into light-industry and services.[13] In the short term, however, it is also an employment creating measure, making it one of the region's most popular policies politically. It is popular with the electorate because, as one official from the *Staatskanzlei* of NRW explained, "It's more advantageous politically to help someone set up a small business than to put him on the dole" (Fischer Interview). From the viewpoint of economic planners, promoting SMEs is attractive because it diversifies the risk of unemployment in a global economy. Whereas the traditional economic structure of the region linked a very large portion of total employment to the fortunes of a handful of firms in heavy industry, a structure based on SMEs would diversify employment across many small employers. The region as a whole would not be so vulnerable to changes in the global market.

Technology policy, another mainstay of endogenous growth strategies, has figured ever more prominently in NRW. As one NRW policy analyst put it, "Whenever we discuss the problems we have in terms of unemployment and competitiveness, the answer very quickly becomes tech and hi-tech" (Lehner Interview 1997). Technology policy began to assume a central role in NRW's economic policy in the late 1980s, when the region started construction of a network of technology centers concentrated in the Ruhr Valley, which as home to the coal and steel industries had been the locus of dramatic economic decline.[14] Since 1988, when the region's various technology initiatives began, some forty-eight technology centers have been built. As with technology initiatives undertaken by other governments, the stated rationale for the Emscher Park project and the *Technologieinitiative* was to facilitate the transfer of knowledge and technology from universities and research institutes to the private sector. According to this vision of technology policy, the government coordinates networks of knowledge, in essence lowering the cost of innovation and R&D for regional firms through the provision of scientific infrastructure.

In terms of its orientation and consequences, however, NRW's technology policy is a good deal broader than this. As one official from the *Staatskanzlei* put it, "NRW's technology policy is at the same time a form of industrial policy in the real sense of the word" (Messalla interview 1997). Regardless of their eventual success in developing new technologies, the various science parks have already created many jobs (Messalla interview 1997). More than just providing the scientific infrastructure for regional firms to be innovative, technology policy has often sought to create new regional industries. The NRW's attempt to create a regional hub in multimedia technologies in Cologne is a good example.

The third way in which NRW's *Strukturwandel* draws on the endogenous growth model is in its attempt to reorganize relations between business and the regional state.[15] Here, we have in mind the so-called regionalized structural policy (*regionalisierte Strukturpolitik*). NRW's regionalized structural policy began in May 1987 as an attempt to restructure coal and steel industries through a policy of decentralization (Jochimsen 1992). The Ruhr Valley was divided into subregions, in which regional state officials would seek to coordinate local projects at economic restructuring rather than dictating policy from above. As part of the program, which was called the Future Initiative for Mining Regions (Zukunftsinitiative Montanregionen), 290 projects were supported at a cost of 1.07 billion DM (Ministerium für Wirtschaft 1992). Little over a year after this strategy was introduced for the lagging mining areas, it was spread to the whole region (Messalla interview 1997).

To borrow from the terminology of Herrigel, the regionalized structural policy is an attempt to shift from an autarkic to a decentralized industrial order. The goal is to create a self-sustaining network of small and medium sized firms, which pool the risks and costs of innovation and market building via the guiding hand of the regional state. As such, it seeks to provide a governance framework within which SME and technology policy can lead to endogenous growth. Or, as described in a paper published by the Ministry for the Economy, the regionalized structural policy was designed to "exploit specific local and regional potential as well as synergy effects associated with them, to mobilize endogenous local expertise, and to improve political accountability for the structural policy" (Ministerium für Wirtschaft 1992, 16). Whereas before policy was decided by the center and communicated to the local level, the new regionalized policy was meant to communicate the expertise and knowledge of local-level actors to policymakers at the center. As the Ministry for the Economy wrote, "The novelty in the structural policy of the Land was not only the joint deliberation of different departments about the goals of structural policy, rather it was the intensive participation of the local areas in the shaping of the program" (Ministerium für Wirtschaft 1992, 15).

It is important, however, to note that, while the regionalized structural policy is intended to bring NRW closer to some version of the Tuscan model, the kind of reform it entails could only be imagined in one of the German Länder. In essence, NRW is attempting to reconfigure its industrial base, and to do so, it is radically changing its educational policies, underwriting technological entrepreneurship in new sectors, and providing the infrastructure for a new SME sector in an economy until recently dominated by large-scale firms. Such a radical reform would not be possible in a region without the formal powers and inward-looking character of NRW.

Changes in the economic development strategy of Tuscany have been far less radical than in North Rhine-Westphalia, though not insignificant. If the goal in NRW has been to move toward greater decentralization, Tuscany has sought to preserve and enhance its tradition of decentralization. As a regional economic researcher told us: "The continuum in Tuscany between past and present is based on the regional philosophy of endogenous development which, based on SMEs, has been developed with a strongly 'bottom-up' orientation toward both the industrial and nonindustrial sectors" (Grassi interview 1997). In accordance with these objectives, regional development in Tuscany is comprised of a variety of strategies which in a more general sense correspond to four primary challenges the region sees itself as confronting: (1) the rejuvenation of local systems of production; (2) maintenance of the region's technological advantages; (3) the basic problems of developing and maintaining coordination; and (4) labor market adjustment.

Among regional officials there is a sense that the Tuscan regional productive system is nearing the end of its capacity for spontaneous regeneration. According to Siliani:

> Greater opening means looking for new markets but also finding an internal organization that allows for better and greater collaboration. Obviously, globalization imposes maximum openness . . . so with this change, traditional ways of doing things are no longer satisfactory and have to be changed to keep up with new technology and become competitive in new areas such as tourism and cultural services (Siliani interview 1997).

While regional policymakers suffer considerable constraints in their capacity as "development engineers," they recognize that regional government serves as an important facilitator of "collective entrepreneurship" and innovation. They aim to promote regional "incubators" to help open new markets and diffuse new strategies and innovation within the region. The development of twelve semipublic business service centers—the highest number of any Italian region—demonstrates one attempt to promote intraregional collaboration (Garmise 1994).

The second substantial challenge facing the region involves its ability to create strategies that will enhance *technological development*. In recent regional legislation on territorial governance, there is a clear emphasis on technical restructuring and information systems (*Norme per la governanza del territorio toscano: L.R.* 16/1/95, n. 5). Traditionally, innovation has been founded largely on original uses of existing technology rather than innovation through technological advances. As Doccioli (1993) notes, this has led to a de facto practice of "innovation without research." While Tuscany's associational networks have been able to generate agglomeration in productive outputs while retaining the advantages of localization, the maintenance of this system may be increasingly dependent on more advanced organizational and technological innovations. This is especially true of the region's SMEs that have more difficulty in developing both processual and technological innovation (Siliani interview 1997).

Regional officials believe that in order to meet these challenges, the region needs to support and expand global networks, including the internationalization of Tuscan businesses and the promotion of export-oriented activity. According to Siliani, "An important strategy of the region is to give support to the internationalization of businesses and export production . . . and help districts to systematize, for example, in networking or facilitating cooperation between enterprises" (Siliani interview 1997). This is particularly important in light of the high costs of technology and the lack of adequate state funding.

In pursuing these strategies, Tuscan officials seek to preserve the benefits of the "old" system by upgrading and "innovating" within traditional parameters. Within this context, technology is aimed at improving resources and organizational structures already present rather than developing new industries centered on specific uses such as media technology in NRW. In recent years Tuscany has become active in cultivating applied research geared toward modernizing the production process, improving products, and diffusing new knowledge. Extensive interaction between research centers, universities, industry, and labor unions concentrated around Siena, Pisa, and Florence have created a high-technology network. Although limited in scope, these high-technology networks create the opportunity to develop a disaggregated innovation pole. Furthermore, regional officials have concentrated on information and service exchange (marketing in particular) as essential factors in diversifying Tuscany's business networks. The region has developed a computerized information-dissemination system, the *Sistema Informativo sulle Politiche Comunitarie*, which was originally designed to distribute information about European finance opportunities but has subsequently been expanded to provide an institutional link between the regional government and private sector actors for development planning (Piattoni and Smyrl 1998).

The third set of regional development strategies, and perhaps Tuscany's most significant challenge, is to promote regional welfare while both preserving solidarity and preventing centralization. According to regional officials, the goal is to develop *system-wide cooperative mechanisms* that permit competition to advantage local production without restricting the coordination of resources. Inevitably this entails resolving the question of how to collectivize costs while encouraging collective action. Regional officials have pursued both private and public institutional support for their regional development strategy. As expressed by Doccioli (1993), the idea that the region should be able to balance private interests with public means provides a central focal point for Tuscan regional planning.

Traditionally, regional enterprises have engaged in cooperative endeavors that have included pooling resources to employ export consultants, joint purchasing of raw materials, and a coordinated "putting out" system (Amin and Thrift 1992). Yet, as Grassi points out, the increasing competition caused by larger firms mimicking the Tuscan model of flexible specialization poses a challenge to the system by threatening to inject divisiveness into informal cooperation networks (Grassi interview 1997). Regional officials recognize that in order to meet this challenge, collaborative ventures must transcend their traditional function as support structures for surviving crisis periods. They also emphasize the importance of collaborative interaction with elements outside the region and with developing a regional form of territorial marketing. To achieve these ends, they are attempting to promote network leaders that can guide local coordination without generating rigid and hierarchical structures (Grassi interview 1997). Tuscany's regional director of International Relations, Fabrizio Pizzanelli, states that one of the region's key strategies in dealing with globalization involves the reinforcement of regional institutions and associations to facilitate a program of commercial promotion for the region (Pizzanelli interview 1997).

The fourth major challenge confronting Tuscany is its ability to maintain its *productive labor force*. According to regional officials, the younger generation is less willing to continue in their parents' occupational footsteps. At present there has been a substantial growth in professional mobility as well as a movement from the industrial to third sectors among more established members of the labor force. In addition, more young people are going to the University and choosing to enter the service sector (Sforzi 1994). Together, these developments have reduced the pool of industrial labor available, offering a considerable contrast to the employment problems facing NRW. While unemployment remains a concern for Tuscany, it has focused on the long-term need to retool its labor force by upgrading its skill base.

Considering that a high proportion of its work force is engaged in craft-oriented and highly skilled specialty occupations requiring a high degree of hands-on knowledge, these trends represent important challenges for Tuscany. As Grassi notes:

> the skills needed in the information age are quite weak in Tuscany. Human capital has to try to develop more formal or scholastic knowledge outside of the experience of the "shop" in addition to emphasizing the need for continual education and skill acquisition. This is a significant step for the Tuscan economy (Grassi interview 1997).

In attempting to deal with these issues, the region has already developed strong programs geared toward diffusing information to targeted populations such as youth and women. Supporting its commitment to develop "professionalization," Tuscan regional development emphasizes continuous education and skill acquisition, facilitated by EU sponsored projects such as COMMET, aimed specifically at enhancing professional training for businesses. Also, while the region's ability to introduce elements of flexibility into the labor force remains highly restricted, Siliani indicates that Tuscany will begin proposing measures that experiment with the reduction of work hours and organization of the service sector (Siliani interview 1997).

Although both Tuscany and NRW have focused on similar policy goals, their implementation was determined not only by the rhetoric of endogenous development and the necessities of globalization, but also by the presence of a political rationale. In NRW, the primary political concern was the persistent problem of unemployment; in Tuscany, it was the attempt to maintain a balance between social and economic goals. Regional economic strategies in both NRW and Tuscany were shaped by officials' conception of the regional government's role in developing the economy. In NRW, the regional economy is defined by political sovereignty over a particular, bounded territory; in Tuscany it is viewed more as an integrated system of spatially concentrated social and economic networks. NRW's recent reforms emphasize *decentralization*. Tuscany is already quite decentralized in terms of its demography, industrial districts, and policy domains. As opposed to NRW,

Tuscany emphasizes *reintegration*. It focuses on expanding local networks to deal with internationalization. NRW has developed an overarching plan to deal with globalization, a radical restructuring of its economy and governance. The old autarkism is no longer economically or politically sustainable, but nevertheless constrains attempts at reform. In comparison, Tuscany is tinkering with an economically successful and politically popular model.

External Linkages: EU-Subnational Relations

So far, we have examined subnational perceptions of globalization and contemporary regional development strategy. In this final section, we consider how these perceptions and strategies shape relations between subnational governments and the EU. We find that whereas NRW tends to cultivate dyadic relations and views the European Union with suspicion, Tuscany cultivates multiple ties, identifying itself as part of a larger project of European integration.

Because globalization has led to an inward-looking strategy of radical restructuring, and because it has brought high unemployment in heavy industry, the relationship between NRW and the EU is instrumental and limited. It is instrumental because, like many other regions in Europe, NRW depends increasingly on the EU to finance its economic policies. The most important source of such EU aid is the EU's European Regional Development Fund (ERDF), where NRW qualifies for Objective 2 funds for its declining coal and steel industries. The relationship is limited because, as one official from the Economics Ministry of NRW put it, "Though we support the EU, we are also quite critical" (Jakoby interview 1997).

From the outset of the EU's forays into regional policy in 1975, NRW was distinctly standoffish. As Jeffrey Anderson describes the first ten years after the establishment of the Structural Funds, "Generally speaking, NRW efforts to tap the ERDF revealed much more hesitancy than those launched in Saarland [another of the major Objective 2 regions in western Germany]" (Anderson 1992, 174). In this period, NRW received 9.7 percent of the total German allotment from the Structural Funds, but as Anderson writes, "This translated into a per capita share of 12 ecus, ninth best of the ten *Flachenländer* [contiguous regions]" (Anderson 1992, 174). As Anderson observes, the reason for NRW's standoffishness was the region's unwillingness to sacrifice policymaking autonomy in return for funds: "To NRW officials, the

EC appeared as a double-edged sword: an alternative yet elusive source of largess to an increasingly unresponsive central government, and an additional source of constraints on independent action" (Anderson 1992, 175). While the same ambivalence to the EU is apparent today in other policy areas, the NRW has long since forgotten its hesitations about participating in the Structural Funds. As one official in NRW's Office for Federal and European Affairs put it, "Basically, our work is lobbying, in the purest sense of the word really. We don't have a status that is different from that of any other economic lobbying group in Brussels" (Engels interview 1997).

Apart from lobbying for Structural Funds, however, NRW tends to guard jealously against EU encroachment on its constitutional powers. Officials in the regional state often described the EU as overly bureaucratic and too quick to intervene in the affairs of the regions. Confident in its own capacity to make economic policy, NRW maintains a largely critical attitude to the EU. To quote the same official from the region's Ministry for Federal and European Affairs:

> The problem that we're having is that the European Commission is dealing with too many things. . . . The Commission is much too strict in a large number of policy areas and restricts our freedom to pursue our own policies—and in a lot of things where we think it's absolutely unnecessary. There is no reason why certain policy areas are dealt with at the European level, or at least not in the sense that they're now being dealt with at the European level. (Engel interview 1997)

In terms of the EU and globalization, the EU is not seen as a great help in furthering regional strategy. First, some officials maintained that the EU itself has not fully grasped the challenges posed by globalization. In agriculture, for example, EU food prices are uncompetitive on the world market and are subsidized at the expense of largely nonagricultural regions such as NRW. Second, the EU makes it easier for companies to leave the region. For example, the NRW chemical industry is very successful but has relocated much of its operations out of the region (Fischer interview 1997).

In keeping with its idea of limited relations with the EU, NRW favors those EU policies that are the least interventionist and redistributive. In interviews, government officials in NRW viewed the introduction of a single European currency as one of the primary benefits of the European Union (Messalla interview 1997). In their eyes, the Euro will devalue the traditionally very strong D-mark and thereby improve the competitiveness of regional companies abroad. The hope that the Euro will be weaker than the D-mark exemplifies the passive view that regional officials in Germany take of the relationship between the regions and the EU. First, devaluing the D-mark is not regional policy even in the loosest sense of the term, nor even the primary objective of monetary union. Rather, it is a side effect of a policy designed to benefit all by lowering the costs of doing business. Second, among the various policy instruments for promoting economic growth, currency devaluation is surely one of the most passive.

NRW views itself as a region in terms of its status as one of the federal German Bundesländer rather than as a part of the European Union. As one official described the Länder's image of themselves as regions:

> Until the last few years, the German Länder were unwilling to consider themselves regions in the European framework. We always said that from a European point of view we may be regions, but we are also states in our own right, like the states in the U.S. It was only in the process of the Maastricht negotiations that there came a change of attitude on the part of the German Länder, in saying that we need to have partners and to accept that they are different from us. We have had to accept that we must work with British counties and French regions, which in reality are nowhere near what we are. We have had to change our attitude and accept that although we are federal units, in the European framework, we are regions and nothing more. (Engel interview 1997)

Thus, in NRW, accepting the EU label of region represented a limitation on the status afforded by the Germany's federal constitution. Because they associated it with more weakly defined regions in other member-states, the Bundesländer were taking a step down in status by entering into the EU's project of a "Europe of the Regions." Even if the idea of being a European region rather than a German Bundesland has become more acceptable than it was several years ago, it is still far from being enthusiastically embraced in NRW.

In terms of representation, NRW's relationship with the EU is limited insofar as the region relies primarily on national channels, i.e. the federal Bundesrat, for most of its dealings with the EU. Only on issues in which its interests may differ from those of the majority of the other Bundesländer does the NRW seek external representation. As an official from the NRW

Ministry for Federal and European Affairs stated, on issues important to the region, such as a coal and steel policy, the regional government engages in its own politicking outside of the federal arena. These are areas where NRW cannot be sure that its interests will match those of the other Bundesländer (Engels interview 1997).

Finally, NRW's understanding of a "Europe of the Regions" is not one in which interregional relations are set up along the lines of a hub-and-spokes model. That is to say, NRW does not use the EU as an intermediary institution through which to form policy linkages with other regions. Rather, NRW has defined its relations with other regions bilaterally, or in other words, outside of the sponsorship of the EU. In fact, NRW has often built coalitions with other regions for the purpose of lobbying the EU, an activity that, naturally enough, discourages regions from the EU-as-chaperone model of regional association. Again the Structural funds are a good example:

> One of the things we're doing strongly is working with Objective 2 regions in other member-states. This leads us directly to the regions because you don't have a whole member state that is Objective 2. You have whole member-states that are Objective 1, like Ireland, Portugal, and Greece. You have different regions that are Objective 2. In Belgium, it's Wallonia. So this leads you directly to coalition-forming, coalition-building among the Objective 2 regions. This has to be done together with other regions. (Interview with Engel)

To summarize, in its relations with the EU North Rhine-Westphalia seeks to limit EU encroachment on its powers as one of the Bundesländer at the same time that it tries to maximize its share of EU resources for financing the Strukturwandel. It has a hard time accepting the mantle of "European region," but is eager to preserve its status as an "Objective 2 region." Outside of those EU programs closely fitted to the needs of its regional policy, NRW prefers the general and noninterventionist policies of the EU, such as trade expansion and monetary union. Such policies are noncoercive and nonredistributive. Its version of a "Europe of the Regions" is not based on a model of interregional interaction mediated through a centralized EU institutional structure. Rather, NRW prefers to develop direct linkages with other regions (particularly Objective 2 regions), often for the purpose of building coalitions to pressure the EU. Thus, NRW's relationship with the EU is at once limited and narrowly self-interested.

In contrast to NRW, Tuscan regional officials do not conceive of the EU as an external hierarchical entity, but rather, a "networked polity" within which Tuscany serves as a key node. The EU's organization, policy style, and most importantly, its approach to regional development are perceived as mapping onto Tuscany's own strategies to promote endogenous development and connect the region to external production and communication networks. As Siliani notes:

> we are developing essentially a parallel modality of planning to that of the EU which precedes both top-down, targeting certain sectors and so forth, but also bottom-up, looking at territorial aspects and seeking a financial balance. Tuscany is trying, similarly to the EU, to cultivate relations with regions and provincial localities through these two modes in order to develop an internal balance (Interview 1997).

In this way, Tuscany sees the EU as a cooperative partner in helping it to achieve its regional development goals.

Tuscany's primary relations with the EU are through program networks that provide information and resource linkages. Most of these networks are the creation of programs initiated at the EU level either directly through the Structural Funds or indirectly through the financing of target projects to achieve more specific goals. The first type includes, for example, programs to combat long-term unemployment and facilitate professionalization. Two notable examples are COMETT (business training for youths) and Metamorfosi (University education in biotechnology and engineering). The second form of EU-regional relations is driven by more macro-level considerations, focusing on areas of European economic concern within the region. Within this domain, EU contributions have facilitated numerous interventions within particular sectors, for example textiles and the environment. Although largely formulated from the top-down, there is a perception among regional officials that these EU sponsored programs have complemented regional objectives.

In regard to the European Regional Development Funds (ERDF), Tuscany has Objective 5b (rural underdevelopment) and Objective 2 (industrial restructuring) status. Yet, unlike in the south of Italy and in NRW, the ERDF are not the primary locus of Tuscan involvement with the EU. Indirect benefits through relationships established by the EU are equally significant. For example, Tuscany plays an active role in organizations like the Confer-

ence of the Regions, the Association of Maritime regions, and the Assembly
of European Regions. According to regional officials, each of these associations provide key international linkages enabling the region to exchange its
expertise (predominately the "Tuscan model of development") for information about foreign regional administration and technological innovation.

In essence, multilateral relations are seen as maximizing Tuscany's access
to experiences and resources from abroad. Moreover, as Pizzanelli suggests,
the region also provides a service for the EU (Pizzanelli interview 1997). In
exchange for the manifold benefits the EU provides for the region, Tuscany
helps to ameliorate the democratic deficit and promote a "citizen-friendly"
version of Europe. In this sense, Tuscan officials tend to see the region as
engaged in reciprocal relations with the EU.

From Tuscany's perspective, the EU promotes regional goals domestically
as well as internationally. As a consequence, its relationship with the EU is
perceived as both collaborative and exchange-based. In addition to assisting
the region in tapping external resources and gaining international recognition, the EU enhances regional influence within Italy and helps promote
further institutional reform. Thus, contrary to NRW, Tuscany perceives the
EU as generating predominately positive benefits for the region, not only
from direct financial and material advantages but perhaps more importantly
through the legitimacy it provides. This latter contribution is particularly
valuable in reinforcing regional efforts to revitalize its traditional comparative advantage in productive localization while at the same time facilitating
commercial promotion and cooperative activities abroad.

In economic terms, the EU has become part of Tuscany's strategy to
respond to globalization. It serves as a potential resource base, providing
compensatory elements such as economies of scale and technical transfers.
In addition it is seen as promoting adaptive strategies by validating the need
to find innovative solutions and programs in order to increase competitiveness and ultimately efficiency. This sentiment is captured by Pizzanelli, who
asserts:

> At this time, I don't see any great disadvantages from the EU. Gains
> are there for all. [In Tuscany] our regional networks have gained
> greatly and have been given a great push from cooperative programs
> emanating from the EU. . . . without Europe, I would say, Tuscany
> would be poorer. The EU provides for stronger competition between
> regions which is ultimately beneficial. We have to adapt to higher

standards, for example those comparable to the German Land (Pizzanelli Interview 1997).

Because regional officials view EU pressure for economic changes in the region as an evolutionary step toward a common market rather than a threat that requires defensive measures, they view Tuscany as receiving positive benefits from its position within European networks.

To understand this regional perspective, it is important to look at Tuscany's position within Italy and its relations with the national government. One of the most important factors here is the discrepancy between formal limitations and informal competencies. Due to institutional limitations on subnational competence, external relations have been considerably restricted. While Italian regions have a bearing on the formulation of the national position on given international issues, until recently they were legally excluded from participating in the decisionmaking process of European affairs—an obstacle that delayed the opening of a Tuscan regional lobbying office in Brussels until 1996. Poor institutional coordination between central and subnational governments reflects not only the extreme fragmentation of the Italian administrative system in general but also the lack of formal participation of the subnational governments in the policy process. As a result, the Italian government has been unwilling or unable to act as an intermediary for subnational interests in the international community.

Overall, regional problems with the central government have been viewed by Tuscan authorities as constraining and impeding regional development. This is exemplified by the fact that a portion of the European Regional Development Funds (ERDF) is forfeited regularly because Italian administrative agencies cannot manage to propose projects within the time allotted to them (Del Colle 1993; Giuliani 1996; Spotts and Wiesor 1986). In addition, national applications for the ERDF are often rejected by the European Commission because of their generality and for not taking into account practical considerations involved in implementation. While Tuscany has demonstrated a capacity (in terms of spending and allocation) to utilize EU funds, national administrative failures have consistently led to an underemployment of money coming from Brussels. These deficiencies of the national administrative system have become all the more intolerable to the subnational governments as their indirect dealings with the EU have increased.

With this background in mind, decentralization in Italy has been explicitly linked to European integration. Tuscany's regional presidents, in particular, have used the regional executive as a platform to campaign for a "Europe of the Regions." Both current Regional President Vanino Chiti and his predecessor Gianfranco Bartolini are strong advocates of political and administrative devolution within Italy as well as closer regional ties to the EU. Chiti holds the presidency of the Assembly of European Regions and is heavily involved in both European and Regional associations connected to the EU. In addition, Siliani notes that Tuscan officials are working hard to push for changes in the EU's Committee of Regions to allow subnational entities to play a greater legislative role and have a greater say in financial and governing issues within Europe (Siliani interview 1997).

In sum, the EU is perceived as giving Tuscany an enhanced status that it does not enjoy within the national context. Instructively, Siliani notes:

> If the EU did not exist, Tuscany's regional development strategies would be greatly altered because we would not have the ability to gain financing from other sources besides the state. Also we would miss the perspective of European integration that pushes in the direction of broader administrative experience and maximum openness to the market. We would therefore be dramatically more restricted economically and culturally (Siliani interview 1997).

Through its regional office in Brussels, its participation in the Committee of the Regions, and its involvement in European interest associations, Tuscany sees itself as taking part in the construction of Europe. At the same time, it also benefits from EU programs and resources that reinforce its own development strategies and objectives. Regional officials' conceptualizations of Tuscany as a networked region have enabled them to pursue multifaceted relations with the EU, serving to simultaneously promote internal development and regional self-reliance.

EU–regional relations differ considerably between Tuscany and NRW. We see three important differences. First, there are diverging perspectives on the connection between globalization and europeanization. NRW officials tend to equate the two and see them both as predominately economic in nature, whereas Tuscany sees the EU as a political response to globalization. Second, EU regional policy has a greater affinity with Tuscan development strategies than it does with those of NRW. This carries over to policy styles. NRW prefers dyadic relations and engages in cooperative interaction in a more intergovernmental manner that presumes clearly bounded and specified interests. In contrast, Tuscany is more process-oriented, preferring multilateral relations that are cooperative, open-ended, and continuously negotiated. Finally, NRW takes a defensive stance toward the EU while Tuscany's stance is more proactive. European integration is perceived as a decrease in autonomy for NRW but an increase in autonomy for Tuscany. These perspectives largely flow from different positions in national institutions. The NRW enjoys significant constitutional powers in a well-established federal system, while Italy is weakly connected to the national level and seeks external sources of validation to improve its legitimacy and position of authority.

Conclusion

To outline the major points of this comparison, we found that the *decentralization* and *europeanization* of regional development policy have favored a strategy of endogenous growth—the utilization and development of indigenous resources to create self-sustaining regional economic development. However, as our comparison of Tuscany and NRW has shown, regional differences are still important. Our comparison shows that historical patterns of the organization of the subnational state and economy have important consequences for the actual implementation of endogenous growth strategies. Traditionally statist regions, such as NRW, have a different conception of endogenous growth than traditionally networked regions, such as Tuscany.

We trace this difference through three main areas: perceptions of globalization, the implementation of regional economic policy, and the relationship between the subnational government and the EU. In our interviews, officials in both regions emphasized the importance of globalization and export-led growth. Both regions were supporting SMEs, pursuing policies of technological development, and trying to facilitate public-private cooperation. And both were deepening their relationship with the EU. However, beneath these similarities—all of which are consonant with endogenous growth—significant differences were apparent. NRW is undergoing major structural changes under the direction of its regional state. These changes are an attempt to protect NRW's economy from globalization, especially the loss of jobs to foreign competitors. Tuscany, on the other hand, envisions endogenous growth policy as an extension of its traditional model of regional development. Rather than wholesale restructuring, it is elaborating policies already in place. Though greater in number than in the past, NRW's ties with the EU still lack the depth of Tuscany's. For NRW, the EU is seen not only as a source of economic subsidies but also as a threat to policymaking autonomy. In contrast, Tuscany sees the EU as an institution parallel to its own regional state, facilitating market networks on a European-wide scale.

In summary, we have argued that NRW exemplifies a "statist" approach and Tuscany a "network" approach to regional economic development. We have attributed these divergent styles to the different institutional settings in which the two regions are situated. One important variable derives from the different constitutional contexts of each region. While the quite limited powers and capabilities of Italian regions encourage a facilitative and mediating role, the German Länder embrace all the governing prerogatives guaranteed by their semi-sovereign status. A second important variable derives from the institutional legacies associated with their different regional economic histories. Whereas Tuscan government has traditionally operated in the context of a decentralized "network" economy, the North Rhine-Westphalian state inherits a regional economy characterized by traditional large-scale industry. Without being able to disentangle the relative importance of these political or economic variables, both factors point to the enduring importance of extant institutional context in shaping the response of regions to both globalization and europeanization.[16]

Endnotes

1. For overviews and discussion of this dual process of decentralization and europeanization of regional development policy, see Bachtler (1997); Balme et al. (1994); Blacksell and Williams (1994); Clout (1987); Conzelmann (1998); Jones and Keating (1995); Keating (1998); Nanetti (1996); and Palard (1993).

2. See Mellors and Copperthwaite (1990) on regional disparities and the aims of cohesion and Vanhove and Klaasen (1987) concerning the "integrated approach" and its connection to ideas of endogenous development and flexible specialization as part of European Regional Policy.

3. An analysis of the development plans of Objective 2 regions found significant variation in development objectives. However, with respect to business development: "the focus is predominantly on enhancing indigenous growth potential" (Bachtler and Taylor 1996). Mimesis may also play an important role in convergence on an endogenous development strategy since regions often model their development strategies on the programs and policies of successful regions.

4. Professor Beate Kohler-Koch of the University of Mannheim has been conducting a major comparative study of regional governance. The study distinguishes between two forms of regional governance—a "statist" mode and a "cooperative" mode (Kohler-Koch 1997).

5. This argument has been influenced by a number of current discussions treating local economies and interfirm relations in network terms (Boissot and Child 1996; Castells 1996; Crewe 1996; Locke 1995; Saxenian 1996) as well as current discussions about social networks and network organizations (Nohria and Eccles 1992; Podolny and Page 1998; Powell 1990; Uzzi, 1996), "network governance" (Chisholm 1989; Hakansson and Johanson 1993; Jones, Hesterly and Borgatti 1997; Scharpf 1993), policy networks (Kickert, Klijn and Koppenjan 1997; Knoke 1996; Lauman and Knoke 1987). A number of authors have already begun to call attention to the network characteristics of subnational governance (Anderson 1992; Conzelmann, 1995; Cook and Morgan 1993; Deeg 1996; Knodt 1997; Le Galès 1997; Macleod 1996; Smith 1995; Stohr 1992).

6. On this point, see Lane and Maxfield's (1996) discussion of the strategy of building "generative relationships"—productive relationships where the "sources of value cannot be foreseen in advance."

7. For an interesting discussion of the "rigid specialization" of the Ruhr economy and the difficulties this presented for economic adaptation, see Grabher (1993).

8. Bennett Harrison, however, has argued that "Everywhere in the world, we can now find examples of a shift away from agglomerated, fragmented, symmetrically powerful, mainly small firm production systems to core-ring systems— some agglomerated and some dispersed, but commonly organized around powerful lead firms" (Harrison 1994, 147). He gives special attention to Northern Italian industrial districts, including Tuscany's Prato district.

9. An exception to this general trend is found in literature on regional development policy that emphasizes the region as the locus of important social, economic, and institutional processes within Italy (e.g., Bartolini 1995; Cavalieri 1995; Leonardi and Nanetti 1994; Nanetti 1988; Piattoni and Smyrl 1998).

10. According to King (1987) over 90 percent of regional funding in Italy originates from the central government. Although this figure drops to 70 percent in Tuscany (Siliani interview 1997), it nonetheless represents a considerably higher percentage of central government funding when compared to the German case.

11. In their study of Tuscan industrial districts, Amin and Thrift (1992) view this trend as threatening to industrial districts like Santa Croce. Discussing the Santa Croce case in particular Amin and Tomaney (1995) reiterate that the inevitable interconnectedness of local economies in global networks means that despite the most innovative of policy measures, the conditions for Marshallian growth are extremely difficult to recapture. For other discussions of the threat

posed by globalization to the decentralized Tuscan model, see Cossentino, Pyke, and Sengenberger (1996) and Harrison (1994).

12. For an analysis of economic restructuring in North-Rhine Westphalia, see Anderson (1992), Cooke (1995), and Deeg (1996). For a discussion of the changing context of national regional policy, see Anderson (1992), Conzelmann (1998), and Herrigel (1996). Conzelmann (1998) notes that the national region policy (*Gemmeinschaftsaufgabe Verbesserung der regionalen Wirtschaftssrtructur* or GRW) was based on an "export-basis theory" that brings it in conflict with an "endogenous development" approach. A major 1996 reform of the GRW made it more compatible with endogenous development strategies, but ultimately did not change fundamental policy commitments.

13. The parallel to an endogenous strategy at the level of the firm is termed "diversified quality production." See Herrigel (1996, 244–247) and Deeg (1996).

14. For an analysis of the linkages between firms and technology centers in Aachen (in North-Rhine Westphalia), see Grotz and Braun (1997).

15. On the evolution of regional policy networks in North-Rhine Westphalia, see Anderson (1992) and Deeg (1996).

16. Arguably, our explanation might be more parsimoniously "reduced" to either political or economic factors. The differences between Tuscany and NRW might be sufficiently explained by either differences in political structure (constitutionally weak Italian regions versus constitutionally strong German regions) or differences in economic structure (flexible specialization vs. Fordism). However, to disentangle the relative importance of the political versus economic variable, we would need to examine at least two additional cases: an Italian region with a "Fordist" economic legacy and a German region with a legacy of "flexible specialization." Some preliminary inquiries lead us to believe that Piedmont in Italy and Baden-Wurttemberg in Germany might be suitable cases.

References

Amin A. and N. Thrift. 1992. "Neo-Marshallian Nodes in Global Networks." *International Journal of Urban and Regional Research.* 16(4) (December).

Amin, Ash and John Tomaney 1995. *Behind the Myth of the European Union.* London: Routledge.

Anderson, Jeffrey. 1992. *The Territorial Imperative: Pluralism, Corporatism, and Economic Crisis.* Cambridge: Cambridge University Press, 1992.

Ansell, Christopher K. Craig A. Parsons and Keith Darden, 1997. "Dual Networks in European Regional Development Policy." *Journal of Common Market Studies* 35(3): 347–75.

Avantaggiati, Michele. CCRE. 1993. Consiglio dei Comuni e delle Regione d'Europa. La Voce Delle Autonomie. Centralita e tutela delle autonomie locali e regionali all'insegna del principio di sussidiarieta. Le autonomie locali e regionali: la riforma Italiana nel quadro dell Unione Europa. Ottobre 1–2. Viareggio.

Bachtler, John. 1997. "New Dimensions of Regional Policy in Western Europe." In Michael Keating and John Loughlin, eds. *The Political Economy of Regionalism*. London: Frank Cass.

Bachtler, John and Sandra Taylor. 1996. "Regional Development Strategies in Objective 2 Regions: A Comparative Assessment." *Regional Studies* 30(8): 723–33.

Bagnasco, Arnaldo. 1977. *Le Tre Italie*. Bologna: Il Mulino.

Bagnasco, Arnaldo. 1988. *La construzione sociale del Mercato*. Bologna: Il Mulino.

Balme, R., P. Garraud, V. Hoffmann-Martinot, S. Le May, and E. Ritaine. 1994. "Analysing Territorial Politics in Western Europe—the Case of France, Germany, Italy, and Spain." *European Journal of Political Research* 25 (4): 389–411.

Bartolini, Gianfranco. 1995. *Il governo regionale*. Mario Badii Fabrizio e Gigli Poalo Ranfagni. Firenze: Presentazione di Giorgio Napolitano, Regione Toscane.

Behrens, P. and M. Smyrl. 1997. "EU Regional Policy in Theory and Practice." Paper presented at the European Community Studies Association meeting, Seattle, May 1997.

Blacksell, Mark and Allan M. Willliams. 1994. "The Development of the European Community: Its Spatial Development." In Blacksell and Williams, eds., *The European Challenge: Geography and the Development in the European Community*. Oxford: Oxford University Press.

Benelli, Paolo. 1993. "Interventi." In La Voce Della Autonomie. 283–284.

Boisot, Max and John Child. 1996. "From Fiefs to Clans and Network Capitalism: Explaining China's Emerging Economic Order." *Administrative Science Quarterly* 41; 600–628.

Castells, Manuel. 1996. *The Rise of Network Society*. Oxford: Blackwell.

Cavalieri, Alessandro (ed.) 1995. *L'internazionalizzatione del processo produttivo nei sistemi locali di piccola impresa in Toscana*. IRPET. Milano: Franco Angeli.

Chisholm, Donald. 1989. *Coordination without Hierarchy: Informal Structures in Multiorganizational Systems*. Berkeley: University of California Press.

Clout, Hugh D. 1987. *Regional Development in Western Europe*. London: David Fulton Publishers.

Coffey W. and M. Polese. 1984. "The Concept of Local Development: A Stages Model of Endogenous Regional Growth." Papers in Regional Science Association, 55: 7–12.

Coffey, W. and M. Polese. 1985. "Local Development: Conceptual Bases and Policy Implications." *Regional Studies* 19: 85–93.

Conzelmann, Thomas. 1995. "Networking and the Politics of EU Regional Policy: Lessons from North Rhine-Westphalia, Nord-Pas de Calais and North West England." *Regional & Federal Studies* 5(2): 134–72.

Conzelmann, Thomas. 1998. "Europeanisation of Regional Development Policies? Linking the Multi-level Governance Approach with Theories of Policy Learning and Policy Change." *European Integration Online Papers* 2(4). http:// eiop.or.at/eiop/texte/1998–004a.htm.

Cooke, Philip, Adam Price, and Kevin Morgan 1995. "Regulating Regional Economies: Wales and Baden-Wurttemberg in Transition." In Martin Rhodes (ed.), *The Regions and the New Europe*. Manchester: Manchester University Press.

Cooke, Philip, ed. 1995. *The Rise of the Rustbelt*. London: UCL Press.

Cooke, P. and K. Morgan. 1993. "The Network Paradigm: New Departures in Corporate and Regional Development." *Environment and Planning D-Society & Space* 11 (5): 543–564.

Cossentino, Francesco, Frank Pyke, and Werner Sengenberger. 1996. *Local and Regional Response to Global Pressure: The Case of Italy and its Industrial Districts*. Geneva: International Institute for Labour Studies, Research Series (103).

Cox, K. 1996. *The Global and the Local: Making the Connections*. London: Longman.

Crewe, Louise. 1996. "Material Culture: Embedded Firms, Organizational Networks, and the Local Economic Development of a Fashion Quarter." *Regional Studies* 30 (3): 257–73.

Deeg, Richard. 1996. "Economic Globalization and the Shifting Boundaries of German Federalism." *Publius* 26 (1): 27–53.

Del Colle, Vincenzo. 1993. "L'attuazione del principio di sussidiarieta e la riforma istituzionale italiana nella prospettiva dell'Unione europa" In *La Voce delle Autonomie*. 1993. pg. 237–44.

Dente, Bruno. 1997. "Sub-national Governments in the Long Italian Transition." *West European Politics* 20(1): 176–93.

Desideri, Carlo. 1995. "Italian Regions in the European Community." In Barry Jones and Michael Keating, eds). *The European Union and the Regions*. Clarendon Press, Oxford.

Doccioli, Paulo. 1993. *Aspetti geografici die recenti processi di trasformazione dell'economia toscana*. Universita delgi Studi di Cagliari, Dipartimento di Economia: Polistampa.

Dunford Mick and Grigoris Kafkalas, eds. 1992. *Cities and Regions in the New Europe: The Global-Local Interplay and the Spatial Development Strategies*. London: Belhaven Press.

Evans, Peter. 1995. *Embedded Autonomy: States & Industrial Transformation*. Princeton: Princeton University Press.

Ferrelli, Nino and G Mario Scali. 1992. Ruolo delle regioni nella elaborazione delle norme communitarie: Conference of state-regions at committee of the regions.

Freddi, Giorgio. 1980. "Regional Devolution, Administrative Decentralization and Bureaucratic Performance in Italy, *Policy and Politics* 8(4): 383–398.

Garfoli, G. 1992. *Endogenous Development and Southern Europe*. Avebury: Aldershot.

Garmise, Shari. 1994. "Convergence in the European Community: the case of Tuscany." In Robert Leonardi and Raffaella Nanetti (eds.) *Regional Development in a Modern European Economy: A Case of Tuscany*. Pinter: London.

Giovannini, Paolo e Angela Perulli. 1995. "Crisi, Deindustrializzazione e declino industriale: Un Concetto Per Ogni Area? Alcune Riflessioni Finali." In Crisi, Deindustrializzazione e declino industriale in Toscana: I Percorsi di Mobilita Dei Lavoratori A Prato, Piombino e Massa. Firenze: Oservatorio regionale sul mercato del lavoro (ORML), Giunta Regionale.

Giuliani, Marco. 1996. Italy and the European Union: Internal Dynamism and External Stagnation? Paper presented at the International Colloquium of "Politics and Public Management" Paris, June 20–21.

Grabher, Gernot. 1993. "The Weakness of Strong Ties: The Lock-in of Regional Development in the Ruhr Area." In Gernot Grabher (ed.) *The Embedded Firm: On the Socioeconomics of Industrial Networks*. London: Routledge.

Grotz, Reinhold and Boris Braun 1997. "Territorial or trans-territorial networking: spatial aspects of technology-oriented co-operation with the German Mechanical engineering industry." *Regional Studies* 31 (6): 545–57.

Hakansson, Hakan and Jan Johanson,. 1993. "The Network as a Governance Structure: Interfirm Cooperation Beyond Markets and Hierarchies." In G. Grabher, ed. *The Embedded Firm: On the Socioeconomics of Industrial Networks*. London: Routledge.

Harrison, Bennett. 1994. *Lean and Mean: The Changing Landscape of Corporate Power in the Age of Flexibility*. New York: Basic Books.

Herrigel, Gary. 1996. *Industrial Constructions: The Sources of German Industrial Power*. New York: Cambridge University Press.

Hine, David. 1993. *Governing Italy: The Politics of Bargained Pluralism*. Oxford: Clarendon Press.

Hooghe, Liesbet, ed. 1996. *Cohesion Policy and European Integration: Building Multilevel Governance*. Oxford: Oxford University Press.

Hooghe, Liesbet and Gary Marks. "Europe with Regions": Channels of Regional Representation in the European Union." *Publius* 26(1): 73–92.

Jessop, B. 1993. "Towards a Schumpeterian workfare state? Preliminary remarks on post-Fordist political economy." *Studies in Political Economy* 4: 7–39.

Jochimsen, Reimut. 1992. "The Regionalisation of Structural Policy: North-Rhine Westphalia in the Europe of the Regions." *German Politics* 1: 82–101.

Jones, Barry and Michael Keating. 1995. *The European Union and the Regions.* New York: Oxford University Press.

Jones, Candace, William S. Hesterly, and Stephen P. Borgatti. 1997. "A General Theory of Network Governance: Exchange Conditions and Social Mechanisms." *Academy of Management Journal,* 22 (4): 911–46.

Keating, Michael. 1998. *The New Regionalism in Western Europe: Territorial Restructuring and Political Change.* Cheltenham: E. Elgar.

Kickert, Walter J.M., Erik-Hans Klijn, and Joop F.M. Koppenjan 1997. *Managing Complex Networks: Strategies for the Public Sector.* London: Sage Publications.

Kilper, Heiderose (ed.). 1996. *Wegweiser in die Zukunft: Perspektiven und Konzepte fuer den Strukturwandel im Ruhrgebiet.* Essen: Klartext Verlag.

Kilper, Heiderose. 1994. "Strukturpolitik als Suchprozess." *Passage* no. 2, pp. 28–39.

King, R.L. 1987. "Regional Government: The Italian Experience." *Environment and Planning C.* Government and Policy 5.

Knodt, Michèle. 1997. "Regional Policy Styles and Regional Propensity to go European." Paper presented to the European Community Studies Association, Seattle, May 28-June 1, 1997.

Knoke, David. 1996. *Comparing Policy Networks: Labor Politics in the U.S., Germany, and Japan.* Cambridge: Cambridge University Press.

Kohler-Koch, Beate. 1997. "Interactive Governance: Regions in the Network of European Politics." Paper presented to the European Community Studies Association, Seattle, May 28–June 1, 1997.

Labriola, Silvano. 1993. "Interventi." In *La Voce delle Autonomie.* 281–282.

Landesentwicklungsbericht Nordrhein-Westfalen no. 53, 1994. *Der Stand der Dinge: Initiativen und Projekte in der ersten Hdlfte der 90e Jahre.* Düsseldorf: Schriftenreihe des Ministerprdsidenten des Landes Nordrhein-Westfalen.

Landesentwicklungsbericht Nordrhein-Westfalen no. 54, 1996. *Verld-liche Politik in einer Zeit des Umbruchs: Ziele, Perspektiven und Handlungsschwerpunkte in der 12. Legislaturperiode* Düsseldorf: Schriftenreihe des Ministerprdsidenten des Landes Nordrhein-Westfalen.

Lane, David and Robert Maxfield. 1996. "Strategy under Complexity: Fostering Generative Relationships." *Long Range Planning* 29(2): 215–31.

La Toscana Europa. N 13/ Dic. 93.

Laumann Edward O. and David Knoke. 1987. *The Organizational State: Social Choice in National Policy Domains.* Madison: University of Wisconsin Press.

Le Galès, Patrick. 1997. "Urban Governance and Policy Networks: A Case Study." Paper presented at the annual meeting of the American Political Science Association, Washington, D.C., August 28–31, 1997.

Lehner, Franz. 1994. "Alte Industriekultur neue Technologien" *Passage* no. 2, 1994, pp. 12–19.

Leonardi, Robert. 1994. "Introduction: the role of Tuscany in the European Community." Robert Leonardi and Raffaella Nanetti (eds.) *Regional Development in a Modern European Economy: A Case of Tuscany*. London: Pinter.

Leonardi, Robert. 1994. "Networking and the European Single Market: Tuscany as the vanguard Mediterranean region." Robert Leonardi and Raffaella Nanetti, eds. *Regional Development in a Modern European Economy: A Case of Tuscany*. London: Pinter.

Locke, Richard. 1995. *Remaking the Italian Economy*. New York: Cornell University Press.

Macleod, Gordon. 1996. "The Cult of Enterprise in a Networked, Learning Region? Governing Business and Skills in Lowland Scotland." *Regional Studies*, 30(8): 749–56.

Marks, Gary, Liesbet Hooghe, and Kermit Blank, 1996, "European Integration from the 1980s: State-Centric v. Multi-level Governance." *Journal of Common Market Studies* 34(3): 341–78.

Mellors, Colin and Nigel Copperthwaite (eds.). 1990. *Regional Policy*. London: Routledge.

Ministerium für Wirtschaft, Mittelstand und Technologie des Landes Nordrhein-Westfalen 1992. *Regionalisierung: neu Wege in der Strukturpolitik Nordrhein-Westfalens*. Düsseldorf.

Ministerium für Wirtschaft, Mittelstand und Technologie des Landes Nordrhein-Westfalen 1995. *NRW-EU-Programme zur Fvrderung des Strukturwandels in Industrieregionen*. Düsseldorf.

Molle, Willem and Riccardo Cappellin, ed. 1988. *Regional Impact of Community Policies in Europe*. Avebury: Great Britain.

Musyck, Bernard. 1995. "Autonomous Industrialization in South West Flanders: Continuity and Transformation." *Regional Studies*, 29(7): 619–34.

Nanetti, Raffaella. 1988. *Growth and Territorial Policies: The Italian Model of Social Capitalism*. New York: Pinter Publishers.

Nanetti, Raffaella. 1994. "Regional policy-making in the European context." Robert Leonardi and Raffaella Nanetti, eds. *Regional Development in a Modern European Economy: A Case of Tuscany*. London: Pinter.

Nanetti, Raffaella Y, Robert Leonardi, and Robert Putnam. 1987. "The Management of Regional Policies: Endogenous Explanations of Performance." In Louis Picard and Raphael Zariski, eds. *Subnational Politics in the 1980's: Organization, reorganization and economic development*. London: Praeger.

Nanetti, Raffaella. 1996. "EU Cohesion and Territorial Restructuring." In Liesbet Hooghe, *Cohesion Policy and European Integration: Building Multi-Level Governance*." Oxford: Clarendon Press.

Nohria, N. and R. Eccles eds. 1992. *Networks and Organizations: Structure, Form, and Action*. Cambridge: Harvard Business School Press.

Norme per la governanza del territorio toscano: Legge Regionale. 16 Gennaio 1995 (5. Circolare illustrativa del titolo 3. Raccolta normativa a cura del Dipartimento Politiche del Territorio. Regione Toscana. Giunta Regionale.

Palard, Jacques. 1993. "Structural and Regional Planning Confronted with Decentralization and European Integration." *Regional Politics & Policy*, 3(3): 192–210.

Pasquino, Gianfranco. 1996. "Italy: A democratic regime under reform." In Joseph M. Colomer (ed.). *Political Institutions in Europe*. London: Routledge.

Piattoni, Simona and Marc Smyrl. 1998. "Regional Governance in Italy: Beyond the North-South Divide." Paper prepared for Council for European Studies Bi-Annual Conference of Europeanists (February 1998).

Pinna, Pietro. 1993. La Cooperazione fra Le regioni in Europa. *Rassegna Parlamentare. Attualita*. Luglio/Agosto. 3: 173–198.

Piore Michael J. and Charles F. Sabel. 1984. *The Second Industrial Divide: Possibilities for Prosperity*. New York: Basic Books.

Podolny, J. and K. Page. 1998. "Network Forms of Organization." *Annual Review of Sociology*, 22 (1): 57–77.

Powell, Walter W. 1990. "Neither Market Nor Hierarchy: Network Forms of Organization." *Research in Organizational Behavior* 12: 295–336.

Putnam, Robert. 1993. *Making Democracy Work: Civic Traditions in Modern Italy*. New Jersey: Princeton University Press.

Rehfeld, Dieter. 1994. "Aufloesung und Neuordnung" *Passage* no. 2, 1994, pp. 20–27.

Rhodes, Marti. 1995. "The Viability of Regional Strategies." In Martin Rhodes (ed.), *The Regions and the New Europe*. Manchester: Manchester University Press.

Ronzitti, Natalino. 1987. "European Policy Formula in the Italian Administrative System" *International Spectator*, 22; 207–215.

Rose, Richard. 1985. "From Government at the Centre to Nationwide Government." In Y. Meny and W. Wright, eds., *Centre-Periphery Relations in Western Europe*. London: Allen and Unwin.

Sabel, Charles. 1989. "Flexible Specialization and the Re-emergence of Regional Economies" in P. Hirst and J. Zeitlin eds. *Reversing Industrial Decline*. London: MacMillan.

Saxenian, Annalee. 1996. *Regional Advantage: Culture and Competition in Silicon Valley and Route 128*. Cambridge: Harvard University Press.

Sanantonio, Enzo. 1987. "Italy." In Edward C. Page and Michael J. Goldsmith eds. *Central and Local Government Relations: A Comparative Analsysis of West European Unitary States*. London: SAGE.

Scharpf, Fritz, ed. 1993. *Games in Hierarchies and Networks: Analytical and Empirical Approaches to the Study of Governance Institutions*. Boulder: Westview Press.

Sforzi, Fabio. 1994. "The Tuscan model: an interpretation in light of recent trends." In Robert Leonardi and Raffaella Nanetti, eds. *Regional Development in a Modern European Economy. The Case of Tuscany*. London: Pinter.

Smith, Andy. 1995. "Going beyond the Democratic Deficit: The European Union and Rural Development in Networked Societies." *Regional & Federal Studies* 5(1): Spring 45–66.

Spotts, T and T. Wiesor. 1986. *Italy: A Difficult Democracy*. New York: Cambridge University Press.

Stohr, W. 1990. *Global Challenge and Local Response*. London: Mansell.

Stohr, W. 1992. "Local initiative networks as an instrument for the development of peripheral areas." In Markku Tykkylaminen, ed. *Development Issues and Strategies in the New Europe*. Avebury: Aldershot.

Storper, Michael. 1992 "The Limits to Globalization: Technology Districts and International Trade." *Economic Geography* 68 (1): 60–93.

Storper M. & A. Scott. 1989. "The Geographical Foundations and Social Regulation of Flexible Production Complexes, in J. Wolch and M. Dear eds. *The Power of Geography*. London: Unwin Hyman.

Swyngedouw, Erik. "Reconstructing Citizenship, the Re-scaling of the State and the New Authoritarianism: Closing the Belgian Mines." *Urban Studies* 33 (8): 1499–1522.

Trigilia, Carlo. 1986. *Grandi partiti e piccole imprese*. Bologna: Il Mulino.

Uzzi, Brian. 1996. "The Sources and Consequences of Embeddedness for Economic Performance of Organizations: The Network Effect." *American Sociological Review* 61: 674–98.

Vanhove, Norbert and L.H. Klassen eds. 1987. *Regional Policy: A European Approach*. Averbury: Aldershot.

Volcic, Demetrio. 1995. Intervista sul federalismo: le ragioni delle regioni: il caso Toscana.

Wilson, Patricia. 1995. "Embracing Locality in Local Economic Development." *Urban Studies* 32 (4–5): 645–659.

Interviews

Engel, Dr. Christian, Ministry for Federal and European Affairs of NRW, Bonn: July 7, 1997.

Fischer, Annett. Land Office of North Rhine-Westphalia, Düsseldorf: June 12, 1997.

Grassi, Mauro. Associate Researcher. Istituto Regionale per la Programmazione Economica della Toscana (IRPET). Florence, Italy, June 26, 1997.

Jakoby, Dr. Herbert. Head of Unit for EU Affairs, Ministry for the Economy, Technology, and Transportation, Düsseldorf: June 25, 1997.

Lehner, Dr. Franz. President, Institute for Work and Technology, Gelsenkirchen: June 23, 1997.

Messalla, Peter. Land Office of North Rhine-Westphalia, Düsseldorf: June 16, 1997.

Noll, Wulf. Regional Policy Section, Ministry for the Economy, Technology, and Transportation, Düsseldorf: July 2, 1997.

Pizzanelli, Fabrizio. Director of the Office of International Relations. Department of General Activity of the President and of Legilative and Judicial Affairs. Tuscan Regional Government. Florence, Italy, June 26, 1997.

Siliani, Simone. Councelor of Institutional Reform and Relations with local entities. Tuscan Regional Government. Florence, Italy June 30, 1997.

3 Convergence or Divergence?

Globalization, Neoliberalism and Fiscal Policy
in Postcommunist Europe

John L. Campbell

Are the world's governments converging on a common set of neoliberal policies that favor, among other things, steep reductions in spending and taxing, balanced to avoid budget deficits? Some scholars insist that the increasingly global nature of economic and political activity is causing a neoliberal convergence (Crouch and Streeck 1997; Meyer et al. 1997; Reich 1991; Strange 1997; Waters 1995). They argue, for example, that as capital flows across national borders with increasing ease, governments seek to accommodate investors and international creditors by pursuing all sorts of neoliberal practices, including austere fiscal policies (Cerny 1997; Greider 1997; Ohmae 1990). Critics argue that divergence remains the rule rather than the exception because nationally specific politics and political institutions mediate the degree to which these global pressures affect public policy making and thus militate against convergence (Berger 1996; Garrett and Lange 1996; Hirst and Thompson 1996; Kitschelt et al. 1999; Milner and Keohane 1996).

The debate has been based almost entirely on analyses of countries that have *well-established* political systems, particularly those in North America, Western Europe, and the Pacific Rim. Thus, even if the critics are right about the importance of mitigating political circumstances, if there is any credence to the globalization thesis, then evidence of neoliberal convergence should be evident in the European postcommunist countries. After all, since the collapse of their communist regimes they have been dismantling their old political institutions and creating new ones, which are still very fragile (Elster et al. 1998, 17) and thus unlikely to provide an effective buffer against global pressures toward convergence. Moreover, powerful international organizations, operating at both the global and European levels, have urged national postcommunist governments to adopt neoliberal fiscal policies (Lavigne 1995, ch. 9; Pereira et al. 1993, 6).

As a result, I begin with the basic hypothesis that international pressures—at both the global and European levels—should have produced convergent fiscal reforms and outcomes among the postcommunist countries. Because I have not interviewed the key postcommunist policymakers, it is difficult in this analysis to disentangle the relative effects of global and European-level pressures on fiscal reform. Nevertheless, as discussed below, what is important to recognize here is that both global and European-level influences pushed in the *same* direction, that is, toward a common set of neoliberal reforms marked by fiscal restraint and balanced budgets.

In fact, although many postcommunist governments initially pursued the same neoliberal fiscal reforms, not all sustained them. Those that succeeded avoided serious budget deficits; those that failed did not. Of course, balanced budgets are only one part of the broader neoliberal program, which also includes privatization of state enterprises, deregulation of economic activity, increased reliance on markets, reductions in state financed social programs, and so on. Nevertheless, because balanced budgets are an important element of neoliberal reform, deficits provide a good indication that a government is having trouble adhering to at least this part of the neoliberal package. Furthermore, if some governments experience deficits and others do not, then fiscal policies have not converged on the neoliberal standard. By comparing the budgetary experiences of several postcommunist European governments this essay sheds light on how global and European-level pressures for neoliberal reform interact with national politics and institutions and affect the degree to which governments converge on a common set of neoliberal policies.

I begin by reviewing the conventional macroeconomic explanation of postcommunist budget deficits and argue that a better account is required that takes seriously the interaction between international pressures for neoliberal convergence and national political factors that may offer resistance. As a result, raising questions about the globalization thesis also provides an opportunity to challenge the conventional wisdom regarding postcommunist budget deficits. Next, I outline briefly the global and European-level pressures for neoliberal fiscal reform that postcommunist governments experienced and then examine in more detail the national political forces that mediated these pressures and caused variation in the degree to which post-communist governments in Poland, Hungary, and Czechoslovakia (subsequently the Czech Republic) sustained these reforms and avoided budget deficits. I draw comparisons both *cross-nationally* and *overtime* within these countries through the mid-1990s. A few scholars have argued that political factors have affected fiscal outcomes in postcommunist Europe (e.g., Campbell 1996, 1992; Kornai 1992; Przeworski 1993) but no one has used the insight to render either a comparative or historical analysis of fiscal problems in the region based on intensive case studies. For reasons discussed below, my focus is primarily on the problem of controlling government expenditures. Finally, I explore the theoretical implications of the analysis.

I argue that the diffusion of a common, neoliberal fiscal reform model from the global and European levels to the national level explains the *similarities* across countries in fiscal policy, but the manner in which domestic politics constrained fiscal reform accounts for the *variation*. Specifically, the new postcommunist governments in Poland, Hungary, and Czechoslovakia each favored cutting taxes and spending, but union opposition prevented spending cuts from being sustained initially in Poland and serious budget deficits emerged. Intense electoral competition had similar effects in Hungary. However, in the Czech case unions were weaker and electoral competition was relatively subdued, so there was less opposition to fiscal reform and budget deficits were largely avoided. In each case, particularly during the early years, the unique political institutional legacies inherited from the old communist regimes shaped the political context within which governments made fiscal policy. Still, when and wherever national-level tripartite bargaining over policy developed, as it did at various moments in each country, it tended either to temper these political conflicts or mitigate their effects and enabled governments to more effectively control their budgets. In other words, tripartism appears to have been an antidote for some of the political conflicts surrounding fiscal reform.

I focus on fiscal reforms in Poland, Hungary, and the Czech Republic for several reasons. First, these are the countries that have progressed the farthest in their transformation process and thus afford the best historical perspective on the factors that affect fiscal reform in postcommunist states. Second, although there has been variation in the speed with which some reforms, such as privatization, have been initiated in these countries, they are generally considered to be "fast reformers" relative to others in the region

(Coricelli 1997, 23). Notably, all three adopted at about the same time fiscal reform packages that resembled those typically recommended by the International Monetary Fund (Lavigne 1995, 118). Many analyses of fiscal reform compare fast reformers against slow ones and thus understate, if not obscure, important differences within each group that may yield important insights about the determinants of fiscal reform and its potential problems (e.g., Ambrus-Lakatos and Schaffer 1997).

The Conventional Account of Postcommunist Fiscal Problems

During the early 1990s most observers argued that postcommunist budget deficits were caused by the recessions that these countries experienced as they began to transform their political economies. Revenues fell as a result of declining enterprise and personal income taxes, and rising unemployment increased the costs of unemployment benefits and social programs. Virtually everyone agreed that budget deficits stemmed from macroeconomic contraction. However, more recent experience suggests that fluctuations in these deficits were not nearly as dependent on economic performance as scholars initially believed (Dabrowski 1997). For example, table 3.1 indicates that deficits emerged initially with recession in Poland, but as economic growth resumed in 1992 and unemployment held steady at about 15% the deficit continued to deteriorate to 8% of GDP and persisted although at more manageable levels. Similarly, in Hungary as the economy began to improve in 1992 and achieved real growth in 1994 the deficit increased to 7.6% and as growth slowed in 1995 the deficit shrank dramatically. Moreover, after 1993 unemployment and deficits appeared to vary inversely. Finally, in Czechoslovakia (and subsequently the Czech Republic) relatively modest deficits ranging only up to 3.8% occurred during a very deep recession in 1991–1992 and as the Czech economy began to grow after 1993 the government experienced small but worsening deficits that bore no clear relationship to unemployment, which remained stable.

Certainly there *is* some merit to the macroeconomic analysis, particularly for the early 1990s, but enough anomalies remain that a substantially revised account is necessary. A useful starting point is to ask why the macroeconomic view has not been able to fully explain these cases. One problem is that it neglects the effects that national political conditions have on fiscal policy

TABLE 3.1 Budgetary and Economic Performance in Poland, Hungary,
Czechoslovakia and the Czech Republic

	1990	1991	1992	1993	1994	1995
Poland						
Surplus or Deficit (% GDP)	3.3	−6.7	−8.0	−4.0	−2.0	−2.7
Economic Growth (% change GDP)	−11.6	−7.0	2.6	3.8	6.0	6.5
Unemployment (% labor force)	6.1	11.5	15.0	15.7	16.2	15.5
Hungary						
Surplus or Deficit (% GDP)	0.9	−3.0	−6.8	−6.3	−7.6	−3.7
Economic Growth (% change GDP)	−3.5	−11.9	−3.0	−0.8	2.9	1.9
Unemployment (% labor force)	1.6	7.5	12.3	12.1	10.4	12.0
Czechoslovakia/CzechRepublica						
Surplus or Deficit (% GDP)	0.1	−0.2	−3.8	1.4	−1.3	−2.1
Economic Growth (% change GDP)	−0.4	−15.9	−8.5	−0.9	2.6	5.0
Unemployment (% labor force)	1.0	6.8	2.6	3.5	3.2	4.0

[a]Data for 1990−1992 are for Czechoslovakia.

Note: Deficits are indicted by a negative sign.

Sources: For economic growth, International Monetary Fund, *World Economic Outlook*, May 1996, p. 125. For unemployment, Organization for Economic Cooperation and Development, *OECD Economic Outlook*, 1993, p. 113 (for 1990–1992), 1995, p. 111 (for 1993–1995). For Polish and Hungarian surplus/deficit, International Monetary Fund, *World Econmic Outlook*, May 1996, p. 78 (for 1989–1992), October 1996, p. 29 (for 1993–1995). For Czechoslovakian surplus/deficit, International Monetary Fund, *World Economic Outlook*, May 1993, p. 59 (for 1990), October 1993, p. 86 (for 1991–1992). For Czech Republic surplus/deficit, International Monetary Fund, *World Economic Outlook*, October 1996, p. 29 (for 1993–1995).

making in general and government expenditures in particular (e.g., Dabrowski 1997). This is a surprising omission insofar as scholars have shown that political factors are important determinants of budgetary problems in the West (Campbell 1993; Rose and Peters 1978) and there is plenty of evidence that political resistance to fiscal reform has been commonplace historically (Levi 1988). Another problem is that the macroeconomic view often overlooks how national politics may conflict with pressures from powerful international actors for neoliberal reform. This too is surprising because scholars have recognized these effects in newly industrializing countries (Haggard and Kaufman 1992; Kahler 1992). The analysis that follows takes all of this into account.

Budget deficits depend on the ratio of revenues to expenditures. However, I focus primarily on expenditures for several reasons. First, the inability to control spending rather than revenues is generally viewed as the chief cause of budget deficits for postcommunist governments (Coricelli 1997, 19–22). Second, the correlation between revenues and economic performance is much stronger than that between expenditures and economic performance (Dabrowski 1997, 11). Because the revenue side of the story *is* tied more closely to economic performance in ways suggested by the standard macroeconomic account, it requires less explanation. Third, although revenue declines depend on poor economic performance, they have also been affected by a mixture of tax cuts and tax evasion whose effects on budgets are extremely hard to estimate. This is especially true for tax evasion. It is clear that tax evasion was rampant everywhere in the postcommunist region (OECD 1997, 43–44, 96), but it is not clear how much revenue was lost as a result or how much variation there was across countries in the severity of these losses. For example, the Polish finance minister lamented in 1996 that substantial revenues were being lost through tax evasion but did not indicate how much (Kolodko 1996, 122, 134). Conservative estimates suggest that about 3 million people earned untaxed income in Poland and as many as half of them paid no taxes at all. The rate of tax evasion was probably about the same in the Czech Republic and perhaps somewhat higher in Hungary but nobody knows for sure (Kramer 1997, 58). What is clear, however, is that in some countries, tax collection problems were so serious that governments scaled back tax cuts and even raised tax rates, which may have aggravated the situation by increasing the incentives for further tax evasion (Kosterna 1997, 37). The point is that because it is so hard to assess revenue fluctuations my argument about budget deficits per se is necessarily tentative, even though it sheds new light on those factors that are least understood by conventional macroeconomic accounts of deficits, that is, state expenditures. More important, the analysis shows how global, European, and national-level forces interact to constitute fiscal reform in postcommunist European countries and, as a result, it provides fresh insights about the broader question of global convergence.

Global and European Pressures for Convergent Fiscal Reform

The East European communist regimes were typically characterized during the late 1980s by levels of taxation that were about 14 percent higher than the OECD average, spending that was 10 percent higher and modest budget deficits of 1–2 percent of GDP that were about half the OECD average (Campbell 1996). This changed dramatically as the new postcommunist governments adopted fiscal reforms that were *initially* similar and that sought to cut taxes and spending while maintaining balanced budgets (Lavigne 1995, 122–129). Scholars generally agree that the neoliberal approach was embraced for several reasons (e.g., Campbell 1996; Przeworski 1995, 1–5). First, at the global level, international lending agencies, particularly the International Monetary Fund (IMF), tried to *coerce* these governments into pursuing neoliberal policies by demanding balanced reductions in taxes and spending as a quid pro quo for financial assistance. The willingness of western governments, banks, and financial markets to provide financial assistance often turned on the IMF's approval of a postcommunist government's reform program (Lavigne 1995, 234). Second, the IMF, World Bank, OECD, top western universities and other institutions convened many conferences designed to familiarize postcommunist officials with *normatively appropriate* western fiscal policy (e.g., OECD 1991; Tanzi 1992). The general thrust of their recommendations favored neoliberalism (Lavigne 1995, 37–38, 153–54). Similarly, some especially influential East European reformers, including Czechoslovakia's Vaclav Klaus, who became Czechoslovakia's first postcommunist minister of finance and an eventual prime minister, and Leszek Balcerowicz, chief architect of Poland's initial reform program, were exposed to the neoliberal model during economic studies in the United States, Britain, and West Germany (Greskovits 1998, 38). Finally, these governments were eager to join Western organizations, such as the OECD, GATT, and NATO, to curry favor with Western investors, and to develop some sort of market economy. They were quick to *mimic* Western practices in order to do so (Lavigne 1995, 153–154). Among other things, the goal of developing market economies required them to liberalize prices, control the inflation that often ensued, and thus try to balance budgets through neoliberal reform. In sum, the same sort of coercive, normative, and mimetic mechanisms operated here that sociologists and political scientists have identified as precipitating the diffusion of common practices among fields of organizations or nation states (Boli and Thomas 1999; DiMaggio and Powell 1983; Finnemore 1996).

Similar forces for neoliberal fiscal reform were at work at the European level (e.g., Lavigne 1995, 191–231). Almost immediately after the old regimes collapsed, Poland, Hungary, and Czechoslovakia aspired to European Union membership. In the early 1990s they signed free-trade agreements among themselves in order to facilitate this goal. Furthermore, in 1991 each country signed separate "Europe Agreements" with the EC to harmonize competition laws and advance free-trade agreements that were viewed as constituting a quid pro quo for consideration later for EU membership. A meeting of the European Council in Copenhagen in 1993 further elaborated these expectations. Among other things, membership would require that these countries accomplish fiscal harmonization and meet the Maastricht "convergence criteria," including budget deficits not greater than 3 percent of GDP.

Coercive, normative, and mimetic effects were more balanced in these countries than in Latin America where several countries pursued neoliberal reforms during the 1970s (Greskovits, 1998, ch. 4). However, they still did not operate equally in each postcommunist country. In particular, Poland and Hungary, because of the large external debts they had inherited from their old regimes, were relatively more susceptible to coercion than Czechoslovakia. By 1989, Poland had $43 billion in outstanding debt (55% of GNP), Hungary had $20 billion (73% of GNP) and Czechoslovakia had $8 billion (17% of GNP) (World Bank 1997, 180, 268, 432). Notably, the Hungarians had borrowed heavily from western creditors during the 1980s in order to modernize their economy and had joined the IMF in 1982. Poland joined in 1986. In part due to IMF encouragement, the Hungarian communist government had already started to liberalize some prices and adopt western-style value-added and personal income taxes a year *before* the old regime collapsed. In both postcommunist Poland and Hungary IMF pressure to pursue neoliberal reforms was substantial and effective, because compliance was viewed by policymakers as necessary in order not to upset western creditors. Conversely Czechoslovakia, which was not heavily indebted to the West when it began its transformation, did not face this sort of pressure. Although the postcommunist Czechoslovakian government called upon the IMF in the early days it was more for advice than financial assistance (EIU 1990c, 14). Nonetheless, the Czechs still espoused a neoliberal agenda, but for different reasons. Many of their early postcommunist political leaders were economists who had been exposed to conservative economics in the West and were intellectually committed to this approach (Lavigne 1995, ch. 7; Wolchik 1995). In fact, during the late 1980s several of them were permitted to establish independent research institutes, were consulted by the communist government when it became apparent that major economic reforms were inevitable, and eventually assumed prominent positions in the transitional "Government of National Understanding" as well as the first freely elected postcommunist governments (EIU 1988b; 1988c, 11; 1989b). Among these economists was Vaclav Klaus.

In any case, during the early 1990s officials in Poland, Hungary, and Czechoslovakia reduced taxes on enterprise profits and introduced western-style corporate income taxation, simplified the tax code, and shifted taxes from enterprises to individuals. In each case, total revenues declined sharply in real terms due in part to these changes (IMF 1994, 75–77). Furthermore, all three slashed enterprise subsidies and capital investment, generally the largest budget category under the old regimes. However, in Hungary and Poland, but not Czechoslovakia, officials were unable to keep total expenditures in line with revenues. In particular, they had difficulty controlling spending on pensions, unemployment benefits, health care, and other social outlays and serious budget deficits resulted (Newbery 1995, 9–12). Understanding how these national experiences diverged requires an analysis of politics.

Collective Action: Poland's Confrontational Politics

Labor union opposition was pivotal to Poland's early budgetary problems. Indeed, unions posed a far more serious obstacle to neoliberal reform than electoral competition, which was critical in other countries. Of course, Poland's labor movement was among the strongest in the region and famous for having brought the communist regime to its knees in the late 1980s.

As Poland entered the postcommunist era it had two strong labor unions, Solidarity and the official communist union (OPZZ), an institutionalized tradition of union-government bargaining and a history of strikes led by Solidarity against the government (Gorniak and Jerschina 1995, 174; Pedersen et al. 1996). By the end of 1988 the government in collaboration with the unions had begun reducing state enterprise taxes in order to provide enterprises with more autonomy over their own affairs, and enterprise subsidies and social programs in order to maintain a balanced budget. However, by mid-1989 the Solidarity opposition demanded and won through round table talks more social spending than originally planned. As a result, budget deficits started to emerge after the first postcommunist government came to power in September 1989. This foreshadowed events to come.

The new government, which was already predisposed toward neoliberalism, entered negotiations with the IMF and other foreign creditors and engaged western economists to advise them on economic reform. The result was the famous Balcerowicz "shock therapy" program, launched in January 1990, which epitomized austere neoliberalism (Przeworski 1993, 148–149). Tax reform was initiated. Enterprise subsidies were cut radically in part to minimize budget deficits and reduce hyper-inflationary pressures. Because many social programs were provided by the enterprises this meant that workers and their families experienced sharp reductions in health care, food subsidies, and other benefits. Nevertheless, most citizens supported the reforms because they believed that it was the right thing to do and because the government stressed that experts rather than politicians were in charge. Significantly, there was little public pressure on the government to do otherwise because Solidarity had formed the new ruling party and there were no social partners to demand anything different (Kowalik 1995). Things seemed fine as the budget experienced a 3.3% surplus in 1990, although this was due largely to a one-time windfall in enterprise tax revenue associated with the sale of commodities at deregulated and highly inflated prices.

However, as citizens began to suffer the effects of inflation and reduced social programs, they turned against the Balcerowicz plan. When the plan was first implemented more than 90 percent of the population supported it, but that figure slipped to 32 percent by October 1991 and enthusiasm for state-financed social programs soared (Gorniak and Jerschina 1995; Przeworski 1996). By 1993 34 percent of those surveyed expected their lives to get worse as the reforms continued—twice the number as in 1990 (Bobinska 1994). Moreover, a wave of labor unrest developed. Between 1990 and 1993 the number of strikes and lockouts skyrocketed from 250 to 7,443 per year and the number of workers involved annually more than tripled to 383,200 (ILO 1997). Most of these involved demands for higher wages or continued enterprise subsidies to preserve jobs and social programs (Kloc 1992).

These efforts were successful. For instance, the announcement of salary cuts for teachers provoked strikes to which the minister of education reacted by backing off and promising to stop cost cutting without first consulting with teachers. Local unions and workers began to win protection for their jobs and assistance from the government in regions such as Lodz, which were particularly hard hit by the reforms (Gorniak and Jerschina 1995). The result was that serious deficits emerged again in 1991 and soared to 8 percent of GDP by 1992. Although both revenues and expenditures declined in real terms, revenue declines outpaced expenditure declines because collective action had undermined the sustained and full implementation of the neo-liberal plan. Policymakers had ignored IMF conditionality requirements and succumbed to public pressure for more spending (Lavigne 1995, 137). IMF officials recognized the problem and agreed to more lenient deficit levels (Bjork 1995, 107).

Unions also upset fiscal stability by undermining the restructuring and privatization of large state-owned enterprises, which lagged far behind schedule by 1994 (Kramer 1997, 65). Trade unions in these enterprises were strong and a primary reason for delays because they feared that restructuring and privatization would bring lower wages and benefits and higher unemployment (U.S. Department of Commerce 1997a). Failure to restructure and privatize these enterprises created budgetary pressures by perpetuating some of the old enterprise subsidies and undermining the revenue base insofar as many of these enterprises were not very profitable and, therefore, did not pay much in taxes.[1]

In contrast to the unions' clout, although competitive electoral politics quickly became important, they did *not* have much effect initially on budgetary politics. The first free parliamentary elections were held in October 1991, by which time public support for shock therapy was in decline. But because there were so many fragmented and weakly organized political parties competing for seats, 29 parties won representation, of which the Solidarity party was clearly the strongest and best organized (Przeworski 1995, 55). So, although there was considerable interparty conflict, it was so fragmented and disorganized that Solidarity managed to cobble together successive albeit fractious governments with slim majorities over the next few years and pursue the neoliberal agenda.

By the next national election parties had to receive at least 5 percent of the vote in order to win representation. This new rule effectively reduced the number of opposition parties to about a half dozen and increased their influence (*East European Politics and Societies* 1994; Millard 1994). Therefore, in the 1993 parliamentary election only seven parties won seats and another coalition government was elected, this time comprising two oppo-

sition parties. The Democratic Left Alliance (SLD) was the big winner and
a party that represented a coalition made up mostly of successor parties to
the old communist party. The SLD represented a social democratic perspective, capitalized on the declining popularity of the Solidarity government's reform program, criticized it severely, and vowed to be more attentive
to the needs of workers and peasants. Its coalition partner was the Polish
Peasant Party (*The Economist* 1994).

The deficits that ensued under the new government were much less severe than they had been previously, hovering around 2.5% of GDP in 1994
and 1995. In part, this was due to strong economic growth, but it was also
the result of a new *tripartite* form of politics that emerged in the wake of
the 1993 national election. The SLD had won the election with strong
backing from business elites, the OPZZ union and even some renegades
from the Solidarity union (Orenstein 1996). The new government drew on
its support base and formed a Tripartite Commission, which brought together unions, employers associations and government representatives and
quickly became the primary forum for discussing wages and benefits, social
security reform, and other social and economic policy matters. Tripartism
was designed to reduce social conflict by moving away from the Solidarity
government's approach of *imposing* rather than *negotiating* austerity policies
(Kolodko 1996, 15–19).

The results were impressive. First, strikes and lockouts plummeted from
their peak in 1993 to 42 by 1995 and involved only about 18,300 workers
(ILO 1997). Second, the government brought expenditures for social security programs under control by initiating reforms that tightened eligibility
requirements and benefits for pensions, unemployment compensation,
health insurance, and other programs (Kolodko 1996, 49–54). Expenditures
for transfer payments, including pensions and other social security programs,
which had grown from 10.4% of GDP in 1989 to 20.6% by 1993—the fastest
growing of all budget categories—rose to only 21.6% in 1994 and then
shrank slightly to 21% a year later (Kosterna 1997, 29). Indeed, the new
government believed that controlling this spending was imperative for restoring the country's fiscal integrity (Kolodko 1996, 26).

Over all, then, recognizing that mass protests had translated into fiscal
crisis for the Solidarity government, the SLD began to rechannel public
concerns in ways that enabled it to rein in expenditures more effectively.
Although the unions were as strong as ever and electoral competition had
become less fragmented and better organized—a situation that might oth-

erwise have made it much more difficult to control spending—the development of tripartite institutions that facilitated bargaining instead of confrontation provided a counterweight to the politics that had previously led to budget deficits. As a result, deficits resumed a fairly comfortable and stable level even as unemployment, if not economic growth, remained a serious problem.

Party Competition: Hungary's Electoral Politics

Whereas domestic opposition to the communist regime in Poland was mass based and rooted in a powerful union movement that confronted ruling elites, opposition in Hungary was more a matter of negotiation between elite opposition groups and the ruling party. Mass-based unions were not a factor (Offe 1997, 141–42). In turn, Hungary's postcommunist political situation was one where political parties emerged early, became stronger politically, and successfully monopolized postcommunist political life. Except for Solidarity, parties were much weaker in Poland (Agh 1997, 19). As a result, the political dynamics surrounding Hungarian budgetary politics differed in important ways from those in Poland.

By 1989 only about 30 percent of the labor force was unionized and unions were considerably more fragmented in Hungary, where there were eight major trade union confederations, than in Poland, where there were two (Bruszt 1995; Reutter 1996). The new postcommunist unions were especially weak (U.S. Department of Commerce 1997b; EIU 1988a, 9; Barany 1995, 180). For this reason although neoliberal reforms were attempted initially by the first postcommunist government they triggered less than 10 strikes per year through 1994 and most of them were extremely small, especially by Polish standards (ILO 1997). The few strikes and other demonstrations that did occur were often spontaneous rather than organized by the unions, such as the famous Budapest taxi drivers' strike of October 1990 that erupted in response to increased gasoline prices and caught the government very much off guard.

Instead, electoral politics provided the obstacle to neoliberalism. During the late 1980s the reform-minded communist government permitted opposition groups to emerge. Notably, the Hungarian Democratic Forum (HDF) was established in 1988 as a moderate opposition party and was permitted to consult with the regime. Although the HDF was somewhat neoliberal in orientation it also favored a rather paternalist state. The same year additional parties were formed, including the Alliance of Free Democrats (AFD) that favored more extreme neoliberalism and the Federation of Young Democrats (FYD), a youth oriented party with a similar agenda. In June 1989, the communist government invited seven opposition groups, including HDF, to enter round table talks to consider major reforms, which quickly led to the collapse of the old regime and the scheduling of national elections. Thus, after the old regime resigned there was already a small handful of established political parties in competition, including HDF, AFD, FYD, and the Hungarian Socialist Party, a reformed version of the old communist party that consisted of a mixture of neoliberal reformers and social democrats (Muravchik 1989). Most of these were broad-based parties without clear programs and did not become full-fledged parties in the western sense for a few years (Barany 1995, 183). Nevertheless, this was still much different from the Polish situation where, instead of inheriting a relatively well organized system of parties prepared to engage in electoral competition, Solidarity came to power and had to contend with a fragmented mass of small, often poorly organized parties. The fact that the first Hungarian elections transpired under a threshold rule similar to that eventually adopted in Poland also helped limit the number of parties that contested the elections (EIU 1989a, 7).

The first national postcommunist elections were held in spring 1990 and led to the creation of a coalition government consisting of HDF, the major winner, and two new parties, the Christian Democrats and the Small Holders Party. Due to Hungary's new electoral rules, the coalition won 60 percent of the seats in parliament but garnered only 45 percent of the vote. Furthermore, local elections were held later that year in which the Alliance of Free Democrats and the Federation of Young Democrats scored major victories. The HDF coalition captured only 36 percent of the local vote. As a result, despite its healthy parliamentary majority, the coalition was sensitive to its rather modest base of electoral support and announced that it would not take a very aggressive approach to neoliberal reform (EIU, 1990b, 8). By the end of 1990 the ruling government of Joszef Antall pursued neoliberal fiscal reform, but it did so carefully out of concern for the next election four years away and intent on avoiding any confrontation that might jeopardize its electoral fortunes (Bruszt 1995; Kramer 1997, 66; Voszka 1995). Hence, by the end of 1990 Hungarian officials had decided to pursue neoliberalism more cautiously than their Polish counterparts (EIU, 1990a, 11).

Their concerns were compounded by public reaction to the manner in which the government pursued structural reform. First, it tried to centralize and insulate decisionmaking from parliament, enterprise managers, and workers by shifting authority over the reform program to the prime minister and his technocrats and experts. Second, it appointed boards of directors, many of whom were people with close ties to the HDF, to monitor the activities of state owned enterprises and established a State Property Company to return control over state enterprises to the central government in order to protect their assets from being stripped prior to privatization. All of this alienated the public and the government's popularity ratings began to decline (Bruszt 1995). By late 1991, less than 20 percent of Hungarians viewed the government's performance positively (EIU 1991b) and although the unions remained weak and fragmented labor unrest increased during the summer (EIU 1991a).

Growing concern within the HDF over its electoral future caused deviations from neoliberal principles. Although the HDF government passed stringent bankruptcy laws, these were soon eased in order to delay the layoffs that would result. Perhaps most important, planned reductions in government spending were either dropped or delayed. Failing state enterprises received financial bailouts and debt forgiveness as a means of preserving jobs. Pension expenditures rose sharply because the government encouraged early retirement in order to avoid the official unemployment that would otherwise occur due to enterprise restructuring and privatization (Kramer 1997, 83). Patronage and pork barrel projects were awarded to appease the coalition partners and keep the government together (Bruszt 1995). As a result, by 1994 the Hungarian government still had total expenditures of 62 percent of GDP, by far the highest of the East European countries (Kosterna 1997, 29). Thus, even after Hungary began to recover from its severe recession deficits lingered just under 8 percent of GDP in 1994 as government spending remained much higher than initially envisioned under the neoliberal approach.

Despite such spending public discontent continued to mount. By early 1994 more than half of Hungarians considered life to have been better under the old communist regime (*New Statesman and Society* 1994). Disagreements over reform had deepened within the ruling coalition and its parliamentary majority had become razor thin because several of its members in parliament had defected to other parties (EIU 1993a, 8). Later that year a new coalition government was elected with 72 percent of the seats in parliament and led by the Hungarian Socialist Party (HSP) that garnered 54 percent of the vote. The HSP was initially hesitant to pursue a radical neo-liberal program even though its junior partner, the liberal Alliance of Free Democrats, as well as some of its own members advocated such a course. The election campaign focused largely on economic issues and the decline in living standards since 1990, so many in the new government were elected to soften the pain of reform (*The Economist* 1995a; U.S. Department of Commerce 1997b). However, this would be impossible due to the onset of a financial crisis and intense international pressure.

Hungary's first postcommunist government inherited $20 billion in foreign debt that increased to over $28 billion by 1994. Moreover, interest payments on the debt increased steadily to 8.4% of GDP by 1994 and the ratio of debt service to exports, an indication of the government's capacity to manage its debt obligations, had nearly doubled to 49 percent during that period—substantially higher than 30 percent, the threshold above which the international financial community began to worry about the possibility of default (Kosterna 1997, 29; World Bank 1997, 268). Much of the new debt was incurred in order to finance spending and budget deficits but as interest payments came due and increased, tripling between 1990 and 1995, they contributed to the expanding deficit in a vicious cycle. In contrast, although Poland carried roughly twice as much debt into the postcommunist period, its interest payments and debt service ratios were about half the size of Hungary's through 1995 in part because Polish officials signed agreements in 1991 with the Paris Club of government creditors and in 1994 with the London Club of private creditors that led to substantial rescheduling and forgiveness of its debt (Lavigne 1995, 143–144). Hungary struggled hard to maintain its international financial credibility by avoiding such measures (Kramer 1997, 65; Kovrig 1995, 39). Of course, rescheduling and forgiveness in the Polish case was facilitated in part by the fact that the vast bulk of Poland's debt was held by government and multilateral rather than private creditors—just the opposite of Hungary (World Bank 1997, 268, 432). Public lenders tend to be more amenable to rescheduling and forgiveness than private ones (Stallings 1992, 49).

The twin problems of debt and budget deficits reached a critical stage when the IMF suspended its 1993 loan agreement with Hungary and with-held $400 million after the Antall government failed to fulfill its debt and deficit reduction commitments (EIU 1995b, 16). More significant, however, was that in September 1994 the IMF and World Bank formally expressed their concern about the situation to the new government and the IMF announced that the deficit must be reduced, especially through cuts in social programs, wages, and other forms of public spending, if any *new* loan agreements were to be negotiated (EIU 1994a, 16–17). The IMF had toughened its stance and concerns within the international financial community over Hungary's ability to service its debt mounted (EIU 1995a, 31).

In response, under the leadership of the new finance minister, Lajos Bokros, the government introduced a radical stabilization program in March 1995, which included major changes in welfare benefits, in order to curb Hungary's massive budget deficits. As in Poland, to obtain political support, the government pursued tripartite negotiations with the trade union confederations and employers associations, who accepted the program (Hethy 1996). Nevertheless, the public was outraged as polls reported that two-thirds of Hungarians strongly opposed the plan and only 4 percent believed that it would improve the country's finances (*The Economist* 1995b). Bokros suffered relentless political pressure from within as well as outside the ruling coalition and in October 1995 watched as the Constitutional Court struck down several important parts of his package, including some of the proposed welfare benefit cuts. However, he still managed to reduce transfer payments from 22.2% of GDP in 1994 to 18.8% in 1995, subsidies from 4.5% of GDP to 3.5%, and ultimately the budget deficit from 7.6% of GDP to 3.7% (Kosterna 1997, 29). Deficit reduction was accomplished largely by cutting social security spending, including unemployment benefits, family support, social assistance and social insurance, restraining public sector wages, and increasing privatization revenues from $1.4 billion in 1994 to $3.8 billion in 1995 by speeding up the privatization process (OECD 1997). Despite these successes, Bokros was forced to resign in early 1996 (Kramer 1997, 66–69).

The new government pursued neoliberalism more aggressively than the old one for several reasons. First, IMF pressure to do so had increased and was facilitated by Hungary's worsening debt situation. Second, the ruling coalition was in a stronger political position than its predecessor to take potentially unpopular policy measures, having won a much larger share of the vote in the national elections. Moreover, unlike the HDF in 1990, the HSP also did quite well in local elections in December 1994, winning majorities in all but one county (EIU 1995a, 11). As a result, disgruntled politicians within the HSP were not likely to break ranks because there were few prospects of political survival outside the party (EIU 1995b, 4). Third, the HSP's junior partner, the Alliance of Free Democrats, had always favored an aggressive neoliberal program. Fourth, although the unions had become better organized in recent years and grumbled about wage restraint, they were willing to continue negotiations over the austerity program in part due to the new government's tripartite approach. Finally, the obvious severity of the deficit and debt situation made it difficult for any social group or party to raise serious objections to the government's program (EIU 1995b; 1994a, 17).

Consensual Politics: Czechoslovakian Exceptionalism

Whereas Poland's problems controlling spending and deficits were attributable largely to union-based resistance and Hungary's problems stemmed largely from electoral competition, Czechoslovakia and later the Czech Republic generally avoided fiscal problems due to the weakness of organized labor and the relative absence of electoral competition.

Because the old regime in Czechoslovakia was particularly repressive compared to Poland or Hungary, during the late 1980s Czechoslovakian unions were organizationally fragmented, politically weak, and contributed little to the opposition movement against the old regime (Reutter 1996, 67; Rychetnik 1995). Moreover, to ensure social peace as it launched its neoliberal program the first postcommunist government, established in 1990, created tripartite bargaining structures that included representatives from government, unions, and enterprise management to negotiate implementation of the reform plan (Cziria 1995; Reutter 1996). During the early years, the unions were willing partners to these reforms. Their cooperation stemmed from the fact that they were initially weak, prone to bickering, had difficulty achieving consensus on most economic issues and remained a group of loose and fragmented confederations for several years (EIU 1990d, 6; 1990e, 7, 11, 1995c). They were also vehemently anti-communist and favored neoliberalism over anything that even remotely resembled social democracy or socialism (Adam 1995; EIU 1990e, 12).

As a result, labor unrest was extremely rare and the unions posed little threat to austerity policies (U.S. Department of Commerce 1997c). Since 1990, the number of strikes and lockouts, workers involved in such actions, and time lost due to such actions was significantly lower in Czechoslovakia and subsequently the Czech Republic than in Poland and in some years even Hungary (ILO 1997). Notably, and in stark contrast to Poland, there was virtually no reaction from the unions when the government established wage controls in 1991 or 1993 to control inflation (EIU 1991c; 1991d; 1993d, 14–15; Kramer 1997, 89).

With respect to competitive party politics there had been little of the organized opposition to the old regime seen in Hungary. Communist repression ensured that there were few well-organized interest groups or opposition movements at all by the late 1980s (Wolchik 1995, 166–68). In fact, when the first postcommunist national election was held in 1990, it was won by candidates sponsored by two groups that had not yet established formal parties, the Civic Forum from the Czech Republic and Public Against Violence from Slovakia. Both were umbrella organizations representing a broad spectrum of citizens and interest groups. They formed a coalition government with the newly organized Christian Democratic Party and launched their neoliberal program in January 1991. For the next four years most political parties were extremely weak, poorly organized, and lacked coherent alternatives with which to challenge neoliberalism so, with one exception, there were no serious challengers and electoral politics did not constitute a strong constraint on policymakers until late 1995 (Agh 1997; Wolchik 1995, 166–68).

The exception came in the run up to the 1992 national elections. Several parties opposed neoliberalism but the best organized was the Movement for Democratic Socialism (MDS), a social democratic party whose support was located in Slovakia where the brunt of the recession was being felt. MDS won a plurality of the Slovakian vote while the Civic Democratic Party (CDP), the formal party that replaced the Civic Forum, won a plurality in the Czech Republic (EIU 1992, 11; Rychetnik 1995). The stage was set for a political showdown over fiscal policy but the confrontation never occurred because the two winners chose instead to negotiate a separation of the republics, effective January 1, 1993, after which each was free to pursue their own reform strategies.

With virtually no significant opposition from either the unions or parties after the separation the new Czech government, led by finance minister Vaclav Klaus, enjoyed a free hand to pursue neoliberal fiscal reform (EIU 1990d). However, because Klaus was deeply concerned that neoliberalism not jeopardize social peace, which in turn was vital to its success, he moved aggressively to minimize unemployment (EIU 1989b, 12; OECD 1996, 4). First, the government adopted wage controls in part to keep production costs low, stimulate exports, and boost the economy by maintaining a wide gap between Czech and West European wages (EIU 1994b, 9; 1995c, 19). Currency devaluation in 1991 was another way the government tried to boost exports and minimize unemployment. Second, in contrast to Poland and Hungary, rather than just provide unemployment benefits the government initiated more active labor market policies in 1992 that also sought to retrain and relocate unemployed workers (EIU 1992, 16; Kramer 1997, 90). Third, the government created incentives for unemployed workers to seek new jobs by maintaining one of the most restrictive unemployment benefit regimes in the region (EIU 1993b, 16–17; Kramer 1997, 90). Finally, the government often delayed implementation of bankruptcy laws and took additional steps to protect large firms in order to prevent the lay ffs that would ensue from their demise (EIU 1994c, 8–9; 1993c, 14).

With unemployment in check the government controlled social spending better than either Poland or Hungary. From 1989 to 1995 government subsidies decreased more in the Czech Republic than in the other two countries (Kosterna 1997, 29). Furthermore, social spending increased much less. In Czechoslovakia social spending rose from 17.5% of GNP to 20.5% from 1989 to 1995 but in Hungary it grew from 19.8% to 31.8% and in Poland from 10% to 25.8% of GNP during the same period (Kramer 1997, 73). Certainly, the ability to keep unemployment, spending and thus budget deficits low was enhanced by the fact that the Czech Republic had a strong tourist industry, a skilled labor force that could tap German and Austrian labor markets and a relatively modern manufacturing and technological base that helped mitigate the enormous declines in output and employment that neighboring postcommunist countries, including Slovakia, experienced (e.g., Kramer 1997, 88–92). Indeed, separation from Slovakia made managing the budget substantially easier than it would have been otherwise, particularly insofar as a hefty proportion of revenues were transferred from the federal budget to Slovakia while the two countries were still united. These idiosyncrasies not withstanding, the absence of union and political party opposition helped the government stick to its neoliberal principles better than either Poland or Hungary. In 1993 the budget was in surplus and in 1994 it experienced only a slight deficit of about 1 percent of GDP.

However, by 1995 the government began to experience political opposition and the situation began to deteriorate. First, perhaps because his party's political position, as well as his own, seemed more secure now that Slovakia had been jettisoned, Klaus started ignoring tripartism in 1993 arguing that most important economic policy issues were none of the unions' business

(EIU 1995e, 20–22). In turn, union militancy began to emerge, particularly in response to planned pension reforms and low wages in the public sector. In December 1994 unions staged a warning strike against the government's proposed pension cuts that involved 450,000 workers. In mid-1995 the teachers' union demanded a 20 percent pay increase and a strike was averted only when the government agreed to a 16.5% pay hike. Rail workers also threatened to strike for higher wages but Klaus, now prime minister, agreed to a hefty pay raise funded in part through the state budget. Second, the Social Democratic Party had emerged as a strong opposition party due to increasing support from disgruntled public sector workers. By August 1995, less than a year before the next national election, Klaus's CDP and the Social Democratic Party topped the polls in a virtual dead heat (EIU 1995c, 9–14; 1995d, 13; 1995e).

Raising public sector wages in the run-up to the 1996 election failed to keep the political tide from turning. The ruling coalition lost its parliamentary majority by one seat and the CDP had to share cabinet positions with members of two minor parties and bargain over most policy proposals with the Social Democrats (EIU 1996a, 10). Moreover, budget deficits appeared in 1994, grew in 1995, and were expected to persist as at least 2–3 percent of GDP in 1997 and 1998. This was due partly to declining export demand from Western Europe, slower economic growth, and lower than expected tax revenues and partly to rising public sector wages and political resistance to further spending cuts. The new government, suspecting that the deficit problem was becoming chronic, was prepared to cut more infrastructure spending and enterprise subsidies, but not the pay increases that preceded the election. This would have been too dangerous politically because senate elections were about to occur (EIU 1997b, 14; 1996b, 25).

Making matters worse, wage growth was becoming a problem in 1995 and 1996, exacerbated, of course, by the recent public sector wage concessions. Since 1994 Czech wages were higher than in any other postcommunist country except Hungary (IMF 1997, 100). Wage growth increased consumer demand for imports and undermined trade and current account balances in 1995 and 1996 (EIU 1996a). By November 1996 the trade and current account deficits had swollen to $5.1 billion and $1.4 billion, respectively (EIU 1997a, 20). This raised concerns that devaluation might be coming to stimulate exports and that it might trigger a currency crisis if foreign investment responded by fleeing the country. The Czech Republic was vulnerable in this regard because it had attracted more foreign direct investment ($6.4 billion by 1996) than any other postcommunist country except Hungary (IMF 1997, 106–7). Klaus resisted devaluation to avoid inflation, refused protectionism to keep markets open, and opposed export credits on neoliberal fiscal principles (EIU 1997a). But as the financial crisis gathered momentum, devaluation occurred and Klaus was forced in 1997 to pursue increasingly austere fiscal policies, including a public sector wage freeze and deep spending cuts, that were aimed at curbing the demand that drove up imports in the first place.

Between 1995 and 1997 the political context shifted dramatically. Unions were more militant and a viable opposition party emerged. Both challenged a government that had experienced few serious obstacles to its policies since 1990. Resistance made it difficult for the government to control public sector wages and social spending, and budget deficits emerged (EIU 1997b; 1997c). But just as domestic politics was forcing the government off its neoliberal path, international financial considerations emerged and for the first time exerted real pressure on the government to stay the neoliberal course. Although the details were different, in broad terms the Czechs were beginning to experience the same conflicting international and domestic fiscal pressures that the Hungarians and Poles had encountered years earlier. This was reflected in the fact that the popularity of both Klaus and the CDP declined sharply after 1995 and Klaus was forced to resign in late 1997 (EIU 1997b, 1997c).

Discussion

To review, I am not arguing that macroeconomic conditions were irrelevant to the budgets of these countries. Recessions did undermine revenues, trigger demands for social spending, and contribute to deviation from the neoliberal goals of reduced government spending and balanced budgets. However, in all three countries domestic politics, initially shaped by legacies of past political opposition (or the lack thereof), and relationships with the international financial community were critically important. Furthermore, without recognizing that neoliberalism emanated at the global and European levels and diffused across the postcommunist countries it is difficult to explain why all three countries initially embraced *similar* neoliberal fiscal reform strategies. Conversely, without acknowledging the significance of unique national political contexts it is difficult to see why effective resistance to the implementation of these reforms *varied* cross-nationally and over time within countries. In other words, in order to understand the fiscal reforms of postcommunist Europe we need to understand the interaction among global, European, and national-level forces. Focusing on any one alone is insufficient. Without this sort of multilevel perspective it is also difficult to decipher why neoliberal fiscal strategies had such unanticipated and troubling practical consequences.

This analysis provides several insights about the debate on globalization. First, and most obviously, it supports those who have argued that tendencies toward globalization and convergence are mediated heavily by national politics (e.g., Berger 1996, 23–24; Kitschelt et al. 1999). Clearly, the ideology of neoliberalism diffused across Poland, Hungary, and Czechoslovakia, but its *sustained* implementation was more varied precisely for this reason. Insofar as strong global and European-level pressures toward neoliberal fiscal convergence were operating, the fact that significant divergence resulted in the end across cases and over time suggests that national-level mediating factors are particularly important indeed. Scholars studying the adoption of austere economic stabilization programs in other parts of the world have made similar arguments noting in particular that government expenditure policies are among the most visible and thus most likely to be politicized and prone to obstruction during implementation (Stallings 1992, 74). Certainly this was true in postcommunist Europe. Whether the forces I have identified can also account for the diffusion and mediation of ideas in other policy areas, such as privatization, banking, or constitutional reform, requires further study. Of course, to the extent that convergence on a common global or European policy standard may be a phenomenon that takes decades to unfold, examining a longer reform period might lead to different conclusions. Nevertheless, my analysis indicates that to argue that global or even European-level forces are sweeping across national political economies in Europe and causing them all to converge on a common set of policies is far too simple an argument to sustain empirically—even in countries where one might expect few obstacles to neoliberalism because political systems are not well-established.

Second, some scholars have argued that neoliberal reform tends to be more difficult to initiate and sustain when the electoral system is fragmented and marked by many competing political parties due, for instance, to systems of proportional representation with low thresholds for representation. In short, the more fragmented the system, the more difficult are neoliberal reforms (Haggard and Kaufman 1992; Haggard and Kaufman 1995, 170). The cases examined here do not entirely support this view. In both Poland during the early 1990s and the Czech Republic immediately after its separation from Slovakia, the party system was extremely fragmented and most parties were so small and weak that they could not muster an effective challenge to neoliberal austerity. Only after the weakest parties had fallen by the wayside and the opposition had been consolidated in a smaller number of parties did electoral competition raise significant obstacles to neoliberal reform. In other words, the more fragmented the system, the *less* difficult were neoliberal reforms. Why the postcommunist cases contradict the received wisdom is unclear, but it may suggest that it is a mistake to assume there is a linear relationship between fragmentation and the capacity for neoliberal reform. Instead, a curvilinear relationship may obtain where under circumstances of either extreme fragmentation or extreme consolidation neoliberal reform is more sustainable at least insofar as a single very dominant party or strong coalition can control the situation, but under more moderate circumstances where there is more balanced and well-organized multiparty competition, neoliberalism is likely to be the object of more serious contention and perhaps, therefore, moderation, as in Hungary during the early 1990s. Of course, regardless of the degree of fragmentation in the electoral system, many have suggested that centralized bargaining over macroeconomic policy, notably through tripartite arrangements, tends to counteract these sorts of problems (e.g., Cameron 1985; but see Smith 1992, ch. 7)—an argument supported here.

Third, this analysis supports the view that not only politics, but also political institutions refract global pressures and produce divergent national responses (Garrett 1998; Garrett and Lange 1996). Notably, even in the presence of well-organized unions and stiff electoral competition, governments had more success sustaining neoliberal reform when it was negotiated through tripartism, as occurred, for example, in Poland under the SLD government. Without such mechanisms for consensus building, when opposition groups were strong, as they were during Poland's Solidarity government, Hungary's HDF government, and after Klaus abandoned tripartism in the Czech Republic, neoliberalism floundered. Others have drawn similar conclusions about developing countries arguing that neoliberal reform is more likely to be sustained when state or party institutions have coopted societal groups, particularly labor or business (Haggard and Kaufman 1992). Furthermore, this suggests that tripartite concertation sustains neoliberal reform better than other more autocratic but nonetheless democratic policy styles because it builds political bases and support for reform. In turn, this also indicates that neoliberalism need not precede democratization in order to succeed (Pereira 1993; Przeworski 1995).

Fourth, some globalization theorists have argued that the diffusion of policies from the global to the national level occurs primarily as a result of the influences on national governments of a fragmented, decentralized set of international organizations or market forces and often through noncoercive means (Meyer et al. 1997; Ohmae 1990). To an extent this was true To an extent this was true—especially in the Czech case, where at first political elites initiated neoliberal reforms because many of them believed that neoliberalism was based on the best economic science, was most acceptable within the West European community to which they aspired, and was the best way to attract foreign investment and develop market-based economies (EIU 1990c, 14; Lavigne 1995, ch. 7; Wolchik 1995). Therefore, the reforms were not in response to the coercive pressures of the IMF or other international actors, who had less leverage over the Czechoslovakian government because Czech debt to western creditors was minuscule compared to Poland and Hungary (World Bank 1997, 180, 268, 432). Nonetheless, it is clear that another very important source of global influence was a small handful of powerful international financial organizations, especially the IMF, that offered substantial and much needed financial assistance, if postcommunist governments adopted the neoliberal policies that these organizations favored. In other words, much global pressure emanated from a more centralized, unified, and coercive source as critics of the globalization thesis and students of economic development have shown (e.g., Berger and Dore 1996; Haggard et al. 1993, 180; Stallings 1992). This is important because it indicates that the fiscal policies of these countries were not somehow dictated by universal economic laws or naturally derivative of human nature, but were instead part of a broad, historically specific, political-economic project that emphasized neoliberal principles and that had very real and powerful proponents (see also Campbell and Pedersen, forthcoming).

Fifth, in contrast to the globalization thesis, which claims that the convergent pressures of capital mobility and international competition are steadily *rising* and overpowering whatever national resistance there might be (e.g., Cerny 1997; Waters 1995, ch. 5), the postcommunist cases suggest that all of this has been much more variable. At the *national* level, for example, the emergence of stable, well-organized political party systems and trade union movements *increased* the possibility that neoliberal reform would run into trouble, although developing tripartite bargaining counteracted these tendencies. At the *global* level, the intensity of international pressure itself fluctuated, often depending on the relationship between the national political economy and the international financial community. As globalization theorists would predict, foreign direct investment increased in the Czech Republic and the government came under increasing international pressure to tow the neoliberal line. In contrast, however, the level of external debt *declined* in Poland and, as a result, so did the international financial community's ability to press policymakers to adopt a particular policy stance. In turn, the government's relationship with the IMF changed. Although government officials still met with the IMF on a regular basis after 1994, rather than doing so out of a need for financial aid, they used these meetings more as an opportunity to elicit IMF approval and, therefore, public legitimacy for policies that they fully intended to pursue anyway. In other words, rather than seeking to appease the IMF, they began using the agency for their own domestic political purposes.[2] This suggests that the ability of institutions like the IMF to use coercive rather than other means is more contingent than is often recognized (see also Kahler 1992). The more important point is that the forces for and against convergence ebb and flow over time, which means that convergence and divergence are highly contingent processes.

Finally, all of this indicates that the debate over whether or not the world's political economies are converging through the global diffusion of a neoliberal model is the wrong one to have. Rather than arguing about whether or not convergence is occurring, a more constructive approach is to investigate the conditions under which convergence is more or less likely to occur. Posing the issue in this way would lead us to attend more closely to the relationships between international and national processes that facilitate and inhibit the globalization of economic ideas and practices.

Acknowledgments

Thanks go to Michael Allen, Ellen Comisso, Beverly Crawford, Frank Dobbin, John Hall, Eva Fodor, Herbert Kitschelt, Misagh Parsa, Ove Pedersen, Guy Peters, Robert Jenkins, Akos Rona-Tas and Mike Smith for comments on previous versions of the argument and to Amir Nahai and Karen Yen for research assistance. Financial support was provided by the Center for German and European Studies at the University of California-Berkeley and the Presidential Scholars Program at Dartmouth College. Correspondence to: John Campbell, Department of Sociology, Dartmouth College, Hanover, New Hampshire 03755, USA. E-Mail: John.L.Campbell@ Dartmouth.Edu.

Endnotes

1. Interview with the chief economic advisor to the Polish Minister of Finance, May 1997. See also Kolodko (1996, 122).
2. Interview with the chief economic advisor to the Polish Minister of Finance, May 1997.

References

Adam, Jan. 1995. "Transition to a Market Economy n the Former Czechoslovakia." In *Strategic Choice and Path-Dependency in Post-Socialism*, eds. Jerzy Hausner, Bob Jessop and Klaus Nielsen. Aldershot: Edward Elgar, pp. 193–217.

Agh, Attila. 1997. "Globalization and Regionalization in Central Europe: Positive and Negative Responses to the Global Challenge." Budapest Papers on Democratic Transition, No. 204. Hungarian Center for Democracy Studies Foundation, Department of Political Science, Budapest University of Economics.

Ambrus-Lakatos, Lorand and Mark E. Schaffer. 1997. "Conclusions and Recommendations." In *Fiscal Policy in Transition*, eds. Lorand Ambarus-Lakatos and Mark E. Schaffer. New York: Center for Economic Policy Research/Institute for EastWest Studies, pp. 69–73.

Barany, Zoltan. 1995. "Hungary." In *The Legacies of Communism in Eastern Europe*, eds. Zoltan Barany and Ivan Volgyes. Baltimore: The Johns Hopkins University Press, pp. 177–97.

Berger, Suzanne. 1996. "Introduction." In *National Diversity and Global Capitalism*, eds. Suzanne Berger and Ronald Dore. Ithaca, N.Y.: Cornell University Press, pp. 1–25.

Berger, Suzanne and Ronald Dore, editors. 1996. *National Diversity and Global Capitalism*. Ithaca, N.Y.: Cornell University Press.

Bjork, James. 1995. "The Uses of Conditionality: Poland and the IMF." *East European Quarterly* 29 (March): 89–119.

Bobinska, Lena Kolarska. 1994. "Social Interests and their Political Representation: Poland in Transition." *British Journal of Sociology* 45 (March): 109–26.

Boli, John and George M. Thomas. 1999. *Constructing World Culture*. Stanford, CA: Stanford University Press.

Bruszt, Laszlo. 1995. "Reforming Alliances: Labor, Management and State Bureaucracy in Hungary's Economic Transformation." In *Strategic Choice and Path-Dependency in Post-Socialism*, eds. Jerzy Hausner, Bob Jessop and Klaus Nielsen. Aldershot: Edward Elgar, pp. 261–86.

Cameron, David R. 1985. "Does Government Cause Inflation? Taxes, Spending, and Deficits." In *The Politics of Inflation and Economic Stagnation*, eds. Leon N. Lindberg and Charles S. Maier. Washington, DC: The Brookings Institution, pp. 224–79.

Campbell, John L. 1992. "The Fiscal Crisis of Post-Communist States." *Telos* 93:89–110.

———. 1993. "The State and Fiscal Sociology." *Annual Review of Sociology* 19:163–85.

———. 1996. "Institutional Analysis and Fiscal Reform in Postcommunist Europe." *Theory and Society* 25:45–84.

Campbell, John L. and Ove K. Pedersen. forthcoming. "The Second Movement in Institutional Analysis." In *The Second Movement in Institutional Analysis: Neoliberalism in Perspective*, eds. John L. Campbell and Ove K. Pedersen. Princeton: Princeton University Press.

Cerny, Philip G. 1997. "International Finance and the Erosion of Capitalist Diversity." In *Political Economy of Modern Capitalism: Mapping Convergence and Diversity*, eds. Colin Crouch and Wolfgang Streeck. Thousand Oaks, CA: Sage, pp. 173–81.

Coricelli, Fabrizio. 1997. "Fiscal Policy: A Long-Term View." In *Fiscal Policy in Transition*, eds. Lorand Ambrus-Lakatos and Mark E. Schaffer. New York: Center for Economic Policy Research/Institute for EastWest Studies, pp. 39–52.

Crouch, Colin and Wolfgang Streeck. 1997. "Introduction: The Future of Capitalist Diversity." In *Political Economy of Modern Capitalism: Mapping Convergence and Diversity*, eds. Colin Crouch and Wolfgang Streeck. Thousand Oaks, CA: Sage, pp. 1–18.

Cziria, Ludovit. 1995. "The Czech and Slovak Republics." In *Labor Relations and Political Change in Eastern Europe*, eds. John Thirkell, Richard Scase and Sarah Vickerstaff. Ithaca, NY: Cornell University Press, pp. 61–80.

Dabrowski, Marek. 1997. "Dynamics of Fiscal Developments During Transition." In *Fiscal Policy in Transition*, eds. Lorand Ambrus-Lakatos and Mark E. Schaffer. New York: Center for Economic Policy Research/institute for EastWest Studies, pp. 3–15.

DiMaggio Paul and Walter Powell. 1983. "The Iron Cage Revisited: Institutional Isomorphism and Collective Rationality in Organizational Fields." *American Sociological Review* 48:147–60.

East European Politics and Societies. 1994. "Bulletin of Electoral Statistics and Public Opinion Research Data." 8 (Spring): 369–79.

The Economist. 1994. "The Fading of the Red." January 14, p. 56.

———. 1995a. "Horn's Dilemma." January 28, pp. 46–47.

———. 1995b. "Radical at Last." April 1, pp. 45–46.

The Economist Intelligence Unit. 1988a. *Country Report: Hungary* (4th quarter).

———. 1988b. *Country Report: Czechoslovakia* (1st quarter).

———. 1988c. *Country Report: Czechoslovakia* (3rd quarter).

———. 1989a. *Country Report: Hungary* (4th quarter).

———. 1989b. *Country Report: Czechoslovakia* (1st quarter).

———. 1990a. *Country Report: Hungary* (3rd quarter).

———. 1990b. *Country Report: Hungary* (4th quarter).

———. 1990c. *Country Report: Czechoslovakia* (1st quarter).

———. 1990d. *Country Report: Czechoslovakia* (2nd quarter).

———. 1990e. *Country Report: Czechoslovakia* (4th quarter).

———. 1991a. *Hungary: Country Profile.*

———. 1991b.*Country Report: Hungary* (3rd quarter).

———. 1991c. *Country Report: Czechoslovakia* (2nd quarter).

———. 1991d. *Country Report: Czechoslovakia* (3rd quarter).

———. 1992. *Country Report: Czechoslovakia* (3rd quarter).

———. 1993a. *Country Report: Hungary* (4th quarter).

———. 1993b. *Country Report: Czechoslovakia* (1st quarter).

———. 1993c. *Country Report: Czechoslovakia* (3rd quarter).

———. 1993d. *Country Report: Czechoslovakia* (4th quarter).

———. 1994a. *Country Report: Hungary* (4th quarter).

———. 1994b. *Country Report: Czechoslovakia* (2nd quarter).

———. 1994c. *Country Report: Czechoslovakia* (3rd quarter).

———. 1995a. *Country Report: Hungary* (1st quarter).

———. 1995b. *Country Report: Hungary* (2nd quarter).

———. 1995c. *Country Report: Czechoslovakia* (1st quarter).

———. 1995d. *Country Report: Czechoslovakia* (3rd quarter).

———. 1995e. *Country Report: Czechoslovakia* (4th quarter).

———. 1996a. *Country Report: Czechoslovakia* (3rd quarter).

———. 1996b. *Country Report: Czechoslovakia* (4th quarter).

———. 1997a. *Country Report: Czechoslovakia* (1st quarter).

———. 1997b. *Country Report: Czechoslovakia* (3rd quarter).

———. 1997c. *Country Report: Czechoslovakia* (4th quarter).

Elster, Jon, Claus Offe and Ulrich K. Preuss. 1998. *Institutional Design in Post-Communist Societies.* New York: Cambridge University Press.

Finnemore, Martha. 1996. "Norms, Culture, and World Politics: Insights from Sociology's Institutionalism." *International Organization* 50 (2): 325–47.

Garrett, Geoffrey. 1998. *Partisan Politics in the Global Economy*. New York: Cambridge University Press.

———— and Peter Lange. 1996. "Internationalization, Institutions and Political Change." *International and Domestic Politics*, eds. Robert O. Keohane and Helen V. Milner. New York: Cambridge University Press, pp. 48–75.

Gorniak, Jaroslaw and Jan Jerschina. 1995. "From Corporatism to . . . Corporatism: The Transformation of Interest Representation in Poland." In *Strategic Choice and Path-Dependency in Post-Socialism*, eds. Jerzy Hausner, Bob Jessop and Klaus Nielsen. Aldershot: Edward Elgar, pp. 168–90.

Greider, William. 1997. *One World Ready or Not: The Manic Logic of Global Capitalism*. New York: Simon and Schuster.

Greskovits, Bela. 1998. *The Political Economy of Protest and Patience: East European and Latin American Transformations Compared*. Budapest: Central European University Press.

Haggard, Stephan and Robert R. Kaufman. 1995. *The Political Economy of Democratic Transitions*. Princeton: Princeton University Press.

————. 1992. "Institutions and Economic Adjustment." In *The Politics of Economic Adjustment*, eds. Stephan Haggard and Robert R. Kaufman. Princeton: Princeton University Press, pp. 3–37.

Haggard, Stephan, Marc Levy, Andres Moravcsik and Kalypso Nicolaidis. 1993. "Integrating the Two Halves of Europe: theories of Interests, Bargaining and Institutions." In *After the Cold War*, eds. Robert Keohane, Joseph Nye and Stanley Hoffmann. Cambridge, MA: Harvard University Press, pp. 173–95.

Hethy, Lajos. 1996. "Negotiated Social Peace: An Attempt to Reach a Social and Economic Agreement in Hungary." In *Parliaments and Organized Interests: The Second Steps*, eds. Attila Agh and Garbriella Ilonszki. Budapest: Hungarian Center for Democracy Studies Foundation, pp. 147–57

Hirst, Paul and Grahame Thompson. 1996. *Globalization in Question*. Cambridge: Polity Press.

International Labor Organization. 1997. *Yearbook of Labor Statistics, 1996*. Geneva.

International Monetary Fund. 1997. *World Economic Outlook, May 1997*. Washington D.C.

————. 1993a. *World Economic Outlook, May 1993*. Washington D.C.

————. 1993b. *World Economic Outlook, October 1993*. Washington D.C.

————. 1994. *World Economic Outlook, October 1994*. Washington D.C.

————. 1996a. *World Economic Outlook, May 1996*. Washington D.C.

————. 1996b. *World Economic Outlook, October 1996*. Washington D.C.

Kahler, Miles. 1992. "External Influence, Conditionality, and the Politics of chAdjustment." In *The Politics of Economic Adjustment*, eds. Stephan Haggard and Robert R. Kaufman. Princeton: Princeton University Press, pp. 89–136.

Kitschelt, Herbert, Peter Lange, Gary Marks and John D. Stephens. 1999. "Convergence and Divergence in advanced Capitalist Democracies." In *Continuity and Change in Contemporary Capitalism*, eds. Herbert Kitschelt, Peter Lange, Gary Marks and John D. Stephens. New York: Cambridge University Press, pp. 427–60.

Kloc, Kazimierz. 1992. "Polish Labor in Transition (1990–1992)." *Telos* 92: 139–48.

Kolodko, Grzegorz W. 1996. *Poland 2000: The New Economic Strategy*. Warsaw: Poltext.

Kornai, Janos. 1992. "The Postsocialist Transition and the State: Reflections in the Light of the Hungarian Fiscal Problems." *American Economic Review* 82 (2): 1–21.

Kosterna, Urszula. 1997. "The Fiscal Policy Stance in Central and Eastern Europe in Comparison to European Union Countries." In *Fiscal Policy in Transition*, eds. Lorand Ambrus-Lakatos and Mark E. Schaffer. New York: Center for Economic Policy Research/Institute for EastWest Studies, pp. 53–68.

Kovrig, Bennett. 1995. "Marginality Reinforced." In *Strategic Choice and Path-Dependency in Post-Socialism*, eds. Jerzy Hausner, Bob Jessop and Klaus Nielsen. Aldershot: Edward Elgar, pp. 23–41 in *The Legacies of Communism in Eastern Europe*, eds. Zoltan Barany and Ivan Volgyes. Baltimore: The Johns Hopkins University Press.

Kowalik, Tadeusz. 1995. "The Free Market or a Social Contract as Bases for Systemic Transformation." pp. 131–48.

Kramer, Mark. 1997. "Social Protection Policies and Safety Nets in East-Central Europe: Dilemmas of the Postcommunist Transformation." In *Sustaining the Transition: The Social Safety Net in Postcommunist Europe*, eds. Ethan B. Kapstein and Michael Mandelbaum. New York: Council on Foreign Relations Press, pp. 46–123.

Lavigne, Marie. 1995. *The Economics of Transition: From Socialist Economy to Market Economy*. New York: St. Martin's Press.

Levi, Margaret. 1988. *Of Rule and Revenue*. Berkeley: University of California Press.

Meyer, John, John Boli, George M. Thomas and Francisco O. Ramirez. 1997. "World Society and the Nation State." *American Journal of Sociology* 103 (1): 144–81.

Millard, Frances. 1994. "The Shaping of the Polish Party System." *East European Politics and Societies* 8 (Fall).

Milner, Helen V. and Robert O. Keohane. 1996. "Internationalization and Domestic Politics: An Introduction." In *Internationalization and Domestic Politics*, eds. Robert O. Keohane and Helen V. Milner. New York: Cambridge University Press, pp. 3–24.

Muravchik, Joshua, editor. 1989. *World Affairs* (special issue on "Democratic Transformation in Hungary" 151 (4).

New Statesman and Society. 1994. "Hungarian Right in Fix." February 18, pp. 10–11.

Newbery, David M. G. 1995. "Tax and Benefit Reform in Central and Eastern Europe." In *Tax and Benefit Reform in Central and Eastern Europe*, eds. David Newbery. London: Center for Economic and Policy Research, pp. 1–18.

OECD. 1991. *OECD Economic Surveys: Hungary.* Paris.

——. 1993. *OECD Economic Outlook* (December). Paris.

——. 1995. *OECD Economic Outlook* (June). Paris.

——. 1996. *OECD Economic Surveys: Czech Republic.* Paris.

——. 1997. *The Role of Tax Reform in Central and Eastern European Economies.* Paris.

Offe, Claus. 1997. *Varieties of Transition.* Cambridge, Mass. Massachusetts Institute of Technology Press.

Ohmae, Kenichi. 1990. *The Borderless World: Power and Strategy in the Interlinked Economy.* New York: Harper Collins.

Orenstein, Mitchell. 1996. "A Genealogy of Communist Successor parties in East Central Europe and the Determinants of Their Success." Paper presented to the Tenth International Conference of Europeanists, Chicago.

Pedersen, Ove K., Karsten Ronit and Ivan Suhij. 1996. "The State and Organized Interests in the Labor Market: Experiences from Postcommunist Europe." In *Legacies of Change: Transformations of Postcommunist European Economies*, eds. John L. Campbell and Ove K. Pedersen. New York: Aldine de Gruyter, pp. 109–36.

Pereira, Luiz Carlos Bresser, Jose Maria Maravall and Adam Przeworski. 1993. *Economic Reforms in New Democracies: A Social-Democratic Approach.* New York: Cambridge University Press.

Przeworski, Adam. 1993. "Economic Reforms, Public Opinion and political Institutions: Poland and the Eastern European Perspective." In *Economic Reforms in New Democracies: A Social-Democratic Approach*, eds. Caralos Bresser Pereira, Jose Maria Maravall and Adam Przeworski. New York: Cambridge University Press, pp. 132–98.

——. 1996. "Public Support for Economic Reforms in Poland." *Comparative Political Studies* 29 (October): 520–43.

——. 1995. *Sustainable Democracy.* New York: Cambridge University Press.

Reich, Robert. 1991. *The Work of Nations.* New York: Vintage.

Reutter, Werner. 1996. "Tripartism without Corporatism: Trade Unions in Central and Eastern Europe." In *Parliaments and Organized Interests: the Second Steps*, eds. Attila Agh and Gabriella Ilonszki. Budapest: Hungarian Center for Democracy Studies Foundation, pp. 59–78.

Rose, Richard and Guy Peters. 1978. *Can Government Go Bankrupt?* New York: Basic Books.

Rychetnik, Ludek. 1995. "Can the Czech Republic Develop a Negotiated Economy?" In *Strategic Choice and Path-Dependency in Post-Socialism*, eds. Jerzy Hausner, Bob Jessop and Klaus Nielsen. Aldershot: Edward Elgar, pp. 230–60.

Smith, Michael R. 1992. *Power, Norms and Inflation: A Skeptical Treatment*. New York: Aldine de Gruyter.

Stallings, Barbara. 1992. "International Influence on Economic Policy: Debt, Stabilization and Structural Reform." In *The Politics of Economic Adjustment*, eds. Stephan Haggard and Robert Kaufman. Princeton, N.J.: Princeton University Press, pp. 41–88.

Strange, Susan. 1997. "The Future of Global Capitalism; Or, Will Divergence Persist Forever?" In *Political Economy of Modern Capitalism: Mapping Convergence and Diversity*, eds. Colin Crouch and Wolfgang Streeck. Thousand Oaks, CA: Sage, pp. 182–91.

Tanzi, Vito, editor. 1992. *Fiscal Policies in Economies in Transition*. Washington D.C.: International Monetary Fund.

U.S. Department of Commerce, Economics and Statistics Administration, Office of Business Analysis. 1997a. *Poland: Economic Trends and Outlook*. National Trade Data Bank CD-ROM (April). Washington D.C.

———. 1997b. *Hungary: Economic Trends and Outlook*. National Trade Data Bank CD-ROM (April). Washington D.C.

———. 1997c. *Czech Republic: Economic Trends and Outlook*. National Trade Data Bank CD-ROM (April). Washington D.C.

Voszka, Eva. 1995. "Centralization, Re-Nationalization, and Redistribution: Government's Role in Changing Hungary's Ownership Structure." In *Strategic Choice and Path-Dependency in Post-Socialism*, eds. Jerzy Hausner, Bob Jessop and Klaus Nielsen. Aldershot: Edward Elgar, pp. 287–308.

Waters, Malcolm. 1995. *Globalization*. London: Routledge.

Wolchik, Sharon L. 1995. "The Czech Republic and Slovakia." In *The Legacies of Communism in Eastern Europe*, eds. Zoltan Barany and Ivan Volgyes. Baltimore: The Johns Hopkins University Press, pp. 152–76.

World Bank. 1997. *Global Development Finance*, Vol. 2. Washington D.C.

4 Creating a Pan-European Equity Market

Steven Weber and Elliot Posner

1. Introduction

To create a new stock market is an audacious act. Since late 1996, Europe has created at least a dozen new stock markets aimed specifically at the entrepreneurial, high-growth company sector. The first of these was EASDAQ (European Association of Security Dealers Automated Quotation), a pan-European enterprise market that began trading in November 1996. EASDAQ is a significant innovation for Europe's capital markets. With the partial exception of Britain, EU states have not had substantial markets in which startup companies can raise equity finance effectively. EASDAQ is an attempt to create such a market, and on a pan-European basis.

Equity markets are crucial institutions in capitalist societies. The means by which an economy allocates capital has wide-ranging implications for social and political policies and structures (Gerschenkron, 1962; Zysman, 1983).[1] Equity financing, as opposed to financing through banks or corporate bonds, has become especially relevant because it is well suited to the high risks of commercializing cutting-edge technology. Clearly, the American market for high growth, entrepreneurial companies—NASDAQ—has had an enormous influence on U.S. political economy and social policy. NASDAQ and the explosion of growth among the kinds of firms that tend to list there are part of what differentiates the American economy from continental European economies, where equity markets in general are far less developed, fewer households own stocks, and entrepreneurs find it much more difficult to raise money. The comparative weakness of bio- and information technology sectors in Europe reflects, at least in part, the lack of finance opportunities much more readily available to risk-acceptant entrepreneurs and venture capitalists in the U.S. By some accounts, NASDAQ listed firms are responsible for much of the rapid job creation that has been a major characteristic of the American economy—and not of continental European economies—since the 1980s (Krueger and Pischke, 1997; OECD, 1997:150–72; *Economist*, 1997b).

The creation of EASDAQ set off further changes in European finance, as national governments and stock markets responded by building enterprise markets of their own. The creation of these new markets is one piece of a general restructuring process in the institutional framework of finance, but it is in some ways the most challenging practically and theoretically. To create this new kind of stock market requires the coming together of a range of auxiliary institutions which run the gamut from brokers to market makers to venture capital firms to research services and more.[2] It depends also on more abstract societal characteristics—so called "equity cultures" (do individuals like to buy stocks?), risk propensities (of individuals and institutions), the social context of failure (is it a scarlet letter or a badge of honor to be an entrepreneur with ten bankruptcies behind you?). Much more so than proposed (and quite limited) alliances between existing national market systems like the London and Frankfurt Stock Exchanges, the concept of EASDAQ (particularly its true pan-European status and its concentration on entrepreneurial companies) reaches deeply into the social and political fabric of bargains that underlie European political economy.

Taking into account the perceived successes of the NASDAQ market in America, it is not surprising that some Europeans considered creating an enterprise market of their own. Indeed, EASDAQ is not the first attempt to do something along these lines in Europe—although it is different from previous efforts in important ways. The most striking differences from the past are two: the pan-European scope of the market, and the very clear attempt to "copy" NASDAQ practices, rules, regulations, and even (for the most part) NASDAQ's name. For a group of countries that often seeks (at least in rhetoric) to distinguish its political-economic culture and practices from the so-called "Anglo-Saxon" model, this *is* surprising: of the many alternatives, why would the creators of a new enterprise market in Europe choose the pan-European, NASDAQ form?

One potential explanation for the creation, timing, and form of EASDAQ seems self-evident and is an obvious null hypothesis. EASDAQ could be a simple institutional convergence phenomenon accompanying "globalization." A stark version of this argument would see a triumph of market forces, pushing toward convergence around "best practice" as a result of intensified competition that results, in large part, from capital mobility (but also from the increased mobility of technology and ideas). Efficiency is the driving force, and EASDAQ follows NASDAQ as the next step in a globalizing, Weberian rationalization of economies, subject only to delays and detours imposed by national differences that are slow to give way to a process of institutional change (Unger and Van Waarden, 1995; Keohane and Milner, 1996).[3] This kind of explanation appears simple and parsimonious—it has a single driving force and could in principle account for the major empirical characteristics of EASDAQ. But it is misleading in several ways.

In this essay, we develop and evaluate alternatives to this a priori globalization story about institutional isomorphism (the observed similarity of institutions across different national contexts). We argue first that the "globalization/efficiency" argument needs to be refined. It is not adequate, even as a null hypothesis, because it lacks the clarity and complexity necessary for generating specific hypotheses which we could test against the historical evidence of EASDAQ's creation. We develop discrete variants of this argument and specify for each variant the actors and mechanisms we expect to observe, if the explanation is valid. We introduce two other potential explanations for institutional isomorphism (cooperation in standard-setting, and ideological "hegemony") and develop from each similar testable implications.

We then evaluate the expectations of each argument within the historical evidence. Our hypotheses, reflecting widely held arguments, expect different combinations of international market forces, powerful international actors, and global mechanisms to effect change in financial institutions. While elements of these hypotheses do appear in the causal story, they miss the central driving force. We instead found at the core of the EASDAQ story European Union institutional actors, who enabled a politically weak group of European venture capitalists to create a new financial market. The critical actors are EU institutions. Their motivations derive from European problems and politics, and the ensuing process of institutional change they instigate is deeply embedded in the politics of European integration.

The narrative details these empirical findings. We show that the origins of EASDAQ are rooted in a broad European political discourse primarily about jobs and competitiveness. First, European states and the EU as a whole were suffering from a major and worsening unemployment crisis. By 1993 unemployment was the single most salient political issue for the European Union, and for many of its member states as well. Second was the problem of technology. Europeans have not matched the explosive growth of new industries in America which might have alleviated, at least in part, the high levels of unemployment. Europe's lack of new industries has been widely associated with the inability to commercialize basic science into cutting-edge technologies. The story of EASDAQ's origins begins with a discourse expressing a "felt need" among Europeans to find solutions to the two connected problems of high levels of unemployment and an inability to commercialize technology. The means for "solving" these perceived problems were (and are) poorly understood, and this uncertainty prompted a search for ideas. Many of the proposed solutions — particularly, increasing the "flexibility" of labor markets — remain politically precarious.

We show in the narrative that the European Commission saw in EASDAQ both a potential alternative solution to these problems, and a vehicle for promoting broader political goals. European venture capitalists, a politically inconsequential group in Europe, had tried (and failed) to create enterprise markets in the 1980s. They also failed to attract the Commission's direct participation in those earlier efforts. A few key players within the venture capital community, however, correctly discerned an opportunity in the new political environment of the 1990s. Believing they could now attract the support of the Commission, they proposed a new enterprise market based largely on NASDAQ. The Commission organized, supported, and modified in important ways the proposal for a European NASDAQ. Commission officials believed they could portray the creation of a new enterprise market as a positive sum solution to Europe's unemployment and technology problems. Changing the financial structure for new companies was a much more politically attractive option than pressing for more "flexible" labor markets. In the public mind, the latter phrase evoked an image of American style labor markets that includes declining wages, high insecurity, and the lack of a serious social safety net.[4] EASDAQ, in stark contrast, could be portrayed as a win-win solution where investors, entrepreneurs, market players, and job-seekers would all benefit from virtuous circles of investment, technological innovation, and profit.

The Commission also saw in EASDAQ a valuable opportunity to promote a key integration goal connected to Europe's new legal environment in financial services. The European Union's 1993 Investment Services Directive (ISD) heralded a major change in the European financial environment. Under the ISD, an investment services firm licensed to operate under the regulations of its home country would essentially be able to operate throughout the EU. The ISD went quite far toward creating a single market for investment services, but the document's ambiguities made certain that implementation by member states would be a contentious process. For the Commission, EASDAQ became a way to push the envelope of securities market liberalization and, even more importantly, integration within the EU. In particular, the Commission saw in EASDAQ a vehicle for pressing member states on ISD implementation, and for finding out just how serious the remaining impediments to cross border trading would turn out to be in the post ISD environment.

The narrative reveals how the origin of EASDAQ is fundamentally a story about a series of creative actions taken by the European Commission in pursuit of these two objectives. Throughout the 1980s and 1990s, the Commission and other EU institutions facilitated and helped foster the broad political discourse which made the connections between unemployment, perceived technological backwardness, and the difficulties European small and medium sized enterprises (SME's) have in obtaining capital. More specifically, the Commission sponsored and organized symposia and programs designed to improve the financing structures for SMEs. It brought together prominent venture capitalists and prompted them to form the European Venture Capital Association (EVCA) which later became the vehicle for creating EASDAQ. In 1993 and 94, the Commission urged the venture capitalists to move forward on EASDAQ, backed a proposal with a pan-European rather than a national network structure, and gave financial support first for feasibility studies and then to get the project off the ground.

Global market forces did not create EASDAQ in any meaningful sense. Political actors did; especially the European Commission. This argument rests on the following explicit counterfactual: minus the EU and minus the active role of the European Commission, it is almost certain that EASDAQ, in particular, would not have happened and that the creation of any new enterprise market would not have occurred at this time and in this form. It is also certain that capital market reform in Europe would have taken a very different path.

In the conclusion, we consider the implications of the EASDAQ story for general arguments about globalization, as well as for understanding the role of the European Commission. A standard view in the globalization literature depicts institutions as obstacles that push backwards against the grain to block or channel economic forces that drive change. In this perspective, institutions are principally resistive forces—"blocking international price signals," "freezing" political coalitions, or trying to insulate extant arrangements (Keohane and Milner, 1996). The EASDAQ story suggests a central, *creative* and *catalytic* role of political institutions and particularly the European Commission. This is consistent with some recent arguments about the role of the Commission in European integration (Nugent 1997; Pollack, 1997, 1998; Sandholtz, 1998; Sandholtz and Stone Sweet, 1998). While economic forces that globalization arguments emphasize are present in the EASDAQ story, it is not the case that the EU acted simply as a political "pipeline" transmitting these forces in a passive way. The European Commission was the necessary catalyst, and the other elements in this story, including global forces, could not have created EASDAQ without it

The notion of a catalytic actor underscores the European Commission's effort to position itself for three major objectives: to bring together strategic coalitions, to be indispensable to that process, and to remain substantially independent in the pursuit of its own goals through those coalitions (Lind, 1992). The Commission played the key role in creating a legal and political environment in which EASDAQ became possible. It brought together a coalition of public and private actors necessary to make EASDAQ happen. And it shaped many of the major elements of the evolving rivalry between EASDAQ and older, nationally based, vested institutional interests which are threatened by financial market innovation.

We develop the EASDAQ story and its implications in the four sections of this paper. In the next section we generate specific hypotheses about EASDAQ from several plausible arguments about institutional isomorphism. Section 3 is the detailed historical narrative tracing the origins and the development of EASDAQ in the context of those theoretical expectations. Section 4 summarizes the results and situates our explanation in the context of globalization arguments.

2. Discrete Hypotheses for Institutional Isomorphism

Institutional change occurs through the efforts of real actors. Systemic economic forces, even when measured accurately, may influence institutional outcomes, but they do not determine them. This point is frequently lost in popular discourse, where it is often said that "markets cause" a policy or institutional change. But it is also a problem in the academic literature. Strange refers to the "impersonal forces of world markets" (Strange, 1996:4).[5] Keohane and Milner focus on how changes in relative prices within markets may affect the preferences of particular sets of actors, but say very little about political processes of changing policies or institutions that result (Keohane and Milner, 1996:7).[6] Hypotheses set up to test globalization explanations need to specify who the actors are and by what mechanism they bring about institutional change.

The EASDAQ case falls under the broad category of institutional change and, in particular, it is an instance of institutional isomorphism—the similarity of institutions across different national contexts. In this section we delineate three general mechanisms that could drive institutional isomorphism. For each, we identify the actors and specify the mechanisms we expect to observe if the explanation were valid. We differentiate the arguments according to the way in which they answer these two central questions:

- Who identifies "the problem" to which institutional change is supposed to be a solution? Who is demanding change?
- What is the range of proposed "solutions" that are put out on the table, and why is a particular solution "chosen"?

The chart below is a summary of our hypotheses and the empirical expectations that connect to them about EASDAQ. We expand on these in the subsequent text.

a. Isomorphism Driven by Competition

The starkest definition of "globalization" is that it represents simply an increase in mobility of capital, goods, technology, and ideas (Weber, this volume, 2000; Clark, 1997; Scholte, 1997). The more easily each of these things can move across political and geographic boundaries, according to the logic of globalization, the higher the level of ambient competition in markets. Competition is supposed to drive change in institutional structures

CHART 4.1 Summary of Our Hypotheses

	Who Identifies the Problem?	Why is a Particular Solution Chosen?
Competition *Profound* *Convergence*	Financial Firms, High Tech companies, and large investors face increased competitive pressures and feel the need to support high tech industry. They demand action by official decision makers who sense Europe's competitiveness eroding in a globalizing market.	Efficient Institutions Squeeze out Alternatives
Mimesis		Satisficing—Actors copy NASDAQ because it works in the U.S.
Cooperation	Large institutional investors and governments want to reduce transaction costs and other costs associated with doing business across different financial systems. They interpret the problem as a coordination problem and seek a focal point around which to create a common standard.	NASDAQ is the 'first mover' and the salient focal point to resolve a coordination problem. Existing standards facilitate joint action and confer legitimacy on new entrants.
Ideology	The "solution" is what matters: universal principles (to be a modern economy means having a technologically-sophisticated enterprise market) inform people of the appropriate way to do things.	NASDAQ is a solution that identifies a problem. U.S. actors proselytize the notion that NASDAQ is the rational, progressive, and modern 'future' of capital markets and European elites accept it.

and practices among organizations that in the past were relatively insulated from each other and, in some sense, from the market.

Too-simple versions of this kind of argument have been the subject of intense (and justified) criticism. But there is a core explanation here that could account for EASDAQ through at least two clear causal pathways. First, assume that business ideas are distributed more or less randomly throughout the human population while the location of an idea (and the entrepreneur who carries it) is now becoming a weaker determinant of how it is developed and commercialized. In a world of increased mobility, ideas will migrate to whatever location is most conducive to their development and commercialization. Europe is an uncompetitive location, in part because of the lack of financing mechanisms for entrepreneurs. So new ideas are expected to migrate to America, leaving Europe disadvantaged in the ability to foster new high-technology (and high value added) industries that are essential to growth and prosperity for developed economies. Competition should thus create a strong felt need in Europe—among governments, financial firms, and large institutional investors—to improve financing structures for small entrepreneurial companies in order to retain and support technology startups.

Second, competition creates new opportunities for consulting and financial firms, mostly U.S.-based, to extend the range of their reach and operations into new places where the potential for profits is tremendous. American firms should respond to Europe's felt need, taking advantage of enhanced mobility to push the NASDAQ model as a solution to the problem, simply because it offers them a huge competitive advantage in an enormous potential market (since European firms are much less experienced in this kind of finance).

The fullest version of the competition hypothesis foresees profound convergence toward an efficient outcome (Ohmae, 1990).[7] According to this version, Europe's capital markets simply are uncompetitive and uncompetitive institutions can not be sustained in an open world economy. EASDAQ would thus represent the first step in a broad restructuring of capital markets as well as corporate finance and governance and ultimately equity cultures, toward a single best equilibrium close to the American model. The expectation of the profound convergence story is that the founders of EASDAQ would create a new enterprise equity market and choose the pan-European, NASDAQ form for reasons of efficiency. They would be pushed forward by mostly American financial firms coercing, persuading, and bribing them to accept the NASDAQ model as a solution to the problem Europe faces (DiMaggio and Powell, 1991:70–74). This model would squeeze out alternatives because it was a demonstrably more efficient means of capital allocation in a modern political economy.

There is a "softer" version of institutional change caused by competition that depends less on efficiency as a major driving force. This is "mimesis under uncertainty" (DiMaggio and Powell, 1991:69–70). Here the pressures of competition prompt actors to find solutions to their problems through the mechanism of *copying*. As in the fullest version, the relevant European actors should demonstrate a felt need to support entrepreneurs and startups. But, in this version, "markets" per se are not expected to identify an efficient or even necessarily a best-practice means for doing that. Put differently, the goal of facilitating high-tech innovation is clear, but the means to do so are poorly understood and ambiguous (Saxenian, 1994). In this extraordinarily complicated environment, the expectation is that Europe simply copies NASDAQ as a standard response: it seems to have worked to inspire high-tech in the U.S., so it makes sense to try it in Europe. Mimetic change carries no presumption of optimality or efficiency. It is closer to a satisficing move that rests heavily on a perception of adequate success among institutions that already exist. The creators of EASDAQ copy NASDAQ in response to competitive pressures on extant institutions, because NASDAQ seems to work well enough in the United States.

b. Isomorphism Driven by Cooperation and Interdependence

Cooperation can also be a driving force behind isomorphism. The central expectation here is that increasing interdependence and interaction between economies based in different national institutional environments makes the high costs of doing business across different systems insupportable. Globalization enhances incentives for cooperation—since the promise of common standards for equity markets (even, eventually, a boundaryless market) is substantial. This creates strong incentives to converge on *some* standard, precisely so that cooperation will become easier across political boundaries.

The difference with competition mechanisms is clear. A new entrant *competing* with existing organizational forms would take what exists as a baseline, and would have to do better—that is, be more efficient—in order to prosper. Older organizations would then converge "upwards" onto the new and more competitive form, leading to an upgrading of efficiency overall. In contrast, if cooperation is the driving force behind isomorphism, a new entrant has no incentive to exceed the efficiency of existing organizations or otherwise try to improve upon them. The incentive is simply to converge on existing standards so as to facilitate joint action and interchange with extant organizations.

Thus, the cooperation mechanism expects the NASDAQ model to be chosen not because it is efficient or competitive, but because it is the salient focal point for cooperation (Schelling, 1960). Isomorphism would result principally from a coordination-type game in which NASDAQ is the big, relatively successful, first-mover and hence the obvious focal point as well as a powerful source of institutional legitimacy for any new efforts. In the cooperation hypothesis, then, large institutional investors, governments, and other major actors are expected to choose the NASDAQ model as part of an effort to create one big world market for entrepreneurial companies. The impetus to cooperate is the source of a felt need among these actors to create a nearly common financial infrastructure for "global" business across political boundaries.

c. Isomorphism Driven by Ideology

Ideology can also be a driving force behind institutional isomorphism. There is a theoretical overlap here between institutional sociologists who focus on the diffusion of "world culture" and Gramscian IR scholars who see the emergence of a Gramscian hegemony of ideas at the international level (Boli and Thomas, 1999; Gill, 1990, 1997).[8] The major difference is that Gramscian hegemony is tied to the interests of a specific dominant class, even though it seems "natural" to everyone (Cox, 1993).[9] What these perspectives share is the notion that there exist sets of universal principles that tell people the appropriate and legitimate ways for doing things. These ideas are powerful drivers of behavior, more fundamental than demonstrable efficiency or other measures of material interest. To be a modern, developed economy at the start of the twenty-first century would mean having a technologically sophisticated market system for entrepreneurial and venture-type equity finance (Finnemore 1996b; Thomas et al, 1987). NASDAQ becomes a central symbolic target for an ideological wave, pulling other institutions towards it like iron filings to an institutional magnet.

The essential content of this ideological wave is modern "liberalism." The state's role in the allocation of capital should be reduced. So should the role of meso-corporatist capital market cartels, a fair description of many aspects of the existing corporate finance system in Europe. Stock markets, like other institutions, should be impartially regulated on the basis of codified rules with formal, juridical enforcement (Moran, 1994). Barriers to entry should be brought down because this constitutes rational, progressive, and modern change. Gramscian scholars, more so than "world polity" institutional sociologists, see embedded within this wave the interests of a specific dominant class which in some accounts is American, and in others is a transnational coalition of finance and high-technology corporations.[10] But in all cases, the key point about ideology as a driving force is that "solutions," such as to create an equity market along the NASDAQ model, are more important than, and have causal priority over, "problems."

Ideas will be present in all accounts of institutional change. If ideology is a *primary* driver in this case, then the idea of a market would be logically prior. European elites should adopt the institutional structure and practices associated with NASDAQ as an ideologically charged solution that seeks out and identifies a problem.[11] U.S. institutions like the Securities and Exchange Commission, multinational financial and consulting firms, and economists would be seen proselytizing their solutions. They would seek to spread their arguments about what is rational, progressive, and modern, to virgin territory (Finnemore, 1996a). They would offer to Europe the NASDAQ model as "the future" of capital markets, and European elites would accept it on that basis.

* * *

Each of these hypotheses is broadly consistent with general, systemic globalization arguments. The specific hypotheses differ in respect to who are the major actors and what are the primary mechanisms that push institutional change and shape the selection among options. The next section tells the empirical story of how EASDAQ came to be, and evaluates that history in the context of the expectations outlined above. Remember that each hypothesis isolates and privileges a single causal mechanism, for the sake of analytic clarity. It is possible (indeed likely) that more than one will manifest in the real data.

More than one causal mechanism is, in fact, demonstrable in the history. Competition is an important driving force, but the kind of competition in evidence is closer to the "mimesis under uncertainty" mechanism than it is to an efficiency mechanism leading to profound convergence. There is some evidence for the cooperation mechanism as well. Incentives to coordinate on something close to a single standard for an enterprise market structure reinforce what is already happening through mimesis. In contrast, we find very little evidence for ideological mechanisms as a primary driving force. To the extent that forces associated with globalization explain the origins of

EASDAQ, it is a "softer" version of global market forces that create incentives to copy what already seems to work well enough, to satisfice, and to coordinate with large, existing, and legitimate institutional structures like NASDAQ.

What stands out most strongly in the evidence, however, is the role of political institutions and particularly a political actor that lies outside the expectations of globalization-style arguments. We argue that the European Commission emerges as the key catalytic actor, putting together and supporting the coalitions that make EASDAQ happen. This role begins in the structuring of discourse and extends to the creation of laws, regulations, financing, and other concrete measures. The European Commission, more than any causal force derived from globalization arguments, shapes the environment within which EASDAQ emerges and is ultimately responsible for its creation.

We discuss in the conclusion broader conceptual implications of this finding. Our argument is consistent in part with other arguments that stress the primary causal importance of political institutions in governance structure changes associated with globalization.[12] But in stressing the catalytic role of EU institutions in particular, we part from globalization arguments that focus on the role of the state and come closer to perspectives on European integration that stress the autonomous and catalytic role of the Commission (Nugent 1997; Pollack, 1997, 1998; Sandholtz, 1998; Sandholtz and Stone Sweet, 1998). In fact, states resist the change at first and later try to redirect it into channels that promise to recapture their previous position. The struggle over creating new enterprise markets in Europe emerges as a microcosm of the politics of European integration, a re-enactment of struggles between supra-nationalist and intergovernmentalist principles which are at the core of debates about the future of the European Union.

3. The History of EASDAQ

a. Early Efforts

Equity markets for smaller companies (enterprise markets) have a history in postwar Europe. Italy opened its "Mercato Ristretto," in 1978. The Unlisted Securities Market (USM) began trading in Britain in 1980. France opened its Second Market in 1983. These markets were small, lightly regulated "over the counter" (OTC) exchanges that focused on attracting local companies and domestic investors. But with the partial exception of Britain's USM, they attracted relatively few of either. From 1963 to 1986 less than 600 companies listed on second-tier markets in the EC (in comparison, NASDAQ listed more than 5000 stocks from 1974 to 1984) (*Euromoney*, 1986b). And without substantial interest from investors these markets could not promise a viable "exit mechanism" for venture capitalists, who need to recoup their early and risky investments in startup firms by selling the successful ones on markets once they have "matured" sufficiently. These nationally based second-tier markets were too small and illiquid to generate the kind of trading volumes that would make for an efficient and desirable investment vehicle.

Two problems plagued the European second-tier markets and thus led to these low levels of participation and liquidity. First was the problem of insufficient regulation. Light regulation made it cheap for companies to sell their shares, but it also led to abuse and fraud that further chastened already wary potential investors. Second, the second-tier markets were not independent. The national European exchanges owned and managed the second-tier markets, preferring this arrangement as a means to limit potential competition. The lack of independence had two negative effects. Instead of a sustained commitment to the success of the new markets, the national exchanges approached the promotion of second-tier markets with ambivalence. There was also an adverse selection problem resulting from the perception that the national exchanges supported second-tier markets primarily as "feeder" or "nursery" markets for themselves. Since "successful" stocks on the OTC markets were expected to graduate to a "real" market listing, this tended to leave on the OTC markets a higher concentration of less successful stocks (Akerlof 1970). Light regulation only made the adverse selection problem worse (*Euromoney*, 1986a).

In 1985 a small group of European venture capitalists began to discuss openly the failure of these markets. The venture capital industry in Europe, small to start with, was being hindered by the lack of exit mechanisms for risky investments in startups. European "venture capital" firms were thus doing business primarily with existing companies, funding mergers and acquisitions rather than supporting new companies and entrepreneurial efforts. Meanwhile, U.S. venture capital firms were enjoying unprecedented success in the new industries of Silicon Valley, "exiting" with spectacularly profitable IPOs on the American NASDAQ market, and spurring the creation of new industrial sectors in high-tech computing and related technologies.

Eugene Schulman and Andrew Sundberg (of the Swiss consulting firms ELBAssociates and Consultex, respectively) in 1985 suggested that finance firms in Europe join together and create a self-regulating body, which they called EASD (European Association of Securities Dealers), to organize an OTC market for startup companies on a Europe-wide basis. They promoted the idea of trading in ECUs as a key to facilitating cross-order investing. While the issue of currency denominations would turn out to be an overly simplistic notion of the real impediments to pan-European trading, the ECU-EASD idea did attract some attention among other European venture capitalists as well as some American financial firms (particularly Baring Bros. Hambrecht and Quist and First Chicago). These firms purchased a multi-client study that ELBAssociates and Consultex completed in December 1985. While the study noted the partial success of Britain's USM and smaller analogues in Netherlands and France, it also pointed out that these markets had only one percent of the turnover of NASDAQ and thus did not constitute a viable exit mechanism. This explained the tendency for what European risk capital there was to go to the U.S. (*Financial Times*, 1985c; ELBAssociates and Consultex, 1985). The study did recognize the significant institutional and political obstacles to cross-border trading, but it emphasized the idea of ECU denomination as a way of making it somewhat easier to compare companies internationally.

The ECU-EASD study prompted some discussions within the venture capital industry, but the issue did not gain much traction beyond this small and politically weak group of actors.[13] Despite Schulman and Sundberg's considerable effort to win the support of the European Commission, the study did not attract the participation of the Commission, other EU institutions or national governments.[14] The October 1987 market crash brought even these limited discussions to an end (at least temporarily). Second-tier markets suffered in this crash much more than did the major markets. And while the national exchanges recovered rather quickly, the second-tier markets did not (Lerner, 1996: 2–3; Graham Bannock, 1994).

The 1987 crash exacerbated the problems of the second-tier markets and led to their demise. The national exchanges, which were running these markets as something of a sideshow, demonstrated very little commitment to keeping the second-tier markets alive and liquid (for example, by aggressively marketing their stocks) when the going got rough. And in a downturn, the already visible adverse selection problem only got worse. These issues surely were foreseen as risks before the 1987 crash, but the established markets remained opposed to the idea of creating truly independent and highly regulated OTC markets mainly because real success would have posed a threat to their traditional—and quite profitable—near-monopoly on securities dealing at a time when it was still essentially unchallenged (*Euromoney*, 1986a). Ultimately, success would have been more threatening to established markets than failure was.

The European Commission (as mentioned) did not participate directly in the ECU-EASD study and did not offer its support, but parts of the Commission had been closely involved since at least the early 1980s with related efforts to spur the venture capital industry in Europe. As the mid 1970s recession lingered on, the Commission began to take a more active role in the debate on the financing of technology and innovation, as a key issue for growth and competitiveness. The Commission sponsored between 1980 and 1982 at least three very large symposia on this subject for banks, venture capital firms, and other companies. Part of what emerged from these symposia was a broad consensus that small and medium sized enterprises (SMEs) would be increasingly important in developing and disseminating new technologies in Europe. But because banks were reluctant to lend to startups, and the established markets' conditions for listing stocks required long histories of profitability, it was clear that venture capital and viable "exit mechanisms" would have to take on a more prominent role in financing these firms. Reports from these meetings endorsed the idea of creating new markets to trade equities in startups, and suggested that governments ease restrictions on pension funds and insurance companies so that these large institutional investors could place more of their assets in such risky (but potentially high return) investments (Commission, 1980, 1981, 1982).

The Commission also convened and organized a working group of venture capitalists and bankers to develop plans for a formal organization promoting the interests of venture capital. In June 1983 this group presented its plan to a Commission-sponsored meeting of sixty major financial institutions, which approved the creation of a professional organization called the European Venture Capitalist Association (EVCA). While EVCA was set up as an independent organization, it acknowledges its founding as "the joint initiative of the industry and the European Commission" (*Business Week*, 1983; Commission, 1983; EVCA, 1998). From the outset EVCA developed its plans in conjunction with various Community initiatives, particularly programs for innovation and technology dissemination under DG-XIII's SPRINT (Strategic Programme for Innovation and Technological

Transfer) program (Commission, 1983, 1988:10). EVCA cooperated with the Commission on a number of projects during the 1980s, including a joint equity financing scheme for startups called the "Innovation Finance Project" (*Financial Times*, 1985a, 1985b, 1986; *International Management*, 1987).[15] While both EVCA and the Commission remained active in promoting the idea of a venture capital industry in Europe, their efforts, like those of the second-tier markets, were hampered by the 1987 market crash and the ensuing languor in European markets. The underlying issue—Europe's institutional weakness in financing the growth of high-tech startups—remained.

b. The Genesis of the Idea

The London Stock Exchange (LSE) decided in 1992 that it would close its second-tier market, the USM, due to poor performance and lackluster interest from the investing community.[16] A group of City finance figures responded by organizing CISCO (City Group for Smaller Companies) to lobby for a replacement. In September 1993 the LSE came back with a proposal for a new market, the Alternative Investment Market (AIM), to replace the USM, and CISCO accepted the idea of AIM as a "feeder market" to the LSE list, as better than nothing. But by this time CISCO had already dismissed the idea that a market with second-tier status and light regulation could address effectively the problems facing smaller companies.

At the time of the AIM announcement, in fact, CISCO had for several months been developing alternative sets of ideas for an independent entrepreneurial market. In discussions with NASDAQ official John Wall (who would later become a director of EASDAQ), several CISCO members had begun to develop a proposal for a free-standing "Enterprise Market" in the UK that would be modeled closely on NASDAQ. This new market would be a British market based in London but independent of the LSE (in ownership and regulation) and would use state of the art electronic trading. In June 1993, Ronald Cohen (with APAX Partners, a prominent venture capital firm) presented the idea, which he called EASDAQ-UK, to the annual meeting of the EVCA.

Cohen's proposal gained a sympathetic hearing at EVCA, although there was concern about the *national* basis and scope of the EASDAQ-UK idea. The lesson of the 1980s, at least for some EVCA members, was that the next effort at creating an enterprise market would not only have to be independent of existing markets. It would also have to be done on a pan-European basis in order to gain sufficient visibility and liquidity.

In summer 1993, Jos Peeters (of Capricorn Venture Partners, another prominent venture capital firm) wrote a plan for what was essentially a pan-European version of Cohen's idea. Although Cohen envisioned an eventual network of nationally based markets, Peeters proposed a pan-European market with a single integrated order and settlement system, as well as unified accounting and disclosure requirements making it possible to compare companies across national borders. Peeters believed that a network of subsidiary markets, regulated in their respective countries, would prove difficult and expensive. It would also give national market authorities an opportunity to abuse regulatory powers in order to inhibit the growth of a new market that might be in competition with the existing major national market.

In fact, the notion of building a pan-European market through "networking" of nationally based markets was not new. The European Commission's 1985 White Paper on Completing the Internal Market proposed exactly this model for securities trading. This led to the development of "Euroquote," which was basically an electronic quotation system across the Community. Using Euroquote, traders in Frankfurt could read off their screens the prices on the Paris Bourse. What they could not do was to easily buy and sell those stocks.[17] The conceptual flaw here was that illiquid and protected national markets do not become liquid or integrated in any real sense by linking them together through price quotations. Euroquote had no compelling commercial or economic logic and it soon fell out of favor.

Peeters and his EVCA colleagues certainly understood this problem. What was different in the summer of 1993 was that they now had at hand a possible solution, as a result of changes in Community law. Under the newly passed Investment Services Directive (ISD), EASDAQ could be set up in a single European state and still operate on a pan-European basis.

The Community's ISD passed the Council in May 1993. Although it would not come into effect until the beginning of 1996, it was clear in 1993 that the ISD heralded a major change in the European investment environment. ISD went quite far toward creating a single market for investment services (although not as far as some early proposals had hoped) (Steil, et al., 1996). The basic notion behind ISD was to create a "single passport" for investment services under the principle of mutual recognition. An investment services firm, licensed to operate under the regulations of its home country, would now be able to operate throughout the EU. Its right to do so effectively would be further insured by "host country" rules of conduct aimed at preventing states from favoring domestic firms. In conjunction with the Prospectus directive (passed in April 1989) which coordinated requirements for issuing a prospectus for the sale of securities, ISD was about to change the legal environment for cross border trading in Europe in a significant way.

The logic of the potential single passport for a new enterprise market was a compelling one for Peeters and his venture capitalist colleagues. Instead of subsidiaries having to pass muster of regulatory authorities in each member state, EASDAQ could now be set up under the rules of one state and could use the single passport mechanism to operate on a pan-European basis. In 1993, there was no shortage of innovative proposals for new enterprise markets.[18] The venture capitalists chose EASDAQ because they saw in it a way to save money; and more importantly, a way to bypass national regulatory authorities that they expected would try to protect existing national markets from competition. They also saw in the NASDAQ model a way to attract instant legitimacy. The missing ingredient was money to set up the market. Peeters and his colleagues approached the major national exchanges looking for financial support, but were turned away (as they expected to be). The necessary support would come, instead, from the European Commission. This is another principal reason the venture capitalists chose EASDAQ. Commission officials had expressed interest in a NASDAQ-like trading facility at a February 1993 EVCA seminar. Peeters and his colleagues had reason to believe EASDAQ's pan-European form would attract the Commission's support (Peeters, 1994).

c. The European Commission and the ISD

The single passport approach was indeed compelling from the point of view of the European Commission. Commission officials made the next move in July 1993, when they convened a series of informal discussions with Peeters, Cohen, and representatives of other major financial companies, to push the pan-European approach that they favored. With the promise of Commission support (financial and otherwise) behind them, the participants agreed that the logical next step would be to organize EASDAQ as the first pan-European market under the ISD.

Negotiating the ISD had taken the Council of Ministers nearly four years. It was clearly not a perfect document and the remaining ambiguities made it certain that implementation by member states would be contentious. For the Commission, supporting a pan-European enterprise market became a way to push the envelope of securities market liberalization, press member states on ISD implementation, and find out just how serious remaining impediments to cross border trading would turn out to be in the post ISD environment (*AFX*, 1995).[19] The Commission officials saw in EASDAQ a vehicle for promoting some of the principles of ISD—especially cross-border trading and venture capital financing in Europe—and for "learning by doing" about the practical impediments that stood in the way of these principles. Through the EASDAQ creation process that culminated with the start of trading in Autumn 1996, they would come to understand at least five serious impediments to cross border trading and venture capital financing in Europe—impediments that would have to be removed through political action.

The first challenge was the need to raise awareness of how difficult it really was for small companies to raise equity finance in Europe. European stock markets catered to the biggest firms (in 1995, the ten largest firms made up 23% of LSE capitalization, 25% in Paris, 74% in Amsterdam; in Frankfurt more than 80% of trades were in the 30 largest companies) and had very little interest in small firms (Commission, 1995: 5). Venture capital was extremely weak, in large part because of the lack of a stock market "exit" route for venture investments. In 1994, emerging companies in Europe attracted just over 300 million ECU in startup capital; that number more than doubled (to 653 million ECU) in 1995 but remained a small fraction of the 8 billion dollars of comparable business in the U.S. that year (*Financial Times*, 1996c). In practice, what are called venture capital firms in Europe tend to do more funding of mergers and acquisitions in existing companies, and much less funding of startups, than do their American counterparts. (In 1990–95 around 7% of European venture capital funds were invested in startups, compared with about 25% in the U.S.) (*Eurowatch*, 1996).[20] Less than 2% of European venture capital goes to biotech and less than 16% into computers and communications (comparable U.S. numbers are 24% and 46%). The conservatism of Europe's venture capital industry has often been described as having a cultural basis in risk aversion. While this is surely part of the explanation, it is clear that a multifaceted institutional problem was also central.

As a result of this weakness, an increasing number of promising European technology companies began to seek listings on NASDAQ. This was the core of a second challenge—to keep European companies at "home." In the first years of the 1990s, about 10% of new listings on NASDAQ were European firms. A few particularly visible examples of European companies choosing to list on NASDAQ (notably the French firm, Business Objects, a flashy and successful software startup), raised the political salience of issues of techno-nationalism (*Economist*, 1996). Particularly for small companies, geography matters greatly when it comes to raising capital. To list on NASDAQ, a foreign firm needs to develop a substantial presence in the United States. It will likely employ American investment banks and underwriters to handle the listing and accounting firms to adapt its books to American disclosure rules. Because it will want to sustain interest in its stock and promote an active community of researchers and brokers who follow the company, it will have clear incentives to locate more of its facilities and activities in America. Put simply, there is a tendency for ideas to migrate toward capital markets just as much as the reverse.

Apart from its impact on Europe's technology base, the migration of European firms to the U.S presented a real challenge to achieving the aims of ISD. If the most promising European companies with an international outlook would increasingly choose to list on NASDAQ, this could create a new adverse selection problem for European markets, which would stunt their growth. Smaller companies or those unable to break into the American market would be left without options, freezing their development. To avoid this, EASDAQ would have to manage a complex cooperative and competitive relationship with the much more powerful NASDAQ.

The third challenge concerned the demand for shares among investors. Even if promising companies listed on a pan-European enterprise market, would investors buy their shares? The key challenge here was to attract institutional investors—insurance firms, mutual funds or their equivalents, pension funds, and so on.[21] Large American institutional investors were interested in expanding their business in Europe—in the first half of 1996 at least four major U.S. investment firms specializing in NASDAQ-type stocks opened offices in London, and a major new joint venture between Hambrecht & Quist with Financiere Saint-Dominique (prominent U.S. and French venture capital firms) was announced. But EASDAQ could not rely too heavily on American investment, since beyond a certain point this would put the new market in competition with NASDAQ. To be successful

EASDAQ would have to tap new sources of investment—most importantly, European pension and investment funds.

Although most of the major European institutional investors continued to purchase bonds, property, and fixed income vehicles in preference to stocks, pressures for change were mounting as the gap in performance with relatively free-wheeling U.S. institutional investment firms grew over the course of the 1990s. The political problem here lay in a multitude of laws and restrictions that in most continental European countries tightly restrict the investment practices of pension funds. (In Germany for example, externally financed pension funds, of which there are relatively few, may hold only 20% of their assets in foreign investments, and only about 35% of assets can be invested in equities). An arcane set of accounting practices and tax regulations generally make it even less attractive for these funds to hold equities, and in practice their investments have been more conservative than mandated by law (Buxbaum, 1991; Steil et. al., 1996). While some of these restrictions were justifiably prudential, others were clearly obsolete in terms of modern investment theory and remained on the books mainly as protectionist measures. And while the demography of an aging population headed for retirement combined with a decline in the yield of fixed investments was putting pressure on pension funds in particular to seek higher returns, the political sensitivities surrounding this issue remained extreme and the consensus in Europe was that reform would be gradual.

The bright side of this picture was the opportunity for EASDAQ. In principle, the demand for higher risk equities was healthy in Europe—87% of European financial institutions held NASDAQ shares in 1995, and European investors regularly buy around 20% of NASDAQ IPOs (when the listing is for a European company, closer to 35%) (Commission, 1995:6). A 1995 survey by Coopers and Lybrand found that approximately two-thirds of 100 big European institutional investors would in principle consider purchasing EASDAQ shares (although in small numbers to start, until the prospects for the market were clearer). The key issues for investors were liquidity and transparency of the market, the availability of high-quality research on the listed companies, and market independence. EASDAQ would be designed around those requirements. A major advantage of a pan-European market would be increased trading volumes along with active participation by a large number of market makers, together contributing to liquidity. Independence was assured by setting up the new market outside of existing national markets. And the Commission was committed to supporting the development of new research capacities in European investment firms, brokerage houses, and market makers (*Economist*, 1995).

The fourth challenge was to accelerate the implementation of ISD in practice. The ISD in principle would remove many (but by no means all) legal, tax, and regulatory impediments to a pan European securities market. In the eyes of the Commission officials, EASDAQ became a means to "learn by doing" about the remaining obstacles to efficient cross-border trading, such as differences in tax practices regarding capital gains, corporate takeover rules, and the like. Commission officials believed they could attempt to force the issue by creating a new vehicle that would exert pressure on national governments. The guiding principle for EASDAQ was national treatment. An investor buying shares in a company listed on the pan-European exchange should receive treatment no less favorable than if the investment were made in a domestic capital market. But transforming this abstract principle into practical arrangements would be a major challenge for the new market. No one could really foresee in advance the full range of legal, regulatory and tax issues that might arise.

The fifth challenge was broader, more ambiguous, but ultimately most significant for the potential impact of EASDAQ on the European political economy. The creators of this market and their supporters in the European Commission are quite unabashed in arguing the need for Europe to move toward what they call an "equity culture."[22] Households in continental European countries are much less apt to invest in stocks than are Americans (about 5% of German households own stock, as compared to about 50% of American households) (Steil et. al., 1996:16). Mutual funds and other collective investment schemes are still the exception in most countries. Pension funds (as we noted before) are biased heavily toward conservative fixed-income investments. A consequence is that continental Europe's major stock markets have very low capitalizations relative to the size of economies, compared with the U.S. and the UK.[23] Relatively few companies are listed and even fewer are actively traded (Steil et. al., 1996:16).[24]

This is consequential for financing and corporate governance, as well as for general issues of distribution of economic benefits and power throughout societies (Blair, 1995). Clearly, signs of gradual change were emerging particularly in France and Germany, where the heavily publicized flotation of Deutsche Telekom shares in November 1996 caught a wave of interest in stocks among institutional and individual investors (Ziegler, 2000, in this volume). But change in behavior is slow and corporate governance issues connected to shareholding, as well as tax and takeover laws, have changed much less. More generally, risk-aversion is still the rule for most investors and many potential entrepreneurs. Whereas American venture capitalists and entrepreneurs are comfortable with the knowledge that many of their efforts will collapse, failure and bankruptcy remain a scarlet letter in most of Europe.

A single new institution like EASDAQ will not by itself revolutionize deeply held cultural practices that are embedded in many other existing institutions. But if those cultural practices are indeed starting to change, then EASDAQ could take advantage of that opening and also become a driving force to push change forward more broadly and rapidly. The success of NASDAQ had precisely this effect in the U.S., helping to drive reform at the NYSE and elsewhere, changing (probably forever) the investment environment for institutions and individuals, and creating opportunities for entrepreneurs in emerging industries. This is the ultimate motivation behind EASDAQ's corporate and private supporters. For the Commission, it was this *plus* the important element of pushing forward European integration through EASDAQ as the first real pan-European stock market. And Commission support would be essential to manipulating the debates and the political environment around these five challenges so that EASDAQ could get started.

d. The European Commission and the Political Environment for EASDAQ

Pushing forward the ISD was not the Commission's only objective in facilitating early discussions about EASDAQ. The Commission's role in the process was also part of a much wider set of relevant EU initiatives in the early 1990s. These initiatives grew out of a broader political discourse focusing on corporate finance and competitiveness in Europe, and they brought various EU bodies deeply into the process of creating EASDAQ in a way that had not happened in earlier pan-European efforts of the mid 1980s.

Two problems, interconnected to some degree, were central in that discourse. The first and most important was the *jobs and unemployment* issue. By 1993 unemployment was the single most salient political issue for the European Union, and for many of its member states as well. The gradual end of Europe's lingering 1980s recession had brought recovery to corporate profits, but not to jobs. Unemployment in Europe, with the partial exception of Britain, remained stubbornly high and looked set to get worse. While the U.S. economy had created 19 million jobs during the 1980s, Europe had created only 6 million jobs (the majority of which on net were in the public sector) bringing the unemployment rate in the EU to 10.7% in 1993 (OECD, 1996; 1994:54). Excitement over the potential of the single-market project and its 1992 target (which had been high at the end of the 1980s) was wearing thin by 1992, as the jobs problem did not seem to benefit much (if at all) from liberalization.

The second issue was about *technology*, a long-standing concern for the EU (Sandholtz, 1992). The explosive growth of new industries in 1990s America, symbolized by (but not limited to) bio, information, and communications technologies, was not matched in Europe. "Completing" the single market had not made a substantial difference here, either. And while there was no shortage of contending explanations for this weakness, one politically popular argument held that Europe's weakness was much less in basic science than in the ability to capitalize on and commercialize products of that science. Worse still, potential European entrepreneurs with new ideas were said to be taking those ideas to the U.S. where a vibrant corporate financial infrastructure and an exciting entrepreneurial culture provided just what they needed. The reverse side of fears about a technology brain-drain was a form of techno-nationalism, now extended to the regional (European) level. Europe's competitiveness would depend, supposedly, on keeping some of these new technologies "at home" and developing them into products sold by "European" companies.

The reality of both of these issues was, of course, more complicated than the salient political perceptions. But those perceptions were strong and influential both in the Commission and within many national governments. They were also interconnected, as an article from the *Financial Times* reflects: "A steady stream of mainly technology based European companies is crossing the Atlantic to seek a NASDAQ listing. . . . This flight depletes Europe's indigenous technology base and its ability to create jobs because many of the companies raising capital relocate to the U.S." (*Financial Times*, 1995d).

In the language of the hypotheses from section 2, this made up a "felt need" among European governments and the institutions of the EU, who identified unemployment and the high-technology issue as problems that demanded a solution. But the means for "solving" this compound problem were (and remain) poorly understood. Arguments about competitiveness, how to reduce unemployment, how to foster the growth of high-technology industries, and how to maximize the payoff in jobs from doing that, spawned literally hundreds of reports, studies, and proposals from both private and government sources. Without clear answers, mimesis would be an expected mechanism of isomorphic change as actors search for solutions to their problems through copying of existing institutions. Mimesis does happen, but it happens in the particular context of a European Union political discourse that shapes the selection of possible initiatives.

Some of the things that the Europeans told themselves they would have to do to solve the technology/unemployment problem were politically wrenching and controversial—in particular, increasing the "flexibility" of labor markets and trimming excesses of the welfare state. More attractive were proposals that could be promoted as win-win dynamics, or virtuous circles where practically everyone stood to gain.[25] Efforts to spur investment and programs to improve infrastructure for new technology ventures could be promoted as having this characteristic, at least in principle. In this kind of political environment, it is not surprising that notions about the importance of fostering new technologies, particularly through the creation of SMEs, which were said in turn to be the major engine of job growth, became a central part of the European discourse.

NASDAQ became an important political symbol of how this virtuous circle might have worked in the U.S. A 1995 Commission report on European capital markets made the argument this way: SMEs in Europe suffer a substantial comparative disadvantage because they cannot easily raise equity capital. High-technology and startup companies suffered particularly because (with the exception of biotechnology stocks in London) loss-making firms could not list on European markets (around a third of NASDAQ IPOs come from companies that are not making profits at the time of listing). Even profit-making smaller companies found it hard to list on European exchanges, due to the very high costs of listing and the general lack of interest in small-company stocks. While it was not possible to calculate the opportunity costs or to know with any precision how many of these companies would seek external capital for expansion and growth if they had the opportunity, the explosive growth of small and high-tech American firms listed on NASDAQ pointed to the availability of venture capital and equity financing mechanisms as a key component of growth (Commission, 1995). Closing the virtuous circle were the jobs created by these companies. A widely cited 1995 study argued that while only 0.04% of U.S. companies were listed on NASDAQ, those companies created almost 16% of the new jobs in the American economy in the first four years of the 1990s.[26]

In the early 1990s these kinds of arguments insinuated themselves into EU discourse through a wide swathe of its many different institutions. DG-XIII (and particularly its SPRINT program) which had been closely involved with EVCA in the 1980s continued to play an active role, in part by commissioning a private study of company demand in Europe for a new EASDAQ-type enterprise market (Coopers and Lybrand, 1995). DG-XXIII ("Enterprise Policy, Distributive Trades, Tourism and Cooperatives," created in March 1990) became involved in the context of promoting the growth of the venture capital industry in Europe (Commission, 1998). After securing approval from the Council, DG—XXIII convened a series of round-table discussions with bankers and finance people to push forward the EASDAQ project. In a 1993 memo, the Belgian Presidency for the first time laid out in explicit terms the argument linking equity finance, SMEs, jobs, and technology together. Early in 1994 the European Parliament while discussing the business environment for SMEs called on the Commission to explore the feasibility of a new enterprise market. In July 1994 the Economic and Social Committee made the same request (CES, 1994). The Council in 1994 approved a framework program in research and technology that said in order to improve the dissemination of technology in the EU, Europe needed a more vibrant venture capital industry which in turn needed exit mechanisms for its investments. The second biannual report of the Competitiveness Advisory Group, commonly known as the Ciampi Report, in 1995 stressed the importance of appropriate capital markets for SMEs and specifically endorsed the EASDAQ idea (*Reuter*, 1995).[27] A major 1995 Commission report stressed the potential for job creation by startup firms that could raise money on EASDAQ (Commission, 1995). In May 1996 the Parliament's Economic and Monetary Affairs Committee endorsed EASDAQ, and in July 1996 the entire Parliament adopted a resolution backing EASDAQ (*Reuter*, 1996).

Three arguments appeared repeatedly in these different strands—the link between financing of new high-tech SMEs and employment (jobs); the importance of keeping new technologies in Europe (techno-nationalism); and pushing forward implementation of the ISD (liberalization). The predominant EU discourse about European political economy, shaped by these three arguments, in turn would shape the economic, business, and legal environ-ment in which EASDAQ evolved.

e. EU-Industry Collaboration and the Founding of EASDAQ

In early 1994 representatives from DGs II, XIII, and XXIII met with representatives of EVCA, including Jos Peeters. They decided that the time had come to push the EASDAQ project forward as a priority, mainly because the political environment had become much more auspicious. They would sell the proposal on the merits of the "jobs" argument and use this logic in national capitals to counter resistance from established stock exchanges and banks. Participants at this meeting agreed to commission a feasibility study for EASDAQ, and the contract for the study was given to EVCA in February of 1994. The DGs contributed money for the study and startup expenses (approximately 80,000 ECUs) for a working group. EVCA put up funds of its own and solicited funds from NASDAQ, which began to express a firm interest in the European venture; and from the French market authority, SBF (Societé des Bourses Françaises),[28] which was also enthusiastic about the idea (*Independent*, 1994).[29]

EVCA began its study in early winter 1994. Jos Peeters chaired the key group (Capital Markets Working Group) which met officially three times between February and November of 1994. Proposals became reality very fast. As early as June 1994 in Paris, Peeters' group agreed to create both EASD—an independent European Association of Securities Dealers—and EASDAQ—the market. Clearly this mirrored central elements of the Amer-ican arrangement between NASD and NASDAQ (*Venture Economics*, 1994). But more importantly, EASD was set up specifically as a nonprofit organization, so that it could accept funds from the Commission.

In November 1994, EASD held its inaugural meeting in London. Full members of EASD were market makers and underwriters; associate mem-bership was open to other companies or organizations with an active interest in EASD activities. The organization began with 26 founding members. DGXIII and DGXXIII provided another sum, about ECU 500,000 ($600,000) to help EASD with startup costs during its first few months.[30] Although all the major European stock market authorities were invited to join, none did so. The London Stock Exchange simply ignored EASD's invitation and sped up its own plans for the opening of AIM.

EASD was primarily a political construction. Unlike the American NASD, an organization with regulatory obligations created in the 1930s by the U.S. Congress, EASD is a nonprofit organizational device whose principal purpose, in the early months, was to funnel funds from the Commission to support the EASDAQ project. EASD today advises on market rules and policies, and corporate governance standards, coordinates activities aimed at improving small company finance in Europe, and develops programs to train auxiliary institutions in the skills they would need to make EASDAQ work, but it never had a de facto regulatory role.[31]

This is very different from the relationship that then existed between NASD (the membership and self-regulatory organization) and NASDAQ (the market), which was in 1994 under investigation by the U.S. Securities and Exchange Commission. The SEC was responding to widespread allegations of price collusion among market makers, who make up a large portion of NASD's membership. The dominant position of market makers in NASD and the fact that NASD was the operating authority for NASDAQ supposedly gave NASD incentives to run the market in ways that favored the market makers.[32] Even though the Europeans copied the NASD/NASDAQ relationship in name, they never had to worry about inherent conflicts of interest of this kind. The relationship between EASD and EASDAQ was close, but EASDAQ's regulator is the Belgian Banking and Finance Commission.

The day following EASD's inauguration, Peeters' capital markets working group presented a detailed plan for the EASDAQ market to more than 200 prominent finance people at a meeting in London. The general reaction among private actors was a cautious optimism, seeing EASDAQ as a good idea in principle, and one in which they would get involved if it began to take off.[33] Representatives from the established markets in Europe were much more hesitant. Edmond Israel, President of the Federation of European Stock Exchanges, expressed doubt as to whether there really was a problem to which EASDAQ could be a solution. And if there was a problem, he argued that it would be more sensible to organize markets on a national level, and under the control of existing national markets, which had the "necessary expertise" (*Reuter*, 1994). This prescient comment foreshadowed the reaction of national market authorities to the implicit threat that EASDAQ, if successful, would pose to their very profitable established quasi-monopolies. But as it was early in the process and still more than a year before the coming into force of the ISD, the threat remained amorphous and the defensive response was lackluster. This was important because if the established markets had put substantial energy into obstructing EASDAQ at this time, they certainly could have complicated matters and might have succeeded in blocking the venture.[34]

Twenty-one companies committed themselves in November 1994 to launch EASDAQ as a private, for-profit company. Seven U.S. investment firms, including several major venture capital firms (e.g. Alex, Brown; Montgomery Securities; and Robertson, Stephens) were part of this group. In May 1995 EASDAQ incorporated under Belgian law with central offices just down the street from Berlaymont. Aside from being close to EU institutions (which had a symbolic as well as practical importance), incorporating in Belgium made sense because Belgium did not have a very large and powerful national market to which EASDAQ could be a threat. Also, Belgium was the first country to transpose fully the ISD into national law.[35]

EASDAQ promotes itself as a state-of-the-art institution which provides a distinctive and better forum for raising capital than do other European markets. It is set up to appeal primarily to fast-growing, entrepreneurially managed smaller companies with at least a pan-European (and preferably, an international) outlook wishing to raise funds for expansion. To trade on EASDAQ, a company must have total assets above 3.5 million ECU and capital reserves of at least 2 million ECU. It needs a sponsoring institution and at least two market makers. There are restrictions on the selling of shares by directors and large shareholders for a specified time after listing, and the prospectus must be approved by an EU market authority under the terms of the EU Prospectus Directive.[36]

Most important, companies must meet stringent and uniform reporting requirements modeled after NASDAQ rules—an annual report with audited financial statements, as well as unaudited quarterly reports. Financial information must meet the criteria of either of two international benchmarks—International Accounting Standards (IAS) set by the International Accounting Standards Committee, or U.S. Generally Accepted Accounting Principles (GAAP). These reporting requirements were far more demanding than is the case for reporting on almost all other European stock exchanges. They were also standardized and internationally transparent, specifically to make it possible for EASDAQ stocks to be compared easily across national borders, as well as with NASDAQ stocks (and thus to facilitate cross listing between EASDAQ and NASDAQ) (Tirez, 1997).

EASDAQ also uses a quote-driven trading system with a multiple market-maker structure. As in NASDAQ, at least two market makers openly compete for investor orders in a stock by stating prices at which they are willing to buy and sell that stock on a transparent computer network. (The market making system of trading contrasts with the model of "specialists," used on the New York Stock Exchange, where one individual firm controls the flow of orders in a particular stock.) Competition among market makers is supposed to offer better prices for investors (as compared to what is essentially a monopoly situation when one specialist firm controls prices), although the empirical evidence on this point is controversial enough that it is hard to claim market-making is a more "efficient" system. Even for smaller companies, where market-making has often been assumed to improve liquidity, the evidence is mixed (Bessembinder and Kaufman, 1997; Chan and Lakonishok, 1997). Market makers also have incentives to maintain research coverage of companies and to disseminate information so that investors will purchase shares.[37]

f. The Nationalist Reaction

EASDAQ poses a threat to vested interests and semi-monopolies in European equity markets and has set in motion a series of reactions. These interests (as we discussed earlier) fought against and managed to dilute some of the more liberalizing provisions of the ISD, and they succeeded in postponing its implementation for several years. EASDAQ threatened to bring the battle to their doorsteps more quickly than anticipated.[38] At first most of the established markets and larger investment firms dismissed the idea of a pan-European enterprise market. But as EASDAQ took shape quickly in the autumn of 1994, outsiders began to recalculate and then to react in defense.

Two things are notable about the character of the reaction to EASDAQ. First, very few people specifically denied or even deeply disagreed with the assessment that there existed a substantial socio-economic problem and that EASDAQ was responding to a real, identified need in Europe. Instead, naysayers mostly argued that the problem could be better "solved" through existing institutional channels. This evidence works against seeing ideology as a primary causal driver. Europeans did not have preconceived and consensual notions about an appropriate or legitimate solution or action to take. And they did not readily accept the idea of a NASDAQ equivalent across Europe, or respond on the basis of ideology proselytized by U.S. firms and banks.

A second notable characteristic of the reaction is that EASDAQ did not provoke a nationalist backlash with purely national solutions. Rather it shifted the entire debate toward European solutions, but of different types. The reaction consisted of *nationally based* enterprise markets that would be tied together by a set of limited linkages and flows while remaining under the control of established markets and interests. In contrast to the Commission's vision of pan-European models embodied in EASDAQ, the established stock exchanges responded with an "intergovernmental"-type solution—a European network of national markets.[39] This evidence works against seeing competition driving profound convergence to efficient models. At a minimum, there was considerable uncertainty about what would be "efficient" and how to get there. And established interests were manipulating and shaping outcomes, rather than themselves being shaped by competitive forces in the world economy.

The first reaction to EASDAQ came just following the 1994 agreement by Peeters' group to create EASD and EASDAQ. The London Stock Exchange (LSE) pushed forward the opening date of AIM, at least in part to preempt possible future competition from EASDAQ. From its start in June 1995, however, AIM has not posed a direct competitive challenge to EASDAQ. Although AIM began with a relatively large number of listed companies, it did not attract much attention or interest on the part of institutional investors and market makers. (*Financial Times*, 1997). This is because AIM belongs to the tradition of nationally based "feeder markets"— its listed companies are small, almost entirely UK-based, and spread over an eclectic range of industries. The idea of AIM was still to "graduate" successful companies "upwards" to the LSE.[40] The LSE regulates AIM and although it stiffened regulation somewhat in 1997 (in response to EASDAQ's perceived success as well as a number of confidence-undermining problems at AIM) the market is still too lightly regulated for institutional investors and not a serious challenger (*Global Investment Magazine*, 1997; *Financial Times*, 1995b; Mazars Neville Russell, 1999).[41]

A more significant reaction and one with greater impact on EASDAQ came from the market authority that had been most closely involved with, and supportive of, the EASDAQ project. Just three months after the formal decision to launch EASDAQ, reports began circulating in Paris that the French bourse was reconsidering its support. In January 1995 a Paris study group released a report considering the prospects of a new enterprise market *solely in France*, with a vague future European component. The Roger-

Faurre Report as it was called stressed the potential demand for listing small companies within France and led to discussions in the SBF about creating its own "Marche des Valeurs Nouvelles" (*Financial Times*, 1995a). In February, the Paris bourse announced that it was pulling out of the EASDAQ project and creating its own enterprise market, now called "Nouveau Marche," in Paris (Roger and Faurre, 1995). This decision was taken in consultation with the French Tresor, where officials were uncomfortable specifically with the European Commission's role in EASDAQ.[42]

The original plan for Nouveau Marche called for the market to be owned by SBF. It would aim to list smaller companies and those with primarily a national rather than an international business focus (a Feb. 1995 feasibility study identified more than 100 candidate firms in France) (*Financial Times*, 1995c). Trading would take place via a mixture of market-making and a central order book with two price fixings daily, the latter provision recognizing the possibility of low liquidity for at least some of the potential stocks. Although the proposal in these early stages lacked detailed rules, it was clear that some of the regulations were being designed to inhibit foreign and particularly U.S. securities firms from taking part in the market (*Financial Times*, 1996d).

Nouveau Marche at its inception clearly was a nationalist reaction against EASDAQ. It was driven by a short-term concern that French companies would list on a new pan-European market, and a longer term concern about the threat that a successful pan-European market would pose to the established complex of institutions in the French market system (including perceived "control" of French technology companies). When the SBF announced formal rules for the Nouveau Marche in September 1995, it was quite explicit about this motivation and the competition with EASDAQ. Dominique Le Blanc, chief executive of Nouveau Marche, said that Europe needed enterprise markets but that "a market must be based on national character" (*Observer*, 1995). That meant continued control of the market by established institutions: the Nouveau Marche would have a nominally independent operating authority, but that authority (Societe du Nouveau Marche) would be set up as a wholly owned subsidiary of SBF. Two questions still needed answers: would the Nouveau Marche be substantially different from the nationally based efforts of the 1980s (which had failed)? and why, given that experience, would companies and investors find the new market attractive?

Possible answers to these questions started to take shape over the course of the next year. Early in 1996, the established markets in Germany, Belgium, and Italy each announced that they too were planning to open "second markets" like the Nouveau Marche. (The Netherlands and Austria made similar announcements in September and November, respectively.) As in France, vested interests from the national financial systems, with the support of their governments, created these new markets to divert the challenge that EASDAQ posed to nationally based, quasi-monopolistic arrangements. The major German banks, for example, were particularly strong opponents of EASDAQ. While they acknowledged explicitly a need to develop new mechanisms for venture capital investment, they strongly preferred that all of this happen within national channels that they could continue to control. (*Financial Times*, 1996b).[43] The German government supported the creation of a national market for SME's as part of its own broader agenda in financial market liberalization (as well as the beginning of a more serious discussion about the future of pension funds) but it too focused on the nationally based alternative. By the spring of 1997, Germany, Belgium, the Netherlands, and Italy had all opened their new national markets for small companies.

Anticipating the growth of these national enterprise markets and the competition from EASDAQ, the SBF in March 1996 took a first step toward clarifying its original vision of a European arrangement—a European "network" of national enterprise markets, dubbed Euro.NM. The idea of Euro.NM is to establish limited cooperation between national, autonomous markets (rather than the single, pan-European model of EASDAQ).[44] An official of the Societe du Noveau Marche put it this way: "The concept hinges on the belief that many companies, institutions, and intermediaries still have nationalistic mind-sets and will therefore prefer a domestic market for their listings, although they may want pan-European 'exposure.' "[45] Pan-European exposure means that each national market in Euro.NM will maintain electronic links with its partners, so that traders in one country could in principle sell and buy shares traded on another country's exchange.

The network presently consists of five new markets—France's Nouveau Marche, Germany's Neuer Markt, Euro.NM Belgium, the Netherland's Nieuwe Markt, and Italy's Nuovo Mercato. The new or future markets in Denmark, Sweden, Switzerland, Finland, and Norway said they would join soon (*Financial Times*, 1998j; *Wall Street Journal*, 1999a; *Financial Times*, 1999a). As of October 1999, Euro.NM had 300 listed companies, including 40 cross-border listings and 23 dual listings, mostly with Nasdaq.

Euro-NM at its inception sought to preserve national listing and regulatory requirements. For example, there were no plans to harmonize accounting standards across the markets. Euro.NM members also agreed that national markets would not compete for each other's domestic companies when seeking initial public offerings of stock (IPOs). These and other beginning rules were designed to protect national market institutions and limit competition. The downside was that the economic rationale for Euro.NM remained doubtful for the same reasons that the Euro-quote initiative of the late 1980s failed: illiquid and protected national markets do not become liquid or integrated through electronic linkages alone. Under pressure from EASDAQ, the shortcomings of Euro.NM had already come into focus by late 1996 and this led to a set of changes in market rules.

The French Nouveau Marche in its first few months of trading attracted more than twenty companies, but most were very small, and not in particularly high-tech or growth oriented sectors.[46] The early performance of these shares was mediocre, and there were a few spectacular losses. In November 1996 Nouveau Marche announced changes in its rules that unmistakingly moved it closer to the EASDAQ model. First, it tightened regulation and oversight of potential listings, including stricter reporting requirements and restrictions on the disposition of original shareholdings. It also announced a new preference for companies in high-tech sectors as well as somewhat larger companies, although still mainly with a national focus. Finally, the Nouveau Marche began to focus more on the possibility of dual listings with NASDAQ (*Financial Times*, 1996d).

When the Deutsche Boerse (Germany's main stock exchange) created the Neuer Markt in March 1997, it paid close attention to the burgeoning competition among the new markets and avoided many of the early mistakes of the Nouveau Marche. Of the Euro.NM markets, the Neuer Markt is closest to the EASDAQ/NASDAQ model in its rules and its focus on high-quality entrepreneurial companies. Most important are the disclosure requirements—at least transitional accounts to IAS or U.S.-GAAP and quarterly reports—and a highly selective admissions process.

Like the Nouveau Marche, the Euro.NM network has continuously announced intended changes to its original design, though there are reasons to doubt the most difficult of these will be fully implemented. As of June 1999, Euro.NM had announced three harmonization agreements and had made the most progress in the areas of admissions criteria (*FinancialTimes*, 1998b; Euro.NM, 1999). If implemented, the remaining changes would move Euro.NM even further toward the EASDAQ model. They include, for instance, compulsory quarterly reports.

But the exact commitment of the member markets has from the start been vague,[47] and two recent developments have cast doubt over the durability of Euro.NM: the Neuer Markt's rapid growth has eclipsed the other Euro.NM markets, and the parent exchanges of the Euro.NM members have formed two rival blocs in competition over trading of Europe's largest companies.[48] There are still a host of additional national regulatory differences that perpetuate the segmentation of the member markets. With the partial exception of the Neuer Markt, participation on the Euro.NM markets is still largely national.[49] Ultimately, Euro.NM officials (unlike EASDAQ's) do not believe that elimination of barriers to cross-border trading is a necessary ingredient of a successful enterprise market and they have not made this a priority (Economist, 1998b). As Euro.NM's director of marketing explains: "Clearly it would be very helpful if there was a common regulatory approach in place across Europe, but we don't feel it impacts on the development of Euro.NM."[50] This suggests, again, the weakness of ideology as a primary driving force, as well as the deficiencies of profound convergence arguments that rely on competition as the primary cause.

A competition is certainly in the works between EASDAQ and Euro.NM.[51] But there is little evidence to suggest that profound convergence around efficient models will be the result. In one of the latest rounds, EASDAQ filed a complaint with the EU over French and Italian tax laws which, it claimed, favor investment in national markets. The Commission ruled in EASDAQ's favor, but the French market authorities have delayed any change in the offending rules. (*AFX*, 1998; *Financial Times*, 1998i;).[52] The tax issue represents the extent to which EASDAQ has become a vehicle for "learning by doing" about the practical impediments that stand in the way of achieving ISD's goals. National governments and financial communities have formidable resources at their disposal, including (but not limited to) tax incentives and the recent success of the Euro.NM markets, especially the Neuer Markt, in attracting new listings, in part, reflects these advantages—which stem more from the political context of the competition than they do from efficiency criteria.

It is also clear that legitimacy of institutional forms and cooperation with large and highly legitimate existing institutions have become central issues in this ongoing rivalry. The officials at both EASDAQ and Euro.NM make public efforts to demonstrate how their new markets are cooperating effectively with NASDAQ, which includes attempts to match its institutional form. EASDAQ appears to have won this round of the competition, but not without making changes of its own. The success of the Euro.NM markets in listing larger numbers of national companies has finally brought into the picture the large American investment banks.[53] The banks recently invested in EASDAQ in an attempt to stop the growing fragmentation of the new European high-tech company segment. Part of their strategy is to turn EASDAQ into the single European trading platform, not just for companies that launch their initial public offerings on EASDAQ, but also for Euro.NM companies with dual-listings and American companies who want exposure to European capital.[54] The recent investment of American banks in EASDAQ is evidence for isomorphism through cooperation and standard setting. The American banks invested in EASDAQ, not in the Euro.NM markets, because the EASDAQ model is familiar. It is what they know and think is legitimate.

It is true that the new markets are trying to reduce costs and, more broadly, transaction costs. The banks probably did reason that EASDAQ would save them money. But this is not because the EASDAQ model is more efficient than integrated national markets. The banks believed EASDAQ could save them money because its model complied with the NASDAQ standard they already use. And this contrasted sharply with the Euro.NM markets. Recent research casts serious doubt about the relative efficiency of the NASDAQ model, and even more serious doubt about the ability of market participants to assess its efficiency. Several studies conclude that, through the historical period when NASDAQ was expanding within the U.S., trading costs actually were higher on NASDAQ than on the NYSE. It was precisely during this period that EASDAQ's founders copied large parts of the NASDAQ model (Bessembinder and Kaufman, 1997; Christie and Schultz, 1994; Huang and Stoll, 1996). In fact, since 1987 U.S. regulators, in response to unfair trading practices, have forced the NASDAQ model to undergo three sets of major changes.[55]

The creators of new markets in Europe believe that sending signals about coordination on a salient, legitimate focal point, will lead to levels of market participation and liquidity necessary for effective financing of high-growth startups and will prove critical to their success. This is certainly not news for EASDAQ officials, who consciously selected the NASDAQ model from the start in part for this reason. NASDAQ may not have been the most "efficient" means to solve the problem of finance and/or corporate governance for venture-type enterprises. But NASDAQ had been successful enough in the U.S. to become a salient focal point for the creators of EASDAQ to emulate, and cooperate with. NASDAQ was the first mover. EASDAQ's creators recognized the legitimacy that accompanied this and saw in a pan-European copy of NASDAQ a vehicle for promoting broader political goals and a possible solution to European problems, especially regarding jobs and technology. Europe's traditional equity markets were perceived as highly protected, meso-corporatist, insular institutions which provided semi-monopoly profits to big investment houses but impeded the growth of companies, and particularly those in emerging technology sectors, that can and do create new jobs. The creators of EASDAQ believed that traditional equity markets had lost legitimacy. This opened the door in their eyes to new institutions, which could gain early legitimacy from copying the NASDAQ model and real economic advantages from cooperating with it.

But promoting Euro.NM on the basis of its similarities to NASDAQ marks a dramatic shift of institutional strategies in a very short window of time. Euro.NM officials now claim they have "modeled a lot of [their] regulatory framework on NASDAQ, designed to meet the needs of Europe."[56] This was not part of the initial objective of the member markets of Euro.NM whose priorities lay in protecting the vested interests of idiosyncratic national financial systems, rather than attracting institutional investors familiar with the NASDAQ model.

One thing is certain. In catalyzing the creation of EASDAQ the Commission provoked a process that may now be heading in unintended directions. Competition has become an important cause of institutional change at present and probably in the future, but it is not the kind of competition envisaged in globalization arguments. It is a competition with EASDAQ, which itself was the product of a Commission-inspired process embedded much more tightly in European political economy and the politics of European integration. And the ultimate outcome will likely be close to the Commission's original goals in two important ways. Small European entrepreneurial companies will have better access to equity financing, and national financial markets for high-growth companies will have become more European.

g. The Hypotheses and the Evidence

We differentiated our starting hypotheses from each other, in terms of how each answers two questions—who identifies the problem, and how is a particular solution selected? In response to the first question, the evidence at first cut supports a variant of the competition mechanism. There clearly was a "felt need" among politically weak financial actors, especially venture capitalists, who were prompted into action by LSE's closure of the USM and by the continued urgings of the European Commission. More important, however, was the "felt need" among European governments and the institutions of the EU. The point is that understanding of the problem was deeply embedded within a particular political discourse, catalyzed by the Commission, that linked together unemployment, technological competitiveness, and financial liberalization. Competition may be a key underlying cause of change but it does not explain very much about a process that was set off more directly by the actions of the Commission.

The evidence is not as strong in support of the cooperation mechanism. NASDAQ did offer early support for the EASDAQ project and its intent in doing so was to reduce the obstacles and costs to trading by extending its model across the Atlantic. While this is consistent with expectations we derived from the cooperation hypothesis, NASDAQ did not play a leading role in the creation process. Also contrary to the expectations of the cooperation hypothesis is our finding that, one, large institutional investors (with clear incentives to facilitate cross-border trading) did not have a substantial role in EASDAQ's creation. And, two, governments along with EU institutions believed the problems of unemployment, technological backwardness, and European financial integration were more critical than the need to facilitate cross-Atlantic trading.

There is relatively little evidence to support expectations of the ideology hypothesis. Europeans first identified problems and only subsequently sought solutions to those problems. They do not appear to have been driven by a strong ideological attachment to the idea of equity markets as a primary driver, and there is very little evidence of successful proselytizing of the idea by American or multinational firms early on in the history. The ideas that mattered in the causal process are more closely tied to the Commission and its assessment of the political economy of European integration, than they are to a "world culture" or Gramscian-style hegemonic wave associated with modern liberalism.

The second general question that differentiates our hypotheses, is why a particular solution is chosen. The evidence on this question strongly supports the mimesis under uncertainty mechanism. Uncertainty hampered the ability of European governments and EU institutions to "select" the most efficient model or even to be certain about "best practice," despite their recognition of the need to support entrepreneurs and startups. The creators of EASDAQ copied much of the NASDAQ model because of the perception that it had contributed to a virtuous circle of jobs and technology through financing for entrepreneurial companies in the U.S. A new European market could gain early legitimacy from copying the well-established NASDAQ model, regardless of its generic "efficiency" or optimality in a European setting. This is precisely the kind of causal process that sociological arguments about mimesis specify.

Cooperation mechanisms seem to play a supporting causal role in this stage of the process. NASDAQ was able to promote its own model to Europe, in part because it represented a focal point on which other big players with whom EASDAQ would need to cooperate had already settled. Some of the major U.S. venture capital and high-tech investment banks clearly preferred the NASDAQ model because they were well positioned to benefit from a market that resembled the one they knew best. They brought with them to Europe a trading system and set of practices which they understood, not necessarily because it was efficient but precisely because they were expert in it and could reap economies of scale from standardization. The promise of common standards for equity markets (perhaps, eventually, an effectively boundaryless world market), is substantial. Indeed, the ongoing reforms in Euro.NM markets illustrate some of the power of this causal force.

Overall there is very little evidence to support the simplest competition hypothesis, the story of profound convergence toward an efficient outcome. Efficiency matters in some ultimate sense, but the creators of EASDAQ could not have known what the most efficient "solution" to their understood problem would be. Finance theory and evidence is inconclusive on the relative merits of NASDAQ and other models of financing; recent work has tended to find a set of incentives built into the NASDAQ model that lead to noncompetitive pricing practices (and are thus inefficient). The literature continues to raise more questions on this score.[57] That is not surprising, given the ambiguous nature of EASDAQ's aims. But it is still worth noting in the context of a debate about globalization and institutional change that takes efficiency criteria seriously in many contexts, as a benchmark or baseline against which institutional change can be measured. By some accounts, financial markets would seem to be a relatively straightforward setting for efficiency criteria since a "price" looks like a precise metric. It is, but what a price actually measures—even in financial markets—is not clear.

In sum, aspects of globalization-style mechanisms are demonstrable in the history. Competition is an important driving force for institutional change, but the kind of competition in evidence looks more like a mimetic mechanism than it does like an efficiency mechanism. Cooperation is also a driving force, as actors respond to incentives to coordinate on something close to a single standard for an enterprise market and reinforce what is already happening through mimesis. But these arguments, even after we refined and differentiated them, take too much for granted. They bypass the critical role of political institutions and specifically the European Commission, which in the EASDAQ case set the context within which the other driving forces play themselves out. The Commission played the key role in creating a legal and political environment for EASDAQ. It brought together an unusual coalition of public and private actors that together made it happen. And it shaped many of the elements of the rivalry between EASDAQ and the nationally based competitors that EASDAQ spawned. The conclusion further develops the general point about political catalysis, and situates it within other arguments that emphasize the role of political institutions as major catalysts in this kind of process.

4. Conclusion

Two important points frequently get buried in both popular and academic discussions about globalization. First, institutional change requires actors. There is no such thing as "market-driven" change in the absence of what those actors do. This is just as true in the creation of new equity markets as anywhere else. Second, in any particular instance of institutional change, it is difficult to determine a priori who the critical actors will be and by what mechanism they will drive institutional change. Most analyses assume that institutional change is the result of pressures from *economic* actors who stand to benefit from increased international mobility of capital, goods, technology, and ideas. These arguments tend to treat national institutions and political institutional actors as channeling or *resistive* forces (Keohane and Milner, 1996). Other analyses assume *national* institutional actors promote change (Moran, 1991; Helleiner, 1994).

While institutional actors often have a fundamental role in promoting change, they are not, however, always national. The EASDAQ story brings institutional actors back into the picture in clear focus, in part by highlighting the pitfalls of making presuppositions about who the critical actors are. It also illustrates a special role for the European Commission, a *regional* European institutional actor—not as a blockading institution, but as a catalysis for change.

To highlight these points, we compare the origins of EASDAQ to recent related research on the contemporary reform of *existing* equity markets.[58] (Sobel, 1994; Vogel, 1996). The modal explanation of the LSE's "big bang" reform in 1986 and less substantial but still significant reforms in French and German markets focuses on actors who are empowered by their relative position in the international economy. (Cerny, 1989; Kapstein, 1992; Moran, 1991, 1994; Sobel, 1994; Vogel, 1996). The key actors are "customers"—the large institutional investors who control big blocks of money and can now move that money easily across borders. Capital mobility and advances in information technology shift power toward these customers at the expense of "suppliers"—that is, the equity markets—which are still nationally based. Institutional investors use their new power to demand reform that suits their interests—generally, liberalization accompanied by standardized, transparent, and more efficient regulation (Vogel, 1996). This demand is met primarily by states, because no other body (neither private actors nor international organizations) has the power, authority, or legitimacy to supply in a credible way the desired reforms. National regulators in many cases seek to match international regulatory standards, to promote the international role of their financial centers (Moran, 1991; Vogel, 1996).

The reform process is thus characterized as strategic interaction and particularly a coordination game among big actors, over the ultimate form of the institutional changes. The complexity of markets and the uncertainties attached to "efficiency" ensures that the processes of defining the problem and offering up solutions will be social and political as well as economic in nature (Moran, 1991; Sobel, 1994; Vogel, 1996). U.S.-based actors, particularly U.S.-based institutional investors, the Securities and Exchange Commission and the Treasury Department, (sometimes in collaboration with London-based actors) in the end are said to use their market power to influence the shape of equity market reform programs (Kapstein, 1992; Moran, 1991).

The creation of new European enterprise markets reflects some of the dynamics that these market reform arguments identify. But the process differs also in two interesting ways. First, EASDAQ (and the Euro.NM markets as well) were not pushed forward by "customers", who then pressured national governments for change. European institutional investors are less powerful than those in the U.S. And they did not play an important role in the early stages of the new markets" conception and creation. Their interest in EASDAQ early on was tentative at best. Instead it was European venture capitalists that were the key economic players in the creation of EASDAQ. This historical fact raises a central question: how could a small and not very powerful interest group (European venture capitalists) generate the driving forces behind EASDAQ?

The answer lies in the empowering and catalytic role of European Union institutions, as well as the political discourse about competitiveness, jobs, and technology that those institutions fostered and shaped. This is the second way the EASDAQ story differs from the modal explanation for change in equity markets. EASDAQ was not the outcome of strategic interaction among big international or state actors responding to the new incentives of a globalized economy. Global forces are in the background. EASDAQ's creation, timing, and form were much more clearly and deeply embedded in the politics and discourse of European integration. The European Commission played the central causal role by fostering a favorable political environment, bringing together a coalition of public and private actors, providing resources and shaping the nature of the ensuing rivalry between EASDAQ and Euro.NM.

As in many other contexts, "pan-European" in this budding rivalry means a serious challenge to established vested interests that are nationally based. Brokerage houses, banks, and equity markets in most continental European states have been to a considerable degree insulated from serious competition. EASDAQ threatens many established (and quite lucrative) relationships among those actors. It is no surprise that many established market institutions oppose EASDAQ. Clearly, the established institutions know that the business environment for equity markets in Europe is going to change. The surprise of EASDAQ was that it happened so fast and that the challenge came so quickly. For the most part, the established national institutions do not deny the significance of the problem that EASDAQ is directed at. Instead, they seek to redirect "solutions" into national channels that they can still hope to control, at least in part, for a longer time. A battle over vying regional forms now defines the national vs. pan-European market rivalry, and this ensures, as in the case of EASDAQ's creation, that the process of institutional change will continue to be deeply embedded in the political dynamics of European integration—at least as much as in the economic driving forces of globalization.

The central role of EU politics in the creation of EASDAQ illustrates a creative and catalytic role for political institutions in processes of globalization. Catalysis means that the EU seeks to bring together strategic coalitions and to be indispensable to that process, while remaining substantially independent in the pursuit of its own goals through those coalitions (Lind, 1992). The European Commission was the focal point for a broad discourse about jobs, technology, and competitiveness that set the political-economic environment for EASDAQ. Changing the financing structure for new companies was a much more politically attractive option for responding to unemployment and technology concerns than pressing for more "flexible" labor markets or greater public funding of research and development. In that context, EASDAQ looked like a positive-sum solution. The EU set the legal environment for EASDAQ. The ISD made a pan-European effort feasible, and Commission officials pushed efforts in that direction and away from a network model in part as a way of driving forward ISD implementation. The Commission took very practical measures to catalyze the process of creating EASDAQ. It seeded the early discussions among venture capitalists, financed the creation of EVCA, and provided both support and financing for EASD as well as direct support to EASDAQ. All of this fit within the context of broader EU goals—principally, liberalization of financial markets, and on a pan-European basis.

Elements of several of our globalization hypotheses are present in this history, but in the final analysis global market forces and the mechanisms associated with them did not create EASDAQ. Nor were American venture capital firms and investment banks central in the early conceptualization of EASDAQ, despite the compelling logic of moving toward one big "world" enterprise market, a quasi-global NASDAQ. It is true that EASDAQ is now part of an increasingly international set of rules and institutional norms in equity markets. Convergence, in this sense, is like a coordination game— NASDAQ as the big and successful first mover has become the focal point for coordination, and a strong source of institutional legitimacy for a new institution like EASDAQ.[59] But European actors chose "convergence" to address regional problems, promote regional political agendas, and create rapid legitimacy for new institutional solutions—not primarily to reduce transaction costs amidst international competition.

Established national markets and their auxiliary institutions were at first mostly impassive toward EASDAQ (with the exception of the SBF, an early supporter). That changed as the new market rapidly took shape and the threat was clarified. The SBF dropped its support for EASDAQ and began the move toward nationally based enterprise markets (later, in a regional network model) that would compete with EASDAQ. A competition between EASDAQ and Euro.NM continues, but that competition appears to be in large part about who will be able to coordinate most effectively with NASDAQ. Cooperation, not competition, has always defined EASDAQ's relationship with NASDAQ. It now appears that the same dynamic (effective cooperation with NASDAQ) will define the terms of rivalry between EASDAQ and Euro.NM.

The EU confronts resistance in its efforts to promote integration of European capital markets. Nationally based market actors are playing a role that is much more familiar in the globalization literature—impeding change and trying to protect extant relationships by controlling the challenge. The Commission is in a delicate position, intensified by the emergence of the Euro.NM effort. EU officials strive to appear even-handed about EASDAQ and Euro.NM but their preferences for EASDAQ are clear (Commission, 1995).[60] If the EU continues to play an active role in this process, it will probably shape many elements of the evolving rivalry between these two strands of institutional change, just as it has up till now.

Acknowledgments

For criticism and comments, we thank Karen Adelberger, Chris Ansell, Michael Barnett, Aaron Belkin, Melani Cammett, Nicolas Jabko, Peter Katzenstein, Paulette Kurzer, Benjamin Read, AnnaLee Saxenian, Steven Vogel, and J. Nicholas Ziegler

Endnotes

1. These range from corporate governance, to what individuals do with the money they earn, to how societies plan to take care of retired persons, to what kinds of businesses are viable, and beyond.

2. A market maker is a company that "makes markets" in a particular security. Market makers use their own capital, research, retail and/or systems resources to represent a stock. They compete with each other for investor orders to buy and sell the stocks they represent.

3. See counterarguments in Berger and Dore, 1996 and Weiss, 1998.

4.   These are some of the images of American labor markets publicly held in Europe. We are not taking a position, one way or the other, on their accuracy.

5.   For example: "The argument put forward is that the impersonal forces of world markets, integrated over the postwar period more by private enterprise in finance, industry, and trade than by the cooperative decisions of governments, are now more powerful than the states." (Strange, 1996:4).

6.   Keohane and Milner recognize that changing preferences do not translate directly into political coalitions, bargaining power, or policy outcomes, but relegate the intervening processes here to a status of "exogenous" factors. (Keohane and Milner, 1996:7). Garrett and Lange (1996) take an additional step by isolating a couple of arguments about particular institutions.

7.   For a critical analysis see Boyer, 1996.

8.   Some institutional sociologists now refer to World Culture Theory as World Polity Institutionalist Theory (WPIT).

9.   Gramscian IR scholars disagree over the nature of the contemporary international order. For contrasting views, see Gill 1997 and Cox 1997.

10. See Gill 1997 for an elaboration of the distinction.

11. Gramscians would expect to see these institutional structures and practices wrapped in an ideology that is closely identified as "American" or "Anglo-Saxon." World polity institutional sociologists would expect the ideology to have become separate from any individual national actor, and to have taken on more autonomy (perhaps through International Organizations)

12. For examples, see Helleiner 1994, Moran 1991, and Vogel 1996.

13. Author's interview with a European Commission official, June 1997.

14. There was renewed interest in the ECU-EASD in 1989, which ended in a similar failure to attract support. Schulman and Sundberg participated in a roundtable in Brussels in June 1989 where Commission officials showed support and requested a proposal for a pilot project. (ELBAssociates and Consultex, 1985, 1989; ELBAssociates et al. 1989)

15. This was renamed the Venture Consort Scheme in late 1985, after the Commission increased its overall contribution.

16. It was widely believed that the LSE went out of its way to kill the USM. Critics argued that the LSE wanted the Official List to be the platform for entrepreneurial companies for two reasons: It would mean that the LSE could ignore the financing needs of smaller quoted companies and it would stave off future competition from other markets. The LSE claimed the USM had become redundant when new EU rules forced the LSE to loosen its listing requirements. (*Financial Times*, 1994; Interview with CISCO official, April 1999; interview with LSE official, April 1999.)

17. They would have had to have a physical presence and legal status in France. Other obstacles included differing accounting standards, regulatory differences and various protectionist measures.

18. In addition to EASDAQ, there were, among others: the European Private Eq-
     uity Exchange (EPEE) proposed by Baring Venture Partners, the European
     Communities Automated Securities Exchange (ECASE) proposed by Madden
     & Co, a European arm of NASDAQ, and the Dutch Participation Exchange
     (PAREX) of the Dutch Venture Capital Association. (EVCJ, 1993, 2: 14–16.)

19. Author's interviews with European Commission officials, June 1997.

20. This was true even in England, where a single VC firm (3i) did the majority
     of startup funding.

21. Individual investors were not expected to be important buyers for some time —
     far fewer households in Europe than in America own equities, and for those
     that do there is a pronounced tendency to invest in "blue-chip" stocks (Coopers
     and Lybrand, 1995:8

22. Author's interviews with European Commission officials, June 1997.

23. End of March 1997 market capitalizations as % of GDP: UK 160, U.S. 118,
     France 45, Germany 40 (*Economist*, 1997a).

24. In 1995 Germany for example, of 810 listed companies, 400 are classified as
     illiquid (annual trading turnover less than 15 million Dmarks) and trading in
     just three stocks (trading Deutsche Bank, Daimler Benz, and Siemens) ac-
     counted for about one-third of total trades.

25. Or at least no large, organized interest groups (like labor unions) would lose
     in a highly visible way.

26. Cognetics Inc., June 1995 quoted in Commission, 1995:5.

27. Named after the former Italian prime minister who headed this "blue ribbon"
     group.

28. The SBF changed its name to Parisbourse in 1999.

29. Author's interviews with European Commission officials, June 1997

30. Ibid.

31. EVCA venture capitalists at this point were primarily concerned about gener-
     ating funds. Even with the Commission's first contribution, they were having
     trouble paying the small staff and the many legal and financial consultants they
     had hired. They created EASD to make it easy for the Commission to make
     further contributions. (Author's interview with former EVCA official, April
     1999)

32. These issues, first made public in an academic study, were prominent in 1994
     and led to a class action suit and a series of SEC, DOJ, and independent
     committee investigations. In 1995 NASDAQ underwent a number of reforms
     aimed at upgrading regulation surveillance and enforcement, tightening
     spreads between bid and ask prices, and dividing into two separate entities
     NASD's dual roles of regulating the member firms and operating the NASDAQ
     market. In 1996 the SEC adopted new rules that change the way NASDAQ
     handles customer limit orders (Christie and Schultz, 1994; Christie, Harris and

Schultz, 1994; *Economist*, 1998a; *New York Times*, 1997a, 1997b; Smith et al, 1997; United States Securities and Exchange Commission, 1996).

33. Author's interview with EASDAQ official, June 1997.

34. Author's interview with European Commission officials, June 1997.

35. In accordance with the ISD, two bodies are responsible for regulating activity on EASDAQ. The first is the internal EASDAQ Market Authority. The second is the Belgian Banking and Finance Commission.

36. Under the Prospectus Directive, each EU state names a regulatory body as its "competent authority" with the power to vet prospectuses. Once a prospectus is approved by a competent authority, it can be issued across the EU.

37. In Autumn 1995 EASDAQ contracted with the International Securities Market Association to develop and operate the quotation and trading system, which would be based on TRAX (an existing trading system for Eurobonds). The new trading system is linked directly to Intersettle, a cross-border settlement system run by a consortium of Swiss banks. This integrated system promised to reduce the transaction costs of trading to a minimum. But EASDAQ recently announced it would replace Intersettle with Euroclear and Cedel Bank, the two biggest clearing and settlement systems used by international investors, and it also planning to replace its trading system. EASDAQ officials attributed the changes to growth in trading and Intersettle's relatively smaller client list. Others claim the original trading and settlement systems were a mistake because EASDAQ's traders do not have accounts with Intersettle (*Financial Times*, 1998h; *Securities Industry News*, 1998; *Securities Industry News*, 1999).

38. Author's interviews with European Commission officials, June 1997.

39. For contemporary examples of the "intergovernmental vs supranationalist" debate, see Moravcsik, 1991 and Cameron, 1992.

40. Indeed, many people inside the LSE were never convinced that AIM was a necessary intermediate step, because they believed that the LSE itself could meet the needs of smaller companies. Author's interview with LSE official April 1999; Author's interview with CISCO official, March 1999.

41. The LSE created a second new market, Techmark, in 1999, in effect acknowledging the failure of AIM to compete.

42. Author's Interview with French Treasury (Tresor) official, June 1999.

43. Author's interview with EASD official, May 1999. The discussion picked up steam after Qiagen, a German biotech firm, became the first German company to list on NASDAQ, in the summer of 1996. The German Neur Markt is not even nominally independent—it operates directly under the aegis of the Deutsche Börse.

44. Again, there is an obvious analogy here with broader arguments about the nature of intergovernmental versus supranational politics in the EU. See endnote 39.

45. Clive Pedder, quoted in *European Venture Capital Journal*, 1996. He was Euro.NM's director of marketing but has recently moved over to EASDAQ (*Financial Times*,1998g).

46. In March 1997 the Nouveau Marche listed 22 companies, with a total market capitalization of just 1.5 bn dollars. EASDAQ listings were on average 3 times as large.

47. The press release following the second harmonization agreement announced that "Member markets have committed to implement these new conditions within their individual rulebooks *as quickly as possible*" (Euro.NM, 1999); italics added.

48. The LSE and the Deutsche Boerse have agreed to merge, pending the approval of their respective members. In its current form, the merger (to be called iX) would terminate the Euro.NM, as it would combine London's new Techmark and the Neuer Markt into a Frankfurt-based partnership with Nasdaq. Meanwhile, the owners of three of the other Euro.NM markets—the national exchanges in Paris, the Netherlands and Belgium—have also agreed to merge into a rival exchange called Euronex (Economist 2000).

49. One of the biggest obstacles to closer linkages has been the differing trading systems. Here the issues are similar to the conflicts which broke apart negotiations over the creation of a single platform for Europe's 300 biggest firms. Several exchanges, including the LSE, Deutsche Boerse, and the French Bourse, have recently invested large sums in new electronic trading systems. They cannot agree on whose system should be used. (*Financial Times*, 1999b, 1999c)

50. Clive Pedder (now head of marketing and communications at EASDAQ) quoted in *Financial Times*, 1998a.

51. Officials from both markets sometimes say this explicitly and at other times deny it.

52. Author's interview with EASDAQ official, May 1999.

53. EASDAQ's new investors include Morgan Stanley Dean Witter and Goldman Sachs. J.P. Morgan and Merrill Lynch invested indirectly via Tradepoint.) Knight/Trimark (the largest market maker on NASDAQ) also invested in EASDAQ at the same time. (Financial Times, 1999d)

54. The United States Securities and Exchange Commission (SEC) recently agreed to let American companies list on EASDAQ without registering with the SEC. (New York Times, 1999b)

55. In the first set of changes, following the aftermath of the 1987 market crash, the Small Order Execution System (SOES) became mandatory, thus diminishing the power of NASDAQ market makers to ignore small orders. The 1994–96 price-fixing scandal prompted the second set of changes including the reorganization of the NASD/NASDAQ relationship (see endnote 32). Fi-

nally, the SEC has recently increased competition by making it easier for Electronic Communications Networks (ECNs) to trade stocks in what was once a market maker monopoly and has announced its desire for a single national quotation that would include ECN as well as trades executed through the NASDAQ system (Smith, et. al., 1998; New York Times, 1999a).

56. Clive Pedder quoted in *Financial Times*, 1998a.

57. Barclay 1997; Bessembinder and Kaufman, 1997; Chan and Lakonishok, 1997; Huang and Stoll, 1996; La Plante and Muscarella, 1997.

58. In one sense, the creation of new enterprise markets is a piece of a general and ongoing restructuring process in European equity markets (*Financial Times*, 1995d, 1998f; *Wall Street Journal*, 1998).

59. Although hard to quantify, status, prestige and legitimacy are important components in a company's decision to list on a particular market (Baker and Johnson, 1990). A common analogy is to hospitals which try to attract physicians, who in turn bring in the business (patients). Markets try to attract companies to list, which in turn bring in the investors.

60. Author's interviews with European Commission officials, June 1997.

References

AFX 1995. "Commission aims to ease startup for EASDAQ, Nouveau Marche Stock Markets." *AFX News*, October 27.

———. 1998. "EASDAQ files complaint with EU over French, Italian market access." *AFX News*, June 30.

Akerlof, George 1970. "The market for "lemons": Quality, uncertainty and the market mechanism." *Quarterly Journal of Economics* 84, August.

Baker, H. Kent and Johnson, Martha 1990. "A survey of Management views on exchange listing." *Quarterly Journal of Business and Economics*, 29(4) (Autumn): 3–20.

Barclay, Michael J. 1997. "Bid-ask spreads and the avoidance of odd-eighth quotes on NASDAQ: An examination of exchange listings." *Journal of Financial Economics* 45:35–60.

Berger, Suzanne and Dore, Ronald, 1996. eds, *National Diversity and Global Capitalism*, Ithaca: Cornell University Press.

Bessembinder, Hendrik and Herbert M. Kaufman 1997. "A comparison of trade execution costs for NYSE and NASDAQ-listed stocks." *Journal of Financial and Quantitative Analysis* 32(3) (September): 287–310.

Best, Michael 1990. *The New Competition*, Cambridge: Harvard University Press.

Blair, Margaret 1995. *Ownership and Control: Rethinking Corporate Governance for the Twenty-first Century*, Washington, D. C.: Brookings Institute.

Boli, John and George M. Thomas 1999. eds. *Constructing World Culture: International Nongovernmental Organizations Since 1875*, Stanford, CA: Stanford University Press.

Boyer, Robert 1996. "The convergence hypothesis revisited: Globalization but still the century of nations?" in *National Diversity and Global Capitalism*, edited by Suzanne Berger and Ronald Dore, Ithaca: Cornell University Press.

Business Week 1983. "Entrepreneurs come of age on the continent." *Business Week*, December 12, 45–48.

Buxbaum, Richard M. 1991. "Institutional owners and corporate managers: A comparative perspective." *Brooklyn Law Review* 57: 1–53.

Cameron, David 1992. "The 1992 Initiative: Causes and consequences." In Alberta M Sbragia, ed. *Euro-politics: Institutions and Policymaking in the "New" European Community*, Washington, D. C.: Brookings Institution.

Cerny, P. G. 1989. "The "Little Big Bang" in Paris: Financial market deregulation in a *Dirigiste* System." *European Journal of Political Research* 17(2): 169–192.

CES 1994. Economic and Social Committee Opinion, CES Opinion IND 521, European Union, July.

Chan, Louis K. C. and Lakonishok, Josef 1997. "Institutional equity trading costs: NYSE versus NASDAQ." *The Journal of Finance* 5(2) (June): 713–35.

Christie, William G. and Paul H. Schultz 1994. "Why do NASDAQ market makers avoid odd-eighth quotes?" *Journal of Finance* 4(9) (December): 1813–40.

Christie, William G., Jeffrey H. Harris, and Paul H. Schultz 1994. "Why did NASDAQ market makers stop avoiding odd-eighth quotes?" *The Journal of Finance*, 4(9) (December): 1841–1860.

Clark, Ian 1997. *Globalization and Fragmentation*, Oxford: Oxford University Press.

Coleman, William D. 1996. *Financial Services, Globalization, and Domestic Policy Change*, New York: St. Martin's Press.

Commission 1980. Bull EC (or Bull EU), European Commission Bulletin of the European Union/European Community, France, Bull EC 9–1980, 2. 1. 95.

———. 1981. Bull EC (or Bull EU), European Commission Bulletin of the European Union/European Community, France, Bull EC 12–1981, 2. 1. 18.

———. 1982. Bull EC (or Bull EU), European Commission Bulletin of the European Union/European Community, France, Bull EC 11–1982, 2. 1. 24.

———. 1983. Bull EC (or Bull EU), European Commission Bulletin of the European Union/European Community, France, Bull EC6–1983, 2. 1. 46.

———. 1988. "Proposal for a Council decision concerning the implementation at Community level of the main phase of the strategic programme for innovation and technology transfer (SPRINT), 1989–1993." Commission of the European Union, Brussels, COM(88)426 final, 20. 7. 1988.

———. 1995. "Reporting on the feasibility of the creation of a European capital market for smaller entrepreneurial managed growing companies." Commission of the European Union, Brussels, COM(95)498 final, 25. 10. 1995.

———. 1998. Web: *www.europa.eu.int/en/comm/dg23/guide"en/general.html*, DG-XXIII, European Commission.

Coopers and Lybrand 1995. *Corporate Finance: EASDAQ—a New Opportunity?*

Cox, Robert W. 1993. "Gramsci, hegemony and international relations: An essay in method." In Stephen Gill, *Gramsci, Historical Materialism and International Relations.* Cambridge: Cambridge University Press, pp. 49–66.

——— 1997. "Introduction." In Cox, Robert W. *The New Realism: Perspectives on Multilateralism and World Order,* New York: St. Martin's Press.

DiMaggio, Paul J. and Walter W. Powell 1991. "The iron cage revisited: Institutional isomorphism and collective rationality in organizational fields." In DiMaggio and Powell, eds., *The New Institutionalism in Organizational Analysis,* Chicago: University of Chicago Press, pp. 63–82

EASDAQ 1999. *www.easdaq.be/pc/enc"02.htm,* January 20.

Economist 1995. "Europe's second markets: Small but not yet beautiful." February 25, 80.

———. 1996. "Not quite the right moral." July 13.

———. 1997a. May 24, 74.

———. 1997b. "Behind America's small-business success story." December 13, 51–53.

———. 1998a. "Collusion in the stockmarket." January 17, 71.

———. 1998b. "Europe's equity markets: Nothing Ventured." April 4, 79–80.

———. 1998c. "Europe's great experiment." June 13, 67–8.

Economy, Elizabeth and Miranda A. Shreurs 1997. eds. *The Internationalization of Environmental Protection.* Cambridge, UK: Cambridge University Press.

ELBASSOCIATES S. A. and Consultex S. A. 1985. *The feasibility of creating ECU-EASD: A European Association of Securities Dealers to trade over the counter in ECU denominated shares,* Switzerland.

———. (July 1989), *Creating EASD & EOTC: The European Association of Securities Dealers who will create a European over the counter market to trade securities denominated in ECUS,* Switzerland.

ELBASSOCIATES S. A. et al. (September 1989), ELBASSOCIATES S. A., Consultex S. A. Scottish Financial Enterprise, *Creating the European Association of Securities Dealers and an integrated European securities market: A proposal to manage a programme for the European Commission,* Switzerland.

Euromoney 1986a. "Innovation in international capital markets." January, 125–27.

———. 1986b. "Europe's fragmented over the counter markets are about to be swept along by the tide of internationalization now flowing over most listed capital markets." March 11.

Euro. NM 1999. Website: *www.euro-nm.com/pressreleases/pr980422.html*, November 8.

European Venture Capital Journal 1996. "Latest Developments in Europe's New Growth Companies Markets." May 1.

Eurowatch 1996. " Why European Venture Capitalists Want Their Own NASDAQ." (8) April 1.

Evans, Peter 1997. "The Eclipse of the state? Reflections on stateness in an era of globalization." *World Politics* 50: 62–87.

EVCA 1998. Web: evca.com/overview.html, European Venture Capital Association, March 16.

EVCJ 1993. European Venture Capital Journal, 26, EVCA, Brussels.

Extel Examiner 1998. "Nouveau Marche, Euro. NM Belgium hook up; herald Europe-wide main bourse net." February 18.

Financial Times 1985a. "EEC to take venture capital stakes." March 25, 4.

———. 1985b. "Commission likely to increase venture capital scheme funds." December 20, 2.

———. 1985c. "Support found for over the counter market." December 24, 2.

———. 1986. "Venture capital companies seek funding from EEC." March 25, 3.

———. 1994. "Special care for young companies." March 8.

———. 1995a. "Paris may set up exchange for small companies." January 13, 18.

———. 1995b. "Lex Column: Small Companies." February 16, 22.

———. 1995c. "Paris is hoping small is beautiful." February 21, 27.

———. 1995d. "EASDAQ gets a step closer." March 14, 16.

———. 1995e. "French and German exchanges to set up joint trading system." October 31, 23.

———. 1996a. "The Nouveau Marché." *Financial Times Financial Regulation Report*, March.

———. 1996b. "Proposals to boost markets in Germany." July 10, 3.

———. 1996c. "At last, a pipeline opens." September 20, 3.

———. 1996d. "Nouveau Marché rule change." October 30, 28.

———. 1997. "Initial public offerings." October 10, 6.

———. 1998a. "EASDAQ's aim is to break down the barriers." March 24, 7.

———. 1998b. "Euro. NM to harmonise regulations ahead of euro." April 22, 40.

———. 1998c. "Chemunex to list on EASDAQ and Euro. NM." June 17, 40.

———. 1998d. "Gloves come off for Europe's answer to NASDAQ." June 22, 30.

———. 1998e. "TelDaFax joins EASDAQ." July 2, 34.

———. 1998f. July 13, 23.

———. 1998g. "Moving places." October 6, 17.

———. 1998h. "EASDAQ names Euroclear for settlement, clearing." October 9, 30.

———. 1998i. "Brussels probes Paris, Milan." November 11, 2.

———. 1998j. "Three more countries join Euro. NM." December 18, 36.

———. 1999a. "SE sets criteria for joining Techmark." September 17, 22.

———. 1999b. "Technology row splits bourses." September 21, 22.

———. 1999c. "Plan for single Europe bourse shelved." 24, September, 19.

———. 1999d. "Securities leaders lift EASDAQ." July 30, 17.

Finnemore, Martha 1996a. *National Interests in International Society*, Ithaca: Cornell University Press.

Finnemore, Martha 1996b. "Norms, culture, and world politics: Insights from sociology's institutionalism." *International Organization* 50: 325–47.

Garrett, Geoffrey and Lange, Peter 1996. "Internationalization, Institutions and Political Change." In *Internationalization and Domestic Politics*, edited by Robert O. Keohane and Helen V. Milner, . Cambridge (England), New York: Cambridge University Press, pp. 48–78.

Gerschenkron, Alexander 1962. *Economic Backwardness in Historical Perspective, a Book of Essays*. Cambridge: Belknap Press of Harvard University Press.

Gill, Stephen 1990. *American Hegemony and the Trilateral Commission*. Cambridge, UK: Cambridge University Press.

———. 1997. "Global Structural Change and Multilateralism." In Gill, Stephen, ed. *Globalization, Democratization and Multilateralism*. New York: St. Martin's Press.

Global Investment Magazine 1997 (December): 44.

Graham, Bannock 1994. *European Second-tier Markets for NTBFs*, London: Graham Bannock and Partners.

Helleiner, Eric. 1994. *States and the Reembergence of Global Finance: From Bretton Woods to the 1990s*. Ithaca: Cornell University Press.

Huang, Roger D. and Hans R. Stoll 1996. "Dealer versus auction markets: A paired comparison of execution costs on NASDAQ and the NYSE." *Journal of Financial Economics* 41: 313–57.

The Independent. 1994. "NASDAQ plans Euro market." October 25, 34.

International Management 1987. "Venture capital seeks pan-European base." April, 52–4.

James, Scott C. and David A. Lake 1989. "The second face of hegemony: Britain's repeal of the Corn Laws and the American Walker Tariff of 1846." *International Organization* 43: 1–29.

Kapstein, Ethan 1992. "Between power and purpose: Central bankers and the politics of regulatory convergence" (Special Issue: "Knowledge, power, and the international policy coordination), *International Organization* 4(6): 265–287.

Keohane, Robert O. and Helen V. Milner. 1996. "Internationalization and Domestic Politics." In Keohane and Milner, eds. *Internationalization and domestic politics*. Cambridge (England), New York: Cambridge University Press, pp. 3–24.

Krueger, Alan B. and Jörn-Steffen Pischke 1997. "Observations and conjectures on the U. S. employment miracle." Cambridge, MA: National Bureau of Economic Research, Working Paper 6146.

LaPlante, Michele and Chris J. Muscarella 1997. "Do institutions receive comparable execution in the NYSE and NASDAQ markets? A transaction study of block trades." *Journal of Financial Economics* 45, 97–134.

Lerner, Josh 1996. "The European Association of Security Dealers: November 1994." Harvard Business School 9–295–116, Rev. Sept. 25, 1996. Cambridge.

Lind, Michael 1992. "The catalytic state." *The National Interest* (Spring): 3–12.

Mazars, Neville Russell 1999. "AIM Past, Present and Future: 1999 AIM Survey Results." London.

Moran, Michael 1991. *The Politics of the Financial Services Revolution: The USA, UK, and Japan,* New York: St. Martin's.

———. 1994. "The state and the financial services revolution: A comparative analysis." *West European Politics* (Special issue: "The state in Western Europe: Retreat or redefinition?" Edited by Wolfgang C. Müller and Vincent Wright. 1(7) (July): 158–77, London: Frank Cass.

Moravcsik, Andrew 1991. "Negotiating the Single European Act: National Interests and Conventional Statecraft in the European Community." *International Organization* 45: 19–56.

Muzyka, Daniel F. Benoit Leleux and Nathalie Guegan 1998. *European New Issues Markets: A Preliminary Review,* November, Fountainebleau, France: INSEAD & 3i Venturelab.

New York Times 1997a. "Marketplace: NASDAQ must wait a little longer for its new market-maker rules." January 9, C6.

———. 1997b. January 14, C11.

———. 1998a. "A European infatuation: Investors aglow over entrepreneurs." June 5, C1.

———. 1998b. "A joy ride, so far, in Euroland." June 14, Section 3, 1,5.

———. 1999a. "S. E. C. chief wants one site for posting all stock prices." September 24, A1.

———. 1999b. "EASDAQ listings get new rule." July 29, C12.

Nouveau Marché 1998. *www.nouveau*-marche.fr/bourse/nm/foncti/etre-cote-gb.html, September 15.

Nugent, Neill, ed. 1997. *At the Heart of the Union: Studies of the European Commission,* New York: St. Martin's Press, pp. 1–26.

Observer 1995. "New small companies market reflects French savoir faire." September 10, 3.

OECD 1994. OECD, SG/NR (94) 54.

———. 1996. OECD Labor Force Statistics.

———. 1997. OECD *Economic Survey, 1996–1997, United States,* November, Paris.

Ohmae, Kenichi 1990. *The Borderless World: Power and Strategy in the Interlinked Economy*, New York: HarperBusiness.

Peeters, Jos B. 1994. "A European market for entrepreneurial companies." In William D. Bygrave, Michael Hay, and Jos B. Peeters, eds. *Realizing Investment Value*. London: Financial Times/Pitman Publishing.

Pollack, Mark A. 1997. "The Commission as an Agent." In Neill Nugent, ed. *At the heart of the Union: Studies of the European Commission*. New York: St. Martin's Press, pp. 109–128.

———. 1998. "The engines of integration? Supranational autonomy and influence in the European Union." In Wayne Sandholtz and Alec Stone Sweet, eds. *European Integration and Supranational Governance*, New York: Oxford University Press, pp. 217–49.

Roger, Bruno and Faurre, Pierre 1995. "Rapport du groupe travail: "Nouveau Marché." February, SBF-Bourse de Paris: Paris.

Reuter 1994. "Euro bourse chief questions need for EASDAQ." *Reuter European Community Report*, November 22, 1.

———. 1995. " Euro-NASDAQ-type exchange to start with fifty firms." *Reuter European Community Report*, June 23.

———. 1996. "Parliament backs EU bourse for fast growing firms." *Reuter European Community Report*, July 4.

Sandholtz, Wayne 1992. *High-tech Europe: The Politics of International Cooperation*, Berkeley: University of California Press.

———. 1998. "The emergence of a supranational telecommunications regime." In Wayne Sandholtz and Alec Stone Sweet 1998. eds. *European Integration and Supranational Governance*. New York: Oxford University Press, pp. 134–63.

———. and Alec Stone Sweet 1998. "Integration, supranational governance, and the institutionalization of the European polity." In Sandholtz and Sweet,. eds. *European Integration and Supranational Governance*, New York: Oxford University Press, pp. 1–26.

Saxenian, Annalee 1994. *Regional Advantage: Culture and competition in Silicon Valley and Route 128*, Cambridge: Harvard University Press.

Schelling, Thomas C 1960. *The strategy of conflict*, Cambridge: Harvard University Press.

Scholte, Jan Aart 1997. "Global capitalism and the state." *International Affairs* 73: 427–52.

Securities Industry News 1998. "Euroclear Wins Race to Settle U. S. Equities." November 23, 1.

———. 1999. "Brussels" EASDAQ hunts for new trading system." January 4, 6.

Smith, Jeffrey W. James P. Selway III, Lorraine Reilly, and Timothy D. McCormick 1997. "NASD data relating to the NASDAQ Stock Market, Inc. and its listed companies." NASD Working Paper 97–01. Washington, D.C.: NASD Economic Research Department.

———, James P. Selway III, and Timothy D. McCormick 1998. "The NASDAQ Stock Market: Historical background and current operation." NASD Working Paper 98–01. Washington, D. C.: NASD Economic Research Department.

Sobel, Andrew C 1994. "Breaching the levee, waiting for the flood: Testing beliefs about the internationalization of securities markets." *International Interactions* 19: 311–38.

Steil, Benn et. al. 1996. *The European equity markets: The state of the union and an agenda for the millennium.* London: RIIA, 1996, chapter 4.

Strange, Susan 1996. *The Retreat of the State*, Cambridge: Cambridge University Press.

Thomas, George M., John W. Meyer, Francisco O. Ramirez, and John Boli. 1987. *Institutional Structure: Constituting State, Society, and the Individual.* Newbury Park, CA: Sage Publications.

Tirez, Dirk 1997. "EASDAQ benefits from European Framework." *International Financial Law Review* 1(61): 11–15.

Unger, Brigitte and Frans Van Waarden, eds. 1995. *Convergence or Diversity? Internationalization and Economic Policy Response.* Brookfield, USA: Averbury Publications.

United States Securities and Exchange Commission 1996. "Report pursuant to Section 21(a) of the Securities Exchange Act of 1934 regarding the NASD and the NASDAQ Market, August 8, 1996."

Venture Economics 1994. "EVCA launches EASD to build Europe's new IPO market." January, 2.

———. *Venture Economics* 1995. "Paris and London markets challenge for EASDAQ." December 19, 19.

Vogel, Steven K. 1996. *Freer Markets, More Rules: Regulatory Reform in Advanced Industrial Countries*, Ithaca: Cornell University Press.

Wall Street Journal 1998. June 23, C18. (about Deutsche Boerse and NASDAQ alliance)

———. 1999a. "High-growth markets, corporate deals are some trends seen for Europe in "99." January 5, B5A.

———. 1999b. "Stock Market Alliances Get Under way." January 5, A15.

Weiss, Linda 1998. The Myth of the Powerless state. Ithaca: Cornell University Press.

Ziegler, J. Nicholas 2000. Chapter in this book.

Zysman, John 1983. *Government, Markets, and Growth: Financial Systems and the Politics of Industrial Change.* Ithaca: Cornell University Press.

5 Corporate Governance in Germany: Toward a New Transnational Politics?

J. Nicholas Ziegler

The rules of corporate governance became a surprisingly contentious question in European politics in the late 1990s. Since these rules specify the rights and obligations of owners, managers, and employers, they are central to the practical meaning of property in industrial economies. Once the preserve of legal specialists, these rules now rank among the central determinants of who owns what in Europe's economic landscape.

Germany is a critical case for the definition of industrial property rights because its approach to corporate governance differs dramatically from the Anglo-American model. Over the last several decades, the U.S. and British business communities have consolidated a financial conception of control in which shareholder value is the primary objective of management.[1] Germany's institutions of social partnership have by contrast provided the clearest case among advanced industrial democracies where long-term stakeholders—including banks and employee groups—have a regular voice in corporate affairs. In accordance with this stakeholder approach to the firm, German law treats the firm as a constitutional construction for structuring a process of ongoing negotiation among different groups within the firm.[2] During most of the 1980s, Germany's relational approach to corporate governance appeared more successful than the "short-termism" from which U.S. firms seemed to suffer. In the 1990s, however, a number of German firms have encountered serious financial difficulties that went undetected by German banks until they necessitated conspicuous rescue packages which in turn threw Germany's stakeholder model of corporate governance into question.

The German approach to corporate governance poses a revealing problem for one of the central components in economic globalization, capital mobility. As usually defined, globalization entails a lowering of barriers to cross-border transactions. Lower barriers expose producers to increased competition from outside national boundaries. Just as purchasers of retail and industrial products gain a larger choice of suppliers in an increasingly international economy, purchasers of corporate assets also have a larger choice of assets to invest in. When holders of capital search over a broader geographic domain for attractive investments, they presumably look for a better return on their investment. The ability of investors to predict the return on their ownership shares is largely defined by the rules of corporate governance. Unlike the relatively simple criteria by which capital holders measure return on investment, however, the rules by which enterprises are financed, managed, and organized are among the institutional features where national economies differ most sharply. Because capital holders have such a clear interest in these rules, corporate governance is an area where capital confronts national institutional arrangements particularly starkly.

The literature on globalization and its political consequences has hinged precisely on this question—the convergence or continued diversity of existing institutions. This approach has been crucial in illuminating and delimiting the consequences of international economic change.[3] At the same time, this formulation has often pushed the debate toward two dichotomous alternatives: either that globalization has become a dominant process overwhelming other forms of politics, or that globalization is inconsequential. More recent contributions have articulated a growing consensus that, while globalization matters and matters very much, it is hardly an anonymous force which proceeds automatically or with uniform effects everywhere. Instead, globalization is a complex process, itself comprised of numerous political choices, which leave plenty of latitude for alternative strategies of economic growth and adjustment.[4]

This essay argues that the increasingly international scope of competition is indeed exerting strong pressure on the rules and practice of corporate governance in Germany. The effects of this process are, however, far from uniform. Even though cross-border capital mobility is central to the force of globalization, corporate governance is an issue where the political interests of capital are much less coherent than those of labor. Organized labor in Germany has consistently tried to maintain the distinctive legal provisions that give German employees an institutionalized voice in business enterprises. Within Germany's business community, some firms are likely to benefit more than others from access to non-German sources of capital. But this distinction has not yet led to any lasting cleavages—for instance between large and small firms, financial and industrial enterprises, or export and import oriented firms. Instead, individual firms are assessing and reassessing their interests in surprisingly piecemeal fashion.

Amidst the business community's fragmented preferences, one pattern is clearly emerging. The politics of corporate governance are becoming more transnational as domestic actors seek political allies outside Germany to support their preferred institutional agendas at home. If globalization refers to an economic process, it is not automatically forcing changes in domestic institutional arrangements. Instead, it is provoking a parallel political process of transnational alliance-building, in which domestic actors find allies abroad. Although their preferences on the issue of corporate governance are fragmented, business firms have shown significantly more success than labor in concluding transnational ties. The actors for whom transnational ties appear most effective, however, are a set of less well-known organizations—including shareholder membership associations and certain state agencies—that seek to bring German institutions of economic governance closer to the Anglo-American model. The evolution of corporate governance in Germany therefore depends critically on the relative ability of domestic actors to create transnational coalitions. If the proponents of neoliberal reform can use transnational coalitions to enhance their influence within Germany, they will be able to circumvent Germany's customary politics of social partnership and shift the country's rules of corporate governance more decisively toward the Anglo-American model.

This chapter illustrates the incipient transnational politics of property rights in three steps. First, it reviews the received model of corporate governance in Germany and contrasts it with the Anglo-American model. Second, it examines the main mechanisms which might link the economic processes that make up globalization to changes in the institutions of corporate governance. Third, it analyzes three types of politics that surround changes in the rules and practice of corporate governance in Germany. These cases show clearly that formal-legal change has been limited, but that the customary patterns of social partnership in Germany are vulnerable to erosion from a persistent campaign by the proponents of neoliberal reform to create a culture and a set of institutions more conducive to Anglo-American arrangements for financing and running industrial enterprises.

1. The German Model of Corporate Governance

Germany's framework for governing industrial firms closely approximates the concept of the stakeholder firm. This concept became popular in the early 1990s among English-speaking critics of the financial conception of control that prevailed in the Anglo-American economies.[5] Germany's stakeholder features stem less from recent reforms than from a century of workplace struggle in which labor and owners have found mechanisms for industrial peace and regularized consultation. The two principal features of this approach to corporate governance include a legally institutionalized role for employees and a pattern of ownership concentrated among long-term shareholders, particularly the universal banks. These features by no means provide an exhaustive account of relevant laws and practices,[6] but they are the key features that underpin Germany's model of organized private enterprise at the firm level. As portrayed by Andrew Shonfield in the 1960s, this model of organized capitalism included a complex set of producer organizations that facilitated tripartite peak bargaining between industry associations, national labor organizations, and the state. This pattern of peak bargaining—which culminated in the regular meetings for Concerted Action (*Konzertierte Aktion*) in the 1970s—provided Germany's clearest example of neocorporatist wage bargaining and facilitated a pattern of negotiated industrial change. As such, the pattern of peak bargaining—and the firm-level arrangements that accompanied it—was closely associated with Germany's successful industrial adjustment in the 1970s and early 1980s.[7]

Labor's role in these arrangements rests on the principle of codetermination (*Mitbestimmung*), or joint decisionmaking. Codetermination includes both top-down cooperation between management and labor in the supervisory boards (*Aufsichtsräte*) of large stock companies (*Aktiengesellschaften*) as well as bottom-up representation of labor in works councils (*Betriebsräte*) at the plant level. These two aspects reflect specific principles of organization—constitutionalism and more radical workplace democracy—that collided in the Weimar period and have remained in tension in Germany's legislation since 1945. A strong form of codetermination reappeared quickly after World War Two in the coal and steel sectors (*Montanindustrie*) where unions obtained equal representation on the supervisory boards in 1951. One of organized labor's key goals for the next 25 years was to extend the strong provisions of *Montanmitbestimmung* to all sectors of the German economy.[8] In 1952, the Works Constitution Act (*Betriebsverfassungsgesetz*) followed a more paternalistic concept of Catholic-conservative constitutionalism by giving employees only one-third of the seats on the supervisory boards and guaranteeing strict procedural independence of the works councils from the unions.[9] Only when this legislation was broadened in 1972 and 1976 did labor achieve roughly equal representation on supervisory boards of large firms (more than 2,000 employees)—though without the neutral tie-breaking procedures that had been stipulated in 1951 for the coal and steel sectors. The laws of the 1970s also allowed closer links between unions and the works councils and gave the latter extensive rights on decisions affecting hiring, layoffs, overtime, and vacations, as well as access to detailed information (though not joint decisionmaking authority) on company finances and investments.[10]

Germany's large universal banks gained their key role in industrial governance in the final third of the nineteenth century—well before the works councils of the Weimar period gave labor recognized representation. As Alexander Gerschenkron pointed out, the universal banks were founded by German industrialists for the explicit purpose of accumulating and concentrating the capital needed to finance Germany's rapid industrialization. Without legal requirements to separate equity holding from other banking activities, the banks quickly moved into retail banking, current-account services for large clients, and long-term lending as well as equity financing. Andrew Shonfield showed how the universal banks reconsolidated their power in the postwar period by maintaining equity positions in Germany's large joint-stock companies. The centrality of the banks rested partly on the distinctive two-board structure of Germany's large stock companies: the managing board (*Vorstand*) handled operational management, while the supervisory board (*Aufsichtsrat*) approved major investment and personnel decisions. The supervisory board of most major firms included several senior bank executives and was typically chaired by a representative of the company's lead bank. In addition to their own equity stakes in such firms, the large banks customarily held and exercised proxy voting rights (*Depotstimmrechte*) for their retail customers. Since the large universal banks such as Deutsche Bank, Dresdner Bank, and Commerzbank typically voted together, they were often able to exercise substantial majorities of a large enterprise's shares.[11] In Shonfield's now-classic discussion of the steel industry, this system of interlocking directorates and voting rights allowed the banks to coordinate industrial growth and to prevent the firms under their tutelage from engaging in competition that undercut the health of the sector as a whole.[12]

The legally sanctioned role of banks and labor in Germany' joint-stock companies produced a pattern of corporate governance almost the reverse of the U.S. model. According to the standard account of Adolf Berle and Gardiner Means, the ownership of large American corporations came to be spread across a diffuse collection of small shareholders, thereby giving managers a great deal of discretion. In Germany, by contrast, ownership was concentrated among a much smaller number of banks and other financial institutions. Managers enjoyed considerable insulation from the short-term pressures of an anonymous equity market, but were subject to the ongoing scrutiny of long-term stakeholders represented on the supervisory board. In the United States, neither organized labor nor other stakeholder groups were granted any legal voice in company decisions. These arrangements meant that the primary tension within firms in the United States occurred between dispersed owners and powerful managers.[13] Formal treatments of this tension appeared in principal-agent theory and in the concept of shareholder value, which provided a basis for analyzing the ties between ownership and control of the firm.[14] Taken to its logical conclusion, the shareholder-value approach excluded provisions for employee codetermination, which for shareholders represented a substantial infringement on property rights.[15] Yet it was just these provisions that enabled the large enterprises in Germany to integrate the social partners within the firm.

This view of the large firm—governed by rules that impose long-term consultative strategies on contending social interests—understates the degree of organizational diversity and experimentation in German industry. Although joint-stock companies with 2,000 employees or more include most of Germany's large manufacturing concerns, they account for somewhat less than half of the country's private-sector workforce.[16] The small- and medium-sized firms in the German *Mittelstand* matter because they provide very different adjustment capacities than the large, integrated firms that anchor Germany's more centralized industrial orders.[17] While most manufacturing firms in the *Mittelstand* have some form of codetermination, they fall well outside the purview of the large universal banks. Instead they rely on Germany's complex landscape of public savings banks (both regional and municipal) and cooperative credit societies (mostly municipal). In 1986, the savings banks and cooperative societies accounted for as much as 32% and 18% of loans to Germany's manufacturing industry in 1986, while the main private banks provided 18.8% of such loans. In 1996, the figures were 32.8% for the savings banks, 18.3% for the cooperative societies, and 21.1% for the major private banks. As these figures suggest, firms in the *Mittelstand* have developed a multitude of coordinating and financing mechanisms that rest on local institutions rather than the country-wide perspectives of the universal banks. Indeed, the limits of the universal banks were further revealed after German reunification, when the government Trust Authority (*Treuhandanstalt*) responsible for privatization designed a range of financing measures that left the larger banks free to pursue less risky business elsewhere. Thus, although corporate governance is an issue that most directly affects the larger joint-stock companies, the entire range of smaller and more regionally embedded actors is relevant because they provide much of the organizational experimentation which could generate new recipes to augment or supplant the rules that regulate the large and more visible firms.[18]

2. Mechanisms of Change

Given the complex history of Germany's diverse enterprise forms, one cannot assume that changes in these forms proceed automatically from forces in the international economy. To be sure, there are plenty of signs of pressure to alter the German model of corporate governance. Yet, the sources of this pressure are not self-evident. Moreover, the metaphor of pressure may be inadequate to show how the changes associated with globalization might lead to changes in the rules of corporate governance. Rather than an impersonal force pushing uniformly in all directions, globalization works its effects on domestic legal arrangements through a series of quite specific mechanisms.

The mechanism of change most often invoked by practitioners is competitive selection. This mechanism fits particularly well with the Political Economy Null Hypothesis, as defined in this volume. This hypothesis holds that globalization allows lower price levels by broadening the geographic scope of competition. Analysts following this view argue that the German model of corporate governance is under pressure because it is less efficient than the alternatives. Some authors have found evidence that German firms which rely on close bank ties show a lower return on investment than firms with arms-length financial ties, but these findings have been consistently questioned.[19] Equally important, such studies at the firm level neglect the question of what kind of efficiency is being measured. Authors who focus on distinctive national variants of capitalism argue that the German economy, like the Japanese economy, sacrifices short-term allocative efficiency in order to achieve longer-term efficiencies in coordinating the activities of entire sectors and supply chains.[20]

Another mechanism of convergence in organizational form is coercion, where more powerful organizations impose structures or practices on less powerful organizations. Given that countries retain sovereignty over basic issues in commercial law, it is hard to see how convergence in corporate governance could result through a process of pure coercion. Although the European Commission is promoting a uniform set of guidelines for corporate governance, it has shown a singular inability to extract agreement from member countries on this central issue.[21] A subspecies of the coercive mechanism could, however, occur when firms in one country need access to another country's markets so badly that they would adopt the other country's legal features or regulatory requirements.[22] If German firms displayed such a need to tap U.S. sources of capital and adopted U.S. governance arrangements as a condition, then one might describe this mechanism as a case of market-power tantamount to coercive isomorphism.[23]

A third mechanism of organizational convergence is the diffusion of organizational templates, or mimetic isomorphism. Cases where organizations imitate other presumably successful models exemplify this mechanism. Since they do not rest on coercion or constraint, cases of mimetic isomorphism often indicate a form of voluntaristic industry self-regulation.[24] Such mechanisms were suggested in corporate governance by industry-initiated studies in the U.K. and France, where industrial commissions defined a set of "best-practice" norms that their members then urged firms to adopt voluntarily.[25] Interestingly, such "best-practice" codes have barely appeared in Germany.

Partly because they focus on well-defined populations and fields of organizations, these three mechanisms do not directly illuminate the exercise of power among unlike organizational actors. As a result, political scientists have often presented domestic politics as a distinct mechanism of change.[26] In this form of adjustment, organized actors see themselves as benefitting more or less from particular changes and mobilize accordingly. For changes in the rules of corporate governance, the best evidence for such political mechanisms would include bargained compromises among political parties, unfamiliar coalitions and cleavages, or outright confrontations between opposing interest groups. Recent efforts to change the rules that govern joint-stock companies in Germany show precisely such instances. Such examples of political conflict do not exclude the presence of other mechanisms of adaptation. But they do show that these mechanisms reflect an explicit effort by the leading actors within Germany to redefine the terms on which organized interest groups cooperate in the tasks of economic production.

3. Deliberation, Promotion, and Confrontation

Given the range of processes that are potentially involved, the links between globalization and changes in the German model of corporate governance can best be understood by examining evidence for all of the mechanisms outlined above. The interest-group politics that lead to the enactment of formal-legal changes are crucial. Since a change in corporate governance entails changing the rules by which actors are organized as well as connected to each other, however, interest-group analysis alone is not likely to offer a full explanation. Insofar as the nature of the actors themselves is at issue, these actors are very likely to show contingent and shifting preferences as they debate the underlying purposes and contours of alternative rules. To explore these possibilities, the following subsections examine three different types of political contestation: efforts to alter the formal rules of corporate governance; de facto shifts in the ownership and the administration of corporate assets; and explicit confrontations over changes in the practices associated with the German model.

a. Enactment: Changing the Rules?

The impetus to alter Germany's received model of enterprise governance evolved through two phases in the 1990s. It came initially from the economic liberals in the Free Democratic Party (FDP) as well as Social Democrats (SPD) who who had long opposed the power of the banks. Several spectacular cases of financial distress among major German firms led observers to question the effectiveness of Germany's two-board system—and the monitoring capabilities of bank representatives on the supervisory boards. Since several cases involved firms with particularly close bank connections—Metallgesellschaft, KHD, and the real estate holding company, Jürgen Schneider—critics revived the familiar theme of "bank power" (*Macht der Banken*). Within a few years, however, the neoliberal reformers repackaged their position in terms of the Standortdebatte—the debate over the characteristics necessary to keeping Germany competitive as a site for investment. Questions about the domestic distribution of financial power were reframed in terms of their consequences for international holders of capital assets.

This first phase of discussion began in the fall of 1994, when coalition discussions between the Christian Democrats (CDU) and Free Democrats included plans to improve procedures by which the supervisory boards could monitor their enterprises. By May of 1995, the Ministries of Justice and Economics—both controlled by the economic liberals in the FDP—formed a joint working group to consider reform of Germany's main shareholding law (*Aktiengesetz*). From the beginning, the interests of the reformers was moderate. FDP members anticipated "careful corrections" rather than major revisions.[27]

The working group adopted moderate goals such as disclosing the interests of supervisory board members and improving its ability to obtain information from the lower management board (*Vorstand*). Many of the group's recommendations—which seem self-evident from American practice—had never taken root in the German context of concentrated ownership and consensus management. Thus the working group recommended that supervisory board members be required to inform shareholders of their seats on other company boards; that supervisory boards meet four times per years rather than two; that bank holdings of 5 percent eventually be disclosed and that procedures for independent auditing be strengthened. The recommendation that board size for large firms be reduced from 20 to 12 members was one of the few that encountered opposition—in this case from the trade unions and Labor Ministry. Even though the existing management-labor balance would be preserved, the unions felt that codetermination would suffer from an absolute reduction in the number of employee representatives.[28] All parties, including the FDP, eschewed any changes in the balance of codetermination as a subject that had to remain taboo if compromise on other issues was to remain possible.

As this exercise in policy moderation proceeded within the Ministries, the rhetoric of industrial relations was growing more strident. A number of firms in the metalworking industry protested wage increases in 1996 by opting out of the employers' bargaining association, Gesamtmetall. The head of the BDI (German Federation of Industry), Hans-Olaf Henkel, who had earlier taken IBM-Deutschland out of the regional collective bargaining agreement in Stuttgart, attacked the trade unions explicitly for undermining the spirit of individualism and self-determination that Germany needed.[29]

The second phase of the debate began when the proponents of moderate reform within the FDP-controlled ministries restated their position in terms of the pros and cons of globalization. They argued that improved transparency and accountability in corporate governance were necessary if Germany was remain a competitive investment location (*Standort*) in a worldwide market. In developing their legislative proposals, members of the ministerial working group did not confine themselves to the customary dialog with Germany's organized interest groups. According to participants in the process, they also met directly with the association of international banks in Frankfurt as well as with individual investment banks and foreign pension funds. Among the latter, ministerial officials particularly mentioned the activist pension funds in the United States, such as the California public employees pension organization, Calpers, which was exporting its stance on corporate governance issues to Europe at the time.[30] The Social Democrats meanwhile drafted more far-reaching legislation that would undercut the power of the finance industry directly by limiting banks to an equity stake of 5 percent in any listed company and by ending the banks' practice of exercising proxy rights for shares held by their retail customers.

When the Bundestag held hearings on the two proposals in early 1997, the main social interests lined up in predictable fashion. The large industry associations formed a common front, not only with smaller firms in Chamber of Commerce but also with the sector-specific associations for banking and for insurance. Their common position endorsed most of the changes proposed by the FDP, while opposing the SPD proposal as unnecessarily drastic. The trade union federation (DGB) as well as the white collar union (DAG) showed some support for the more aggressive limits on bank power proposed by the Social Democrats while opposing any reduction in the size of the supervisory boards.[31]

A less familiar set of preferences came from the two shareholder groups, the Deutsche Schutzvereinigung für Wertpapierbesitz, e.V. (German Association for Share Ownership, or DSW) and the Schutzgemeinschaft der Kleinaktionäre, e.V. (Association of Small Shareholders, or SGK). Given the historical weakness of Germany's stock markets, these organizations, dedicated to the protection of individual shareholder rights, were curious actors in the country's political landscape. During the 1990s, however, they became rapidly more prominent. Though generally aligned with the economic liberals, the shareholder associations frequently articulated more forceful protests than did the politicians in Bonn. The SGK deviated from the FDP's position by endorsing limits on bank ownership of industrial firms at 10 percent. The DSW supported most of the FDP's proposals, but also decried the "Japanization" of the German economy caused by interlocking directorates that often put the same individual on the supervisory boards of competing companies.[32] With Otto von Lambsdorff (former head of the Free Democratics) as its honorary chairman, the DSW was one of the few organized constituencies supporting the FDP. Its influence was, however, magnified when the California pension fund, Calpers, announced that its position on legal changes in Germany were best articulated by the DSW.

Yet another set of preferences came from the Green party. The issue of enterprise governance—while hardly ranking among their core concerns—allowed the Greens to criticize established concentrations of economic power as obstacles to desirable types of change. Much like the Social Democrats, the Greens attacked the multiple sources of influence that the large universal banks exercised over German firms. Much like the liberals, they argued ever more pointedly through the 1990s that Germany needed a modern equity market to support entrepreneurs in the small and medium-sized sector. In effect, on issues of finance and economic policy, the Greens bridged the positions of the economic liberals and the modernizing wing of the Social Democrats.[33]

This configuration led to legislation that was remarkable for its incremental nature. Since these changes aimed almost entirely at bolstering accountability and transparency of the supervisory boards, rather than altering the power or participation of the banks in those boards, the law became known as the *Kontrolle und Transparenz Gesetz* (Kontrag). It left the number of board seats that an individual could hold at ten, although chairmanships were henceforth to be double-counted. The law required the supervisory boards to meet four times per year rather than twice. And it required auditors to submit their reports to all members of the supervisory boards rather than only to the managing board as had previously been done. Regarding banking power, the permissible size of a bank's equity share in industrial companies was not reduced, although banks with more than 5 percent of a company's outstanding stock did lose their automatic right to exercise proxy rights for other shareholders. This last provision reinforced efforts already underway at the large banks to reduce their equity holdings in Germany's principal manufacturing firms, but it nonetheless signified a potentially decisive change by allowing alternative organizations, particularly the shareholder associations, to advertise themselves as shareholder representatives and to assume some of the voting power that German banks had long enjoyed as the virtually unquestioned custodians for smaller investors.[34]

The neoliberal reformers had clearly put in place the elements of a transnational coalition for more far-reaching reductions in the power of Germany's banks. Since they largely refrained from mobilizing this coalition in the process leading to enactment, it is hard to avoid the conclusion that the neoliberals ultimately favored only mild and incremental changes in the formal regulation of Germany's capital markets.

b. Promotion: Creating an "Equity Culture"

If the federal government's effort to refine Germany's formal rules of corporate governance dissipated into growing degrees of moderation, its efforts to broaden the public's interest in purchasing equities were more successful. The main actors in this effort were not the social partners, but the state, the large industrial corporations, the banks, and foreign financial-service firms. The European Union was not directly involved, but nonetheless provided important stimuli to the German government's efforts to create an "equity culture."

The German government's interest in promoting a more vibrant equities market had several sources. As European integration proceeded, the question of European financial leadership surfaced. Frankfurt was one of the only competitors to London. But if German politicians were to promote Frankfurt as the EU's leading financial center, Germany's small and high-cost regional stock markets would need to be combined into a much more transparent and liquid market.[35] Beyond wanting to promote Frankfurt's place in the EU, the macroeconomic criteria for the Maastricht Treaty gave the federal government renewed interest in privatizing major state-owned enterprises such as Lufthansa and Deutsche Telekom. In addition to revenues, both privatizations promised to generate fees that the German government wanted to direct to German banks.

One of the first issues raised by these privatizations was the size of the German stock markets. With only about half of the country's top 100 firms listed in Frankfurt,[36] the dynamism and liquidity of the stock markets in

Germany were limited. Counting all domestic firms listed on German exchanges, the market value of Germany's stock market equalled approximately 39% of gross domestic product for 1997, while listed firms on the New York Stock Exchange were valued at 133.6% of U.S. GDP.[37]

The initial privatization of Deutsche Telekom in November 1996 was the single most important event in the government's efforts to strengthen the equity market. The privatization had to be prepared by a complex series of legal and organizational changes, which gave the operation great visibility. In addition, the federal government bankrolled a massive advertising campaign to encourage individual investors to buy shares. The Finance Ministry appointed an international consortium of investment banks, including Goldman Sachs and Merrill Lynch, to conduct a global offering. Partly owing to the government's careful advance promotion, the offering was oversubscribed and shares in Deutsche Telekom rose nearly 20 percent on the first day of trading. As authoritative observer, the *Financial Times* pronounced the Germans ready for their plunge into the world of equities.[38] Immediately after the privatization, Deutsche Telekom had two million shareholders, which made it the most widely held German firm, far ahead of Volkswagen (0.7 million shareholders) and Siemens (0.5 million shareholders).[39]

In addition to dramatically broadening share ownership in Germany, Deutsche Telekom's privatization raised the issue of accounting standards and foreign listings. Deutsche Telekom was only the second German firm, following Daimler Benz, to apply for full listing on the New York Stock Exchange. Non-U.S. firms did not need to follow U.S. laws for board composition or ownership structure in order to list their shares in New York, but they did have to satisfy regulatory requirements for financial accounting and disclosure enforced by the Securities and Exchange Commission (SEC). Combined with its reputation as a regulatory watchdog, the SEC's position as guardian of the world's largest securities markets gave it great influence in setting norms for accounting transparency around the world. German firms had to keep two distinct sets of books in order to comply with U.S. generally accepted accounting principles (GAAP) as well as German accounting conventions. Before Daimler-Benz listed its shares in New York, for example, it had to reveal hidden reserves that created a discrepancy of DM 2.5 billion in profit calculated according to German versus U.S. accounting rules. The discrepancy created bad publicity, but did not harm Daimler's SEC-registered offering in the United States, which was managed by Deutsche Bank and targeted primarily to U.S. investors. Deutsche Telekom was expected to face fewer difficulties in adopting U.S. GAAP, because its pension liabilities were being taken over by the German government and it had no inherited pension or participation reserves. Even so, like Daimler, Deutsche Telekom was obliged to show its accounts in both German GAAP and U.S. GAAP in its 1996 annual report, with substantial differences between the two.[40]

A conspicuous split quickly developed among well-known German companies over the desirability of following SEC requirements to follow U.S. GAAP. German managers generally preferred to avoid disclosure that would encourage shareholder activism or suits. Some larger firms such as Siemens and VW, which had considered stock listings in New York, lost interest after observing the time and expense caused by Daimler's listing. Others, for which an American presence was increasingly important for business reasons, adopted the alternative international accounting standards, IAS, which allowed greater discretion on the reporting of R&D expenses and the valuation of equity investments in such entities as subsidiaries and joint ventures.[41] The pharmaceuticals firm, Bayer, believed that Daimler gave up too much and had "practically capitulated" in its negotiations with the SEC. Deutsche Bank, itself Daimler's lead banker, also chose IAS as opposed to U.S. GAAP.[42]

The large-firm sector was not the only target of the federal government's efforts to promote an equity culture. Since the early 1980s, officials in the Research Ministry had tried to promote entrepreneurship in high-tech sectors by subsidizing startup capital for new firms. Toward the end of the decade, the Ministry initiated new programs for subsidizing equity capital through two public banks, the Kreditanstalt für Wiederaufbau and the Deutsche Ausgleichsbank.[43] These programs aimed explicitly at younger technologists and dovetailed with the appearance of a new venture-capital network in Germany. Although implemented by the Christian-Liberal government in Bonn, such programs found confirmed support from social-democratic experts as well.[44] The decision by the Frankfurt Stock Market authorities (Deutsche Börse) to create a new market (called the Neuer Markt) for initial public offerings, consolidated a public-private effort to bolster a new equity-driven entrepreneurial sector in Germany that was quite different from the traditional Mittelstand.

These efforts to stimulate a culture of stock purchasing were far from superficial. While household savings still went largely into savings accounts and fixed-income securities, share ownership was increasing. According to one study, the number of Germans who held shares increased from under 13 percent in 1996 to 19 percent in 1999. By September of 1999, German savers were investing more in equity accounts than fixed-income accounts for the first time in the postwar era.[45] Equally important, the shareholder associations worked with brokerage houses to provide a deeper infrastructure for individual investors who sought to bypass the large banks. An incipient movement toward investor activism also emerged as the concept of shareholder rights gained more visibility.

c. Confrontation: Challenging the Anglo-American Model

The possibilities suggested by the growth of Germany's equity markets became apparent through the encroachment of Anglo-American takeover tactics in Germany's steel industry. The steel sector carried great symbolic weight because of its place in the country's burstlike industrial growth in the nineteenth century and because it provided the clearest example of the bank-dominated capabilities that Andrew Shonfield celebrated in analyzing German industrial adjustment after World War II. One consequence of this pattern of negotiated adjustment was that banks rarely if ever permitted hostile takeovers. Instead, in periods of growth, they discreetly planned expansions in capacity, while, in periods of recession, they worked closely with labor as well as government officials to manage orderly reductions in capacity. When, in the 1990s, therefore, the banks not only countenanced but seemed to sponsor hostile takeovers, they signaled a major effort to change the unwritten rules by which labor had participated in existing arrangements for sectoral governance.[46]

The stage for confrontation was set by the economic turmoil of the late 1980s. In both the coal and steel sectors, increasing competition and productivity-enhancing innovations put pressure on German firms to cut costs and rationalize capacity. One step in this direction occurred when the Krupp steel company acquired one of North Rhine-Westphalia's other major steel producers, Hoesch, in 1988. Such changes invariably ranked as high politics in North Rhine-Westphalia, where IG Metall remained a major force. Krupp's acquisition of Hoesch was particularly controversial because Krupp's ownership structure, dominated by a family foundation, was exempt from the stronger form of codetermination (*Montanmitbestimmung*) that applied to Hoesch. Following this merger, steel executives and political leaders periodically raised the issue of further rationalization between Krupp and the region's other major producer, Thyssen. Growing impatient with ongoing negotiations, the chairmen of Krupp's supervisory and managing boards, Berthold Beitz and Gerhard Cromme, assembled the financial backing necessary to make an unsolicited tender offer to Thyssen's shareholders in early 1997.[47]

The prospect of a hostile takeover deviated dramatically from the norms of coordinated management that had become deeply rooted in the steel industry. When Krupp's plans were leaked to the press in March 1997, they provoked a storm of protest. Thyssen's chief executive, Dieter Vogel, saw Krupp's offer as a tactic to circumvent more deliberate negotiations. The nature of the banking consortium that financed Krupp's takeover attempt aroused more general protest. Deutsche Bank was widely criticized for a de facto conflict of interest, because its investment banking subsidiary, Morgan Grenfell, advised Krupp even while a Deutsche Bank officer sat silently on Thyssen's supervisory board. Dresdner Bank was also criticized for its ties to both firms. These points mattered because Thyssen's board structure, like Hoesch's, fell under the 1951 legislation for Montanmitbestimmung. Since a takeover by Krupp would remove Thyssen from the full parity provided by Montanmitbestimmung, every vote on Thyssen's supervisory board was potentially crucial. The banks with members on both boards were heavily criticized. The presence of Goldman Sachs among Krupp's advisers provoked further charges that Krupp was importing an Anglo-American type of "casino capitalism" into Germany.[48]

Krupp's plans also triggered an intricate set of negative reactions in the political sphere. Although the regional government in North Rhine-Westphalia had often tried to facilitate rationalization in this industry, it opposed Krupp's use of hostile takeover tactics to accomplish this goal. For one thing, Krupp was more deeply indebted than Thyssen, causing concern in the government about the economic wisdom as well as the political costs of the takeover.[49] The Social Democratic leader of the regional government in North Rhine Westphalia, Johannes Rau, summoned leaders of both firms to a dinner meeting on March 18, one day after the initial press reports, and persuaded them to begin talks toward a quick and mutual resolution. As talks began on March 20, the regional economics minister, Wolfgang Clement, set out the government's goals in a speech to the regional legislature (*Landtag*) in Düsseldorf. Clement claimed a major voice for the regional government in persuading the two companies to reach a mutually acceptable plan (*Konzept*) within eight days. He said that this goal required close communication among the company leadership, the steelworkers represented by IG Metall, and the works councils. Emphasizing the importance of such communication, Clement invoked the term "concerted action" (Konzertierte Aktion), reminiscent of tripartite wage-bargaining in the 1970s. Even as the CDU leaders in Bonn denied that the Krupp-Thyssen talks required any federal involvement, Minister Clement in Düsseldorf emphasized the need for a full-employment solution.[50]

Pressure on the two companies increased dramatically toward the end of the week-long negotiating period. On March 25, roughly 30,000 steelworkers demonstrated in front of Deutsche Bank's headquarters in Frankfurt while another 6,000 demonstrated in Dortmund. According to some reports, Thyssen helped transport the steelworkers to Frankfurt to give them a forum for attacking the "wild west" tactics of Krupp and its financial backers.[51] Even as he negotiated with Krupp's chief executive, Gerhard Cromme, in Düsseldorf, Thyssen's chief executive, Dieter Vogel, helped mobilize the steelworkers to forestall the solution that Krupp had initially wanted. The day after the demonstrations, Krupp and Thyssen issued a joint memorandum, announcing that the two companies would merge their steel operations. Rather than the original model, in which Krupp would control the merged entity, the talks in Düsseldorf generated a solution in which Thyssen would hold 60 percent of the merged company's shares. Both companies renounced the use of involuntary layoffs and announced their intention to meet soon with representatives of the employees and IG Metall. In addition, both chief executives thanked the regional economics minister Clement for helping moderate the talks.[52]

This sequence of events marked a clear setback for the proponents of a more open market for corporate control in Germany. Gerhard Cromme claimed that the solution achieved all of his company's aims for greater efficiency, but he also complained that Germany's financial markets had not been "ready" (reif) for an unsolicited takeover bid and argued for the dismantling of Germany's encrusted structures (verkrustetenStrukturen) of financial management.[53] For Thyssen as well as IG Metall, the mediation of the regional government led to a far more satisfactory outcome. The government's role lessened Krupp's relative power in the merged entity and obliged both companies to negotiate continually with employee representatives over organizational structures and practices for the new firm.

This case clearly contradicts the argument that Germany's economic institutions are inexorably converging on those of Anglo-American style capitalism. At the same time, however, the story is not a simple revival of neo-corporatist social partnership at the regional level. First, the interests of the firms were by no means congruent. Inasmuch as Thyssen invited coopera-tion from IG Metall in opposing Krupp's unsolicited tender, it was as much management as labor that tried to prevent the unrestrained sway of financial power. Second, after the companies agreed to merge, they set up a detailed system of consultation with the works councils and the representatives of IG Metall to help plan and implement specific restructuring measures. These consultative mechanisms at the firm level exemplified a willingness to ex-periment with strategic partnership that went well beyond standard accounts of neocorporatist economic bargaining.[54] In the Krupp-Thyssen case, the union negotiated a series of such "coordinating" bodies for each of the com-pany's functional divisions. These new structures went part of the way toward replacing through contractual means the protections earlier guaranteed to Thyssen employees through Montanmitbestimmung. As one union repre-sentative interpreted it, the Krupp-Thyssen merger represented a victory for the Rhineland variant of negotiated German capitalism, but it also signaled that labor would have to elaborate a range of new consultative policies (*Be-gleitpolitik*) to maintain a day-to-day voice in the industry's restructuring.[55]

4. Conclusion

By documenting the different types of politics that are shaping the future of corporate governance in Germany, these three instances of contestation illustrate the depth of the tension between the Anglo-American conception of property rights and the German conception of the firm as a constitutional construction for balancing the interests of contending social groups. The questions at stake are how widely German firms will adopt the shareholder-value approach and how they will adapt it to their legally required commit-ments to provide a regular voice for employees as well as owners in the running of industrial companies.

The formal legal changes to date show a pattern that appears deceptively similar to previous examples of incrementalism and negotiated change in the Federal Republic.[56] The initial debate over a new law on stock ownership quickly settled into a smaller-scale discussion of the transparency and in-dependence of the supervisory boards. The Free Democrats sometimes claimed to want far-reaching reforms, but ended up by tinkering with existing structures rather than proposing the wholesale reductions in bank power sought by the Social Democrats. In the confrontation over Krupp's takeover effort, the SPD government in North Rhine-Westphalia intervened to moderate any move away from accepted neocorporatist processes of industrial policymaking. And the steelworkers were called out as much by Thyssen's management as by IG Metall, with the purpose of thwarting Krupp's effort to push Germany toward the Anglo-American example of a more freewheeling market for corporate mergers and acquisitions. Of three three cases examined here, the government's efforts to create an "equity culture" through the privatization of Deutsche Telekom had the most far-reaching consequences by deepening the infrastructure for new equity issues and thereby encouraging a significantly broader segment of the German public to purchase shares.

The incremental scope of formal legal change accurately reflects the balance of power among Germany's political parties. Just as they prefer a politics of negotiation among large organized groups in the political arena, both the CDU and the SPD support the representation of contending social interests in large industrial enterprises. From their different ideological traditions, both of the large parties therefore uphold some kind of regularized voice for employees at the company level—thereby putting a brake on any radical efforts to dismantle the laws on codetermination. The Greens, while espousing a Jeffersonian attachment to small-scale enterprise, have not played a prominent role in legislation for corporate organization. As the main party that champions individual choice over large group negotiation in economic policymaking, the FDP is therefore limited to proposing moderate changes in the role of the banks while avoiding any direct assault on the labor's codetermination rights.

A more important reason for the limited extent of formal-legal change comes from the genuine ambivalence and uncertainty among Germany's business leaders about where their interests lie. Individual business leaders have periodically complained about the unwieldy procedures required by codetermination, but the peak employer associations have consistently recognized the importance of works councils in insulating plant-level consultation from collective bargaining and providing important shop-floor information.[57] Labor's role at the supervisory-board level provoked more criticism from business representatives in the debates over corporate governance, but here, too, prominent German employers decided against tinkering with arrangements that conferred many advantages. The case of Daimler-Benz is especially illustrative. When Daimler established a U.S. production plant in Alabama, its Mercedes auto division happily managed the new facility as one of its only nonunion sites.[58] Daimler subsequently emphasized the language of shareholder value in negotiating with U.S. investors and regulators over listing its shares in New York. In Stuttgart, however, the company took great pains to maintain workforce loyalty. When Daimler's merger with Chrysler occurred in 1998, the company chose to maintain its legal status as a German enterprise and made German institutions of social partnership its model for cross-border holdings by accepting a representative of the United Auto Workers on the supervisory board of the merged entity.[59] Similarly, while Deutsche Bank actively champions the openness and transparency that are needed in maintaining Frankfurt's credentials as a European financial center, it also seeks to perpetuate its privileged ties with Germany's largest enterprises. These examples follow a familiar pattern by which German firms tend to emphasize the language of economic liberalism in international negotiations while continuing to invest in the long-term relationships that anchor their positions in the domestic economy.

Such mixed messages are more than an exercise in cross-border public relations. They also reflect a deeper analytic issue. Institutional analyses often distinguish between actors behaving strategically within a known set of rules and actors seeking to alter the rules that govern their interactions.[60] In the debate about corporate governance, actors are not seeking to alter the rules by which they compete but rather the rules by which they and their competitors are themselves constituted. In such a situation, firms are effectively faced with the problem of figuring out which rules might work to their benefit while simultaneously deciding what it should mean to be a firm in the first place. It is hardly surprising that business preferences in such a situation are subject to change. Until the menu of likely institutional alternatives is clarified, firms cannot calculate their payoffs reliably and preferences are not are likely to coalesce.[61] This process of institutional clarification necessarily involves more than jockeying for strategic advantage; it is also a process of deliberation about the underlying goals of economic production and exchange.[62]

The ambiguity of business's interests is one important reason that the politics of corporate governance are shaped by the evolving priorities of the transnational business community.[63] All parties to the German debate seek to preserve the inherited features of German institutions that best fit their needs while espousing those institutional features preferred by the modern and forward-looking camp in international business. Alliances with non-German actors provide the clearest way of displaying the desired bona fides. In the steel merger, for example, Krupp's executives failed to impose their plan for a simple merger, but managed to bring Thyssen to the bargaining table by recruiting non-German banks, Morgan Grenfell and Goldman Sachs. In discussions about listing its shares on the New York Stock Exchange, Daimler-Benz saw advantage in breaking ranks with other German firms by accepting the accounting standards of the U.S. Securities and Exchange Commission. In debating the formal rules of corporate governance, economic liberals in the Ministries of Justice and Economics allowed access to non-German capital holders and helped them align their interests with the domestic German shareholder associations. The transnational dimension suggests that the advocates of neoliberal reform, while weak in the arena of domestic party politics, are potent in the arena of organizational recipes and ideas. By linking their positions to those of activist pension funds and fiduciary organizations abroad, the German shareholder associations can shape the terms of debate by positioning themselves as the most stalwart proponents of a more open and flexible economy.

For all of these reasons, it would be an analytic mistake to underestimate the importance of the shifts that underlie the modest formal-legal changes enacted to date. The highly intentional creation of an "equity culture" in Germany has precipitated more than a shift in attitudes. By extending and literally advertising the rights of individuals to purchase shares, the German state prompted individuals to invest a significantly larger proportion of household financial assets in equities. By reinforcing the language of shareholder value, the new "equity culture" also created openings for aggressive foreign entrants, as shown in Vodafone's bid for Mannesmann in late 1999. The creation of a new market for small entrepreneurial startup firms was also significant, because it gave younger Germans a sense that equity financing on the U.S. model can provide career possibilities that were previously dominated if not monopolized by larger and more established firms. All of these changes favor the continuing growth of the shareholder protection associations, the disaggregation of voting rights, and a limited but significant shift away from the prevailing pattern of block ownership for large enterprises.

What are the possible outcomes? One possibility is the imposition of reform from above. Although it seems like a logical place for the European Commission to assert itself, the likelihood of a pan-European reform enforced by Brussels is "distant."[64] The proponents of neoliberal reform within

Germany often look to the Competition Directorate in Brussels for support, but the Commission's weakness in this debate so far testifies to the great difficulty of finding guidelines acceptable to all member states. Partly owing to this intractability, other international organizations such as the OECD and the World Bank have launched important initiatives on corporate governance. While the OECD initiative is important for Germany, the generic nature of the OECD guidelines suggest that they are meant to prompt further discussion more than to impose new practices.[65] A second possible outcome is continued resilience of German laws and practices in the face of all outside influences. This outcome is also unlikely because almost all groups within Germany agree that some degree of change in the structure of equity markets is desirable.

The third and most likely outcome is a process of ongoing improvisation that occurs as new patterns of interest become clear. These new patterns of interest will rest on several factors: the perceptions of large firms about the relative value of stability versus flexibility in industrial relations; the perceptions of large bank managers about the pros and cons of arms-length versus more integrated ties to the industrial customers; the emerging markets for new financial-services firms; and the opportunities for small entrepreneurs in search of capital. At the level of individual investors, as more Germans hold shares—and vote those shares independently rather than through the banks—there is more chance that they will adopt Anglo-American criteria of shareholder value in evaluating their holdings. Significant as such a shift would be, it would not necessarily imply a wholesale adoption of Anglo-American practices. The spread of American-style compensation schemes is, for example, very likely to be limited by German expectations that prevent the huge disparities in income acceptable in the United States. While continuing change in the rules of corporate governance is highly likely, it will therefore be change of a hybrid sort in which the German view of the firm as a constitutional embodiment of social partnership remains a clear reference point in evaluating the shareholder rights supported by the proponents of more Anglo-American definitions.

This hybrid process of institutional imitation and adaptation shows why very different mechanisms of change will continue to complement each other in linking globalization to the processes of domestic politics. The examples of financial distress, merger, and acquisition in Germany all point to the operation of competitive selection. For corporate governance, however, such instances served more as signals of something amiss than as unambiguous evidence for the superiority of one approach over another. To see how German firms and organizations interpreted these competitive pressures, the mechanisms of coercive and mimetic isomorphism proved most revealing. Some firms—including both Daimler Benz and Telekom—adjusted to the requirements of powerful regulatory agencies abroad such as the American Securities and Exchange Commission. Other organizations—such as the shareholder associations—articulated their goals in terms that made them likely allies for Calpers and other fiduciary actors in the United States. Yet when Krupp retained Goldman Sachs to help plan its hostile takeover of Thyssen, the resort to Anglo-American practice backfired and the merger was accomplished only by improvising on the more familiar formula of high-level negotiations facilitated by the regional government.

In all three cases, direct transnational ties between particular pairs of organizations conveyed norms as well as financial pressures from abroad to the arena of domestic German politics. Such cases show that proponents of neoliberal reform can readily import new ideas from abroad. At the same time, nothing precludes alternatives for firm-level governance from emerging and taking root within Germany. While such homegrown innovations cannot be forecast with certainty, the current diversity in Germany's industrial landscape suggests that they are likely to occur among large firms as well as the smaller and more insulated firms of Germany's *Mittelstand*. This view suggests that pressures from the international economy will provoke changes in the German economy, but that the changes will build upon Germany's inherited institutions for regularized consultation with labor even as the methods and techniques of equity-based financing encroach on sectors previously dominated by German institutions for bank-led financing. Since the interests of different segments of the business community are likely to shift as new institutional possibilities come into view, new ideas may be as valuable as new resources in this debate. Accordingly, the conventional politics of pushing and hauling captures neither the full weight nor the potential for longer-term change at stake in the politics of industrial property rights. The question of corporate governance hinges on more than the changes wrought by competitive selection or the adjustments negotiated by domestic actors pursuing clear goals. Ultimately, it hinges on the ability of domestic actors in different countries to conclude transnational alliances that give their concepts of corporate governance political credibility as well as financial backing.

Acknowledgement

For comments and suggestions on earlier drafts, I thank Fred Block, John Campbell, Neil Fligstein, Peter Hall, Wade Jacoby, Peter Katzenstein, John Leslie, Jutta Kneissel, Suzanne Lütz, William Ocasio, Kathleen Thelen, Sigurt Vitols, Steven Weber, and John Zysman. Financial support for this research was provided by the German Marshall Fund of the United States, the Center for European Studies at Harvard University, and the Center for German and European Studies, Berkeley.

An earlier version of this chapter appeared in *Politics and Society* 28 (2) (June 2000): 195–221. © 2000, Sage Publications, Inc. Reprinted by Permission of Sage Publications.

Endnotes

1. For the process by which the financial conception of control became ascendant, see Neil Fligstein, *The Transformation of Corporate Control* (Cambridge: Harvard University Press, 1990), and Mark J. Roe, *Strong Managers, Weak Owners: The Political Roots of American Corporate Finance* (Princeton: Princeton University Press, 1994).

2. For the historical emergence of Germany's constitutional treatment of the firm versus the approaches taken in other countries, see especially Gregory Jackson, "Corporate Governance in Germany and Japan: Developments within National and International Contexts (Typescript: Max-Planck-Institut für Gesellschaftsforschung, 1997); Sigurt Vitols, Steven Casper, David Soskice and Stephen Woolcock, "Corporate Governance in Large British and German Companies: Comparative Institutional Advantage or Competing for Best Practice" (Anglo-German Foundation for the Study of Industrial Society, London, 1997); and Mary O'Sullivan, "Corporate Governance in Germany: Productive and Financial Challenges" (Annandale-on-Hudson, N.Y.: Jerome Levy Economics Institute, 1998). For selected perspectives from the wide literature on comparative corporate governance, see Richard Buxbaum, "Comparative Aspects of Institutional Investment and Corporate Governance" and other essays in Theodor Baums, Richard M. Buxbaum, Klaus J. Hopt, eds., *Institutional Investors and Corporate Governance* (Berlin: de Gruyter, 1994); and Andrei Shleifer and Robert W. Vishny, "A Survey of Corporate Governance," *Journal of Finance* (June 1997): 737–783.

3. For representative contributions, see Suzanne Berger and Ronald Dore, eds., *National Diversity and Global Capitalism* (Ithaca: Cornell University Press, 1996); Robert Keohane and Helen Milner, eds., *Internationalization and Domestic Politics* (New York: Cambridge University Press, 1996); Rogers Hollingsworth, Philippe Schmitter, and Wolfgang Streeck, eds., *Governing Capitalist Economies: Performance and Control of Economic Sectors* (Oxford: Oxford University press, 1994).

4. For critiques of the idea of globalization as an automatic process, see Fred L. Block, *The Vampire State and Other Myths and Fallacies about the U.S. Economy* (New York: The New Press, 1996); Peter B. Evans, "The Eclipse of the State? Reflections on Stateness in an Era of Globalization," *World Politics* 50 (October 1997): 62–87; Geoffrey Garrett, *Partisan Politics in the Global Economy* (New York: Cambridge University Press, 1998).

5. See especially Will Hutton, *The State We're In* (London: Jonathan Cape, 1995); and Margaret Blair, *Ownership and Control: Rethinking Corporate Ownership for the Twenty-First Century* (Washington, DC: Brookings, 1995).

6. A more comprehensive description would have to include a country's provisions under at least four categories: (1) the formal rules that establish the terms of liability and authority within a firm; (2) the distribution of ownership among different interest groups in a society; (3) the rights of lenders (debt-holders) as opposed to owners (shareholders); (4) the informal patterns of decisionmaking that characterize top management's links to external constituencies as well as internal stakeholders. For these issues, see Jonathan R. Macey and Geoffrey P. Miller, "Corporate Governance and Commercial Banking: A Comparative Examination of Germany, Japan, and the United States," *Stanford Law Review* 48(1) (November 1995): 73–112; and Mark J. Roe, "Some Differences in Corporate Structure in Germany, Japan, and the United States" (Symposium: Economic Competitiveness and the Law), *Yale Law Journal* 102(8) (June 1993): 1927–1003; Roberta Romano, "A Cautionary Note on Drawing Lessons from Comparative Corporate Law (response to article by Mark J. Roe)," *Yale Law Journal* 102(8) (June, 1993): 2021–2037.

7. For representative views on the evolution of the German model, see Andrew Shonfield, *Modern Capitalism: The Changing Balance of Public and Private Power* (London: Oxford University Press, 1965); Fritz W. Scharpf, "Economic and Institutional Constraints of Full-Employment Strategies: Sweden, Austria, and West Germany, 1973–1982," in John H. Goldthorpe, ed., *Order and Conflict in Contemporary Capitalism: Studies in the Political Economy of Western European Nations* (Oxford: Oxford University Press, 1984): Wolfgang Streeck, "Neo-Corporatist Industrial Relations and the Economic Crisis West Germany," in Goldthorpe, ed.; and Peter A. Hall, "The Political Economy of Adjustment in Germany," *WZB Jahrbuch 1997* (Berlin: Sigma, 1997).

8. For these developments, see Andrei S. Markovits, *The Politics of the West German Trade Unions: Strategies of Class and Interest Representation in Growth and Crisis* (New York: Cambridge University Press, 1986), and Kathleen A. Thelen, *Union of Parts: Labor Politics in Postwar Germany* (Ithaca: Cornell University Press, 1991). For the historical roots of labor's commitment to the works councils in the Ruhr region, see Mary Nolan, *Social Democracy and Society: Working-Class Radicalism in Düsseldorf, 1890–1920* (New York: Cambridge University Press, 1981).

9. Alfred L. Thimm, *The False Promise of Codetermination: The Changing Nature of European Workers' Participation.* (Lexington, MA: D.C. Heath and Company, 1980), especially 30–40.

10. See Hans Willy Hohn, *Von der Einheitsgewerkschaft zum Betriebssyndikalismus: Soziale Schließung im dualen System der Interessenvertretung* (Berlin: Sigma, 1988); Peter J. Katzenstein, *Policy and Politics in West Germany: The Growth of a Semisovereign State* (Philadelphia: Temple, 1987); Wolfgang Streeck, "Codetermination: The Fourth Decade," in B. Wilpert and A. Sorge, eds., *International Perspectives on 'Organizational Democracy* (New York: Wiley, 1984), 391–422; and Thelen (note 8).

11. For examples of the banks' voting strength, with and without exercising proxy rights, see Theodor Baums and Fraune, "Institutionelle Anleger und Publikumsgesellschaft," *Die Aktiengesellschaft,* no. 3 (1996): 106.

12. Alexander Gerschenkron, *Economic Backwardness in Historical Perspective* (Cambridge: Harvard University Press, 1962); Andrew Shonfield, *Modern Capitalism: The Changing Balance of Public and Private Power* (London: Oxford University Press, 1965).

13. Mark Roe, *Strong Managers, Weak Owners* (note 1).

14. A. Alchian and H. Demsetz, "Production, Information Costs, and Economic Organization," *American Economic Review* 62 (December 1972): 777–795; M.C. Jensen and W.C. Meckling, "Theory of the Firm: Management Behavior, Agency Costs and Ownership Structure," *Journal of Financial Economics* 3 (1976): 305–360.

15. For an example of this logic, see William Emmons and Frank A. Schmid, "Universal Banking, Control Rights, and Corporate Finance in Germany," *Federal Reserve Bank of St. Louis Review* 80(4) (July–August 1998): 19–42.

16. In 1970, corporations or joint-stock companies (Aktiengesellschaften) employed roughly 33.5% of German workers, but constituted less than 2% of the 1.9 million enterprises in Germany. The others were single proprietorships (91%), partnerships of different types (5.8%), cooperatives (0.7%), non-stock private companies (0.2%), and public companies (0.2%). Figures from Alfred Thimm, "How Far Should German Codetermination Go?" *Challenge* 11 (July/August 1981). For these different organizational forms and their legal status,

see Germany's Commercial Law Code, the Handelsgesetzbuch (HGB), articles 17–37a.

17. On centralized versus decentralized industrial orders in Germany, see Gary Herrigel, *Industrial Constructions: The Sources of German Industrial Power* (New York: Cambridge University Press, 1996).

18. For the different types of banking institutions in Germany, see Richard Deeg, *Finance Capital Unveiled: Banks and the German Political Economy* (Ann Arbor: University of Michigan Press, 1999), 19–21 and 83. For their role in Eastern Germany, see John R. Griffin, "Investment and Ownership in a Volatile Economy: Big Banks and the Case of the East German Economic Transition," *Politics and Society* 22(3) (September 1994): 389–413. For a more general treatment of organizational experimentation and democracy, see Michael C. Dorf and Charles F. Sabel, "A Constitution of Democratic Experimentalism," *Columbia Law Review*, 98(2) (March 1998):267–473.

19. See for example Julie A. Elston and Horst Albach, "Bank Affiliations and Firm Capital Investment in Germany," *IFO-Studien* 41(1) (1995): 3–16; Ulrich Schroeder, "Corporate Governance in Germany: the Changing Role of the Banks," *German Politics* 5(3) (December 1996): 536–370; Emmons and Schmid (note 15 above).

20. For Germany's coordinating capabilities, see David Soskice, "Divergent Production Regimes: Coordinated and Uncoordinated Market Economies in the 1980s and 1990s," in H. Kitschelt, et al., eds., *Continuity and Change in Contemporary Capitalism* (New York: Cambridge University Press, 1999), 101–34. For longer-term "coordination efficiencies," and the problems they pose for arguments from competitive selection, see Block, *The Vampire State* (note 4 above), 53–57. For two complementary views suggesting that competition may remain a dominant selection mechanism without selecting strictly on the basis of efficiency criteria, see Michael T. Hannan and John Freeman, *Organizational Ecology* (Cambridge: Harvard University Press, 1989), especially 35–37; and Neil Fligstein, *Ruling Markets: An Economic Sociology of Capitalist Societies*" (Princeton: Princeton University Press: forthcoming).

21. Karel Lanoo, "A European Perspective on Corporate Governance," *Journal of Common Market Studies* 37(2) (June 1999): 269–94; Martin Rhodes and Bastiaan van Apeldoorn, "Capitalism Unbound? The Transformation of European Corporate Governance," *Journal of European Public Policy* 5(3) (1998); and Richard Deeg and Sofia Perez, "International Capital Mobility and Domestic Institutions: Corporate Finance and governance in Four European Cases," Paper presented at the 1998 American Political Science Convention, Boston, Massachusetts, September 3–6, 1998.

22. For an analysis showing how this pattern also results when dominant powers adopt a regulatory first-mover role, see Beth Simmons, "The International Poli-

tics of Harmonization: The Case of Capital Market Regulation," Paper prepared for the Conference on Globalization and Regulation, Berkeley, December 3–4, 1999.

23. Paul J. DiMaggio and Walter W. Powell, "The Iron Cage Revisited: Institutional Isomorphism and Collective Rationality in Organization Fields," in Walter W. Powell and Paul J. DiMaggio, eds., *The New Institutionalism in Organizational Analysis* (Chicago: University of Chicago Press, 1991): 63–82.

24. DiMaggio and Powell, "The Iron Cage Revisited," especially 69–74.

25. For examples including the Cadbury Report in the U.K. (1992) and the Rapport Vienot in France (1995), see *Le Monde*, July 12, 1995, as well as James P. Hawley, "Comparative Corporate Governance: Explaining Changing Pattern in the Ownership, Control and the Governance of Large Corporations in France and Germany, with a Note on the U.K." Paper presented at the annual meetings of the Pacific Sociological Association, Seattle, Washington, March 22, 1996.

26. For these different mechanisms and the styles of institutionalist analysis from which they derive, see Peter A. Hall and Rosemary C.R. Taylor, "Political Science and the Three New Institutionalisms," *Political Studies* 44(4) (1996): 936–57, and the debate between these authors and Colin Hay and Daniel Wincott in *Political Studies* 46(5) (1998): 951–962.

27. Rainer Funke, parliamentary state secretary of the Justice Ministry, quoted in the *Financial Times* (27 February 1997): 11.

28. "Bonner Regierung scheut Einschnitte in die Eckpfeiler der Bankenmacht," *Süddeutsche Zeitung* (September 14, 1996); Beat Gygi, "Suche nach "besserer" Unternehmenskontrolle: Debatte über die Reform des deutschen Aktienrechts," *Neue Zürcher Zeitung* (November 27, 1996).

29. *Financial Times* (April 11, 1996) and (June 24, 1996).

30. Interview, Ministry of Justice, Bonn, June 1998. The evolving views of Calpers on corporate governance in Japan, France, and Germany are available on its website: www.calpers.ca.gov/invest/corpgov/cggermany.htm
     In 1996, Calpers was primarily concerned with U.S.-based efforts to bring more "outsiders" or nonmanagement directors to American boards—a priority which at best addressed awkwardly the tensions within Germany's two-board system.

31. "Zusammenstellung der Stellungnahmen zur öffentlichen Anhörung des Rechtsausschusses . . . , January 29, 1997 (Bonn: typescript, January 30, 1997).

32. Ibid.

33. Interviews, Office of Margareta Wolf, Green Party spokeswoman for economics, finance, research, and technology, Bonn, June 1999; Office of Hans-Martin Bury, SPD spokesman for economic, finance, and technology, Bonn, June 1999. For the Greens' position on corporate governance, see the published version of a roundtable, held 5 March 1997, in *Das Deutsche Bankensystem:*

Innovationsbremse oder Erfolgsgarant? (Bonn: Bundestagsfraktion BÜNDNIS 90/ Die Grünen, May 1997).

34. *Handelsblatt* (March 6–7, 1997): 6. My thanks to John Cioffi for reminding me of this provision's significance.

35. Karl Otto Pohl, "Frankfurt im Konkurrenzkampf der Finanzplätze neue Rahmenbedingungen sind schnell erforderlich," *Frankfurter Allgemeine Zeitung* (June 24, 1989). For the regional stock markets, see Susanne Lütz, "The Revival of the Nation-State? Stock Exchange Regulation in an Era of Internationalized Financial Markets," Discussion Paper 96/9, Max-Planck-Institut für Gesellschaftsforschung, Cologne, December 1996.

36. *Financial Times* (February 27, 1995): 11.

37. Figures from Lanoo (see above, note 21), page 274. The corresponding figure for the market valuation of all British firms as a proportion of British GDP was 193.7%

38. "Germans Dive into the Equity Culture: Deutsche Telekom Shares Surge," *Financial Times* (November 19, 1996): 1; J. Nicholas Ziegler, "The Politics of Privatization and Restructuring in Germany," Working Paper #3880, MIT Sloan School October 1997.

39. Figures from the dpa (deutsche Presseagentur), November 1996, and available (as of May 1999) at the website for Deutsche Telekom <http://www.dtag.de /untern/inv_relations/forum/right.htm>.

40. In keeping with the more closed nature of financial governance in Germany, the German financial press reported on these cross-listings in notably less detail than English language publications. The best accounts on these particular cross-listings are from *Euromoney* (April 1995), *Euromoney* (May 1995) and *Economist* (September 17, 1994). For the reconciliation of Deutsche Telekom's 1996 accounts, see the company's Geschäftsbericht (Annual Report), 1996.

41. Interviews, Ministry of Justice, Bonn, June, 1999. For a report on the similarities and differences between IAS standards and U.S. GAAP, from the viewpoint of the U.S. Financial Accounting Standards Board (FASB), see Carrie Bloomer, ed., *The IASC-U.S. Comparison Project* (Norwalk, Connecticut: FASB, 1996).

42. *Euromoney,* May 1995, and *Economist,* September 17, 1994.

43. Marianne Kulicke, u.a., *Chancen und Risiken junger Technologieunternehmen: Ergebnisse des Modellversuchs "Förderung technologieorientierter Unternehmensgründungen* (Heidelberg: Physica-Verlag, 1993).

44. Peter Glotz and Uwe Thomas, *Das dritte Wirtschaftswunder: Aufbruch in eine neue Gründerzeit* (Düsseldorf: Econ, 1994).

45. Results of the study, by the Institut für praxisorientierte Sozialforschung (ipos), appeared in the website of the Federal Association of German Banks (Bundesverband Deutshcer Banken)— http:www.bdb.de/presse/interes/aktuell.htm— under the heading "Deutschland: Die Aktienkultur gewinnt an Tiefe" in June

1999. See also "Aktienfonds stehen bei Anlegern an erster Stelle," Süddeutsche Zeitung (November 12, 1999).

46. On the steel industry, see especially Josef Esser and Wolfgang Fach, "Crisis Management 'Made in Germany': The Steel Industry," in Peter J. Katzenstein, *Industry and Politics in West Germany: Toward the Third Republic* (Ithaca: Cornell University Press, 1989), 221–48.

47. This account is based on interviews with representatives of the regional government of North Rhine-Westphalia and IG Metall in Düsseldorf, June 1998, and June, 1999, as well as the documentary sources cited below.

48. Süddeutsche Zeitung (March 26, 1997).

49. Interviews, Landespresseamt, North Rhine-Westphalia, Düsseldorf, June 1999.

50. "Regierungserklärung des Ministers für Wirtschaft und Mittelstand, Technologie und Verkehr, Wolfgang Clement, vor dem Landtag Nordrhein-Westfalen am 20, Marz 1997 zur aktuellen Situation in der Stahlindustrie (issued by the regional government of North Rhine Westphalia, March 20, 1997).

51. Süddeutsche Zeitung (March 26, 1997) and Sunday Times (London) (30 March 1997).

52. "Grundsatzvereinbarung zur Bildung von 'Thyssen Krupp Stahl' unterzeichnet" (Presseerklärung, Düsseldorf/Essen, March 16, 1997).

53. Press conference by Dr. Gerhard Cromme, Villa Hügel, Essen, March 28, 1998.

54. For additional information on new arrangements for labor-management cooperation in firm-level strategy and change, see the important Report of the Commission on Codetermination, Mitbestimmung und neue Unternehmenskulteren (Bertelsmann Stiftung und Hans-Böckler Stiftung, 1998).

55. Interview, IG Metall, Zweigstelle Düsseldorf, June 1998.

56. Peter J. Katzenstein, "Stability and Change in the Emerging Third Republic," in Katzenstein, ed., *Industry and Politics* (note 46).

57. Kathleen Thelen, "Why German Employers Cannot Bring Themselves to Dismantle the German Model," in Torben Iversen, Jonas Pontusson, and David Soskice, eds., *Unions, Employers and Central Banks* (New York: Cambridge University Press), 1999.

58. "The UAW's Next Battleground," *Business Week* (July 26, 1999), 28–29.

59. "Unions to Decide on Daimler Chrysler Seat," *Detroit Free Press* (May 19, 1998); "UAW Wins Seat on Daimler Board," *Detroit Free Press* (May 28, 1998).

60. Douglass C. North, *Institutions, Institutional Change and Economic Performance* (New York: Cambridge University Press, 1990).

61. Choice-theoretic accounts grapple with this problem as an extreme example of the unintended consequences of institutional change, which can disappoint actors who opt for particular institutional alternatives only to find that the chosen arrangements do not produce the expected benefits. For discussion of this

issue in the context of property rights, see Jack Knight and Douglass C. North, "Explaining the Complexity of Institutional Change," in David L. Weimer, ed., *The Political Economy of Property Rights: Institutional Change and Credibility in the Reform of Centrally Planned Economies* (New York: Cambridge University Press, 1997), 354.

62. For the general difficulty involved in imputing "pre-political" preferences and focusing analysis on the way actors with fixed preferences proceed, see Cass R. Sunstein, *Free Markets and Social Justice* (New York: Oxford University Press, 1997), 21–23.

63. For the growing role of transnational society in European politics more generally, see Alec Stone Sweet and Wayne Sandholtz, "Integration, Supranational Governance, and the Institutionalization of the European Polity," in Sweet and Sandholtz, eds., *European Integration and Supranational Governance* (New York: Oxford University Press, 1999), 1–26, esp. 11.

64. Lanoo (above note 21), page 280.

65. The "OECD Principles of Corporate Governance" were developed at the request of the OECD Council meeting of April 27–28, 1998 and published on the OECD website http://oecd.org/dag/governance/principles.htm on May 18, 1999.

6 Discourse and the Legitimation of Economic and Social Policy Change in Europe

Vivien A. Schmidt

National economic and social policy change in European countries has been influenced by a variety of external economic and institutional forces, both at the global and regional levels. The global forces include the competitive pressures resulting from the liberalization of international financial markets and trade and the (de)regulatory pressures coming from liberalizing international trade organizations and negotiations. For European Union member-states, regional-level economic and institutional forces have had an even more significant impact than those at the global level. European integration has acted both as a conduit for global forces and a shield against them by promoting convergence in macroeconomic policies and institutions through the common currency and liberalization in microeconomic policy and institutions through the single market (Schmidt 1999b). These global and regional forces have together spurred European member-states to tighten budgets, open markets, deregulate business, downsize the public sector, and cut back the welfare state. But some countries have gone farther than others in accommodating global and/or Europe-driven policy change, and some have done better than others in reconciling themselves to whatever changes they have instituted (Schmidt 1995). This not only is related to such national level factors as countries' economic vulnerabilities to external economic pressures or their institutional capacities to adapt to external regulatory pressures. It also depends on countries' ability to construct legitimating discourses capable of generating public acceptance for policy change.

Despite the alleged inescapability from global imperatives and the apparent inexorability of European integration (these attesting to another external influence—the ideational) (Hay and Watson 1988; Hay and Marsh 1998; Weiss 1997; Zysman 1996), nothing is inevitable. Nations, just as individuals, exercise choice. And with regard to global and European-related liberalization, much depends upon nations and their citizens choosing openness and integration. This is made easier when the public is convinced that policy change is not just necessary because it makes sense intellectually but also appropriate because it resonates with national values.

These cognitive and normative aspects of discourse naturally differ from one European member-state to the next, given the fact that member-states start from very different economic, political, and cultural specificities. However, member-states' discourses differ not only in terms of ideas but also process. Countries' differing institutional contexts frame the discourse, determining who articulates the discourse, how it is articulated, and toward whom it is primarily directed. This interactive dimension of discourse, which essentially speaks to the ability of policy elites to coordinate the construction of a policy program and to communicate it to the public, is as important to the ultimate success of a discourse as the ideational.

In order to show how discourse works and why it is important, I examine the political-economic discourses of France and Britain. These stand out because whereas French governments of both the left and the right beginning in 1983 consistently failed to find a discourse capable of legitimating their moderate neoliberal policy paradigm, and so have had difficulties with reform efforts in the 1990s, British governments of the right beginning in 1979 developed a legitimating discourse for their more radical neoliberal policy paradigm which has been so successful that it is now in the process of renewal by a government of the left. The comparison is especially instructive because although these countries differ ideationally, they nevertheless bear great resemblance to one another in terms of the interactive dimension of discourse, given the importance in both countries of public communication of policy programs constructed by a restricted, government-centered policy elite. This is in contrast to countries where discourse is the product of a wider policy elite more focused on the coordination of policy construction rather than its communication to the public, such as Germany. For the benefits of comparison, in the initial theoretical section as well as in the conclusion, I briefly discuss the case of Germany, which until recently had managed to maintain its postwar legitimating discourse of the policy paradigm of the social market economy largely intact (see Schmidt 1997).

The Nature of Discourse

The account of discourse elaborated herein draws on the definition developed by James March and Johan Olsen (1995, 46), who see discourse as a central part of democratic governance, helping to consolidate political identity, define political action, and interpret political events. However, my approach is somewhat narrower, since I focus primarily on the discourse of policy elites within a given issues area or policy arena (here, political-economy, but this would apply equally well to defense, citizenship, energy, the nation-state vis-à-vis Europe, etc.) (for more detail, see Schmidt 2000). As such, it resembles a "policy narratives" approach (Gottweis 1999; Larat 1999; Radaelli n/a; Roe 1994), without, however, making claim to that literature's philosophical presuppositions (following from Michel Foucault, Roland Barthes, and others).

My approach also shares with Martin Rein and Donald Schön the assumption that discourse serves to "frame" a complex reality by providing guideposts to "knowing, analyzing, persuading, and acting" (1991, 263, 289; 1994, 22), except that my definition of discourse considers the underlying structure of beliefs, or values, as separate, as in the discourse but not of it. Moreover, although my notion of discourse bears a striking resemblance to the "référentiel," or "ideas in action" developed by French policy analysts such as Bruno Jobert and Pierre Muller (see Faure, Pollet and Warin 1995; Jobert 1992; Muller and Surel 1998), I draw a greater analytic distinction between policy program and discourse. By considering discourse on its own, apart from both the values to which it appeals and the policy program it promotes, I seek to take account of the ways in which discourse may affect values rather than simply reflect them and may be disconnected from the policy program (see Schmidt 1999b).

Finally, my account of discourse has much in common with the extensive literature concerned with the groups responsible for the generation and implementation of policy ideas, whether "epistemic communities" (Haas 1992; Kohler-Koch 1997, 99–101; Mazey and Richardson 1996), "advocacy coalitions" (Sabatier and Jenkins-Smith 1993; Sabatier 1998), "social learning" and "policy paradigms" (Hall 1993), "discourse coalitions" (Wittrock, Wagner, and Wollmann 1991), or the "médiateur" of the "référentiel" (Muller 1995). The focus of most of these approaches, however, tends to be at the coordinative stage of discourse, where the groups at the center of policy construction tend to come up with the ideas and meanings that form the bases for collective action and identity. My approach goes farther than most of these, first of all, by pointing to the different kinds of contexts which frame the discourse and, secondly, by connecting this "coordinative" stage of the discourse to the "communicative," by considering how policy elites persuade the public of the validity of the policy programs they constructed. In this sense, my approach joins Peter Hall's notion of "national political discourses" (1989, 383f) and Gerhard Lehmbruch's "discourse coalitions" (1999), although the focus of Lehmbruch's inquiry is primarily on the ideational rather than the interactive dimension, that is, on the ideas and not on how a policy program is constructed and communicated.

The Ideational Dimension of Discourse

In its ideational dimension, discourse serves two functions: cognitive, by sketching out the basic principles and parameters of a policy program in terms of the issues to be addressed, problems to be solved, goals to be attained, and policy instruments to be used; and normative, by showing how the policy program fits with the polity's basic values, that is, its purposes, goals, and ideals, or builds on them to create something new, better suited to the new realities and more appropriate than the old "public philosophy" (Campbell 1998).

As such, the policy program, much like the classical Kuhnian definition of a paradigm in science (Kuhn 1970), need not be an elaborated structure initially, but rather have great potential for further elaboration. Much like Lakatos' research programs (1970), moreover, such policy paradigms or programs have a "core" — made up of the most basic principles, goals, assumptions about appropriate courses of action, and methods of translating general principles into action — which is likely to change very slowly compared to its "periphery" of policy applications (see Majone 1989).[1] When change in policy paradigm occurs, moreover, as in Kuhnian science, it is likely to appear revolutionary. But unlike in science, where the problems stem almost entirely from the science-related concerns of scientists and the solutions are certified as such by scientists alone, in society, the problems stem from the concerns of the citizens while the solutions are recognized as solutions only if they are accepted as such by the citizens as well as by policymakers (see Schmidt 1988). This is why normative legitimation takes on such importance in society, by contrast with science.

Finally, while in Kuhnian science the picture is of only one dominant paradigm which is then entirely abandoned in favor of the new, in society, although there may be only one dominant paradigm and legitimating discourse in a given issues area, there may be other, minority (opposition) discourses waiting in the wings, proposing alternative policy paradigms and appealing to alternative sets of values in the polity. What is more, even a dominant discourse need not be monolithic: the different parties in a government coalition and/or the different currents in a majority party may have separate discourses which are most often (but certainly not always) complementary.

The Interactive Dimension of Discourse

In its interactive dimension, the discourse also serves two functions: coordinative, by providing a common language and ideational framework through which key policy groups can together construct a policy program, debate its merits, and refine it as it is put into place; and communicative, by serving as the vehicle through which policy elites seek to persuade the public that the policy paradigm is necessary and appropriate.

Although all countries have both coordinative and communicative discourses, the balance in favor of the one or the other tends to depend largely on the institutional context which frames the discursive process. For the framing of the process, much depends upon the relative strength of government vis-à-vis opposition parties, organized interests, and other groups in the polity; the institutional arrangements which underpin the distribution of power; and the discursive practices which reflect the balance of powers and produce differing kinds of discursive interactions.

In some countries, the elaboration of the program is by a restricted, government-centered policy elite, whether a politico-technocratic elite (as in France) or a political party elite (as in Britain), and the discourse is mainly directed toward the general public, to communicate the government's policy decisions. This "communicative discourse" is most prevalent where governmental power is concentrated in the executive (e.g., countries with unitary states and statist policymaking processes, as in Britain and France). In such "single-actor" systems, the relatively small number of actors involved in the construction of the policy program ensures that the coordinative discourse, focused on policy construction, will be much less elaborate than the communicative discourse, which is focused on winning over the general public. In this context, policy elites are likely to be authoritative in discursive practice, as they seek to persuade others of the validity of their view, without expecting to have to accommodate alternative views (although, depending upon the public reaction, they may in fact be accommodating in practice). The process of persuasion itself tends to be similar to that found in judicial decisionmaking (which is equally authoritative in its hierarchical and unilateral communication), because legitimacy also depends upon policy elites providing an explanation which gives "good reasons" based on shared cognitive and normative criteria.

In other countries, the elaboration of the policy program is the product of a much wider cross-section of policy-related elites, encompassing not only governmental political and technocratic elites but also opposition parties and interest group leaders, in particular those from business and labor (as in Germany and the smaller consociational democracies like Switzerland, Austria, and the Netherlands). In such "multi-actors" systems, the discourse tends to be directed toward those very policy elites involved in the original elaboration, as a way of coordinating the policy construction. This "coordinative discourse" is much more the case where governmental power and/or societal representation are more dispersed (e.g., countries with federal states and/or corporatist policymaking processes, as in Germany). The institutional context alone ensures that policy elites need to be more accommodating in discursive practice if they are to succeed in building a common point of view and a mutually agreed-upon policy program. Such practice is generally focused on producing consensus, whether the interaction leading up to consensus is entirely cooperative and "solidaristic" (as has been typical in Austria—Heinisch 1999) or, rather, involves more rational self-interested bargaining and conflict preliminary to arriving at a compromise consensus (more typical in Germany—Scharpf 1997). In either case, the large number of actors necessary to reaching agreement ensures that the coordinative discourse will be quite elaborate.

By the same token, however, the communicative discourse may end up quite thin, since actors' energies are focused on agreeing amongst themselves and on then persuading their own constituencies that the agreement is acceptable according to their own particular group's cognitive and normative criteria. In consequence, the process of persuasion here is more akin to what occurs in contract negotiations (which tend to be nonhierarchical and bi- or multilateral) than judicial decisionmaking, because legitimacy depends upon policy elites convincing their separate constituencies that the outcome is better than what would have happened if the negotiations failed and there were no contract. Depending upon the country, there may be no other discourse than this (e.g., Austria). However, in multi-actor systems where the parties involved in the negotiations do not include all relevant groups and where the government still faces an opposition in public confrontations (e.g., Germany), a communicative discourse akin to the French or British that addresses the wider public with appeals to shared criteria may be necessary. The fact that it comes on top of a much wider coordinative discourse, how- ever, means that it is constrained by the compromises among the bargaining parties in a way that single-actor Britain and France, with their more re- stricted, government-centered elite construction of the discourse, are not.

But whichever way a polity constructs and communicates its discourse, the discourse itself is central not simply to the legitimation of a policy program but to the maintenance of democracy as well. The pursuit of public accep- tance of a policy program by politicians who represent the public they seek to persuade is at the very foundations of representative democracy. And such public attempts at persuasion are an ongoing task, even though elections may consecrate a discourse or bury it. For whatever the cognitive and normative commitments of the policy elite, in a democracy they must be able success- fully to communicate these to the larger public as they coordinate the elab- oration and implementation of the policies with relevant policy players. Fail- ures in communication, in fact, can have dire consequences for democracy.

The Discursive Challenges of European Integration and Globalization

For European countries subject to the global and European pressures, there is an additional discursive issue to add to the ones noted above. It is hard enough to construct and maintain a successful national discourse when policy elites largely have autonomy in their national policymaking and con- trol over national actors. But with European integration, governments have lost significant independence in decisionmaking and influence not simply over the forces at work in the polity but also over the very policies they can institute in response to those forces. In the construction of a policy program, moreover, it is not only that decisions at the EU-level increasingly determine national policies but also that national ideas about national policy options prior to or outside the realm of EU legislation are also affected by the "epistemic communities" or "advocacy coalitions" of transnational, European policy elites which promote mimesis among nations (for example, with the nationally decided restrictive monetary policies which culminated in EMU—see Marcussen 1998). Such policy sectorization, in turn, increases the problems for national governments of creating a discourse which has some coherence across sectors.

The difficulties of reconstructing a national discourse under these circumstances are major. And success depends on whether policy elites are able to argue convincingly that the national economic adjustments and institutional adaptations in response to global and European level forces mesh with the underlying policy paradigm both cognitively and normatively or, if not, whether they can argue persuasively either that is possible to alter the policy paradigm without undermining longstanding national values or, if this is not plausible, that it is beneficial to revise those values along with the policy paradigm.

The importance of constructing or reconstructing a national discourse capable of legitimating the changes in national economies and institutions in response to the global or European level forces cannot be underestimated. Without such a discourse, countries will risk what Wolfgang Streeck has termed the "democracy illusion," in which political opportunism and populist demagoguery will prosper as voters and politicians alike are torn between "refusing to recognize the externalities that increasingly govern national polities, and blaming everything on them—at one time calling for national solutions where these are no longer possible, and at another demanding 'European solutions' while in the name of national sovereignty and diversity refusing integrated Europe the means to deliver them" (Streeck 1996, 311–313). For Streeck, this is inevitable in "democracy under fragmented sovereignty." But this underestimates the power of public discourse as well as the possibility that national policy elites will produce a coherent vision of what integration within a larger Europe and world is and should be, and that is capable of providing the public with a sense of orientation and legitimacy with regard to the economic adjustments and institutional adaptations in response to European and global pressures.

Where the policy responses to global and European pressures can be legitimated within the context of a coherent national discourse, they help round out the vision of the country in a larger Europe and world. Without such a vision, or a sense of how responses to global and European pressures fit within it, discussions of European and global economic imperatives tend to be heard more as rhetorical exhortations, with no greater rationale than as excuses for government policy, and with little lasting message other than that outside incursions are causing change within. At best, in times of prosperity and complacency, the public will accept such exhortations and their rationale with little question, and will respond to the message as a challenge. At worst, in times of recession and malaise, the public may reject the exhortations and the rationale, finding itself left only with the message, which will most likely mainly instill fear and increase public vulnerability to political opportunism and demagoguery. In such cases where national elites fail to provide a sufficiently legitimating account of national economic and institutional responses to global and European pressures, national stability or, worse, national democracy, may be put at risk.

The risk to national democracy stems primarily from the fact that the economic and institutional changes instigated by global and European pressures have struck at the very foundations of European member-states' self-conceptions. This is because such changes challenge popular expectations about the role of the state in the economy, throwing open for question traditional conceptions of economic organization, social welfare, and political democracy and, thereby, also jeopardizing the deeper structures of national identity which are often attached to such traditional conceptions.[2] But they do this differently, of course, given differences among countries not only in terms of their generally very different economic, social, and political specificities but also their different cognitive and normative frameworks and their different coordinative and communicative contexts and practices. For France and Great Britain, as we shall see, these differences make for very different discourses with very different levels of success.

France: In Search of a Discourse

Since 1983, with the adoption of a moderate neoliberal political-economic policy program, French governments have been markedly unsuccessful in constructing a legitimating discourse capable of projecting to the public a convincing vision of how France fits within an integrating Europe and a globalizing world. Ever since the Socialists abandoned their socialist discourse in the early 1980s once they converted to a neoliberal economic policy program and the right failed to sustain their radical neoliberal discourse of the mid 1980s in the face of electoral defeat (see Schmidt 1996), French policy elites have been in search of a new discourse that would serve to legitimate the country's liberalizing economic transformation in terms of national values and identity. In its absence, successive governments have more often than not justified neoliberal policy change by reference to the European and global level pressures, generally by presenting the changes related to European integration as necessary to protect the country against the incursions of globalization while enhancing France's economic power in Europe and the world. In consequence, the public has had to settle for successive communicative discourses that, whether from governments of the right or the left, have all provided the same general policy orientation and justification for why change has been economically necessary (cognitive function) but insufficient legitimation on why it has been appropriate in terms of national values (normative function). Over the course of the 1990s in particular, this became more and more problematic, as the economic adjustments related to the neoliberal policy program and European monetary integration were seen increasingly to conflict with longstanding values related to social solidarity, given continuing high unemployment and cuts in social programs, and to undermine the *"service public"* (public interest services), given rationalization and privatization in public sector infrastructural services and utilities.

In France, where the state is ideal typically strong and societal groups weak, the coordinative discourse tends to be very thin, given that the policy program is generally the product of a small, restricted governmental-technocratic elite. Because power is concentrated in the executive, given a unitary state with statist policymaking processes, governments tend to formulate "heroic" policies largely absent outside input (whether of opposition, social partners, subnational governments, or other societal interests which tend to be the interlocutors in unitary or federal systems with pluralist or corporatist policymaking processes). In consequence, the communicative stage of discourse is especially important. This is when governments authoritatively present their policy program, seeking to convince not only the general public but even those interests most affected by the policy program of its necessity and appropriateness. And this is where governments get their response, either through public acquiescence or protest, whether in words—by way of polemics in the media, by interest group leaders, experts, and the opposition—or in action, whether immediately through demonstrations and strikes or with a time delay, through periodic elections. It is the public reaction, moreover, which leads governments to decide whether to persist with the policy or withdraw it, whether to accommodate the concerns of the most affected interests or to risk confrontation.

In this public arena, however, although the government's pronouncements represent the dominant discourse, it is neither the only discourse, since opposition parties have separate (although since 1983 not really opposing) discourses, nor is it monolithic, since governmental coalition members also tend to have separate (although generally complementary) discourses. Moreover, even president and prime minister may have somewhat different discourses, and especially so where "cohabitation" (when the president and prime minister are of different parties) occurs. With regard to the neoliberal economic program and European monetary integration since 1983, however, the discourses have tended to show few significant differences—with a taboo against criticism of European monetary integration for mainstream parties of the left and the right for much of that period (except for the Maastricht debate and after 1997).

The Postwar Paradigm and Discourse

Until 1983, the dominant political-economic paradigm of the postwar period was *"dirigisme,"* or state interventionism, in which the state was to lead economic growth and industrial development by whatever means it saw fit. Although the paradigm began in the early postwar period, with the planning process directed by the technocratic elite of the state, it did not gain a fully legitimating discourse until Charles de Gaulle became president at the inception of the Fifth Republic in 1958. It was de Gaulle who put the political-economic program at the center of his vision of France becoming a major world power and a leader in Europe. In the discourse, he made appeal to national pride with his talk of French *grandeur* and independence, and sought to build on a sense of France's exceptionalism as well as its history of state interventionism that goes all the way back to Louis XIV and his minister Colbert. The industrial policies that created and promoted the "national champions," the public sector enterprises which were to provide a high level of infrastructural services and perform a public service mission (electricity, air transport, later the railroads and the telephone), and the *grands projets* were all presented as symbols for a France which was to be strong and industrialized enough that it would never again suffer defeat at the hands of Germany or any other power—including the United States. Even after de Gaulle's departure from the scene, his successors used much the same discourse, although by the mid-1970s, the policy program was no longer accomplishing what the discourse proclaimed, as the national champions were coming to be seen as "lame ducks" and the *grands projets*, white elephants.

All the while, however, there were rival discourses, in particular those of the opposition Communists and Socialists, which increasingly overlapped by the 1970s as the two parties of the left made a common front. Their policy program was less a rejection of the ideas contained in the old Gaullist policy paradigm, however, than a reinvigoration of them, as they called for more state interventionism in response to the economic crisis beginning in the mid 1970s through the full-scale nationalization of industry, the return to neo-Keynesianism, and generous socioeconomic policies. The policy program's normative legitimation, however, was completely different from the Gaullist. Although the appeal to traditional political values and national pride remained with regard to the role of the state in restoring French economic prowess, there was also a postwar Marxian ideology which infused the discourse, reflected in talk of the capitalist "wall of money," of CEOs of major firms as exploiters, and of the "break with capitalism" through the nationalization of the means of production (Schmidt 1996, Chapter 4).

Thus, when the Socialists swept into power in 1981, although the discourse changed, the basic political-economic paradigm did not. In fact, the Socialists themselves presented their policy program as a return to the fundamentals of the *dirigiste* paradigm, by contrast with the preceding few years when France had joined the European Monetary System and Prime Minister Raymond Barre instituted a moderate budgetary austerity program. The problem for the Socialists, however, was that neither their renewed *dirigiste* policy program nor their ideologically grounded discourse could stand up to events. Not only was the policy program unsustainable economically, but the discourse itself could neither cognitively account for the failure of the policies to promote growth nor normatively justify the subsequent turn to budgetary austerity in terms of its political and social commitments. And therefore, when the Socialists abandoned their policy program in 1983, they also dropped the discourse.

The 1983 change in policy program and discourse appeared so abrupt, in fact, that it could be characterized as a Kuhnian revolution in paradigm. But even with Kuhnian-like revolutions, the ground has to be prepared ideationally—and was, in the coordinative discourses within political parties and among experts. The policy program itself had increasingly come under attack, and not only in its 1981 socialist incarnation, for its growing failure to deliver on its promises. The second half of the 1970s saw the rise of the "new" economists who questioned the continuing validity of the economics of the *dirigiste* paradigm and the "new" political philosophers who questioned the all-important role of the state, while some politicians on the right, in particular in the political clubs around the UDF, had become converts to neoliberalism (Jobert and Théret 1994). Beginning in 1981 with the victory of the Socialists, moreover, the number of right wing politicians who embraced neoliberalism increased exponentially, not only among the UDF but also among the RPR, the Gaullists who until then had with few exceptions continued to have faith in the powers of the strong French state. And once the Socialists took control of the state, the "retreat of the state" became the new, radical neoliberal ideology of the right as a whole (Baudouin 1990; Schmidt 1996, chapter 5).

Even among the Socialists after their accession to power, however, neoliberalism was gaining ground—although they never called it that. Already between 1981 and 1983, the policy program and its discourse were undergoing subtle changes, as the Socialist government began to liberalize the financial markets, dropped many of their more radical policy promises (e.g., to institute a National Investment Bank or worker self-management), and quickly gave up the attempt to institute neocorporatist concertation with the social partners, labor and business (Jobert and Théret 1994). Moreover, they increasingly justified nationalization in nationalistic (i.e., to save firms from foreign takeover) as opposed to Marxian terms and soon rehabilitated business by calling CEOs no longer "exploiters" but "creators of riches" and by treating profit no longer as a dirty word (Schmidt 1996). As one Socialist put it, "We went from the idea of a break with capitalism to the very different idea of a break with the failures of capitalism" (Zinsou 1985, 61). Economic interest, of course, had everything to do with these changes, given the Socialists' growing concern with deepening economic crisis and double-digit inflation. The Socialists' own political interests, however, also played a large role, since they increasingly recognized that if they did not do something to turn the economy around, they would lose the next election.

The Moderate Neoliberal Paradigm in Search of a Legitimating Discourse

The turning point came in March 1983, as a small group of Socialist party leaders conferred with President Mitterrand on the choice of policy: whether to institute budgetary austerity and stay in the EMS or to pull out, put up protective economic barriers, and seek to maintain French "exceptionalism." The coordinative discourse here was extremely restricted: neither Communist coalition partners nor the larger party was consulted (Bauchard 1986); and Mitterrand himself was alone to decide.

The communicative discourse which followed offered justification for the shift in policy program in terms of the "contrainte extérieure" or the external constraints imposed by globalization and the need to remain in the European Monetary System, which would act as a shield against globalization. In the macroeconomic sphere, this is when "competitive disinflation" and the strong franc (*franc fort*), became the new catchwords; competitiveness became the new imperative, as the government instituted budgetary austerity; and bringing inflation down below that of Germany, in order to ensure that French workers were getting the jobs going to Germany, became the new exhortatory goal. Moreover, in the microeconomic sphere, Laurent Fabius (first as Minister of Industry and then as Prime Minister), talked of the need for the progressive disengagement of the state, put the emphasis on profit (exhorting French firms to "get out of the red") and put his faith in the market (warning that "heads would roll" in companies that failed to return to profitability and that "lame ducks" would no longer be rescued from bankruptcy) (*Le Monde* March 31, 1985). He followed up on his words with action. Moreover, this is when Mitterrand himself began to differentiate his presidential discourse from that of the government, by insisting that his role was not to talk of "rigueur," or austerity, but rather to identify the "grands objectifs," the "projet de civilisa-tion" (Labbé 1990, 155–156) and thus to provide the vision of where France was going. [Later, once Chirac was in office, Mitterrand increasingly sought to emphasize his role as statesman (or "Dieu," as the French jokingly began to call him), as above the fray of party politics, like de Gaulle before him, even though his communicative discourse was as much focused on maintaining his own power vis-à-vis the opposition in government as it was in providing a sense of direction to the French public.]

But while the Socialists made clear how necessary the new political-economic paradigm was to relaunch growth and fight unemployment, they did little to demonstrate its appropriateness in terms of the socialist values they had espoused throughout the postwar period (nor could they). Instead, they fell back on the appeal to French national pride, and spoke of the economic combat for national survival, of national revival and modernization. And although they did continue to speak of social justice (and Mitterrand especially), the definition had changed. Whereas before 1983, it was linked in the Socialists' discourse to equality, and the effort to equalize income disparities, after 1983, Mitterrand and other Socialist leaders spoke increasingly of solidarity, which represented the unarticulated acceptance of the inequalities of income necessitated by a more neoliberal approach to economic management (Jobert and Théret 1994, 72–78).

The Socialists, in fact, instituted a moderate neoliberal program that dared not speak its name, not only because the opposition had claimed neoliberalism for itself but also because the Socialists quite naturally could not for political reasons then or later repudiate their 1981 to 1983 policies or its underlying values in their subsequent discourse, even if they did so in their policy program. This caused them a number of problems with speaking the truth or in altering certain policies that had been ideologically driven, in particular those regarding nationalization. This came out most clearly with the contortions of the "ni-ni" period (1988–1991), when Mitterrand declared that there was to be neither privatization nor nationalization but in fact allowed firms to sell off subsidiaries and trade shares with foreign firms, and of the post "ni-ni" period (1991–1993), when without any official declarations firms gained greater leeway to form strategic alliances with private as well as other public firms and to sell shares to raise capital. It has only been in the late 1990s, with the Jospin government, that the Socialists seem to have come up with a coherent, socialist rationale for privatization, by insisting that theirs (as opposed to that of the right) respected rules of efficiency and equity—by seeking to secure investment as well as to guarantee jobs while involving the unions in the negotiations, in contrast to the right's focus on state disinvestment, regardless of its impact on jobs or on industrial strategy, and lack of worker consultation (Levy n/a).

When the right came to power in 1986 on the basis of a radical neoliberal program, their problems were less with the communicative discourse than with the coordinative discourse within the government coalition. Prime Minister Chirac seemed to spend less of his time trying to communicate to the public about the appropriateness of the retreat of the state through privatization and deregulation as attempting to coordinate a government riven by divisions between ministers who sought to institute radical neoliberal reform (such as shutting down the Ministry of Industry—generally members of the UDF) and others (mostly RPR) who were wed to much more moderate reform (Schmidt 1996, chapter 5). When the right lost the elections in 1988, mainly because it was perceived as more radical and less stable than the Socialists, the right largely abandoned the discourse. But the moderate neoliberal program continued, whether under the Socialists until 1993—even though balanced somewhat by policies in keeping with social solidarity (such as the RMI, the *revenu minimum d'insertion*, which provided a minimum income for the "excluded," and various training programs, internships, and subsidies for the young and long-term unemployed)—or under succeeding right wing governments, as the reform of the welfare state became imperative in the run-up to EMU.

In either case, moreover, the neoliberal policy program lacked a discourse which provided a vision of France in Europe and the world sufficiently legitimated in terms of national values—in particular social values. This was evident in the opinion polls, which noted an increasing sense of dissatisfaction among the general public. In response to the question as to whether they had the impression that people like them lived better or worse than before, in 1966, only 28% responded less well, compared to 50% in 1981, 51% in 1985, 60% in 1993, and 62% in 1994. The sharp rise in dissatisfaction by the early 1990s is also clear from the increase in those who felt that there needed to be a complete change in society, which went from 35% in 1989 to 53% in 1994. It is equally interesting to note that the acceptance of neoliberal economic values, indicated by positive attitudes to profits, business, or capitalism, after rising appreciably in the 1980s diminished in the early 1990s. Profit, for example, which was seen as a more negative than positive thing in 1980 (39% con vs. 37% pro), became more positive than negative in 1983 (42% pro vs. 33%), attaining a majority of positives in 1988 (54% pro vs. 32% con), only to lose ground by 1993 (44% pro vs. 42% con) and to be viewed negatively again in 1994 (49% con vs. 43% pro) (Sofres 1996).

In place of a fully legitimating discourse, the leadership of both right and left spoke of the importance of European integration as a shield against globalization. In the macroeconomic sphere, it was to protect the country against the vagaries of the international financial markets while promoting economic stability and growth. In the microeconomic sphere, deregulation and privatization were presented as necessary to meet the competitive challenges of European integration and globalization. Even in the socioeconomic sphere, once welfare reform began in earnest under the right starting in 1993, the discourse related to Europe was initially invoked in justification.

But although their pro-European and anti-global rhetoric worked for a while, with a permissive consensus assured by the growing economic prosperity, by the early to mid 1990s, the lack of a fully legitimating discourse began to take its toll in the face of economic recession, the 1992 run on the franc, continued high unemployment, and the increasing incursions on the welfare state. The problems did not really come to a head with the debates surrounding the 1992 Maastricht referendum, since these were primarily focused on the political-institutional impact of European Monetary Union (see below), but rather as successive governments began to institute cuts in welfare and social security in the mid 1990s and to deregulate and privatize in the public service arena, as European pressures for deregulation increased in such sectors as telecommunications and energy.

In the macroeconomic sphere, however, the mainstream parties maintained something of a taboo on criticism of the EMU. "La pensée unique," literally, single-minded thought, was what the few political and economic analysts who dared to write critical editorials in the *Le Monde* or publish books questioning the unquestioning support for EMU, termed the injunction against criticizing the EMU. It stymied any thorough-going, open discussion of the potential problems involved, and especially any linkages between the restrictive budgetary policies related to meeting the Maastricht criteria and cuts in the social policy arena. The taboo, or dominant conviction, itself stemmed in large measure from the fact that perseverance with monetary integration had become not only a point of honor for most mainstream politicians of the left and the right, given the sacrifices since the mid 1980s that included suffering high unemployment and too-high interest rates, but also a source of national pride, given France's economic leadership role in the EU that accompanied its perseverance (Schmidt 1997b). Equally importantly, a majority of policy elites, not just politicians but also central bankers, business and labor leaders, saw EMU almost entirely in positive light, although their reasons for support differed (Verdun 1996).

The "pensée unique," in short, ensured that little negative press was forthcoming on EMU. But it also meant that public debate was largely nonexistent, leaving little or no middle ground between accepting all aspects of EMU without question or opposing it, which generally encompassed not just exit from EMU but also from the EU. The result is that before the May 1997 election campaign even those national politicians on the right who initially opposed EMU (although mainly on political-institutional grounds) were largely silent. Moreover, those few politicians who recommended exit tended to be marginal or marginalized, as in the case at one point of Jean-Pierre Chevènement on the left and, of course, Jean-Marie Le Pen of the National Front on the extreme right, the most vocal proponent of exit since the 1980s. And the public, left with little more from mainstream politicians than exhortations to continued sacrifice and incantations on the future benefits of EMU, were therefore more vulnerable to demagoguery from the extreme right (as evident from the continuing electoral strength of the National Front in particular), who were also able to gain strength from the public's concerns about unemployment, insecurity, immigration, and corruption. In fact, concerns about European integration have been very far down the list of explanations for the rise of populism—at 5% compared to 60% for unemployment, 45% for insecurity, 36% for immigration, and 33% for corruption and financial scandals" (Sofres 1996).

With the 1997 election campaign, however, the taboo against criticism of the EMU was lifted and public debate has flourished. On the right, the divisions ran very deep, primarily in the RPR, where a number of powerful politicians broke with the official pro-EMU line. On the left, Jospin has espoused a tolerance for pluralism in the coalition of the left, as an "exercise in the democratic confrontation of ideas" (Cole 1999) and necessarily so, given criticism from within the coalition government, in particular from the Communists.

For mainstream parties of both the left and the right, the problem has been less European integration per se than how to legitimate a neoliberal political-economic program which has increasingly impinged on the socioeconomic sphere. (On the list of things in 1996 that worried people the most for the next few years to come, attacks on their social rights (*les aquis sociaux*) was second, with 43% worried (after racism, at 56%); by contrast the disappearance of the French nation in the European Union was in fifth place with 25% worried—Sofres 1996).[3] This has represented both a cognitive problem, because of the seeming logical contradiction between economic belt-tightening and generous social services, and a normative one, given underlying French concerns with social justice and equality. Social solidarity has been a constant theme in the national political discourse of the Fifth Republic and before, and is intimately tied to the symbol of "l'état républicain," which governmental elites have yet to find a way to reconcile with liberalism. The difficulty for policy reform in this area in particular is that the French remain very attached to their system of social security (in 1993, 85% had confidence in the ability of the social security system to solve the problems they confronted, by contrast with 39% with confidence in the administration, while 69% were unwilling to take out private insurance, 74% were unwilling to pay more social security tax, and 75% unwilling to pay more income tax (1993 Espace Social Européen survey — cited in Jobert and Théret 1994). What is more, the public remained fully in favor of a continued state role in the provision of public interest services. Not only were they against privatization — with 49% against any at all in 1989, and opposed in particular to the privatization of the schools (59%), hospitals (53%), and social security (52%) (Sofres, Jan. 20–24, 1989) — but large majorities of the public also retained great confidence in them, considering that they worked well or had even improved over time, whether telephone (92% in 1989 and 92% in 1995), post (65% in 1989 up to 80% in 1995), railroads (60% in 1989 up to 65% in 1995), hospitals (62% in 1989 up to 63% in 1995), and schools (49% in 1989 up to 57% in 1995), with only the social security administration registering a loss of confidence (52% in 1989 down to 49% in 1995) (Sofres, Sept. 8–9, 1995).

For the French, the attempts to cut the welfare state have generated major political crises, as evidenced not only by the repeated strikes and job actions since 1995 but also the change in majority in the 1997 election. Much of the problem has been in the discursive realm, that is, in governments' inability to persuade the public as to the appropriateness of the reform or to coordinate with the social partners on the substance of the reform. The experience of macro and micro economic reform since the early 1980s — where government promises that just one liberalizing measure more would solve the problems of unemployment proved to be pipedreams, whether it was reducing the inflation rate to bring jobs to France, allowing wages to give way to profits in order for investment and jobs to follow, or enabling employers to fire so that they would be more inclined to hire — have left the public distrustful of further reform in the socioeconomic arena (Levy n/a).

Moreover, the lack of real consultation or coordination with the social partners made labor especially wary of government initiatives in this area. This was patently clear in 1995 in particular, when the public sector strikes in protest against proposed social security reforms and plans for the national railway that paralyzed the country gained such widespread sympathy from a public which was not so much opposed to the content of reform (a majority of French at the time had accepted that the government had to put into place drastic social security reforms—at 51% to 40%) (Sofres 1996), as to the method. This was mainly because Prime Minister Juppé not only ignored the social partners in a reform which he proudly declared was of his construction alone, with perhaps a handful of advisers, but also failed to communicate about the reform to the public at large.

The Socialists in government since June 1997, however, have seemingly done better both in terms of dialogue and concertation—as well as in softening the impact of the neoliberal policy program. Its coordinative discourse has been much more accommodating. The government has opened up policy construction to a less restricted group of policy elites, including not only government coalition members but also the social partners in the case of reforms in social security or industrial relations (e.g., the 35 hour work week); and it has convened experts in advisory commissions in the case of controversial issues. Moreover, its communicative discourse has directly focused on the problems of the fit between neoliberal policy program and social values, by seeking to persuade the public that it is possible to have reforms that can be economically efficient and at the same time promote social equity as well as, in the oft-repeated phrases of governments of right and left, to combat social exclusion and heal the "social fracture." This has been evident in its approach to privatization, as noted above, as well as in its more redistributive fiscal policies, by taxing and eliminating benefits for the rich while reducing the burdens on the poor and by raising taxes on business and lowering them on consumers (rather than the other way around, which had been Juppé's solution), thereby increasing public confidence and consumer spending, which has helped the economy. The government has also been more successful in social security reforms, not only because of the legitimating content of the discourse but also because of the coordinative process, through more "corporatist" negotiation of reform, including the creation of private pension funds administered by the social partners (rather than private companies as the right had sought to do) (Levy n/a). Moreover, even on Europe, the Socialists have managed to be more consistent, in words and action, by seeking to balance the commitment to the EMU with the defense of the "European social model" against the excesses of "Anglo-Saxon liberalism" and U.S.-led globalization, as noted above.

Finally, the Jospin government may even have begun to moderate public expectations about the role of the French state as guarantor of the public good, by deliberately using less heroic language to talk about the choices of government, with the "ni-ni" now being used to suggest that the government will pursue moderate change, with "neither pause nor acceleration" in the pace of reform, neither slashing benefits to the poor nor doing nothing while the social security system goes into deficit; neither declare class warfare on the rich nor allow the privileged not to pay their share; and neither dismantle the welfare state nor fail to address its dysfunctions (Levy n/a). The Jospin government still confronts great difficulties, however, not only because of the economic pressures related to European monetary integration and globalization that reduce socioeconomic capacity but also because of the institutional context that makes productive coordinative discourse with the social partners difficult, and thus hinders reform efforts.

In France, in short, the problem since the early 1980s has been the inability of French governmental elites to fashion a coherent discourse to justify the conversion to a more liberal, open, and market-oriented economy and to a more restricted socio-economy. Without such a justificatory discourse, the loss of socioeconomic capacity in the face of European and global forces has led to public malaise and protest, stymied necessary welfare reform efforts, and contributed to the success of the extreme right. These are problems which Great Britain and Germany have had less of, albeit for very different reasons, given their very different political economic discourses and paradigms.

Britain: Renewing the Discourse

By contrast with France, British governments starting with Thatcher have been most successful in constructing a coherent discourse that projects a convincing vision of Britain in and out of an integrating Europe while thoroughly in a globalizing world. Their pro-global stance, which has roots in the country's more open economic history, in conjunction with their anti-European stance (until the Blair government), which enabled them to gain opt-outs from EMU, the Social Chapter of the Maastricht Treaty, and (until Blair), fit in well with their neoliberal discourse which propounds the rollback of the state in all spheres—socioeconomic as much as macroeconomic and microeconomic. In fact, Britain's loss of socioeconomic capacity finds as much justification in the discourse, which ever since Thatcher has preached the need to dismantle the welfare state, as does the resistance to the loss of autonomy in the macroeconomic sphere due to monetary integration (until Blair, where it is only delayed) or in the microeconomic sphere due to any perceived EU reregulation—which British governments have been able to turn to their political advantage by loudly protesting any new rule which they see as excessive. With the May 1997 change in government, however, the discourse has been in the process of renewal, not only because the Blair government has largely abandoned the Conservatives' anti-Europe stance but also because it has sought to convince the public that "New Labour" has taken a "third way" between the left and the right, and is fulfilling many old Labour aspirations through new Thatcherite policy means.

In Britain, as in France, the communicative stage of discourse is more elaborate than the coordinative. This is again a consequence of the unitary institutional structure, which concentrates power in the executive and statist policymaking processes that ensure the policy program is generally the product of a small, restricted political party elite, and formulated largely absent outside input—whether from the larger party membership or backbench members of Parliament, let alone the opposition or organized societal interests. It is at the communicative stage that governments seek to convince the general public and most affected interests of the necessity and appropriateness of their policy program, and where they get their response—more in words rather than action, however, and mostly through elections rather than protest (given Britain's less contestational political style).

Moreover, in Britain, the communicative discourse is if anything more authoritative than in France, since the majority is a single party rather than a coalition of parties, and the Prime Minister is the sole authority (by contrast with the French dual authorities of President and Prime Minister—especially in the case of cohabitation). And the majority tries to keep its discourse as authoritative as it can, through strictly enforced party discipline enabling the government to speak in one voice, and thereby to project a sense of coherence and vision in policy program as well as to promote the public impression of a government that knows what it is doing, and doing what it promised. This discourse by and large has worked for both Thatcher and Blair (at least so far), by contrast with Major, with his thin majority and his difficulties in maintaining party discipline in particular with regard to the Euroskeptics.

Yet, the discourse is no more monolithic than in France. This is not only because opposition parties tend to have separate, well-developed discourses but also because the British Parliament gives voice to opposing views (including not just the opposition but also those of the "backbenchers" of the ruling party). In addition, the British press tends to be both vibrant and contentious—although its attention seems to have been drawn in recent years more to sexual peccadilloes and scandal than to substantive policy issues.

The Postwar Paradigm and Discourse

In Great Britain, the early postwar period was characterized by a discourse and set of policy prescriptions from the Conservatives and Labour that were so close that they were seen as Tweedledum and Tweedledee. ("Butskellism," under Tory Prime Minister Harold Macmillan, to refer to the fact that the policies of his Chancellor of the Exchequer, Robert Butler, were the same as those of the previous Labour Chancellor Hugh Gaitskell) that lasted from the 1950s to the 1970s. Whether the Conservatives or Labour were in power, a quasi-liberal political-economic policy program held, where liberalism was apparent in the openness of the economy, the generally hands-off policies toward business, and the emphasis on voluntarism in management-labor relations. But it was only quasi-liberal given a more interventionist state which retained a large nationalized sector, engaged in experiments with French planning and Swedish-type social concertation, and periodically attempted to establish incomes policies or imposed wage controls.

The two political parties were in fact quite close in both content and style, even if not in discourse. The Tory paternalists in control of the Conservative party until Thatcher's takeover in the mid 1970s conceived of conservatism as nonideological, neither an "ism" nor even an idea, in the words of Sir Ian Gilmour (Gilmour 1977, 121—cited in Hetzner 1999). They were imbued with a pre-capitalist ethic and the "gentlemanly culture," in which politics was more appropriately done through "the pursuit of the gray areas or Macmillan's famed middle way' " and where "the pursuit of consensus acted as a brake on radical change and as a catalyst to accommodation." And although these Tory "gentlemen" might disagree with their Labour Party counterparts on specific issues, they shared with the Labour "gentlemen" a disdain for business (even though the Conservatives were seen as the "party of business" and that there was a faction of the Conservatives who were pro-capitalist) and a sense of mutual obligation to provide for community welfare (Hetzner 1999, 37–39). Moreover, their policy program was little different from that of Labour, with which they often cooperated, in its neo-Keynesian macroeconomics and in its support for continuing public ownership and social welfare measures. In addition, their consensual policy style was similar to that of Labour, although their discourse differed in emphasis and in imagery, given the paternalism of the Tory view versus the class-based, egalitarian language of Labour (Hetzner 1999, chapter 1).

The differences in policy paradigms and discourse had crystallized by the 1970s, however, with Labour having moved much more to the left beginning in the sixties with its somewhat socialist ideology and its policy program promoting corporatist business-labor-government relationships and neo-Keynesian macroeconomic policies while the Tories had moved to the right with a neoliberal ideology that rejected socialism and corporatism in favor of monetarism and laissez-faire capitalism. In response to the crisis of the 1970s, as the neo-Keynesian and interventionist policy program of Labour proved increasingly incapable of solving the problems of the day, neoliberalism gained ground. In many cases, it was influential supporters of planning and Keynesianism who came to believe in the importance of market forces and a more minimalist state, such as the journalist Samuel Brittan (in a 1973 book) or Sir Keith Joseph, who had been a minister under Heath. Moreover, the neoliberal ideas themselves were popularized through the publications of think tanks such as the Institute of Economic Affairs and the Center for Policy Studies (Hayward and Klein 1994, 96–99), while the financial press played a major role in focalizing dissatisfaction with the economics policies of the day and promoting monetarism (Hall 1993). Although these ideas were clearly not new, given the long history of economic liberalism in Britain going back to Adam Smith and the Scottish economists and more recently to those influenced by the work of Hayek, Friedman, and others, they came back renewed and reinvigorated in the New Right around Thatcher (who became Party head in 1975) and a number of her closest advisers, and in a form not seen before. Thus, whereas in France, the dominant Gaullist discourse gave way to the rival postwar discourse of the Socialists once they gained power in 1981, Britain with the election of Margaret Thatcher in 1979 acquired a brand new discourse and program that broke with the past: Thatcherite neoliberalism which propounded greater laissez-faire capitalism and the rollback of the state in place of Labour's neo-Keynesianism and state interventionism.

The Radical Neoliberal Paradigm and Thatcherite Discourse

Thatcher quite consciously chose to articulate a neoliberal ideology as a counter to Labour's "socialist" and "corporatist" ideology which she abhorred and to the Tory paternalists' wishy-washy approach to economics and governance which she disdained. With her confrontational style and its explicit rejection of consensus politics, her espousal of monetarism against previous governments' neo-Keynesian interventionism in the economy, and her emphasis on competitive capitalism as a counter to the cooperative capitalism of Labour and the Tory paternalists, Thatcher sought to produce a revolution in her own party as much as in the polity. Thus, Thatcher, together with a few other conservative converts to neoliberalism such as Sir Keith Joseph, Sir Geoffrey Howe, Nicholas Ridley, and Norman Tebbit, who saw themselves as "outsiders," sought to impose their ideology on the party while ridding it of its accommodationist tendencies. Policy construction, in consequence, was a confidential affair, with the ideas coming from close allies in the Cabinet and hand-picked advisers in the "Policy Unit" in the Prime Minister's office at 10 Downing Street. In battles internal to the Cabinet once in power, Thatcher was constantly fighting the "wets," whom she saw as soft on state interventionism, on Europe, and on all those things about which she felt it was only appropriate to be "dry." In government, moreover, she was also waging war against the powerful Civil Service, which she distrusted because she held it responsible for the wrong-headed economic policies of the postwar period, and which she was determined to restructure to make it more efficient as well as a more effective tool to implement her programs. And although she did not succeed in politicizing the Civil Service, or destroying its vaunted neutrality, as some have argued, Whitehall did change, with the rewards going to the more dynamic and efficient implementers of government efforts to roll back the state (Hennessey 1989).

In Britain, then, paradigm change came about through the construction of a discourse and policy program by a small political party elite that managed to capture the party leadership and then the election, and then to impose its pro-market, anti-state program via the strong state apparatus. Only half the battle was won with Thatcher's conquest of power, however. The other half was to keep it, which entailed a communicative discourse capable of persuading the public in election after election that the Thatcherite program was not only necessary to put the economy back on its feet but also appropriate because it resonated with long-standing national values.

Thatcher herself had a keen sense of the importance of communicating her policy program to the public, and took every opportunity to do so. First and foremost, she presented her program as revolutionary, not only as a break with past Tory and Labour practice but also as a way of "breaking the consensus and tackling traditionally immune targets," such as the trade unions, local government, and nationalized industries (speech to press, Jan. 18, 1984—cited in Hedetoft and Niss 1991). She talked of the "Revival of Britain" (the title of a collection of speeches) and the need to reverse the decline which had been the focus of much of the economic discourse of the 1960s and 1970s, contrasting her own monetarist paradigm with Ted Heath's earlier failed return to Keynesianism (Hall 1993, 290). She was particularly intent on "rolling back the frontiers of the Welfare State," and promoting an "enterprise culture," in order "to change Britain from a dependent to a self-reliant society. From a give-it-to-me to a do-it-yourself nation; to a get-up-and-go instead of a sit-back-and-wait-for-it Britain" (London Times, Feb. 9, 1984—cited in Hedetoft and Niss 1991). And instead of government being responsible for solving Britain's problems, she sought to shift the onus to the people (Riddell 1989, 1).

However, at the same time that Thatcher claimed to be making a revolutionary break with the recent history of state interventionism, she justified her policy prescriptions in terms of the country's long-standing adherence to a limited state and liberal economic principles (Marquand 1988), with their basis in deep-seated British values—even if these were more Methodist than Church of England, and more from the Midlands than central London. Thatcher herself talked of the need to return to "Victorian" values, which for her included the importance of hard work, self-reliance, living within your income, helping one's neighbor, pride in country (Interview with the BBC, 1983—cited in Hedetoft and Niss 1991). She has been called a "populist authoritarian" because of the mix of values to which she appealed: populist when she argued for the need to combat the oppressive bureaucratic "nanny" state, welfare ideology, and intellectuals or emphasized the importance of self-interest and competitive individualism; and seemingly authoritarian in her insistence on not rolling back the police, defense, and judiciary, or in her actions focused on crushing the unions, on abolishing local government, and refusing to consult with interest groups (S. Hall 1983; 1988).

Thatcher's policy paradigm, as with the Kuhnian notion of paradigm, was only vaguely sketched out initially. The discourse presented a set of neoliberal ideas about what was to be done, which then were developed, sector by sector, largely on an experimental basis, with success in one area encouraging the move to the next. In the 1979 election, the Conservative Manifesto was focused primarily on macroeconomic policy, promising strict control of the money supply and a reduction in public spending, and on industrial relations, with new restrictive rules governing union action and a return to a hands-off policy in pay settlements; although it also offered limited denationalization. Only in the 1983 election was significant privatization promised (of British Telecom, British Airways, British Steel, and more). Resolving the problems of industrial relations once and for all became a major focus around the same time, with the test coming shortly thereafter with the coal miners' strike of 1984. Initiatives on the welfare state came a bit later, and education even later.

While certain policies were implemented in full, moreover, others were barely put into force, depending upon the centrality of the policy to the government's political-economic paradigm as well as the government's view of its potential electoral repercussions. Thus, during her first mandate, Thatcher held true to her monetarist approach to economic management, although it did not turn the economy around nearly as quickly as she had forecast. Fortunately for Thatcher, continued poor economic performance was overshadowed by her great popularity in the aftermath of the Falklands War, with her militaristic incantations of past British military glory and memories of Empire helping usher the Tories back into office, despite public disenchantment with her neoliberal politico-economic paradigm which had so far failed to deliver on its promises.

Thatcher's second mandate went more smoothly. Not only did the macroeconomic program finally appear to be bearing fruit but also the privatization of major utilities along with the sale of council housing also proved popular, even if it did not quite produce a people's capitalism in the stockmarket or turn new homeowners into budding capitalists, and it proceeded with hardly a peep from the now divided Labour Party or the unions. With regard to industrial relations, moreover, Thatcher's hard-nosed approach to the unions turned out to be generally popular to citizens weary of constant crisis and work stoppages and no longer sympathetic since the Winter of Discontent of 1978–79.

Social welfare reform, however, was another matter. In the end, despite her rhetorical attacks on the "culture of dependency," Thatcher actually did surprisingly little to cut overall social welfare expenditures or the National Health Service. This was mainly because of fears of negative reactions from the electorate, which showed little change in their strong support for government responsibility with regard to the National Health Service and social security, even as they seemed to accept other Thatcherite values about individual responsibility, to wit, that the government not be responsible for maintaining full employment or for equalizing incomes.[4] The cumulative effect of incremental welfare reforms, however, has nevertheless moved British pension arrangements toward a more marginal model of welfare and prepared the ground for an expansion of private pension provision, while the National Health Service has changed somewhat with the introduction of market experimentation (Fawcett 1995).

Thatcher's policies and discourse on Europe were another matter. Although her neoliberal paradigm was by its very nature pro-global, given the commitment to open markets and open borders, it was not necessarily pro- or anti-European. Leaving aside political institutional issues related to sovereignty, which were the main complication in the British relationship with the European Community throughout the postwar period (see below), questions related to European integration and its political economic fit were not cut-and-dried either for or against. For Thatcher, Europe represented as much an opportunity—to extend laissez-faire capitalism to the continent— as a threat—with the extension of continental-style state interventionism to Britain. And whereas the opportunity presented itself with the Single Market Act of 1986, with Thatcher using accommodating, "communautaire" language as she sought to lead Europe toward a greater market liberalism, the threat appeared with the proposed Maastricht Treaty beginning in 1988, with its promise of integration in both monetary and social policy.

The threat was perceived as greatest with regard to the Social Chapter, about which Thatcher was in perfect agreement with her closest advisers and Cabinet ministers. For Thatcher and advisers, this constituted an unacceptable violation of neoliberalism because, as she insisted in her famous Bruges speech in September 1988, "we certainly do not need regulations which raise the cost of employment and make Europe's labor market less flexible and less competitive with overseas suppliers. . . . And certainly we in Britain would fight attempts to introduce collectivism and corporatism at the European level." With monetary union, however, the issue was not as clear-cut. Where Thatcher (along with advisers such as Nicholas Ridley) perceived threat, mainly on grounds of loss of national sovereignty and control if the central bank were to become independent and monetary policy were administered by a central European bank (Busch 1994), others saw opportunity (e.g., Geoffrey Howe, Norman Lamont, and Nigel Lawson), on the grounds that this would institute sound neoliberal macroeconomic policy throughout Europe; and they split publicly with her on the issue (Larsen 1997, 66–68). Moreover, there was also strong support for the EMU among the Tories' business constituency, which saw it as ensuring a stable currency and encouraging the generalization of market principles to fiscal and social policy, as well as among British monetary authorities, who wanted to participate in its construction to avoid the problems of the 1970s, when they took on board policies that they had had no part in constructing, and to prevent too much deepening (Verdun 1996). Thatcher's increasingly confrontational stance toward the EC, which threatened to isolate the country, together with growing dissension among the party leadership on her position, ultimately led to her forced resignation as head of the party and Prime Minister.

For John Major, her successor as Prime Minister, therefore, the course was clear: negotiate in a more accommodating manner, but don't give in on the Social Chapter, and be cautious on EMU. The opt-outs on both Social Chapter and EMU accomplished these purposes. After the negotiation of the Maastricht Treaty and the controversy over its ratification, moreover, the government shifted from discussing the big issues to criticizing details of environmental and social legislation and of poor financial control and overzealous bureaucracy (Wallace 1996, 69). The discourse for a long time, therefore, was something of a low pitched, moderately anti-European rhetoric, conveying the image of an ever watchful British government, quick to protest anti-liberal incursions. By the mid 1990s, however, the discourse began to get more strident, as it had during Thatcher's last couple of years in office, in this case because the Euroskeptics were growing ever stronger and Major's majority ever thinner. Add to this the disaster of the mad cow disease (BSE), where Major was valiantly trying to save British cows from slaughter, or more egregious regulatory encroachments by the Commission, such as the extension of the 48-hour work week to Britain on grounds of occupational safety and health, despite the British opt-out from the Social Chapter, and it is understandable that the Major government found it increasingly convenient to point out the dangers of Europeanization without mentioning its other merits, whether in playing to the Euroskeptics in Parliament in order to retain their allegiance or to the Eurocrats in Brussels to broker the best deal.

By contrast with France, then, where criticism of the EMU and even the EU had been largely taboo until 1997, in Britain such criticism had become almost a *sine qua non* of British political life, whether by the government, Parliament, or the newspapers. While Tory backbenchers in particular were increasingly vocal in their criticism of Major's "softness" on Europe, Fleet Street had a field day with EC regulations, with specious headlines, for example, on EU banning of curved bananas and square gin bottles.[5] The danger for Britain was that as the anti-European rhetoric escalated, the rational discourse that with Thatcher had consistently put European integration squarely within the neoliberal vision of Britain's future, as part of a larger, neoliberal Europe and world, was being forgotten—not so much by the elite, and in particular the business elite, which was well aware of the benefits of continued integration for the country's global competitiveness—as by the population, making it more open to demagogic manipulation from the anti-Europe forces. And all of this represented a major challenge for the newly elected Blair government—as the Labour Party found already in the 1997 election campaign, having time and again had to qualify its statements about how much and where Britain would opt back in (in particular with regard to the Social Chapter).

The Major legacy on Europe, in fact, left the Blair government in some difficulty. On other policy issues, by contrast, this was much less the case, mainly because Major did little to depart from Thatcher's legacy—nor has Blair. In effect, on policy issues other than those regarding Europe, although Major took a more consensual, less confrontational approach than Thatcher, he largely proceeded with the further development of her neoliberal political-economic paradigm through continued privatization and deregulation. And although Britain has not thereby become the "enterprise culture" that Thatcher wanted and has not dismantled the welfare state, it has gone a lot farther in the directions Thatcher had hoped than some commentators admit (Crewe 1988, 44—see critique in Hetzner 1999, 121–30). The proof of the success of Thatcher's revolutionary change in paradigm and discourse comes from the fact that the Labour Party was not to win another election until it had thoroughly altered its political-economic paradigm and discourse to come close to the Thatcherite.

The Neoliberal Transformation of Labour's Paradigm and Discourse

While Thatcher, with the Conservative Party firmly in hand, was "selling" her neoliberal political-economic paradigm to the public, the Labour Party was going through its own transformation. When Thatcher first came into office, the Labour Party presented a radically opposing political-economic paradigm to Thatcherite neoliberalism. Much like the Socialists in France, Labour's "Alternative Economic Strategy" proposed socialism in one country, with a mix of protectionism, assistance to nationalized industry, renationalizaton, and reflationary neo-Keynesian spending programs with the express purpose of insulating the country from global economic pressures. This went hand-in-hand with Labour's 1983 Manifesto commitment to withdraw from the EC, given that its policies were in clear opposition to its proposed economic program. Labour's position was thus not only in opposition to globalization but also to European integration, with an anti-global rhetoric to counter Thatcher's pro-global one, and an even more anti-European rhetoric than that of Thatcher. From the 1950s to the 1980s, in fact, the Labour Party was concerned that the EEC was something of a capitalist club for the rich and, especially in the 1950s and 1960s, when parties of the right predominated, worried that it would frustrate socialist policy initiatives in Britain. Moreover, its opposition to EEC entry on "Tory terms" reflected its hostility to the Heath government's economic and industrial relations policies (Daniels 1998).

The transformation of Labour was gradual across the 1980s. By the mid 1980s, with the failure of the French Socialist experiment in 1983, which cast doubts on the viability of their program, many in the Labour Party, in particular the leadership and the "soft" left, had shifted away from their earlier domestic economic strategies based on reflationary policies toward a focus on the EC as the arena for attainment of Labour's economic objectives. In fact, in the Labour Party's coordinative discourse, European integration was used by modernizers as a rhetorical strategy in support of changes in party structure and policy (Geyer 1998, 90). This had not only to do with an acceptance of the inevitability of more neoliberal macroeconomic policy and the benefits of greater economic coordination across countries but also the hope that social policies ruled out at the national level would find greater support at the EC level, with Delors' concept of a "social Europe." This also provided a European cause to use with the electorate against Thatcher (Daniels 1998, 87–88). By the late 1980s, much of the Labour Party, along with the unions, had come to have a more positive attitude toward the EC. By 1989, the Labour Party had committed itself to support the pound's entry into the ERM (even though divisions remained within the party), and in 1993, it supported ratification of the Maastricht Treaty. And when Blair took over the party, he not only supported the macroeconomic orthodoxy of price stability, abandoning once and for all Keynesian demand management policies but also got rid of one of the last vestiges of "socialism." In 1995, he eliminated Clause IV from the Labour Party Constitution, which justified nationalization. Most telling is that once elected, he immediately gave the Bank of England de facto independence, at the same time that he "opted in" on the Social Charter of 1989 (and Social Chapter of the Maastricht Treaty) which had so appalled Thatcher and out of which Major had opted. Moreover, he also adopted a minimum wage—in great contrast to Old Labour's earlier voluntarism. On the euro, however, he has had to exercise caution, in part because the lack of preparation prior to his arrival in power necessitated a delay in order to bring the economy and institutions in line, in part because of the legacy of John Major's increasingly anti-European discourse, and the Euroskeptic press which has had a great influence on the public.

The gradual shift in the Labour Party's view of capitalism as well can be seen not only in the policies but also in the discourse, as the Labour Party moved from clear hostility to the market, to general skepticism, then to general acceptance and, by 1992, to open embrace, with the 1992 election manifesto claiming "not to replace the market but to ensure the market works properly" (Hay and Watson 1998). The changing discourse, however, rather than using a pro-Europe discourse as a rationale for the neoliberal turn (as had the Socialists in France), instead used globalization. This is understandable, not only given the charged political atmosphere with regard to Europe, in particular since Major's increasingly anti-European rhetoric and the popular press's polemics, but also because of the traditional pro-global discourse. Unlike Thatcher's pro-global discourse, though, where opening up to global forces followed from her ideologically-grounded, neoliberal justification for change, Blair's pro-global discourse has presented globalization as the primary rationale for neoliberal reform.

Necessity, rather than ideology, was the key to Blair's discourse on globalization. Blair's stated commitment to "work with the grain of global change" and to have his administration "accept, and indeed embrace, the global market" (Tony Blair, Speech to the Singapore Business Community, Jan. 8, 1996—cited in Hay and Watson 1998) was geared to reassuring the international financial markets, just as was its granting of de facto independence to the Bank of England to set interest rates or its "golden rule" of borrowing only for investment and not consumption, as well as the "sound money" paradigm. With all of this, it sent a signal to the financial markets that, by depoliticizing monetary policy decisions, it would ensure that it would be "tough on inflation, tough on the causes of inflation"—although this was also a signal of the government's commitment to joining EMU sometime in the future. Globalization, as the "necessity" of satisfying the inflation demands of the global foreign exchange markets was also cited as the reason for government policies to attack the real wage (by keeping public sector wages down and urging the private sector to exercise restraint) and the social wage (by downgrading benefit entitlements and redefining welfare as workfare) (Chancellor's budget speeches, July and November 1997— cited in Hay and Watson 1998), while globalization as the challenge to the competitiveness of business was the rationale for promoting greater flexibility in the labor markets.

In the context of the globalization discourse, moreover, the cognitive justification was not, as one might have expected, focused on rejecting the Thatcherite paradigm but, rather, on differentiating the policy program of New Labour from that of Old Labour. In fact, the promoters of "New Labour" seemed mostly intent on suggesting continuity with the Thatcherite paradigm and distancing themselves from the "failed world of Old Labour," by making clear that "good government" was "minimal government," and that it was important to recognize that "choices are constrained; there are no panaceas, and the solutions adopted by left and right may often overlap" (Tony Blair, speech to the BDI, Bonn, Germany, June 18, 1996—cited in Hay and Watson 1998). Blair's new ideas, which come largely from his "guru," Anthony Giddens, a social theoretician, in marked contrast to Thatcher's free market economist, Alan Waters, have helped shape his view of a "third way" between the neoliberal right and the old socialist left. It is an amorphous set of concepts suggesting that globalization means that we all live in a "risk society" in which new conditions demand a new politics of the radical center, with an active, inclusive civil society, in which one must reconstruct the state, rather than shrink or expand it (Featherstone 1999). With this comes a new vocabulary as well, which the *Economist* encapsulated perfectly in a very funny table on the differences in language employed by the right, the left (Old Labour), and the "third way" (New Labour). In the economic realm, where the right speaks of "bosses" and the left of "workers," the third way speaks of "consumers." In welfare, where the right talks of the "feckless" and the left, "the oppressed," the third way talks of "the excluded." Other comparisons are, respectively, small government, big government, clever government; competition, planning, teamwork; silent majorities, vocal minorities, focus groups; market, state, community; and colleague, comrade, contact (*Economist*, December 19, 1998, 40).

But what then of values? The "third way" has been Blair's attempt to differentiate himself from both Thatcher's ideological appeal to the values of individualism and laissez-faire capitalism and old Labour's appeal to values of equality, community, and socialism. It has been criticized for being amorphous—but then, what discursive presentation of values isn't if it is to appeal to a wide cross-section of the electorate. In his speech to the French National Assembly, Blair argued that "we have to be absolute in our basic values, otherwise we have no compass to guide us through change. But we should be infinitely adaptable and imaginative in the means of applying those values. There are no ideological preconditions, no pre-determined veto on means. What counts is what works" (Paris, March 24, 1998). Although his message did not go over well in Paris, it has apparently worked in Britain, to judge from Blair's high ratings in the opinion polls in his first years on office.

With Blair, then, as with Thatcher, there is a clear recognition that a fully developed communicative discourse is of the essence, and that the Prime Minister's primary business is one of public persuasion. The coordinative discourse, by comparison, is almost nonexistent, with the elaboration of the policy program the product of a small group of close advisers and Cabinet ministers. Even more than with Thatcher, party discipline is a major concern of New Labour—so much so that Blair has gone so far as to expel a couple of members from the party in retaliation for speaking out against government policy.

In Britain, then, one policy paradigm, the neoliberal, and one discourse, the Thatcherite, has predominated since 1979. Although it may have taken Thatcher some time to win the public and the politicians over to her view, she largely succeeded, as evidenced by the fact that her Tory successor Major continued her neoliberal program with a somewhat kinder and gentler manner and discourse, and that "New Labour" under Blair has picked up the neoliberal baton, renewing the Thatcherite discourse while giving the policy program new élan rather than rejecting it. Blair's approach may be neoliberalism with a human face, given the greater (at least verbal) attention to the poor and dispossessed, but it is still neoliberalism in its support of a more liberal, open, and market-oriented economy and its acceptance of a more restricted socio-economy. With such a legitimating discourse, successive governments have managed to convert the country without the kind of disruption faced by France in the 1990s and, arguably, with less public dissatisfaction.

Conclusion

France and Britain, in conclusion, started from very different postwar political-economic paradigms and very different legitimating discourses, and have had very different experiences with regard to their responses to European and global level pressures. In France, the postwar political-economic paradigm of state interventionism and its Gaullist discourse was replaced in the early 1980s by a moderate neoliberal policy program and accompanying discourse which was pro-European and anti-global, but which failed to legitimate the policy program sufficiently in terms of national values. Only today does France seem to have finally found the beginnings of a new, credible discourse with Jospin. In Britain, by contrast, the quasi-liberal postwar paradigm and "Butskellite" discourse was replaced in the late 1970s by a radical neoliberal political-economic paradigm and accompanying "Thatcherite" discourse, which was largely pro-global and anti-European, and largely successful in legitimating the policy paradigm. Its success has been such, in fact, that today it is in the process of renewal under "New Labour" Blair.

The contrast with Germany is enlightening. There, unlike both France and Britain, the postwar political-economic paradigm of the social market economy continued without much challenge through most of the 1990s, along with a liberal social-democratic discourse which was both pro-global and pro-European, and fully legitimating. But both the paradigm and the discourse are now in difficulty.

German governments since the late 1950s have been successful, until very recently, in sustaining a coherent national discourse, in this case one that projected a convincing vision of Germany securely ensconced within an integrating Europe and a globalizing world. But that vision has remained within the confines of a postwar, liberal social-democratic discourse that since the mid 1990s has increasingly been fraying at the edges as a result of the economic problems related to unification and the growing pressures from globalization. As long as the German economy flourished and Germany managed to dominate European macroeconomic policy and delay adjusting national microeconomic policy, German governments found it relatively easy to reconcile their pro-European and pro-global stance with a social democratic discourse infused with liberal market notions that served to justify their political-economic paradigm of the "social market economy." But by the mid 1990s, once the country also began to experience a loss of capacity in the socioeconomic realm, increasing deregulation in the micro-economic arena, and difficulties in meeting the strict Maastricht criteria they themselves insisted on, they found it much harder to maintain a social-democratic discourse that appeared increasingly at odds with the neoliberal policies promoted by European and global level forces. But rather than abandoning the discourse, they have attempted to recast it to fit the changing realities, by emphasizing the liberal and de-emphasizing the social in the liberal social-democratic discourse (Schmidt 1997a). The task is in some ways more difficult than in France or Britain, because of the institutional context which privileges the coordinative over the communicative discourse.

In Germany, unlike in France or Britain, the coordinative discourse tends to be much more elaborate than the communicative. Because of Germany's federal structure which disperses power among different branches and levels of government and between government and opposition, and because of its corporatist policymaking processes which bring in the social partners (busi-ness and labor), the state cannot and does not play as strong a leadership role as in unitary, statist France or Britain. Here, construction of the policy program is the product of a wider policy elite, often but not always led by government, and generally forged through accommodating discussions with coalition partners, the opposition (especially if they hold the majority in the Bundesrat), subnational governments (via the Bundesrat), the social part-ners, and other relevant organized interests, depending upon the issue area. It is at the coordinative stage of discourse, in other words, where the job of convincing the participants to the discussion that a given policy program is necessary and appropriate, and often this is a job of mutual persuasion as well as group construction.

Moreover, although the outcome of the discussions is generally consen-sus, the process itself may entail a great deal of conflict, especially at the outset, as each of the parties to the discussion sets out its position. Such conflict may remain private, as it sometimes does in the case of policy agen-das worked out among government coalition partners, or it may spill out into the public sphere, as it often does in particular in the case of government and opposition or business and labor at the preliminary stages of discussion.

Among the social partners, in fact, the rational self-interested bargaining can be seen as "antagonistic cooperation" (Scharpf 1991, 117), with consensus characteristic of the outcome of the bargaining but not the process itself, which may involve tremendous verbal conflict and public posturing and threats outside the meetings but which will be cooperative internal to the closed meetings, especially as compromise draws near. The resulting consensus between the social partners, moreover, is upheld by a rigid legal framework to ensure that the consensus holds, and to preserve order and stability in the labor relations system as a whole (Heinisch 1999). In the case of coalition governments, the consensus is ensured by the threat of government collapse, whereas in the case of agreements between government and opposition, it is more often the fear of electoral sanction that guarantees continued cooperation, given a public which expects cooperation and compromise.

In Germany, in short, the coordinative discourse tends to be the most elaborate and important stage of discourse, by contrast with the communicative, which tends to be much thinner. This is because once the agreements have been worked out, the discourse is essentially over, with the government communicating the outcome in general terms to the larger public, and the other parties to the discourse communicating to their own constituents. There are cases, however, where the communicative discourse is more elaborate: For one, during election years there is generally a more elaborate communicative discourse by government, but then it may work at cross-purposes with the coordinative discourse, as the adversarial rhetoric in the campaign for election may obviate cooperation in the coordinative realm. This was the case in the year running up to the September 1998 elections, when government and opposition were consistently accusing the other of responsibility for the lack of movement with regard to tax and social policy reform. Moreover, where the coordinative discourse breaks down, the government may use the communicative discourse in a manner similar to the French or British, in an effort to convince the general public and the most affected interests of a better course of action. But unlike the French or the British, German governments do not have the power to impose that course of action, just to exhort all parties to the debate to come to the table. This has been the case most recently, as the Schröder government in the face of stalemate in the discussions of the social partners has been taking his message public in the hopes of getting some progress in the Alliance for Jobs talks.

Today, in short, Germany under Schröder has only just started the process of trying to recast its postwar social market paradigm and liberal social-democratic discourse. Success in such an effort is not at all certain, however. This is because any change must take place in an institutional context in which government cannot impose reform or even speak in a single voice, and requires major policy actors together to recast the old policy paradigm and discourse or to forge new ones. In this way, countries such as Britain and France have it easier, given that discourse and paradigm are the product of more restricted, government-centered elites. However, as we have seen, even in these countries it has not been so easy. Britain seems to have been most successful not only because of an institutional context which allowed for the government to speak in one single voice and thereby to deliver a strong communicative message but also because it had a leader who had the courage of her convictions, and was able to persuade the public of the value of the reforms as she imposed them. France has had greater difficulty not only because of an institutional context which left government with a less unified voice but also because its leaders have had fewer clear convictions and thus were less able to deliver a strong communicative message capable of persuading the public of the value of the reforms which they imposed.

In summary, when it comes to legitimating policy change, the national level is paramount. Whatever the external pressures related to global or European forces, these are refracted through national lenses. Any changes must be shown to make sense in terms of national ideas and to resonate with national values. In consequence, global and European forces are themselves portrayed very differently in different countries, depending upon the historical openness to global forces, attitudes toward European integration, and the perceived impact of global and European forces on national economies and institutions. Moreover, the way in which policy change is legitimated also differs depending upon the national institutional context, which affects whether legitimation comes more through coordinative discourses within the wide group of relevant policy elites responsible for policy construction or through communicative discourses constructed by restricted policy elites and addressed to larger publics. In short, whatever the external global or European pressures, these are experienced very differently from one country to the next not only because of differences in how national economies and institutions respond to those pressures but also because of differences in how national legitimating discourses construct and communicate their conceptions of the implications of global and European pressures for economic and social policy change.

Endnotes

1. Another way of describing this distinction is that of Herbert Gottweis (1999), who differentiates between "political metanarratives" and " policy narratives," where metanarratives provide an overall conceptual framework that establish the collective political identity within which the more specific policy narratives proceed.

2. I am not talking here about the general constructions of nation-state identity, which political leaders have for the most part actively sought to reconstruct in their discussions of why to embrace globalization or Europeanization, but about the particular economic and institutional elements that contribute to the more complex entity that is national identity. On the relationship of Europeanization to nation-state identity, see Risse 1997. On the construction of a nation-state identity, or a sense of nationhood, see Greenfeld 1992.

3. It is also important to note here that the public protests related to cutbacks in the welfare state have generally not been focused on EMU, which people seemed to have largely accepted. Opinion polls have found that 58% (vs. 34%) of the French accept that monetary integration justifies sacrifices such as the reduction of public spending and public debt (Schwok 1999, 63).

4. In a survey of British social attitudes, whereas those polled continued to agree that the government should provide for health care for the sick (98% in 1985 and 1990) and for a decent standard of living for the elderly (97% in both years), they showed an erosion in support of government responsibility to reduce inequalities in income between rich and poor (81% in 1985 down to 77% in 1990) or to ensure employment to all those who wanted one (68% down to 60%). (Taylor-Gooby 1991)

5. In actuality, the Commission has never ruled on square gin bottles, or on the curve of bananas, although it has on the dimensions of cucumbers. The cases of gin bottles and bananas were invented by the British papers. But they are nevertheless illustrative of the fears involved, as certain traditions have indeed been challenged by the Commission in the name of public health or safety.

References

Bauchard, Philippe. 1986. *La Guerre des Deux Roses: Du Rêve à la Réalité, 1981–1985*. Paris: Grasset.

Baudouin, J. 1990. "Le 'moment' néo-libéral du RPR." *Revue Francaise de Science Politique* no. 6.

Busch, Andreas. 1994. "Central Bank Independence and the Westminster Model." *West European Politics* 17(1): 53–72.

Campbell, John L. 1998. "Institutional Analysis and the Role of Ideas in Political Economy." *Theory and Society* 27: 377–409.

Cole, Alistair. 1999. "Europeanization, Social-Democracy and the French Polity: Lessons from the Jospin Government." Paper presented to the Sixth ECSA Conference. Pittsburgh, June 2–5.

Crewe, Ivor. 1988. "Has the Electorate become Thatcherite?" in *Thatcherism* ed., Robert Skidelsky. Oxford: Basil Blackwell.

Daniels, Philip. 1998. "From Hostility to 'Constructive Engagement:' The Europeanization of the Labor Party." *West European Politics* 21(1): 72–96.

Faure, Alain, Pollet, Gilles and Warin, Philippe. 1995. *La Construction du Sens dans les Politiques Publiques: Débats autour de la notion de Référentiel.* Paris: L'Harmattan.

Fawcett, Helen. 1995. "The Privatization of Welfare: The Impact of Parties on the Private/Public Mix in Pension Provision." *West European Politics* 18(4): 150–169.

Featherstone, Kevin. 1999. "The British Labor Party from Kinnock to Blair: Europeanism and Europeanization" Paper prepared for presentation for the ECSA Sixth Biennial International Conference. Pittsburgh, PA, June 2–5.

Geyer, Robert. 1998. "Globalization and the Non-Defence of the Welfare State." *West European Politics* 21(3): 77–102.

Gilmour, Sir Ian. 1977. *Inside Right: A Study of Conservatism.* London: Hutchinson.

Gottweis, Herbert. 1999. *Regulating Genetic Engineering in the European Union: A Post-Structuralist Perspective.* London: Routledge.

Greenfeld, Liah. 1992. *Nationalism: Five Roads to Modernity.* Cambridge, MA: Harvard University Press.

Haas, Peter M. 1992. "Introduction: Epistemic Communities and International Policy Coordination." *International Organization* 46: 1–35.

Hall, Peter. 1989. "Conclusion" in *The Political Power of Economic Ideas: Keynesianism Across Nations* ed. Peter A. Hall. Princeton: Princeton University Press.

Hall, Peter. 1993. "Policy Paradigms, Social Learning and the State: The Case of Economic Policy-Making in Britain." *Comparative Politics* 25: 275–96.

Hall, Stuart. 1983. "The Great Moving Right Show." In *The Politics of Thatcherism,* eds. S. Hall and M. Jacques. London: Lawrence & Wishart.

Hall, Stuart. 1988. *The Hard Road to Renewal: Thatcherism and the Crisis of the Left.* London: Verso.

Hay, Colin and Marsh, David, eds. 1998. *Demystifying Globalization.* London: Macmillian.

Hay, Colin and Watson, Matthew. 1998. "Rendering the Contingent Necessary: New Labour's neoliberal Conversion and the Discourse of Globalisation." Paper prepared for presentation to the annual conference of the American Political Science Association. Boston, Sept. 3–6.

Hayward, Jack and Klein, Rudolf. 1994. "Grande-Bretagne: De la Gestion Publique à la Gestion Privée du Déclin" in *Le Tournant Néo-Libéral*, ed., Jobert.

Hedetoft, Ulf and Niss, Hanne. 1991. "Taking Stock of Thatcherism." Department of Languages and Intercultural Studies, Aalborg University, vol. 4.

Heinisch, Reinhard. 1999. "Coping with the Single Market: Corporatist Response Strategies in Germany and Austria." Paper prepared for presentation for the Sixth Biennial Conference of the European Community Studies Association. Pittsburgh, PA., June 2–5.

Hennessy, Peter. 1989. *Whitehall*. London: Fontana.

Hetzner, Candace. 1999. *The Unfinished Business of Thatcherism*. New York: Peter Lang.

Jobert, Bruno. 1992. "Représentations Sociales, Controverses et Débats dans la Conduite des Politiques Publiques." *Revue Française de Science Politique* 42(2): 219–234.

Jobert, Bruno and Théret, Bruno. 1994. "France: La Consécration Républicaine du Néo-Libéralisme." In *Le Tournant Néo-Libéral* ed. Bruno Jobert. Paris: L'Harmattan, pp. 21–86.

Kohler-Koch, Beate. 1997. "Organized Interests in European Integration: The Evolution of a New Type of Governance?" in *Participation and Policymaking in the European Union* ed., A. Young and H. Wallace. Oxford: Oxford University Press.

Kuhn, Thomas S. 1971. *The Structure of Scientific Revolutions*, second edition. Chicago: University of Chicago Press.

Labbé, Dominique. 1990. *Le Vocabulaire de François Mitterrand*. Paris: Presses de la Fondation Nationale des Sciences Politiques.

Lakatos Imre. 1970. "Methodology of Scientific Research Programmes" in *Criticism and the Growth of Knowledge*, ed. Imre Lakatos and Alan Musgrave. Cambridge: Cambridge University Press,.

Larat, Fabrice. 1999. "The Political Dimensions of Narrative." Paper prepared for delivery at the 27th Annual ECPR Joint Session of Workshops. Mannheim University, March 26–31.

Larsen, Henrik. 1997. *Foreign Policy and Discourse Analysis*. London: Routledge.

Lehmbruch, Gerhard. 1999. "The Rise and Change of Discourses on 'Embedded Capitalism' in Germany and Japan and their Institutional Setting." Paper prepared for presentation for the Workshop Project on Germany and Japan organized by Wolfgang Streeck and Ronald Dore. Max Planck Institute, Cologne, June 24–26.

Levy, Jonah. n/a "France: Directing Adjustment?" in *From Vulnerability to Competitiveness: Welfare and Work in the Reform of the Welfare State* eds., Fritz Scharpf and Vivien Schmidt. Oxford: Oxford University Press, forthcoming 2000.

Majone, Giandomenico. 1989. *Evidence, Argument and Persuasion in the Policy Process*. New Haven: Yale University Press.

March, James G. and Olsen, Johan P. 1995. *Democratic Governance*. New York: Free Press.

Marcussen, Martin. 1998. "Central Bankers, the Ideational Life-Cycle and the Social Construction of EMU." EUI Working Papers, Robert Schuman Center RSC no. 98/33

Marquand, David. 1988. *The Unprincipled Society*. London: Fontana.

Mazey, Sonia and Richardson, Jeremy. 1996. "EU Policy-making: A garbage can or an anticipatory and consensual policy style?" In *Adjusting to Europe: The Impact of the European Union on National Institutions and Policies* eds., Yves Mény, Pierre Muller, and Jean-Louis Quermonne. London: Routledge.

Muller, Pierre. 1995. "Les Politiques Publiques comme Construction d'un Rapport au Monde." In Alain Faure, Gielles Pollet, et Philippe Warin, *La Construction du Sens dans les Politiques Publiques: Débats autour de la notion de Référentiel*. Paris: L'Harmattan.

Muller, Pierre and Surel, Yves. 1998. *L'Analyse des Politiques Publiques*. Paris: Monchrestien.

Radaelli, Claudio M.. n/a "The Power of Policy Narratives in the European Union: The Case of Tax Policy." In *The Power of Ideas: Policy Ideas and Policy Change* eds., Dietmar Braun and Andreas Busch. Edward Elgar, forthcoming.

Rein, Martin and Schön, Donald A. 1991. "Frame-Reflective Policy Discourse." In P. Wagner, C.H.Weiss, B. Wittrock, and H. Wollman, eds., *Social Sciences, Modern States, National Experiences, and Theoretical Crossroads*. Cambridge: Cambridge University Press.

Rein, Martin and Schön, Donald A. 1994. *Frame Reflection. Toward the Resolution of Intractable Policy Controversies*. New York: Basic Books.

Riddell, Peter. 1989. *The Thatcher Decade* (Oxford: Blackwell.

Risse, Thomas. 1997. "Who Are We? A Europeanization of National Identities?" Paper presented at the Workshop of "Europeanization and Domestic Change". University of Pittsburgh, 6–8 November.

Roe, Emery. 1994. *Narrative Policy Analysis: Theory and Practice*. Durham: Duke University Press.

Sabatier, Paul A. 1998. "The Advocacy Coalition Framework: Revisions and Relevance for Europe." *Journal of European Public Policy* 5, no. 1. March: 98–130

Sabatier, Paul A. and Jenkins-Smith, H.C. eds. 1993. *Policy Change and Learning: An Advocacy Coalition Approach*. Boulder: Westview.

Scharpf, Fritz. 1991. Crisis and Choice in European Social Democracy. Ithaca: Cornell University Press.

Scharpf, Fritz. 1997. *Games Real Actors Play: Actor-Centered Institutionalism in Policy Research*. Boulder, CO: Westview.

Schmidt, Vivien A. 1988. "Four Models of Explanation." *Methodology and Science* 21(3): 174–201.

Schmidt, Vivien A. 1995. "The New World Order, Incorporated: The Rise of Business and the Decline of the Nation-State." *Daedalus* 124, no. 2. Spring: 75–106.

Schmidt, Vivien A. 1996. *From State to Market?* Cambridge: Cambridge University Press.

Schmidt, Vivien A. 1997a. "Discourse and. DisIntegration in Europe: The Cases of France, Great Britain, and Germany." *Daedalus* 126(3): 167–198.

Schmidt, Vivien A. 1997b. "Economic Policy, Political Discourse, and Democracy in France." *French Politics and Society* 15(2): 37–48.

Schmidt, Vivien A. 1999a. "Politics, Values, and the Power of Discourse in the Reform of Welfare and Work." Paper prepared for presentation for the European Community Studies Association Conference. Pittsburgh, Jun. 2–5.

Schmidt, Vivien A. 1999b. "Convergent Pressures, Divergent Responses: France, Great Britain, and Germany between Globalization and Europeanization" in *States and Sovereignty in the Global Economy* eds., David A. Smith, Dorothy J. Solinger, and Steven Topik. London: Routledge.

Schmidt, Vivien A. 2000. "Democracy and Discourse in an Integrating Europe and a Globalizing World." *European Journal of Law* 5(2. forthcoming.

Schwok, René. 1999. "La France et l'Intégration Européenne: Une Évaluation du "Paradigme Identitariste." *French Politics and Society* 17(1): 56–69.

Sofres 1996. *L'État de l'opinion.* Paris: presses Universitaires de France.

Streeck, Wolfgang. 1996. "Public Power beyond the Nation-State: The case of the European Community." *States against Markets: The Limits of Globalization* ed., Robert Boyer and Daniel Drache. London and New York: Routledge.

Taylor-Gooby, Peter. 1991. "Attachment to the Welfare State." In *British Social Attitudes: The 8th Report* ed., R. Jowell.

Verdun, Amy. 1996. "An 'Assymetrical' Economic and Monetary Union in the EU: Perceptions of Monetary Authorities and Social Partners." Journal of European Integration 20(1): 59–82.f

Wallace, Helen. 1996. "Relations between the European Union and the British Administration" in *Adjusting to Europe: The Impact of the European Union on National Institutions and Policies* eds. Yves Mény, Pierre Muller, and Jean-Louis Quermonne. London: Routledge.

Weiss, Linda. 1997. "Globalization and the Myth of a Powerless State." *New Left Review* 225: 3–27.

Wittrock, Björn, Wagner, Peter, and Wollmann, Hellmut. 1991. "Social Science and the Modern State: Knowledge, Institutions, and Societal Transformations." In *Social Sciences and Modern States: National Experiences and Theoretical Cross-*

roads, eds., Peter Wagner, Carol Hirschon Weiss, and Hellmut Wollmann. Cambridge: Cambridge University Press.

Zinsou, Lionel. 1985. *Le Fer de Lance*. Paris: Olivier Orban.

Zysman, John. 1996. "The Myth of a 'Global' Economy: Enduring National Foundations and Emerging Regional Realities." *New Political Economy* 1(1): 157–84.

Conclusion

Steven Weber

Globalization has had meaningful consequences for governance structures in modern Europe's political economy. The cases in this book tell stories of change in a variety of sectors and practices. In some instances change is significant, perhaps even revolutionary; and in others it is more incremental. In no case does the stark Political Economy Null Hypothesis (PENH) which I proposed as a baseline in the introductory chapter explain adequately the nature of change, or capture the mechanisms of change. That in and of itself is not terribly surprising. It nonetheless is a powerful reminder that simple arguments can distort just as readily as they can reveal important aspects of reality.

The discussion of globalization is about much more than relative prices and convergence vs. divergence among national systems. It is also about the magnitude and nature of changes in mobility, which is the major driving force. It is about the actors whose interests and beliefs are affected in turn, and about the mechanisms through which these actors bring about change in institutions.

The essays in this book focus particularly on the actors and the mechanisms of change, by examining how governance structures are changing in a few notable cases within modern Europe. In the introduction I outlined three possible points of leverage for our arguments:

- To specify the agents and mechanisms of change in governance structures

- To examine obstacles and intervening variables in diffusion processes that shape globalization-induced change in Europe
- To refine and revise our understanding of what globalization means.

The more general question to which we contribute is simply this: what kinds of politics are engendered by globalization?

This concluding chapter explores three sets of findings and implications that emerge. First, I consider what the evidence suggests about whether different change mechanisms do or do not lead institutions toward significantly different outcomes, or places, in real world cases. Precisely what is the value-added in differentiating among mechanisms? Second, I discuss some implications for understanding in a broad theoretical sense what governance structures are, and what they do, in modern political economy. Third, I return to globalization as a cause and consider what role Europe as a highly organized region is playing in response.

These are for the most part implications and hypotheses rather than firm and certain conclusions. The basis of evidence is obviously not sufficient to prove or disprove in a final sense these points. I am confident that the ongoing process of globalization will continue to generate cases and data that can be used to explore in more depth some of the findings that this book suggests.

1. Do Different Mechanisms of Change Lead to Different Outcomes?

The major rationale for distinguishing different mechanisms of change is the expectation of differences in outcomes that would result. Clearly, global driving forces can alter domestic (and other) institutional structures by several different causal pathways. The cases yield four interesting observations on this point.

The first is the importance in each case of political perceptions about the "global" system and the driving forces emanating from it. Ultimately, institutional change happens only when political actors understand a challenge in a particular way and fashion a response. This is simply another reminder that neither markets nor prices nor any other economic variable by itself can cause institutions to change—it is political actors perceiving and responding to economic variables that is the cause. The question then immediately becomes, who is doing the perceiving? Of what? And how accurately?

It's unlikely that deductive models will suffice to answer these questions. There is simply too much variation in individual psychology, group dynamics, and the institutional infrastructure within which groups can organize—as well as uncertainty in conceptualizing and measuring the economic variables themselves—to make this work. Simple a priori distinctions, for example between holders of mobile assets and holders of nonmobile assets, can take the argument just so far.

The "losers" in that argument—that is, people unlucky enough to hold nonmobile assets, or limited to skill sets that are now available on world markets at lower prices—have a lot of leeway in terms of how they perceive and interpret the challenge to their interests. For example, if less-skilled workers in America have seen a reduction in their real wages over the last 25 years, is this a result of technological change, of enhanced competition from workers in developing countries, or something else?[1] Academic economists will continue to argue the logic and evidence on this point. But political entrepreneurs know intuitively that what people believe is a more powerful source of energy for policy and institutional change. Extreme right wing politicians like France's Jean Marie Le Pen and Austria's Jorge Haidar exploit this interpretive space and gain real power from it.

The key question for this book is, does Europe as a highly organized political space have any significance in this process? Do perceptions of the global system and its implications for action differ meaningfully among actors who exist in that European space?

The cases suggest different answers to this question. Ansell, Gonzales, and O'Dwyer portray two European regions in which major political actors perceive and interpret very differently the challenges of globalization. But these perceptions are closely linked to the very real, material circumstances in which these two regions find themselves. North Rhine-Westphalia is indeed more deeply threatened at a very basic level by globalization than is Tuscany, given the differences in industrial structure between the two regions, even before taking into account the differing relationships with national governments and with the EU. And it is the relationship with national governments, rather than with the EU, which in their chapter helps to explain differences in attitude not attributable to brute industrial structure. The EU appears relatively unimportant as a cause (although the regions' respective views of the EU are different, as an effect, which I take up later).

In Campbell's cases, European institutions are merely a backdrop to global institutions (particularly the IMF) which are setting the fundamental terms of the macroeconomic challenge to transition economies. Again, Europe is not significant. The same holds true for Kurzer's account of "sin" laws and practices. Perceptions of the challenge center on global causes, not European ones, although Europe is always at risk of becoming a political scapegoat. Schmidt sees discourse, the medium through which understanding and interpretation happens, as primarily emanating from and situated within national traditions. Like many observers, she does not detect a strong free-standing European level discourse about globalization.

The EASDAQ case looks an exception to this pattern. Posner and I argue that European institutions were critical causes of the shape and timing of the creation of new enterprise markets in Europe, signally a potentially major change in the political economy of finance in the region. We argue that the Commission plays a crucial role in setting the legal and other formal prerequisites but more importantly in fostering a European-level discourse about possible solutions to the unemployment problem through reform of financial markets, taking the emphasis off labor market reform where zerosum perceptions tend to prevail. In this case, the actors and the mechanisms matter a great deal in "selecting" among possible outcomes. If the counterfactual we put forward ("no commission, no EASDAQ, and no euro-n.m. either") is well-founded; and if mimesis is a more significant mechanism than is competition, the character of corporate finance in Europe (and by implication some very important things about the shape of the real economy as well) and perhaps globally will look substantially different five years from now than if the actors and mechanisms had been otherwise.

This signals some significant cross-sectoral variation in the importance of European level causal forces at this step in the argument about the impact of globalization. It may seem surprising that Europe's causal importance seems most prominent in financial market change, simply because finance is usually portrayed as a sector that should come close to a market ideal where transaction costs and efficiency considerations are closer to the surface than almost anywhere else.

With the necessary caveats in place (since this is only one case), I think the operative lesson here is more about the nature and intellectual foundations of the expectations, than it is about a "surprising" finding per se. The EASDAQ story may be an early signal of how Europe's institutions will wield causal importance as catalysts of change. At a minimum it suggests hypotheses that should be kept on board for future research in this area. It also puts in perspective the importance of historical "archaeology" as a crucial element in understanding institutional change. Political institutions and their environments are closely intertwined in a space that is as densely institutionalized as Europe. To imagine that institutions come and go while something called "structure" remains is, in Europe at least, a potentially misleading way to understand the impact of globalization.

It is worth remembering that the process of perception that takes place between the global and the local flows upward as well as downward. "Global" causes do not always present themselves in the form of impersonal market forces. Prices and even markets don't "learn" in any meaningful sense, but institutions—including global actors—do. Campbell's chapter describes how the IMF modified its demands on former Eastern European countries as it gained experience and knowledge about the political economy of transition. A similar process followed on the first phase of the 1998 Asian financial crisis and will likely continue. Precisely because perception is a two-way street, and because global "causes" also must deal with complexity and uncertainty in their operating environment, it is important to resist any temptation to reify the global in hopes of explaining neatly and parsimoniously changes in a purely "dependent" variable. Unfortunately, the arrows go both ways. Feedback is ongoing and a central part of the dynamic of change.

A second observation relates to the importance of ideas in terms of understanding what are feasible and desirable responses to global-level causes. Is Europe significant as a source or nexus of these ideas? Ansell, Gonzales, and O'Dwyer point to the idea of "endogenous growth" as a particular conception of economic development, an intellectual focal point around which strategic thought about development was converging at the regional and European level. Although the idea leaves lots of room for further interpretation and indeed is refracted (as they show) into quite different practical manifestations in NRW as compared to Tuscany, it nonetheless has a core meaning—focusing more on internal technological development than foreign investment, emphasizing small- and medium-sized enterprises, investing in human capital. These ideas do not flow directly from economic change and are not explained by PENH. But where do these ideas come from and who is promulgating them? Posner and I raise a similar question with regard to EASDAQ. Global markets do not determine that equity financing of smaller, entrepreneurial companies is the rational or efficient response to globalization. The general question is, who does push these ideas forward and why do they succeed when they do? The question for this book is, to what extent are the operative ideas European ideas, American ideas, global ideas, or from some other origin?

The evidence on Europe's contribution is again mixed. "Endogenous growth" is not a European idea in any meaningful sense. It may, because of the kinds of policies and possibilities it legitimates, make sense to Europeans and offer ways to think about action in a highly uncertain environment— but this is still an application of an idea with roots elsewhere. Ideas seem more distinctly European in the case of EASDAQ, where the Commission developed a particular set of arguments about how enterprise markets would in fact offer promise for making progress on some of Europe's central political economy dilemmas. Europe appears more as a receptacle for or consumer of ideas in the Kurzer, Campbell, and Ziegler chapters; and even in Schmidt's account of discourse construction the major focus is national and Europe, per se, seems to contribute relatively little. This is not for lack of trying on the part of the Commission and other European institutions that are continually attempting to foster distinctive European dialogues in a number of different issue areas. But the success rate appears to be low.

This is not a crisply positive finding, but it does say something important for Europe about the nature of globalization and ideas. Contra the view that globalization simplifies by bringing the world closer to Walrasian markets, globalization appears not to be making the world simpler but instead making it increasingly complex, at least in Europe. Ideas probably matter more in this environment, in an ironic way. Complexity and uncertainty demand an intellectual compass for navigation, but don't easily provide it. "Efficiency" is not a serious contender for that role, precisely because in a complex and uncertain environment it is not often possible that actors (or analysts, for that matter) will know what is efficient. Remember that less than a decade ago, American analyses of international political economy were dominated by serious scholars who thought that Japan had figured out the "best" way to run a capitalist economy. To say that what works at any given moment is by definition efficient, would be (implicitly) to adopt an extraordinarily naïve view of evolution which crumbles on close examination. This is critical in Ziegler's case, because no one really knows what kind of corporate governance regime will perform best under particular circumstances (even if one could possibly know what kinds of circumstances will arise in the future!).

Mimesis, or copying of what seems to work for others, is one expected consequence. DiMaggio and Powell saw this as a powerful mechanism of institutional isomorphism.[2] It can be that, but it doesn't have to be that. Mimesis does not by itself necessarily imply convergence around a single, stable, institutional equilibrium. In fact in a period of rapidly changing environments and conditions, the opposite might be true. There is an alternative image of mimesis leading to massive *instability*, where people are chasing around "solutions" and trying to copy precisely what worked *yesterday* but fails to work tomorrow.

The major impediment to a process that might generate this kind of instability is political, bureaucratic, cognitive, and emotional resistance to change. These together make for institutional stickiness, by many accounts more strongly in Europe than in other parts of the world. And while rigidity typically is seen as a weakness of Europe, it is easy to see how some rigidity could very well turn out to be an unexpected asset, if the kind of rolling instability I described above is latent. Schmidt's assessment of how countries scramble their way toward a legitimacy discourse to justify change is central here because the success or failure of these attempts would be an important element, perhaps the most important element, in delineating when institutions remain sticky and when in fact they will change. Both cognitive and normative components of discourse matter, because institutions depend ultimately on both kinds of foundational consensus.

A third observation is about the importance of the political process that leads to change. Conventional accounts of globalization in the international relations literature have tended to black-box much about this process.[3] Part of the justification for doing that is to gain parsimony and analytic tractability, but it is not solely a methodological choice. It represents also a bet or implicit claim that politics acts as an "intervening variable." This means that politics channels the institutions under examination to an outcome that is determined predominantly by more fundamental and profound driving forces. Is that a defensible claim? The cases in this book suggest that it may not be, and that politics is much more than an intervening process that only refracts "fundamental" causes on the way to their ultimate effects.

Campbell's study of fiscal reform in three Eastern European cases clearly illustrates this point. To maintain budget discipline in a reforming transition economy is an intensely political process that is not nearly determined by "fundamental" causes at the global level. Poland, Hungary, and the Czech Republic each contain stories of a national politics of fiscal reform, in which governments of the right fail to sustain discipline while more consensual, tripartite based governments of the left are comparatively successful. The variance in government composition within each individual country at different times, as well as among the three countries, suggests that where the political process of transition is more nearly negotiated among stakeholders than coerced, the likelihood of a backlash that undermines fiscal discipline is reduced.[4] Campbell's chapter suggests also the essential dilemma of reform facing transition economies is more than a matter of time-inconsistency of aggregate preferences, although that problem is certainly present.[5] It is also (and perhaps as importantly) a matter of the distribution of benefits along the way—which implies that political processes on that route are critical to any reasonable explanatory claim.

Kurzer's chapter adds a significant element. She shows that while physical arbitrage between states with different legal codes and tax systems is a powerful force for change, arbitrage (even though it is a market metaphor) does not work in a straightforward manner and outside of politics. Certain traditional practices and norms survive mainly because no one talks about them—and that is because it is not politically or socially legitimate to talk about them. There is, prior to arbitrage, relatively little politics surrounding these value-oriented or cultural issues. Societies have successfully insulated these questions from political debate. What arbitrage does in Kurzer's cases is to empower certain domestic interest groups that are motivated for one or another reason to seek change. This happens indirectly, by politicizing and placing on the agenda for discussion and debate, a process or set of issues that state actors would prefer to see remain in a depoliticized status. Once the debate is open, the protective veneer falls away and something much more akin to normal political disagreement and bargaining begins. Physical arbitrage of this sort in a globalizing world can be expected to have similar impact on a broader basis, bringing into the political process of give and take bargaining, issues and practices that were previously insulated from it.

Different political processes of change in NRW vs. Tuscany are the result of the economic structures, internal social and political structures, and the national political structures within which these two regions are situated. Ansell, Gonzales, and O'Dwyer argue that these differences are, in turn, highly consequential for the two regions' respective visions of globalization and their relationships with the European Union in that context. Endogenous growth thus takes on very different meanings in NRW vs. Tuscany. NRW pursues a statist approach, and the region will develop dyadic linkages with other regions in order to build coalitions that seek to pressure the EU and extract redistributed resources. For NRW the EU is a corporate actor with autonomous interests and the relationship is primarily about bargaining for clear advantage. Meanwhile Tuscany pursues what the authors call a network approach, developing open-ended multilateral relationships with other regions and the EU which together serve as a pipeline to the global economy. For Tuscany the EU facilitates connections to market networks at a higher level and with greater competency than the national government of Italy has been able to do. The relationship between the region and the EU is characterized more by diffuse reciprocity and flexibility—as Ansell, Gonzales, and O'Dwyer put it "cooperation is less threatening and more complementary."

A fourth observation concerns the importance of legitimacy for "stable" outcomes. Economic change engenders winners and losers. One person's productivity revolution is for someone else the source of politics of defensiveness and reaction. Particularly during periods of rapid and accelerating change, "price signals" and other supposedly objective measures can be very noisy and hard to interpret. Clearly it is the interpretation that matters most for political action. Change brings displacement, but the measure of how much displacement any person or social group can tolerate (and at what rate) is ultimately a product of the discourse that goes on around it. Individuals, groups, and leaders try to explain to themselves and to others what is actually happening to them and why.[6] People, not markets, decide what kinds of displacements are normatively defensible or tolerable.

Schmidt in her argument locates the sources of legitimacy in political discourse constructed at the national level. Kurzer's chapter illustrates this point with an interesting twist. She argues that particularly distinctive "sin" laws or regulations in Ireland, the Netherlands, and the Nordic countries have been distinguishing characteristics of the modern national identity of each country. Globalization threatens this kind of exceptionalism in large part by making it politically and socially legitimate to challenge the rules. But it does not immediately replace that old distinctiveness with anything new.

Schmidt suggests that the potential loss of a legitimate consensus around identity issues of this kind poses a subtle but real threat to modern democracy. This is closely related to what Wolfgang Streeck calls "democracy illusion." Streeck fears that people will refuse to acknowledge externalities that reduce national political capabilities, while transferring blame for what they don't like to external forces or actors. At the same time they may demand national solutions that are no longer possible, and appeal for European-level responses while remaining highly reluctant to transfer sufficient power to European institutions.[7]

This is clearly an opportunity as well as a threat, and it may have a different character in Europe than elsewhere in the world. As national governments lose influence in some traditional areas of competency, whether it be administrative discretion or central banking, "citizens" will surely look elsewhere for new sources of interest articulation and influence. When states lose elements of cultural or ethical distinctiveness that were central to national identity, people again will surely search for new sources of identity, somewhere else.

Outside of Europe and particularly at the global level, there is relatively little, other than an anonymous market, to connect to. Blame is one component of this dynamic, as became painfully clear at the World Trade Organization ministerial meeting in Seattle at the end of 1999. This does not always play to Europe's advantage. While Malaysians (or at least their Prime Minister) can denounce speculators, markets, and other far-off or ambiguous groups that are somehow held to be responsible for the 1998 downside of the Asian miracle, and NGOs can blame the WTO, Europeans have at hand an even more convenient target. The bureaucrats and parliamentarians of Brussels as well as the very concrete and visible institutions that they represent are natural scapegoats. This is one reason why the collapse of the Santer Commission over mismanagement issues and fraud, but even more deeply over its profound weakness, was quite damaging to the project of European Union.

The EU has struggled almost continuously to position itself as a source of legitimacy located in the intermediate space between the nation-state and the global "system." Measured by opinion polls this effort has not generally been seen as successful, although Europhiles always envision a watershed coming either in the next generation of citizens or in the wake of the next big project of integration (currently EMU).[8] As Schmidt points out, the national level is still very much paramount and connections to Europe (in the French case) or to the global level (in the British case) are still made in terms of how they facilitate national goals.

The persistence of the notion of *acquis communitaire*, in the face of a reality where Europe is both variable geometry *and* multi-speed, is partly a story about Europe trying to say it stands for *something* that is more than what is necessary or even what is efficient. Elsewhere I have argued that Europe's political legitimacy rests on three pillars of normative commitment.

The three are, that there will be no more war between us; we will not sacrifice wholesale our vision of the good society in order to achieve economic integration and competitiveness; and we will make compromises of sovereignty as is necessary to achieve these goals. As of this writing governments of the left are in place among the majority of EU states and are attempting to articulate visions of a "third way" toward integration and development. The EU faces a real challenge that its distinctive potential position as a source of legitimacy could be undermined. It is clearly possible that intergovernmental institutions and processes will offer up a cogent, legitimate rationale to underpin change more quickly and more effectively than will the EU. What is certain is that even a dynamic, evolving equilibrium depends on legitimacy in some way. There is likely to be a continuing competition to provide it.

2. Governance Structures in European Political Economy

Governance structure is a very broad term that can encompass many things. At a minimum the common usage of this term presupposes a set of rules that place boundaries around interaction, by changing the availability of options as well as the costs and benefits accruing to actions that any individual player in a game might choose to take. These rules may or may not be situated within formal institutions. Clearly the analysis of governance structures is easier when formal institutions exist. But even when they do not, shifts in policies and strategies that take place over time and across different actors or different realms of actions sometimes signal in a relatively clear way changes in the broader governance structures or regimes that sit behind these behaviors. The lack of formal institutions is no reason not to pay attention to governance structures.

But this raises the broader question of what governance structures in political economy are fundamentally about, what it is that they are trying to govern, and for what purposes. The answers to these questions are frequently defined by assumption. In mainstream political economy circles, these assumptions have settled around a core "economistic" view that in turn drives a research agenda around the problem of just how it is that markets by and large function pretty well. The key concepts here are opportunistic actors; principle-agent problems; monitoring, compliance, and sanctioning; and high information and transaction costs.

Transaction cost economics is an exemplar of this line of thought, because it specifies through the use of deductive logic an optimal set of governance structures for particular kinds of transactions depending upon specific and well-defined (if often hard to measure) characteristics of the transaction.[9] Although deductive logics of this kind have an inherent tendency to become functionalist arguments in practice, there is no gainsaying the importance and value of analyzing governance structures in this way. Consider, for example, the argument of Milgrom, North, and Weingast about the revival of trade in the Middle Ages.[10] These authors ask, what kinds of governance structures are needed to support a resurgence of trade in an institutionally thin environment, among opportunistic actors who are constrained by high information and transaction costs? Even if the authors do not tell a compelling story of how the question was answered in a historical sense, their argument carefully lays out the minimum requirements for a set of rules—that is, a governance structure—that would make the observed outcome (revival of trade) possible and sustainable.

But this approach, deducing what is necessary to sustain a set of transactions given assumptions about actors as "rational egoists" or "opportunists with guile," is not the only way to conceptualize governance structures. An alternative view lies closer to sociological perspectives and is inspired more by Polanyi and even Chandler than by Coase and Williamson. This view of governance tends to rely on institutional theory of some kind, to make the case that governance structures (and perhaps institutions more generally) are not about bridging market failures or lowering transaction costs per se. Instead they are about creating stability, predictability, and control.

This companion perspective sees governance structures as aimed at stabilizing markets in what would otherwise be a highly uncertain and unstable world. Put simply, governance may not be a means of perfecting markets. Instead, governance is a means of escaping, or transcending, much of what would otherwise happen in markets. Organizations seek to create governance structures around their interactions not to generate efficiencies but precisely so that they can ensure a level of stability that makes it possible to exist more comfortably and with less uncertainty. Neil Fligstein sees this kind of governance emerging as what he calls "conceptions of control" among the major firms in a market. William Lazonick tells a similar story about advanced capitalist systems.[11] All of these arguments are closely linked to Polanyi in an important sense. Just as the welfare state was a response to the instabilities and unsustainable elements of "laissez-faire" national capitalisms, modern governance structures in political economy (including, possibly, elements of the European Union) can be conceptualized in part as a response to globalized capitalism at the end of the century.

Many of the essays in this book show elements of governance structures that seem in accordance with this view. NRW is clearly trying to stabilize its environment. The reaction to EASDAQ by national authorities, and the creation of the alternative Euro-NM network of national markets, represents an attempt to retain control over enterprise markets within the grasp of extant vested interests. The changes in corporate governance that Ziegler describes are just as easily understood within this perspective as within a more economistic perspective. Other authors have reached similar conclusions, although they have not always shared the interpretation. Geoff Garrett, for example, argues that corporatist social democratic regimes in Europe attract investment precisely because they offer the promise of relative stability in the context of high global uncertainty and volatility.[12]

To recast the notion of governance structure in this fashion requires a broadening of analytic perspective. Some readers will oppose this move on the grounds that it sacrifices parsimony and precision. I am not proposing it here as a wholesale change but instead as a complementary argument that takes in alternative possibilities which a more narrow argument does not. As Schmidt says of political discourse, governance structures also serve a cognitive function, a coordinating function, and a communicative function as well as an "economistic" function around transactions in markets.

One important research question, looking forward, is to ask whether these theoretical lenses on governance are two different ways of looking at the problem, each highlighting a particular aspect of institutions and governance. Or, perhaps each captures a distinct kind of phenomenon and thus describes a subset of institutions in the world. If so, then the next step would be to understand whether the balance between these subsets is changing as a result of globalization. I find it hard to settle a priori on a compelling null hypothesis on this score. Capital mobility might increase the need for economistic governance functions since the extension of markets both geographically and to more segments of human activity raises new possibilities for opportunism and incomplete contracts not backed up by social capital and normative "fillers." At the same time, uncertainty and volatility stretches the capacity of human decisionmakers and institutions to be prudent and sensible, much less efficient. Stabilization might be a product of concentrated power but it might also appeal to some of the cognitive, normative, and emotional needs of humans and organizations that are less clearly represented in economistic arguments. Rather than choose one or another perspective as a null hypothesis, a reasonable way forward would be simply to compare these perspectives over time and try to isolate the dynamics of a changing balance between them.

3. Studying the Politics of Globalization in the European Context

Risse, Cowles, and Caporaso present three kinds of models of institutional change that characterize studies of how European integration affects domestic politics.[13] The first, functional and neofunctional models, portray institutional change as driven by consensually recognized social needs, efficiencies, and spillovers. These create a set of possibilities, into which transnational networks built up by policy entrepreneurs pour their energies.

The second image of change is intergovernmental. These models portray institutional change as negotiated outcomes of bargaining between governments. The preferences and bargaining positions of these governments may be motivated by domestic interest groups seeking economic advantage, but change is ultimately a negotiated outcome reflecting more than anything else the power balance between states.[14]

The third image is historical institutionalist. The case studies in this book clearly adopt this stance. We start from the perspective of expecting a deeply contentious political process. We find that only a part of that process is made up of bargaining between governments, and between governments and EU institutions. Similarly, functionalist drivers of change exist in our accounts, but are only part of the story. These emerge mainly as background causes that in and of themselves have limited explanatory power. Most of the chapters in this book see flows of ideas and components of identity (both of which affect preferences) traveling between the global, the European, and the domestic.

The endogeneity of these causal forces in our model make the study somewhat messier but also more realistic. The historical-institutionalist style of explanation almost demands some level of messiness, which it makes up for by careful process tracing. Concepts like principal-agent theory and "unintended consequences" can be imported into these stories, and as heuristics they are useful notions that call attention to some elements of the historical record. But they do not by themselves constitute a good explanation.

Ultimately the notion of unintended consequences, in particular, is a placeholder for variance that does not fit within existing models or cannot be captured in accounts of what the actors *ought* to know. Since the whole notion of structure is about something that intervenes between actors' intentions and behaviors, and the outcomes of their interaction, the so-called "logic" of unintended consequences is not really a logic at all, but is exactly what needs to be explained in most accounts of institutional change. Hence our special attention to mechanisms.

Ziegler's chapter illustrates one significant advantage that we gain in this trade-off. Formal-legal changes in corporate governance within Germany are in the short term heavily constrained by "the conventional politics of pushing and hauling" between interested parties. But the fundamental driving forces behind change remain strong. Ziegler's analysis of the mechanisms by which transnational coalitions bring both normative and financial pressure to bear on existing arrangements demonstrates that the range of possibilities for change in the foreseeable future is significantly more broad than what has happened until now. By identifying the mechanisms behind what he calls an "incipient transnational politics of property rights" Ziegler builds a falsifiable set of propositions about the future course of corporate governance reform in Germany.

Posner and I see the emergence of comparable transnational coalitions in the politics of financial market change. Similar coalitions play a smaller but still significant role in Kurzer's chapter and the Ansell, Gonzales, and O'Dwyer chapter. In some cases these are new debates, energized by transnational connections. In others they are more familiar issues (for example, questions about how societies fund retirement) repackaged as debates about international ties and consequences, which facilitates pulling transnational actors and interests into the discussion in a significant way.

This is not a surprising finding per se in the context of globalization, but it does point to the latent power of these nascent coalitions to drive quite fundamental change in governance structures across a variety of issue-areas. The seeking out of transnational coalitions in each of these accounts is not simply a matter of finding external allies to support previously existing positions. Economic change is creating new possibilities for alignments around quite fundamental and even constitutive questions of political economy. As Ziegler puts it, the question ultimately is what is an industrial enterprise for, and who should therefore own and control it? In Kurzer's study, the question reaches into central identity issues about what it means to be Dutch or Irish or any other nationality.

The consequences of these kinds of discussions are typically kept in check by conventional partisan politics and the bargaining games familiar to national politicians. One of the things that historical institutionalist styles of explanation are able to do well, is to extend the boundaries around possible outcomes and depict the mechanisms by which those boundaries may begin to collapse. The outlier is still Schmidt's account of discourse construction. Here the content and (even more so) the process of discourse around the cognitive and normative foundations for institutions of political economy remain constrained and nationally based.

There is a disequilibrium inherent here, which many others have pointed to on both a national and a global level, between what is happening "on the ground" of institutional change, and the intellectual/emotive foundations of knowledge and discourse that people need to accept the inevitable dislocations. As I suggested earlier, a key opportunity for European-level institutions as causal drivers is to fill that gap in a meaningful way. But they have not, for the most part, yet done so in many areas of concern to citizens.

This is important for studies of globalization, in ways that go beyond the simple notion that public acceptance eventually sets limits on what kind of institutional change is acceptable and sustainable. That is surely correct, but it is in a real sense a minimum position. I wrote in the Introduction that mobility of goods, ideas, capital, and people—a simple definition of globalization—has been increasing unevenly but gradually as a trend line for several hundred years. There is considerable evidence now that capital, and particularly owners of mobile capital, have been empowered by the sharp increases in capital mobility that have taken place over the last two decades.

Can we foresee the next round of sharply increased mobility and hypothesize about its consequences? Of course this is contingent and it is entirely possible that globalization, as it has in the past, will be slowed or perhaps even reversed for a time. That said, the most likely outlook for the next decade is a particularly rapid increase in the mobility of ideas and information relative to capital, goods, and people.

Some of what is happening in electronic commerce in the United States, and the late 1999 "battle in Seattle" around the ministerial conference of the World Trade Organization, provide windows into possible political consequences. It is now commonplace to hear that e-commerce is changing the game in a fundamental way by shifting marketplace power from producers to customers. At the same time it poses threats to central social bargains around issues of privacy, equal access, and the like. Governance structures are under great pressure to respond. In Seattle, trade ministers discovered to their dismay that they no longer had any significant organizational advantage over labor unions, NGOS, and transnational environmental groups.

If power is being reshuffled in this direction, as I believe it is, then the question of how governance structures will respond engages in a serious way a broader swathe of "independent variables" than before. This matters greatly for the possible significance of European-level causes. The institutional struc-ture of the European Union has for the most part been focused on coordi-nating governments and large economic interest groups, primarily business. In the Introduction, I laid out three broad hypotheses about the possible role of Europe as a causal force behind domestic institutional change:

- The EU may be an autonomous source of driving forces that would be significant even in the absence of global-level driving forces.
- The EU may be a strategic environment within which other kinds of causes are played out, and manipulated by actors. Europe is a playing field where states and firms try to moderate and control how they are affected by global driving forces.
- Europe may be a causally "empty" level, simply a pipeline that transmits global causes to states and firms.

The findings of the case-studies within this book vary. In Campbell's chapter the EU appears most like a passive pipeline. In Kurzer's chapter the EU is a major driving force, at a minimum accelerating and focusing global-level causes, but most likely acting as an autonomous source of causation. The remaining chapters blur the distinctions between these three hypoth-eses. The EASDAQ story mixes elements of the first and the second—Eu-rope appears both as an autonomous cause and as a strategic environment. In the Ziegler and Ansell, Gonzales, and O'Dwyer chapters Europe appears sometimes as a strategic environment and other times as a passive pipeline.

We set out in this book to assess and map the variance, which is a nec-essary step before trying to explain it. Still, the cases suggest categories around which to construct a set of hypotheses having to do with differences in the characteristics of issue-areas; differences in the capacities of particular actors; differences in ideas about what governments can and can not do. It is also possible that the variance in outcomes primarily is a matter of timing—in other words, that we are catching a more or less singular process of institutional change at different stages in time, and that the variance will "collapse" in the medium to long term. Designing and conducting a study to evaluate these hypotheses is a clear next step for research in this area.

Finally, what of the debate about convergence? There were always two aspects to this question (although they are not always separated cleanly in the literature). The first aspect is simply convergence yes or no. The second aspect is, if yes, then convergence on what standard or focal point. As Berger and Dore clearly explained, even the starkest neoclassical economic globalization arguments do not require institutional convergence, since there surely are multiple institutional configurations that can match each other's performance in an increasingly competitive world economy. And the notion that convergence necessarily meant convergence toward a least common denominator (so called "race to the bottom") has been discredited in theory as well as in empirical research.[15] It is worth noting that our case studies reaffirm both of these notions.

The Kurzer and Ansell, Gonzales, and O'Dwyer chapters each see a modest convergence, albeit of different kinds. Kurzer shows that cultural norms around alcohol, abortion, and drugs were maintained in each instance by a network of state and other social institutions, while the basis within the public for a deeper underlying social consensus on the wisdom and importance of maintaining these unique policies was deteriorating. Changing policies can be thus be interpreted as "convergence" toward what is actually a majority-supported norm, and away from a default position around tradition (which is its own kind of least common denominator). This raises a related issue, of whether there may be a subtle selection bias in many studies of globalization-induced change, that could lead to an overestimation of the fundamental importance of external pressure. If external pressures (such as arbitrage made possible by increased mobility) acts on many areas of governance, but only has a visible impact on issues where the underlying social consensus is already weak, researchers need to look carefully also at cases where mobility is just as much in play but does not lead to visible changes, and at cases where the social consensus is weak but mobility is not yet in play, to clarify the real importance of these different kinds of causes.

The Ansell, Gonzales, and O'Dwyer chapter illustrates another aspect of the conceptual ambiguity around convergence. While NRW and Tuscany both think of themselves as pursuing a strategy of endogenous growth, they are doing very different things and perceive both the challenge to their current situation and the causal impact of global and European-level forces in different ways. It is possible that the two regions are, in fact, trying to end up in the "same place" in the sense that they are creating "functionally equivalent institutional configurations" that would allow them to succeed by living up to a common competitive standard.[16]

But it is also possible that there is a more dynamic differentiation going on. Once some actors in an open, competitive market have chosen a particular strategy, that probably narrows the field of immediate and close possibilities left to others simply because markets get crowded and congested. At the same time, it may open up new niches for others to populate.[17] Table 2.1 in the Ansell, Gonzales, and O'Dwyer chapter illustrates this point: a proliferation of network-type development strategies may very well open or expand a niche for statist-type development in particular sectors of the economy. Schmidt's analysis of national discourses raises the same idea. Since discourse can sometimes be about uniqueness or at least difference, the prominence of one kind of discourse opens niches and may even increase the premium for other and distinct legitimizing discourses. As a whole, the "system" of European political economy is responding to global-level causes, but whether this can be read as convergence or not seems perhaps to be a question situated in a conceptual framework that is just not quite appropriate to the setting.

Yet there remains a real sense in which some institutions are undergoing change that makes them more rather than less like each other, and that is in and of itself an important phenomenon. Campbell's chapter demonstrates the weight of global-level pressures for convergence around clearly demarcated standards of macroeconomic performance. Because these forces operate on transition-from-communism countries with weakly institutionalized political systems, Campbell expects a potent set of effects and indeed finds them, at least initially. The pressures for divergence come later, and they come from national political dynamics that include but are also broader than formal institutions.

Posner and I see a substantial amount of convergence in enterprise markets. Mimetic mechanisms are powerful means for bringing this kind of convergence to bear in a way that meshes with the peculiarities of European political economy, and particularly the ongoing debate about unemployment and technology. The test going forward in time may now have somewhat less to do with a backlash from extant institutions, and somewhat more to do with a broad confrontation with extraordinarily rapid technological change that is revolutionizing what it means to be a stock market all over the world. Ziegler's chapter reveals somewhat similar current dynamics around corporate governance in Germany, which (like enterprise markets) seems a hard case because of its deep enmeshment with many powerful and traditional institutions central to a national political economy. For Ziegler, transnational coalitions are stretching the boundaries of what seems possible in light of short-term political constraints. The process of change should be expected to be gradual and tortuous, in both equity markets and corporate governance arrangements. But this points up the importance of a point I made earlier in this chapter (and more abstractly), about the possibility that mimetic change might take place too slowly to catch up with a more rapidly changing environment. This is the image of dynamic instability where people and states are chasing yesterday's institutional solutions and copying what worked, but will fail to work by the time it is effectively in place. I believe this needs to be taken seriously as an alternative hypothesis about the consequences of globalization for European political economy.

Endnotes

1. See for example Eli Berman, John Bound, and Stephen Machin, "Implications of Skill Biased Technological Change: International Evidence," National Bureau of Economic Research Working Paper 6166. September 1997.

2. Paul J. DiMaggio and Walter W. Powell, "The Iron Cage Revisited: Institutional Isomorphism and Collective Rationality in Organizational Fields," *American Sociological Review* 48 (1983): 147–60.

3. For details see my introductory chapter.

4. Beverly Crawford developed this argument in her comments on Campbell's paper.

5. Adam Przeworski, *Democracy and the Market: Political and Economic Reforms in Eastern Europe and Latin America* (Cambridge: Cambridge University Press, 1991).

6. See Steven Weber and Elliot Posner, "Emerging Markets: Good for US? Good for Everyone?" *Brown Journal of International Affairs*, Summer 1998

7. Wolfgang Streeck, "Public Power Beyond the Nation-State: The Case of the European Community," in Robert Boyer and Daniel Drache, eds., *States Against Markets* (London and New York: Routledge), pp. 311–13; see also

Colin Crouch and Wolfgang Streeck, eds., *The Political Economy of Modern Capitalism* (London: Sage, 1997).

8. The central importance of these political projects is discussed in Liesbet Hooghe and Gary Marks, "The Making of a Polity: The Struggle over European Integration," in Herbert Kitschelt, Peter Lange, Gary Marks, and John D. Stephens eds., *Continuity and Change in Contemporary Capitalism* (Cambridge: Cambridge University Press, 1999).

9. Oliver E. Williamson, *The Mechanisms of Governance* (New York: Oxford University Press, 1996).

10. Paul R. Milgrom, Douglass C. North, and Barry R. Weingast, "The Role of Institutions in the Revival of Trade: The Law Merchant, Private Judges, and the Champagne Fairs," *Economics and Politics* 1990.

11. Neil Fligstein, "Markets, Politics, and Globalization," Uppsala Lectures in Busines 13. Stockholm: Almquist and Wiksell, 1997; Neil Fligstein, *The Transformation of Corporate Control* (Cambridge: Harvard University Press, 1990); William Lazonick, *Business Organization and the Myth of the Market Economy* (Cambridge: Cambridge University Press, 1991).

12. Geoffrey Garrett, *Partisan Politics in the Global Economy* (Cambridge: Cambridge University Press, 1998), p. 130.

13. Thomas Risse, Maria Green Cowles, and James Caporaso, "Europeanization and Domestic Change: Introduction," in Cowles, Caporaso, and Risse eds., *Europeanization and Domestic Change* (Ithaca: Cornell University Press, 2000).

14. This "liberal" version of intergovernmentalism is explained in Andrew Moravcsik, "Preferences and Power in the European Community: A Liberal Intergovernmentalist Approach," *Journal of Common Market Studies* 31 (1993): 473–524.

15. For examples see Steven K. Vogel, *Freer Markets, More Rules: Regulatory Reform in Advanced Industrial Countries* (Ithaca: Cornell University Press, 1996); David Vogel, *Trading Up: Consumer and Environmental Regulation in a Global Economy* (Cambridge: Harvard University Press, 1995).

16. As in Colin Crouch and Wolfgang Streeck, Introduction, to Crouch and Streeck, eds *The Political Economy of Modern Capitalism* (London: Sage, 1997), pp. 4.

17. Herbert Kitschelt, Peter Lange, Gary Marks, and John D. Stephens make a similar point in "Convergence and Divergence in Advanced Capitalist Democracies," in Kitschelt, et al, eds., *Continuity and Change in Contemporary Capitalism* (Cambridge: Cambridge University Press, 1999).

Index

Page numbers for tables are followed
by t